LOW INCOMES: SOCIAL, HEALTH AND EDUCATIONAL IMPACTS

SOCIAL ISSUES, JUSTICE AND STATUS SERIES

Risk and Social Welfare
Jason L. Powell and Azrini Wahidin (Editors)
2009. ISBN: 978-1-60741-691-3

Handbook on Social Change
Brooke H. Stroud and Scott E. Corbin (Editors)
2009. ISBN: 978-1-60741-222-9

Social Development
Lynda R. Elling (Editors)
2009. ISBN: 978-1-60741-612-8

Low Incomes: Social, Health and Educational Impacts
Jacob K. Levine (Editor)
2009. ISBN: 978-1-60741-175-8

LOW INCOMES: SOCIAL, HEALTH AND EDUCATIONAL IMPACTS

JACOB K. LEVINE
EDITOR

Nova Science Publishers, Inc.
New York

LIBRARY OF CONGRESS CATALOGING-IN-PUBLICATION DATA

Levine, Jacob K.
 Low incomes : social, health, and educational impacts / Jacob K. Levine.
   p. cm.
 Includes index.
 ISBN 978-1-60741-175-8 (hardcover)
 1. Low-income consumers--Case studies. 2. Poor--Social conditions--Case studies. I. Title.
 HC59.3.L48 2009
 305.5'62--dc22
                       2009017370

Published by Nova Science Publishers, Inc. ✦ *New York*

CONTENTS

PREFACE

Although the definition of what constitutes low income varies significantly from one country to the next, it is always below average and people who have it score high on the misery index. This new book brings together leading researchers from around the globe on defining it and seeking solutions.

As discussed in Chapter 1, poverty rates in the United States are determined based on a metric from the 1950s that takes into account the cost of food and is then adjusted for family size (National Center for Children in Poverty, 2008a). Accordingly, in today's economy, a family of four residing on an annual income of $21,200 would be below the federal poverty level. Currently, there are 13 million American children living in families with incomes below the federal poverty level. There are concerns, however, that the metric of determination based on food and income alone is flawed since it does not take into account the cumulative costs of housing, health care, child care and transportation and that, realistically speaking, there are many more children adversely affected by poverty (National Center for Children in Poverty, 2008a).

Historically, the poverty rate in the United States has varied, mirroring national trends of economic growth, stability and downturn. Since 1959, when the poverty rate was first calculated, the percentage of people living below the poverty level has dropped from a high point of 22.4% to its lowest level of 12.3% reported in the 2006 census data (U.S. Census Bureau). The percentage of children living in poverty, however, differs from the population at large, and of the more than 73 million children in the United States, roughly 18% currently live in poor families while another 39% live in low income families (National Center for Children in Poverty, 2008b). Moreover, because parents of younger children tend to have lower incomes due to their younger age and limited work experience, official poverty rates are higher for the youngest, most vulnerable child population. Considering only children under the age of 5, the percentage living in poor families swells to 21% (National Center for Children in Poverty, 2008a).

Poverty is a significant national problem affecting millions of children in the United States, and it should not and cannot be ignored by schools. To put the problem of child poverty in perspective, in 2007 the U.S. Census Bureau indicated that 18% of children under the age of 18 were living in poverty, up from 17.4% in 2006 (U.S. Census Bureau, 2008). This rate represents approximately 13 million children and is higher than the rate for adults ages 18 to 64 and for senior citizens age 65 and older (Whitehouse, 2006). In addition, data from recent years indicates that about 10% of all American families live in poverty, and that more than a quarter of families headed by single mothers are impoverished (DeNavas-Walt et al., 2005). As such, millions of children in our nation's schools are experiencing poverty, indicating that there is an urgent need to disseminate information to school professionals who work with these children (Whitehouse, 2006).

The purpose of Chapter 2 is to discuss poverty, particularly the many deleterious effects it has on children. A social justice perspective on child poverty will be provided, including the notion of providing a school-based "preferential option" for children living in poverty. Finally, a public health approach to school-based interventions for children in poverty will be described, including a framework for how interventions can be provided across multiple levels. The authors begin, however, with a brief overview of poverty.

Since the advent of Head Start in the 1960's, preschool interventions targeted children living in poverty. The findings from some of these programs demonstrate some positive results. While teacher education and other features of child care quality have been found to be an important factor in the improvement of childhood outcomes for children in poverty, the relevance of racial ethnic socialization in child care has not been examined as a potentially crucial element toward improving developmental outcomes for African-American and Mexican immigrant children living in urban poverty. Before determining the impact of child care racial ethnic socialization on childhood outcomes, it is necessary to identify what racial ethnic socialization in child care is. Chapter 3 will address this question by presenting original research that describes racial ethnic socialization practices in professional child care programs that serve poor, urban, racial ethnic minority children[1].

The primary goal of Chapter 4 is to empirically investigate the association among income, health promotion behaviors, and health satisfaction in Korea. The findings obtained in the current study support a clear relationship between self-assessed health status and income in the context of health promotion behaviors. The results confirm that income matters in the health context in that it is associated with health promotion behaviors. However, by income level, the mechanism of income in health differs. Health satisfaction among the rich is higher than that of the poor, and participation in health checkups and regular exercise shows a proportional association with income levels except in the richest group. As for the low income group, the primary reason for poor health stems from low levels of health management in seeking health checkups and engaging in regular exercise, which are associated with income level. For the low income group, the problem of low health satisfaction is mainly due to health management resources while for the richest making money appears to be the first priority. This idiosyncratic nature of the two types sheds an informative light on implementing health policy. In order to increase health satisfaction for the low income groups, the appropriate policy focuses on providing them with financial assistance for health checkups. Regarding a health promotion policy for the richest people, there seems to be little government attention. The action that the richest people need to take is to free themselves from a money-oriented mindset. They should recognize that there might be a trade-off between the amount of money earned and level of health satisfaction.

The main aim of Chapter 5 is to analyse the contribution of unemployment and individual characteristics to welfare durations taking into account different ways of modelling unemployment and including heterogeneity according to participation sequences. The programme studied in this paper is the Minimum Income Integration programme (*IMI*) of the

---

[1] The term "racial ethnicity" is adopted in line with Thorne (2005)

Madrid Government. Administrative records are available from more than eleven years and the number of households and spells is larger than in other studies (over 50,000 spells). The authors estimate different discrete time duration models with alternative ways of controlling unobserved heterogeneity. Their results show that there are clearly differentiated types of recipients depending on the recurrence and duration of welfare participation. The unemployment rate at the moment of entering the programme seems to be a relevant factor for the probability of leaving, but having less weight than that exerted by the recipients' socio-demographic characteristics. There is also a certain degree of duration dependence and the effects of macroeconomic conditions drastically differ depending on the length of the welfare spell.

Chapter 6 looks at the housing experiences of Sri Lanka over the past four decades during which it has adopted both 'top-down', regulated approaches to 'bottom-up' flexible practices to address the issues of low–income housing. It focuses on the issues of social perceptions, engagements, expectations, values and mechanisms of interactions between people and the state that are at the core of the housing problem which often lead to the construction of impoverished and improvised shelter. While the strategies most governments adopt such as low-cost building technologies, enabling the acquisition of land, infra-structure and finance and offering support to resolve the construction issues are useful and important, addressing the underlying social challenges are key to unlocking the potentials that exist in the low-income communities to house themselves well. The paper offers insights into how the complexities of these social challenges have been confronted in Sri Lanka through support housing and will suggest the way forward in dealing with them in order to devise more meaningful and positive interventions n low-income housing.

Chapter 7 deals with health inequalities attributable to economic, social, and cultural factors. It first analyses how social inequalities have increased in many developed countries in the last decade, following a lengthy period of decline since the early 20th century. Secondly, and narrowing its focus to older Italians, it investigates how a low Socio-Economic Status (SES) can be an independent predictor of further risks in terms of health status. Furthermore, the paper tries to explain key aspects of this phenomenon and their impact on older people's needs within society. Finally, the paper attempts to identify policy options for relevant actors, reviewing the current debate on the topic, including recent advances and future research needs.

The healing of human ailments by using therapeutics based on medicines obtained from animals or ultimately derived from them is known as zootherapy. The use of animal-derived medicines as an alternative therapeutic has also been recorded in different parts of the globe, yet little attention has been paid to the cultural, medical, or ecological significance of zootherapeutic practices, even in countries where the use of medicinal animals is well established. Despite their importance, studies on the therapeutic use of animals and animal parts have been neglected, when compared to plants. Chapter 8 discusses some related aspects of the use of animals or parts thereof as medicines in South America, and their implications for public health, ecology and economy. Our review revealed that at least 322 species of animals belonging to 157 families are used in traditional folk medicine in South America. The use of medicinal animals is a fundamental component within traditional health systems and medical practice in South America. Besides being influenced by cultural aspects, the relations between humans and biodiversity in the form of zootherapeutic practices are conditioned by the social and economic relations.

A cross-sectional study of 474 adult (> 18 years) Bengalee male slum dwellers of Kolkata, (India), was undertaken investigate the use of mid-upper arm circumference (MUAC) as a measure of nutritional status and its relationship with current reported morbidity. Height, weight and MUAC were measured using standard techniques. The body mass index (BMI) was computed following the standard formula. Classification of chronic energy deficiency (CED) was done following the WHO guideline of BMI < 18.5 kg/m^2. Results revealed that MUAC of 24 cm was the best cut-off point to distinguish between CED and non-CED individuals with sensitivity (SN), specificity (SP), positive (PPV) and negative (NPV) predictive values of 86.3, 85.1, 73.3 and 92.9, respectively. Moreover, there was a significant (chi-square = 11.834, p < 0.005) difference in the presence of self reported morbidity between the two MUAC groups (MUACGI: MUAC < 24 cm and MUACGII: MUAC ≥ 24 cm) with subjects in MUACGI 2.09 times more likely to be currently morbid compared with those in MUACGII. Furthermore, morbid subjects had significantly lower mean values of weight (p < 0.005), BMI (p < 0.005) and MUAC (p < 0.001) compared to non-morbid individuals. Chapter 9 concludes that a MUAC value of 24 cm can be used as a simple and efficient cut-off point for the determination of CED and morbidity status in this population.

Surgery has long been considered too costly to be part of basic health care packages in low-income countries. Very little data are in fact available from resource-poor settings. Cost-effectiveness analysis is a widely used tool to inform decision makers in the resource allocation process. It is particularly valuable where resources are very scarce. Chapter 10 reports on two cost-effectiveness analyses conducted at two surgical centers of the Italian non-governmental organization Emergency, in Sierra Leone and in Cambodia. Data on both the costing and effectiveness sides were collected and analyzed using the same methodology. The results are presented in dollars per DALY averted. Although both hospitals have a slightly different vocation, they were found to be very cost-effective at $32.78 per DALY averted in Sierra Leone and $77.40 per DALY averted in Cambodia. This compares favorably to other public health interventions in similar contexts, such as vaccination or nutritional supplementation. The reasons for the difference between the two sites, and the significance of the findings are discussed.

Physical inactivity is most prevalent among low-income women, yet a paucity of physical activity research exists with this population. Primary care practitioners can play a critical role in promoting physical activity to decrease adverse health outcomes among low-income women. The purpose of Chapter 11 was to test a stage-matched message developed from the Transtheoretical Model to increase physical activity. From a primary care clinic women (N=32) at or below 185% of poverty level in Contemplation or Preparation stages of change completed measures of physical activity, stage of change, perceived physical activity benefits and barriers, and demographic data. Participants were randomized to receive a stage-matched physical activity message or a standard message with two follow-up phone contacts over 10 weeks. Pre and post difference scores, Mann-Whitney U and independent t-tests were used to analyze data. The groups did not differ pre-intervention on demographic variables, mean number of steps measured by pedometer, benefits or barriers scores. Participants were 78% White, with a mean age of 37.5 years, 11.8 years of education, and BMI of 34. The experimental group progressed significantly more in stage of change (m = 21.24) than the control group (m = 11.13; U = 47.00, p < .000). The experimental group had significantly ($t(30)$ = 2.60, p = .015) higher step counts (m = 7826.24, sd = 4559.45) than the control group

(m = 4137.27, sd = 3280.03) and significantly lower ($t(30)$ = -2.52, p = .017) barriers scores (m = 12.88, sd = 5.13) than the control group (m = 17.47, sd = 5.15) post-intervention. Further research is needed that targets this at-risk population, but it appears that practitioners in primary care settings could implement this counseling approach to increase physical activity in low-income women.

The rent-to-own (RTO) industry is popular among low income consumers in part because it offers immediate access to merchandise along with the ability to cancel a transaction at any point without adverse consequence. Chapter 12 studies consumer use of RTO using a unique data base of more than 11,000 completed transactions originating between 2001 and 2004 inclusive and drawn from four RTO stores in the southeast United States. Descriptive statistics are produced on customer characteristics, e.g., income level and martial status; and on contract structure, e.g., maximum duration and the periodicity of the payment schedule. While it is understood that the main categories of RTO products are appliances, computers, furniture, electronics and jewelry to produce a fuller picture of a typical transaction, the data is used to tabulate the actual merchandise being acquired. Further, contracts must conclude in one of four manners: return, contract payout, early purchase or default (i.e., a "skip"—the customer does not fully discharge their obligation but the store is unable to recover the merchandise). This paper explores the likelihood of these various outcomes using a multinomial logit methodology. This has two advantages. One, the authors are able to see the significance of various customer characteristics and contractual features in impacting these probabilities as well as comparing the direction of any affect against a priori hypotheses. Two, the authors are able to compare and contrast the simulated probabilities of different types of customers, e.g. a single, young, man receiving government aid versus a married, older, female getting no aid. In sum, this paper seeks to add to our understanding of an important but little studied acquisition mechanism. Among other benefits, this piece could play a role in the policy debate about the nature of rent-to-own and its contribution to consumer welfare. Additionally, the paper adds novel insights into the picture of how financially-disadvantaged consumers conduct their affairs while also providing some insights applicable to all consumers whether financially constrained or not.

In: Low Incomes: Social, Health and Educational Impacts   ISBN: 978-1-60741-175-8
Editor: Jacob K. Levine, pp. 1-30   © 2009 Nova Science Publishers, Inc.

Chapter 1

PREVENTING ANTISOCIAL BEHAVIOR: PARENT TRAINING IN LOW-INCOME URBAN SCHOOLS

Kristin D. Sawka-Miller[1] and Barry L. McCurdy[2]
[1] Siena College, Loudonville, NY, USA
[2] Devereux Center for Effective Schools, PA, USA

Abstract

Poverty rates in the United States are determined based on a metric from the 1950s that takes into account the cost of food and is then adjusted for family size (National Center for Children in Poverty, 2008a). Accordingly, in today's economy, a family of four residing on an annual income of $21,200 would be below the federal poverty level. Currently, there are 13 million American children living in families with incomes below the federal poverty level. There are concerns, however, that the metric of determination based on food and income alone is flawed since it does not take into account the cumulative costs of housing, health care, child care and transportation and that, realistically speaking, there are many more children adversely affected by poverty (National Center for Children in Poverty, 2008a).

Historically, the poverty rate in the United States has varied, mirroring national trends of economic growth, stability and downturn. Since 1959, when the poverty rate was first calculated, the percentage of people living below the poverty level has dropped from a high point of 22.4% to its lowest level of 12.3% reported in the 2006 census data (U.S. Census Bureau). The percentage of children living in poverty, however, differs from the population at large, and of the more than 73 million children in the United States, roughly 18% currently live in poor families while another 39% live in low income families (National Center for Children in Poverty, 2008b). Moreover, because parents of younger children tend to have lower incomes due to their younger age and limited work experience, official poverty rates are higher for the youngest, most vulnerable child population. Considering only children under the age of 5, the percentage living in poor families swells to 21% (National Center for Children in Poverty, 2008a).

Poverty and the Risk for Antisocial Behavior

Aggression, delinquency and violence are all strongly linked dimensions of a pattern of behavior generically referred to as "antisocial." Broadly defined, this pattern of behavior is the opposite of prosocial and suggests a willingness to commit rule infractions, defiance of adult authority, and violation of the norms and mores of society (Kazdin, 1995; Reid, 1993; Walker, Ramsey, & Gresham, 2004). Associated behaviors include those considered mildly disturbing such as noncompliance, talking back, and temper tantrums, to those considered more serious and disruptive to the environment such as threatening others, physically harming others, destroying property and even sexual assault. Statistical records show that antisocial behavior among youths has increased over the years due, in large part, to increases in the number of youth gangs and associated gang violence (Achenbach, Dumenci, & Rescorla, 2003; Loeber & Stouthamer-Loeber, 1998; Howell, 2003).

Researchers have identified a myriad of risk factors linked to the development of serious and chronic antisocial behavior, many of which are also associated with socioeconomic disadvantage (Bolger, Patterson, Thompson & Kupersmidt, 1995; Bradley & Whiteside-Mansell, 1997). Persistent poverty, as opposed to transitory poverty, has been found to have detrimental effects on intelligence, school achievement and social-emotional development (McLoyd, 1998; Scaramella, Neppl, Ontai, & Conger, 2008). It is important to note, however, that the effects of poverty are not equally distributed across all three outcomes. Several reviews have shown that although family income is more strongly linked to lower cognitive functioning and poor school performance, it is the social class effects of poverty that appear to impact social/emotional development, particularly the development of externalizing problem behaviors (Bradley & Corwyn, 2002; Bradley & Whiteside-Manssell, 1997; McLoyd, 1990; 1998).

Mediating Processes Linking Poverty to Behavior Problems

Deteriorating Neighborhood Conditions

Families in poverty have limited access to the resources that are essential to healthy development. Many of these families are relegated to living in dilapidated and crowded housing conditions, in neighborhoods that have few resources. For younger children, growing up with less access to stimulating resources, including recreational facilities, may limit their opportunities for socialization. A related concern is for adolescents who, residing in similar neighborhood conditions, are increasingly exposed to deviant peers (Bradley & Corwyn, 2002). In a recent twin study, Caspi, Taylor, Moffitt and Plomin (2000) demonstrated that the effects of neighborhood deprivation, in addition to family environmental factors, was an important variable in accounting for children's emotional and behavioral problems.

Under-resourced Schools

Many families in poverty reside in our nation's urban centers (Rutter, 1981; Wilson, 1987). The extreme and persistent environmental stressors commonly found in inner-city communities, including poverty and its associated factors (i.e., unemployment or underemployment, limited resources, substandard housing, single-parenting combined with a prevalence of female-headed households, and high crime rates) expose children to a greater number of risks for the development of conduct and disruptive behavior disorders (Attar,

Guerra, & Tolan, 1994; Levanthal & Brooks-Gunn, 2000). Compounding the problem is that these children attend under-resourced and often over-taxed inner-city schools - schools under extreme economic and social strain. In a study conducted by the U.S. Department of Education's Office of Educational Research and Improvement (OERI), the analysts found important differences between urban, suburban and rural schools, with urban schools showing a greater number of student behavior problems including, among others, absenteeism, classroom discipline and weapons possession (Lippman, Burns, McArthur, 1996). Not only does student academic performance deteriorate in these challenging conditions, but the environment may actually engender aggressive behavior. For example, Guerra, Huesmann, Tolan, Van Acker and Eron (as cited in Van Acker & Talbott, 1999), conducted a longitudinal study of children from first through fifth grade in low income neighborhoods in Chicago. The authors described a significant increase in the level of teacher-rated aggression as children entered and progressed through school. Accordingly, the percentage of children displaying aggression upon entering first grade (4.9%) was about similar to the national average (4.5%), but that number doubled by second grade and by fifth grade had increased to almost four times the national average.

Teachers' attitudes and expectations for children from low-SES families also contribute to the problem. Children who come to school with less experience with cognitively stimulating materials and/or without good language skills often reinforce teachers' negative stereotypes (McLoyd, 1998). Positive attention and praise for desired academic performance is bestowed less frequently on these students leading them to behave in other, typically more negative, ways to gain teacher attention. As such, reciprocal and negative teacher responses exacerbate the situation, which often serves to further alienate students (and their families) from the schooling experience (Walker et al., 2004).

Inadequate Language Development

Children who do not develop adequate language skills at an early age and are not adept at using those skills at school entry are also at risk for developing social-emotional difficulties. Benner, Nelson and Epstein (2002), in a review of the prevalence of language deficits in children formally identified as having emotional and behavioral difficulties in school, found that nearly three out of four (71%) identified children experienced clinically significant language deficits that included deficiencies in expressive language as well as receptive and pragmatic skills.

There are a number of ways in which growing up poor contributes to deficiencies in language development. Low-SES parents are less likely to purchase reading materials or to read to their children. They are less likely to take their children to educational and cultural events or to regulate the amount of television that children watch (Bradley, Corwyn, Burchinal, McAdoo, & Garcia Coll, 2001). Moreover, children in low-SES families are less likely to experience the high quality adult-child interactions characteristic of higher SES families. In their landmark study of 42 families that span the socioeconomic strata of the United States, Hart and Risley (1995) found that parents from professional and working class families used more words and more different kinds of words with their children, gave their children more affirmative feedback, and responded to them more often and for longer periods of time than parents on welfare. The end result is that children from low-SES families have lesser cumulative experience with language at school entry, which likely affects peer-to-peer socialization as well as interactions with adult staff members.

Harsh, Inconsistent Parenting

Probably the most important factor linking low-SES with poor social-emotional development among children is parenting style. Bradley and Corwyn (2002) link ineffective parenting practices to both stress reactions and health-relevant lifestyles among the poor. Accordingly, parents under the daily strain of living in poverty experience more uncontrollable and threatening events, hazardous conditions, and destabilizing situations (e.g., family breakups and household moves). Additionally, many of these individuals adopt unhealthy patterns of behavior, including the use of alcohol and drugs, and engage in little or no exercise, which serves to exacerbate stress levels and cause parents to be less nurturing toward their children. Parents who are over-stressed are not attuned to their children's behavior, fail to discipline consistently and, when they do, tend to rely on the use of negative control strategies (McCoy, Frick, Loney, & Ellis, 1999; Patterson, 2002; Wahler & Sansbury, 1990). Harsh, punitive styles of parenting have been consistently linked to externalizing behavior problems in childhood (Snyder & Stoolmiller, 2002), and parents who reside in urban communities tend to be more restrictive and punitive in their parenting style (Garbarino, 1995). Parents who raise children in communities rife with violence and where any number of predatory adults may co-exist tend to be overprotective and thereby restrictive and punitive in efforts to keep children under watch and in the confines of the house and neighborhood.

Finally, the interactive mechanism by which externalizing problem behaviors emerge in children and increase over time appears to be bi-directional. Several researchers suggested that the dearth of stimulating materials in the homes of low-SES families contributes to the frustration and boredom of children, who then begin to engage in other non-sanctioned behaviors. These behaviors then lead to coercive parenting practices that have been shown to contribute to and, in fact, strengthen externalizing problem behaviors in children (Patterson, 2002; Wahler & Williams, 1990)

Parent Management Training

One way to buffer the impact of low-SES on social-emotional development is through parent training. There are actually few tested approaches for helping parents to address the oppositional, aggressive and antisocial behaviors of their children. To date, no other approach has been as well investigated as parent management training (PMT; Kazdin, 2005; Kazdin & Weisz, 2003). PMT, also known as behavioral parent training or parent behavior management training, is an approach that teaches social learning techniques, including social reinforcement and modeling concepts, to parents invested in altering the behavior of their children (Kazdin, 2005; Patterson, 1982). PMT is distinguished from other models of parent training and other forms of therapy involving parents by the four defining features described below (Kazdin, 2005).

Theoretical Basis

PMT is based on learning theory and specifically operant conditioning, which posits that behavioral change can be achieved by focusing on the antecedent and consequent events that surround the behavior of interest. Those same events are often used to shape and change child behavior. The focus of PMT is to change how the parent behaves and interacts with the child to ultimately change the child's behavior.

Behavior Principles

Therapists employing this approach focus on teaching parents the basic principles of operant behavior, including reinforcement and punishment, in a manner that promotes prosocial behavior in the child. Parents are taught techniques to apply these principles in everyday situations. The fact that the techniques are based on empirically established principles is important because, at times, a particular technique may prove to be ineffective with a particular child. Therapists in these circumstances can then easily substitute a different, more effective strategy as long as it is supported by the same behavioral principle.

Active Training

In a significant departure from other parent training programs, PMT therapists employ an active training approach to teach parents the techniques of how to interact most effectively with the child in promoting prosocial responding. Active training includes modeling, role play, practice, and feedback, and these strategies are employed whether PMT is delivered in group- or family-based (individual) therapy. Simply providing parents with information on behavior change techniques is insufficient for helping parents to change how they respond to their child's behavior. PMT therapists utilize the same techniques of positive reinforcement, shaping and antecedent intervention to alter the interactions that parents will use with their children.

Ongoing Evaluation

PMT therapists integrate assessment and evaluation with intervention. The overarching goal of treatment is to improve adaptive functioning in the child. Several objectives are targeted to achieve this goal (e.g., complying with basic parent requests) and, as they are attained, new objectives are selected (e.g., homework completion without argument). PMT therapists monitor progress on discrete objectives while working with families so that decisions can be made about what is and is not working.

Finally, it is important to note that the strategies and procedures of PMT are not captured in one therapeutic method or approach or by one model of parent training. What constitutes PMT is defined by the core features above. These features have been combined in different ways, with differing emphases, into a variety of parent training programs - all of which can be subsumed under the general theoretical approach known as PMT (Kazdin, 2005). Table 1 provides a brief description of the different parent training programs that have contributed to the research on PMT.

Table 1. PMT Programs, Populations Served and Brief Descriptions

Model	Target Age	Description
Helping the Non-compliant Child (HNC; McMahon & Forehand, 2003)	3-8	HNC is specifically designed to address noncompliance in children. Noncompliance is considered a "keystone" behavior in the development of child conduct problems. Parenting skills are taught in two phases with the first (Phase I) designed to improve attending skills and to establish a mutually-reinforcing and positive relationship and the second (Phase II) designed to teach primary parenting skills intended to promote compliance. Training is done with individual families, in a clinic setting, with the use of one-way mirrors and bug-in-ear devices to communicate unobtrusively with parents.
Parent-Child Interaction Therapy (PCIT; Brinkmeyer & Eyberg, 2003)	3-6	PCIT is grounded in both social learning and attachment theories. The goals of the program are to improve the parent-child relationship as well as parent management skills. Parents first learn a child-directed interaction (CDI) designed to enhance the nurturing response. CDI is followed by learning the parent-directed interaction (PDI) designed to improve parent behavior management skills.
Incredible Years (Webster-Stratton & Reid, 2003)	3-8	The core program (BASIC) incorporates a standard package of videotape programs demonstrating effective parenting skills. The program is presented to groups of parents during a 12-14 week program. The core program is supplemented with a program of advanced parenting skills (ADVANCE), parenting for school-related topics (SCHOOL), as well as a teacher training and child training (Dina Dinosaur Social Skills and Problem-Solving Curriculum) programs.
Oregon Social Learning Center (OSLC) Parent Training (Patterson, 1975, 1976; Patterson & Forgatch, 1987; Forgatch & Patterson, 1989)	3 – Adolescence	Two of the earliest OSLC parent training programs include *Families* and *Living with Children*. These program booklets provide the conceptual background for parents as a therapist specifically teaches the skills of pinpointing and tracking child behavior, increasing behavior using positive reinforcement and decreasing behavior using mild, negative consequences (time out, response cost). *Parents and Adolescents Together: Parts I and II*, later OSLC publications intended to address the needs of teens, provide a translation of these skills for use with adolescents.
Triple P-Positive Parenting Program (Sanders, Mazzucchelli, & Studman, 2004)	Birth - 16	Triple P is a tiered model of behavioral parent training that incorporates five levels of intervention strategies ranging from universal to intensive support, including: (a) Universal Triple-P; information based strategies using the media and targeting the larger population of parents, (b) Selective Triple-P; a 1-2 session brief consultation conducted by primary healthcare providers, (c) Primary Care Triple-P; a 4 session consultation also conducted by primary healthcare providers, (d) Standard, Group and Self-Help Triple-P; an 8 – 10 session program for parents of children with more serious conduct problems, and (e) Enhanced Triple-P; adjunctive interventions targeting adult adjustment problems (e.g., depression, marital conflict, etc.) that co-occur with parenting concerns.

Empirical Support for PMT

As a treatment procedure, PMT is designed to promote largely positive interactions between parents and children in an effort to strengthen prosocial child behavior while preventing the development or escalation of disruptive and deviant behavior (Kazdin, 2005). The central focus of PMT is to alleviate the parent-child coercive interchange by teaching parents and other caregivers a specific set of skills to address child noncompliance, one of the core ingredients of antisocial behavior.

PMT has been effectively applied in the treatment of child clinical populations, most notably the disruptive behavior disorders of attention-deficit hyperactivity disorder (ADHD), oppositional defiant disorder (ODD), and conduct disorder (CD), as well as juvenile delinquency (Anastopoulos, Shelton, DuPaul, & Guevremont, 1993; Bank, Marlowe, Reid, Patterson, & Weinrott, 1991; Webster-Stratton, Reid, & Hammond, 2004). Several studies incorporating no-treatment or wait-list control conditions have demonstrated positive outcomes for PMT. For example, the application of PMT with child clinical populations has consistently shown marked improvement in behavior to the extent that the improvements are considered "clinically significant" and of a large magnitude ($d = .88 - 1.00$; deGraaf, Speetjens, Smit, Wolff, & Tavecchio, 2008; Webster-Stratton, Hollinsworth, & Kolpacoff, 1989).

Poor parenting practices, usually coupled with harsh and inconsistent punishment, are consistently linked with disruptive child behavior (Granic & Patterson, 2006; Patterson, 2002). Improving parenting skills, therefore, serves to mediate children's externalizing behavior. PMT improves child behavior because it leads to more positive parent-child interactions, less use of physical discipline by parents, and greater parent-child bonding (Reid, Webster-Stratton, & Hammond, 2007; Webster-Stratton, 1992; Webster-Stratton & Hammond, 1997).

Long-term maintenance effects have also resulted from PMT interventions. Studies have shown that PMT leads to positive effects on parent and child behavior that have extended from 1 to 2 years up to and including 6 years after the intervention (Eyberg, Funderburk, Hembree-Kigin, McNeil, Querido, & Hood, 2001; Hood & Eyberg, 2003). In addition, although the outcome research is not as clear in this area, there is evidence to indicate that the effects of PMT on child behavior generalize to other settings, most notably the school (McNeil, Eyberg, Hembree Eisenstadt, Newcomb, & Funderburk, 1991; Reid, Webster-Stratton, & Hammond, 2007).

The wealth of research in support of PMT resulted in its designation as one of the first interventions to meet the stringent criteria of the American Psychological Association (APA) as a "well-established" treatment for child and adolescent conduct problems, including ODD and CD (Brestan & Eyberg, 1998). In advocating a public health approach to the prevention of antisocial behavior, several researchers have called for the universal application of PMT practices (i.e., implemented with an entire population of parents in a given community), particularly in low-income neighborhoods (Sanders, Mazzuchelli, & Studman, 2004; Webster-Stratton, 1997). To illustrate how a universal PMT program can be used with low-income parents in an urban school setting, a pilot project conducted by the authors and known as the Toolbox of Parent Skills is described below.

Toolbox of Parent Skills (TOPS) Pilot Project

Participants

All parents of children attending an urban elementary school serving approximately 400 students in grades Kindergarten through fifth grade were targeted for inclusion in Toolbox of Parent Skills (TOPS), a five-week school-based PMT program. The project was part of a larger prevention initiative funded by a grant from the US Department of Education, Office of Special Education Programs, in which the school was implementing a universal school-wide positive behavior support program. In this program, all students were systematically taught a set of school-wide expectations (Be Cooperative, Be Prepared, Be Respectful, Be Kind) and recognized with praise and tickets for following the expectations throughout the day. Teachers were also provided intensive training and technical assistance for classroom behavioral and instructional management. The TOPS program served as the parent/community outreach component of this larger initiative.

Across three years, 345 families were targeted for participation in TOPS, and intakes (defined as making a verbal invitation to at least one parent in the family and securing completion of a self-report demographic survey) were completed for 307 (89%) parents of children attending the school. Of the parents for whom intakes were completed, approximately 99% were from minority racial-ethnic backgrounds, primarily self-identified as African American (96%). The mean number of children per household was 2.5, and the mean age for children in the household was 7 years. The majority of parents who responded to the survey question related to income reported combined family incomes of less than $20,000 per year, and only 9% reported annual incomes greater than $40,000 (see Table 2). Approximately 50% of parents reported that high school graduation was their highest level of educational attainment, and 28% reported dropping out of high school. Approximately 20% of parents reported completing some college or vocational school, and 2% indicated they earned college degrees.

Table 2. Self-Reported Income of Recruited Parents for TOPS Program

Annual Combined Family Income	Mean % of Respondents Who Answered Question
Below $10,000	25%
$10,001 - $20,000	32%
$20,001 - $30,000	23%
$30,001 - $40,000	12%
$40,001 - $50,000	6%
Greater than $50,000	3%

Note: 262 of 307 parents completing demographic survey responded to this item.

The TOPS Program

Curriculum

The TOPS curriculum was written by a team of psychologists, including the authors, at the Devereux Center for Effective Schools specifically for this project. The curriculum adopted a PMT approach and was divided into five modules. One module was trained per week, and training sessions were one and a half hours per module. General training topics included following directions and giving attention, effective requests and praise for following directions, household rules, reward systems for following directions, and reducing negative behavior. (See Appendix A for a full list of training topics.)

Each module was presented using an active training approach. Specifically, each skill uwas taught using an instruction-modeling-practice-feedback sequence in which the instructor explained and modeled the skill, engaged parents in a role play or other activity, and provided monitoring and feedback to parents as they practiced the skill. In addition, parents were provided optional homework assignments that provided them the opportunity to practice the skill, and time was devoted at the beginning of each session to discussing homework and trouble-shooting reported obstacles to implementation. At the end of each session, parents were provided with a "Refrigerator Note" (i.e., a note to display prominently on the family refrigerator to provide easy access to information) summarizing the major points from the session. Parents were invited to have private meetings (at home or at school) with the parent trainer if they wanted more information about any topic.

Staffing

The project employed one full-time parent trainer and two half-time community liaisons. Two individuals served as parent trainers during the course of the project, both of whom were female, African American, in their late 20's, and had graduate degrees in counseling psychology. The role of the parent trainer was to facilitate all training sessions, manage and participate in recruitment and retention efforts, communicate with school staff about the progress of children of parents participating in training, and supervise two community liaisons.

Community liaisons lived in the school community and had children or grandchildren who attended the school targeted for the project. They were paid $10 an hour and were each employed approximately 20 hours per week by the Devereux Foundation for the duration of the TOPS project. During the project, four females held the position of community liaison. All were African American and three had earned high school diplomas. Their ages ranged from 23 to 62 years. Responsibilities of community liaisons included conducting initial home visits to recruit parents to attend training, participating in parent training sessions, making follow-up phone calls and home visits to individuals who missed a training, and informally communicating with parents regarding the program.

Training

All class-based training sessions were held at the elementary school. Classes were conducted in a small group format (i.e., limited to 10 participants per session) and were offered in the morning, afternoon, and evening several days per week to provide multiple opportunities for parents to attend the 1.5 hour weekly session. If a parent was not able to make a scheduled class-based training session, they were given the option of completing the session in their home, one-on-one (versus small group) at another time at school, or over the phone. Each week parents who did not participate in any of these modes of training were mailed a training handout, the session's "Refrigerator Note", a copy of the homework assignment, and a reminder card for the next session.

Free childcare, meals (breakfast, lunch, or dinner), and door prizes were provided at each session, and bus tokens were made available for parents in need of transportation to the training. Parents earned tickets for attendance (two tickets for in-class attendance and one ticket for a one-to-one class at home or on the phone), completing homework assignments, and speaking up in class or meeting privately with TOPS staff. These tickets were exchanged at the end of each session for opportunities to win a daily door prize. In addition, tickets earned in all sessions across the five weeks of the program were saved for a large prize drawing conducted at the end of the project on "graduation" day.

At the end of the five-week session, parents were invited to a graduation ceremony in front of all students in the school. This assembly also served to recognize students for their efforts in the schoolwide positive behavior support project and often consisted of chants and cheers, a brief review of the expectations, and pubic acknowledgment of individuals or groups of students for noteworthy accomplishments in the program. During this assembly, graduating parents sat with their children and walked across the stage to receive a TOPS diploma when their name was called. In addition, parents were recognized for different levels of graduation. Specifically, a "graduate" attended all five sessions in any combination of in-class, one-on-one, or by phone. An "honors" graduate attended all sessions, with at least three being in-class. Honors graduates were given a gift certificate toward a school uniform. "High honors" graduates attended all the sessions in-class and were awarded a $50 gift certificate to any family establishment of their choice. Following the graduation ceremony, all TOPS graduates and their families had a cake and punch reception.

Recruitment and Retention Procedures

All parents of children attending the school were targeted for participation in the program across three years. Approximately 30 families were targeted per training cohort, for a total of 11 cohorts throughout the course of the project. Participants were clustered into training cohorts based on geographic variables. Specifically, the addresses of all families were plotted on a map prior to the start of the project, and efforts were made to cluster participants who lived closest to one another. At the beginning of the project, all parents were sent a letter by the school explaining the TOPS program and informing them that at some point within the three-year period they would receive an invitation to participate.

Participants in each cohort were sent a letter three weeks prior to the first training explaining the project and letting them know that someone from the project would be coming to their home the following week to answer their questions. Two weeks prior to the first training, the parent trainer and a community liaison made a home visit to introduce themselves, complete the intake interview, and secure the preferred day and time of training. One week prior to training, the community liaison delivered a reminder card with the day and time of the first training session. One day before the session, the parent trainer or a community liaison provided a reminder phone call to the parent.

If a parent did not attend a scheduled session, a community liaison attempted to contact the parent by phone within three working hours to try to schedule another training session. If unable to speak with parents by phone, a community liaison dropped of a "You Were Missed" letter to the parent's home encouraging them to attend the meeting the following week and encouraging them to make-up the current week's training via a one-to-one session at school, home, or by phone. Two more efforts were made to contact parents by phone who did not schedule a make-up by the end of the training week before mailing the missed session's handouts, homework, and "Refrigerator Note" to the parents' residences.

Outcomes

The primary outcome measures evaluated the effects of the project on parental acquisition of knowledge of effective parenting practices, parent satisfaction with the TOPS program, and parental participation and retention rates for training. The specific measures and outcomes are described below.

Knowledge

Participant knowledge of effective parenting skills was measured at the beginning of Module 1 and the end of Module 5 using the same 10-item multiple-choice test. The test was created by the developers of the TOPS curriculum and items were designed to reflect applied knowledge of the major skills covered in the training. The test included questions such as the following:

What is the first tool a parent should use to increase "good" behaviors they want to see more of in their child?

A) Take away a privilege
B) Use positive attention
C) Use a reward system.

Two questions were constructed from each of the five training modules and each question had three choices. In an effort to control for reading skill, the test was read to participants as they completed it. The test was piloted with the community liaisons before being used with parent participants. If a participant was not present for a training session, the parent trainer attempted to secure completion of the test over the phone or through the mail. Pretests were completed by 60% of parents in the school (n=180), and posttests were completed by 49% of all parents (n=149). The average score increased from 51% correct on the pretest to 82% on the posttest.

Satisfaction

Following the completion of the last training session, participants anonymously completed a nine-item program evaluation form created by the developers of the TOPS curriculum. Specifically, parents were asked to rate on a 5-point Likert scale the degree to which they (a) were satisfied with the program, presenters and activities; (b) believed the program helped them and their child; and (c) would recommend the program to other parents. The evaluation form was read to parents as they completed the form. Parents were also encouraged to write additional comments. If a participant was not present for a training session, the parent trainer attempted to secure completion of the test over the phone or through the mail.

The mean score for parents completing the evaluation form was 4.83 (n=144). Parents were strongly in agreement that the trainers were friendly and approachable and that the program was a good use of their time. In addition, they indicated that the activities were fun and helped them learn effective parent management skills. Several parents commented that one of the things they liked best about the program was the graduation ceremony.

Attendance and Retention

Over the course of the project, 307 families were recruited for participation in training and were monitored with respect to the type of training they received. Specifically, each week it was noted if each target participant was exposed to direct training (i.e., class instruction, one-to-one session, phone training) or indirect training in the form of mailed materials. Although mailing materials to all parents who missed a direct training was a component of the TOPS program, it was the expectation of program staff that parents would generally *not* benefit substantially from receiving instructional materials in the mail without any direct training. Retention (i.e., program completion) in the program was defined as attendance at all five training sessions in any direct contact format. Over the course of the entire project, 53% of all parents in the school attended at least one direct training session, and 47% of all parents in the school attended all training sessions in the direct training format. This indicates that 89% of the parents who attended the first session completed the entire training program (i.e., were retained), a figure significantly higher than those reported in other studies. Further, the overwhelming majority of these parents attended their sessions in the class instruction (versus one-to-one or phone training) format.

It is important to note that there was a period during the project in which the recruitment and retention procedures were implemented with low treatment integrity (e.g., reminder calls were not consistently made and there were few attempts to follow-up in person with participants who missed a scheduled training.) The problem was eventually resolved, but in the interim the recruitment and retention procedures for 4 of the 11 cohorts were compromised, and this appeared to substantially impact attendance and retention rates. When the procedures were implemented as intended, 70% of targeted parents attended at least one direct training, and the program completion rate was 62%. When the recruitment and follow-up procedures were compromised, 35% of targeted parents attended at least one training, and the program completion rate was only 25%. This suggested that high fidelity implementation of the recruitment and retention procedures was associated with substantially higher participation and retention rates, and that the aggregated data across the project is a poor indicator of overall program effectiveness.

Limitations

In terms of program evaluation, the TOPS project as described should be considered a pilot study. There are several limitations to the current research methodology that would need to be addressed for a well-controlled evaluation of the program. For example, there was a lack of an experimental design to evaluate outcomes, and - while there were early attempts to include a control school in this pilot study - there were too many differences and uncontrollable variables to allow for meaningful comparison to a non-training site. In addition, there was no evaluation of outcomes at the individual child level. Student behavioral referrals on a whole-school level were evaluated and did diminish substantially during the course of this project. There is no way of knowing, however, if this was due to the PMT program, the school-wide positive behavior support program, some combination of the two, or neither.

Two other important outcomes related to PMT were knowingly not addressed in the TOPS pilot, as they did not relate directly to the goals of the project. First, there was no measure of generalization of parent skills from the training context to the home. That is, there is no way of knowing if parents actually *changed* their behavior and implemented more effective parenting skills in the home as a function of the increased knowledge gained during training. Second, there was no information obtained from parents who never attended training or dropped out of training with respect to reasons for their nonparticipation. Logistical constraints prevented both of theses research questions from being investigated; however, they have been addressed in other studies and those results are summarized elsewhere in this chapter.

Implications

Despite these limitations, results obtained from the TOPS pilot project contribute significantly to the literature on PMT. The TOPS program is one of the few PMT programs applied at a universal, preventive level. Further, it is one of even fewer school-based programs, and it is the only known PMT program to target all parents in a school. Finally, to-date it is the only universal program that has been applied in an urban school setting with a high percentage of low-income, ethnic minority parents.

Perhaps the most striking outcome from the project was its success at recruiting and retaining low-income parents for whom attendance at PMT programs has historically been lowest. Research has clearly demonstrated that PMT programs are effective. Effectively recruiting and sustaining parent involvement in trainings, however, are the primary obstacles to success. In the TOPS program, when the recruitment procedures were followed 70% of target parents attended at least one in-class, individual, or phone training; and throughout the project 89% of parents who attended one training went on to complete the entire training. These figures are unsurpassed and are substantially higher than other universal PMT programs reported in the professional literature. This finding is particularly powerful given the multiple risk factors facing families targeted in the TOPS program.

The following section will address lessons learned from the TOPS pilot project in the context of a research-based discussion on common barriers to parent management training and possible ways to overcome these obstacles.

Overcoming Barriers to Parent Management Training in Low-Income, Urban Communities

The challenge of recruiting, engaging and retaining parents in PMT is substantial, and overall attendance rates across socioeconomic groups typically do not exceed 50% even when compensation is offered for participation (Gross, Julian, & Fogg; 1991; Nock & Kazdin, 2005; Orell-Valente, Pinderhughes, Valente, Laird, & Conduct Problems Prevention Research Group, 1999). These problems are intensified when recruiting populations exposed to multiple risk factors, thus making prevention programs targeting low-income, urban, ethnic minority families particularly challenging (Harachi, Catalano, & Hawkins, 1997). Indeed, research has consistently demonstrated that ethnicity and income are two of the strongest predictors of retention in parent training programs (Coatsworth, Duncan, & Pantin, 2007; Gross, Julion, & Fogg, 2001). Rates of attendance in universal parent training programs is lowest for low-income, ethnic minority families, and parents making a combined income of less than $15,000 annually are the most likely to drop out (Heinrichs, Bertra, & Hahlweg, 2005). For this group, attendance rates typically don't exceed 13% (Gross et al., 2001; Heinrichs et al., 2005; Myers et al., 1992).

Parents from low-income ethnic minority families are more likely to attend parent training programs when they perceive their child as having significant behavior or learning problems (Coatsworth et al., 2005; Kazdin, 1997). In universal prevention programs, however, the goal is to prevent behavior problems from occurring or from escalating into more serious concerns. Therefore, most of the parents invited to attend prevention programs such as TOPS will *not* have children demonstrating severe behavior problems, so one should expect low attendance if additional measures are not taken to address this challenge.

In addition to low socioeconomic status, low participation and retention in parent training programs tend to be systematically related to other risk factors such as single parenthood and lower parent educational levels (Coatsworth et al., 2006; Gross et al., 2001). When targeting caregivers with lower educational levels for training, one cannot underestimate the role of a parent's perceived competence in completing the course. Training curricula often are heavily language-based, requiring prerequisite oral communication, reading, and/or writing skills in order to benefit. Not addressing this fact could result in nonattendance. For example, the following anecdotal note from a TOPS parent trainer was written early in the training sequence:

> "Monique T. came to the TOPS room to let us know she didn't come in last week for the second module because she was planning to drop out of the program. She said she is embarrassed because she cannot read or write and the parents were writing things down. We worked out a plan for participating in class – not necessary to read or write anything, but if others are, the liaison will assist her immediately and other TOPS staff will assist other parents so that all parents are working with a staff member."

The professional literature indicates that ethnic/cultural issues are often neglected in PMT (Kazdin, 1997), and that different recruitment methods may be required to engage high-risk families from socio-economically disadvantaged areas (Dumka, Garza, Roose, & Stoerzinger, 1997; Heinrichs et al., 2005). In the following section of this chapter, specific research-based recommendations for enhancing the quality of universal parent training programs and promoting high levels of parental attendance for families living in low-income, ethnic minority, urban communities are discussed. Emphasis will be placed on the use of parent liaisons, incentive programming, frequent and person-to-person recruitment and follow-up, and the need for a comprehensive home-school approach. Specific examples from the TOPS program will be integrated into this discussion to help illustrate how a universal PMT intervention was used to target and successfully retain families with multiple risk factors (i.e., low income, urban, low educational level, and ethnic minority).

Use Community Liaisons

School-based PMT programs that target families living in low-income, urban areas face unique challenges in establishing and maintaining active parental involvement. Parents may have had negative and/or unsuccessful experiences with school themselves, and as a result may be disengaged from the schooling process for their children (Raffaele & Knoff, 1999). Low-income, ethnic minority parents have cited the personal qualities of the recruiter as being the most important factor in their decision to attend training (Gross et al., 2001), and some research suggests that the more similar participants perceive themselves to the trainer, particularly with respect to ethnicity, the more effective training will be (Dumas, Moreland, Gitter, Pearl, & Nordstrom, 2008; Howland, Anderson, Smiley, & Abbott; 2006; OJJDP, 1999). In fact, it is estimated that 50% to 80% of the effectiveness of a family program is due to the trainer's personal efficacy and characteristics rather than the standardized curriculum (OJJDP, 1999).

Unfortunately, the socioeconomic, educational, and ethnic/cultural differences between the school-based PMT trainer and the low-income, urban parents targeted for program inclusion are often vast, and this can contribute to poor training outcomes (Ouellette & Wilkerson, 2008; Sanders, 2008). Although urban districts enroll almost twice as many students from ethnic minority backgrounds as schools in non-urban areas (Schroth, Pankake, Fullwood, & Gates, 2001), the percentage of urban educators from minority backgrounds is less than half and declining (Howland et al., 2006). This lack of representation of varying cultural perspectives in schools can alienate diverse families from systems already viewed as hierarchical and, often, unwelcoming (Baker, 1997). Additionally, educational and income levels can be vastly different from the predominantly Caucasian, middle-class professionals with whom they must interact. (Boyd & Correa, 2005).

The use of community liaisons (also referred to in the literature as "parent liaisons", "community aides", and "family interviewers") can be an effective way to help connect families with schools and increase participation among low income parents in preventive PMT programs (Dumka et al., 1997; Gross et al., 2001; Harachi, Catalano, & Hawkins, 1997; Howland et al., 2006; Sanders 2008). Community liaisons typically share the same demographic characteristics as the parents targeted for training, and most live in similar communities. As such, community liaisons are sensitive to the contextual issues confronting low-income families. Their endorsement of the program as members of the community can significantly enhance program credibility (Harachi et al., 1997), and is important for helping to establish initial parent trust and cooperation (Gross et al., 2001). Additionally, focus groups with parents who have worked with community liaisons suggests that, when parents previously had negative experiences with their child's school, the liaisons helped develop more positive relationships with school personnel (Howland et al., 2006).

In the TOPS program, two community liaisons were hired who lived in the elementary school community where training was occurring and also had children or grandchildren who attended the school. Their primary roles involved face-to-face recruitment of parents and between-session follow-up, in addition to being present for PMT sessions. Liaisons often were not active participants during PMT training and instead used that time to catch up on paperwork or make follow-up phone calls to parents. They were, however, typically present in the room in which training occurred. On those occasions when the liaison was not present, their absence was clearly noted; parents asked for them and overall engagement (i.e., asking questions, answering questions) during the session was observed to be lower. Other PMT programs with low-income, urban, ethnic minority parents have hired key informal community leaders on an hourly basis who had access to parents, such as church staff or volunteer school crossing guards, to assist in recruitment efforts (Gross et al., 2001; Harachi et al., 1997). The use of bilingual liaisons to assist low-income parents with limited English proficiency has also been associated with high participation rates in universal parent training programs (Dumka et al., 1997; Howland et al, 2006).

When low-income parents participating in PMT programs were specifically asked what made their experience with liaisons successful, parents explicitly emphasized the personal qualities of the liaison. They noted that they enjoyed a deeply personal relationship with the liaison, as opposed to one that was merely professional (Howland et al., 2006). Over 90% of parents indicated that being "trustworthy" was the personal characteristic of the liaisons that mattered most (Gross et al., 2001), and other important attributes included being "compassionate" and "positive" (Howland et al., 2006). Other research findings suggest that cultural responsiveness and community connectedness are two additional liaison attributes that are important to parents (Gross et al., 2001; Howland et al., 2006). The parent liaisons in the TOPS program all grew up in the community in which they lived and were highly connected with the community (e.g., an active church leader, an aide at the school, a hairdresser, and a reformed gang leader who was a visible church leader).

It is important to provide liaisons adequate support in their efforts to reach out to parents, particularly when they are being held accountable for parent outreach (Sanders, 2008). In the TOPS program, liaisons were provided structured training involving instruction, modeling, practice, and feedback to develop mastery of recruitment and retention procedures. For example, following instruction on how to fill out a family contact log, liaisons were required to demonstrate understanding of 8 out of 10 scenarios to move to the next step of training. (Scenarios included questions such as, "It is 6:30pm on Tuesday and Ms. Williams is not at her scheduled training. What do you write on the contact log and what is the next step?") Liaisons were primarily responsible for introducing the TOPS program to parents during the initial home visit; it was therefore important to ensure that they adequately convey all necessary information. To help build this skill, liaisons were provided a general recruitment "script" (see Appendix B) and practiced executing it in mock recruitment sessions with the parent trainer until they demonstrated mastery. The training took approximately six hours and was deemed as time well-invested in ensuring the high-integrity implementation of procedures. Liaisons also commented that they enjoyed the training and felt more confident about their ability to recruit parents after they practiced the procedures in mock sessions.

Maximize Motivation for Participation

Incentive programming is typically incorporated into preventative PMT programs that target low-income parents (e.g., Dumka et al., 1997; Gross et al., 2001). Holding the training in an accessible location or providing transportation, offering training during the day and evening, and providing on-site childcare help reduce logistical barriers to attendance. In addition, it is often recommended that food, prizes, and even payment for attendance be provided when possible to try to attract parents to attend PMT. Interestingly, however, attendance rates often remain low and dropout remains high even with these incentives in place (Heinrichs et al., 2005; Ouellette & Wilkerson, 2008).

The TOPS program utilized all of the methods described above. In addition to incentives, however, parents were provided choices that conceivably increased interest in attending the PMT sessions. For example, when parents scheduled for a 6pm training were given their reminder phone call a day before, they were also invited to put in their specific "order" for Chinese food. When this practice was implemented, 100% of parents who were contacted and placed an "order" for dinner attended class the following evening, despite the outside temperature being below freezing and no heat in the school during the training. Moreover, during each session one parent was awarded a "door prize" of their choice amongst several family games suitable for elementary-aged children (e.g., Chutes and Ladders, Candyland). Similarly, rather than providing a cash incentive, parents who attended all sessions were eligible for a $50 gift certificate to any family establishment of their choice (e.g., restaurants, arcades, amusement park, zoo). Parents commented that they liked this choice, and TOPS attendance and retention rates were higher than for programs that offered a larger cash incentive by paying for attendance at each session (Gross et al. 2001). The research suggests that when individuals are provided choices during activities – even choices with similar outcomes – their engagement in and satisfaction with the activity increases (Kern, Vorndran, Hilt, Ringdahl, Adelman, & Dunlap, 1998). It is therefore recommended that choices be integrated into as many aspects of PMT as possible in an effort to enhance attendance and participation.

Although monetary incentives may be helpful in recruiting or retaining parents in PMT, research suggests they may not be necessary. In one study, low-income, urban, African American parents rated cab fare and financial compensation for attendance as being the least important incentives in their decision to attend PMT training (Gross et al., 2001). Both qualitative and quantitative investigations have found that the most frequent reasons to participate in PMT cited by low-income, ethnic minority parents are to (a) access social support (i.e., meet other parents, make friendships, share experiences) and (b) become a better parent (Cameron, 2002; Gross et al., 2001; Harachi et al., 1997). The desire for and benefits of increased connectedness with others was observed throughout the TOPS program. Parents brought their friends or neighbors to the training, often indicating they were looking for help with their child's behavior. On one occasion, a grandparent (and primary caregiver for her grandchildren enrolled at the school) requested that her $50 gift certificate be changed from the grocery store to an area restaurant so that she could share a meal with her neighbor, another TOPS graduate whom she met during training. At several points during the training, parents who attended a regular time slot organized pot-luck meals, opting to bring and share the food they prepared rather than be provided a free meal by the project.

The collective findings on use of incentives suggests that efforts to promote *meaningful* outcomes for parents, such as becoming a better parent and meeting other parents, will likely motivate parents more than the promise of monetary or tangible gain. It is worth noting that the opportunity to "graduate" on a stage in front of their children and the whole school was deemed the incentive most important to parents who attended the TOPS program. Many of these parents did not graduate from high school and took great pride in this public acknowledgment; they took time off from work to attend, often invited other family members, and dressed formally for the occasion. Many became visibly emotional when receiving their TOPS diploma and audience applause. The idea to offer public graduation as an incentive for attendance came from of one of the parent liaisons, who completing the program herself and had never graduated high school.

Utilize Targeted and Person-to-Person Recruitment Strategies

Attracting parents to a preventive PMT program is challenging. There appear to be some common approaches, however, in programs that have achieved high recruitment rates with low SES, urban families. In particular, strategies such as extending a person-to-person invitation and targeting geographically concentrated areas of parents are recommended.

Extend Person-to-Person Invitations

Urban parents living in low-income neighborhoods have reported that the invitation to attend training is the single most important determinant in their initial attendance (Howland et al., 2006). It is suggested that extending that invitation personally increases the probability of attendance (Dumka et al., 1997; Harachi et al., 1997). This person-to-person contact is important to allow the parent to assess the personal qualities of the recruiter, and research suggests that parents who perceive the recruiter as trustworthy are more likely to come to training (Gross et al., 2001). As previously discussed, utilizing a community liaison in the capacity of recruiter can enhance the credibility of the program and help bridge the gap of educational, socioeconomic and/or ethnic differences between the parent and parent trainer (Howland et al., 2006), as well as allow the invitation to occur within the context of an existing relationship (Harachi et al., 1997).

In the TOPS program, a letter to parents was sent home with their child three weeks prior to the onset of training describing the program and informing the parents that a TOPS staff member would be visiting their home the following week. The three-week timeframe to initiate recruitment was recommended in previous research and provided sufficient lead time to alert parents to allocate the time while not allowing so much lead time that parents become disinterested or forget about the training (Harachi et al., 1997). In the welcome letter, parents were provided a number they could call if they did not wish to be visited at home, although during the three years of the project no parent made this request. Two weeks before training, the parent trainer and a community liaison visited the home of every parent participant. The liaison stood closest to the parent, led the interaction, and extended the invitation to attend. Occasionally the liaison was absent and a parent trainer went for the invite visit alone. It was anecdotally noted that fewer parents opened the door for the solo parent trainer and, when they did, the overall interaction was shorter than when accompanied by liaisons who lived in the community. Parents clearly appeared to be more responsive to the community liaison than the school-based parent trainer.

The TOPS program utilized liaisons in a formal recruitment process. Based on their work with parents living in low-income, urban, ethnic minority communities, however, Harachi et al. (2007) suggest that the use of community liaisons can also provide an effective means of informal recruitment to a PMT program. Specifically, informal community leaders were hired to recruit parents into the program during *naturally occurring* events. For example, church leaders extended invitations during after service coffee hours; socially active parents invited other parents to training during birthday and Tupperware parties; and staff members at the community recreation center conversed with visiting parents (Harachi et al., 2007). The combined findings on initial recruitment of low-income parents to PMT programs suggest that the most effective person-to-person invitation would be a face-to-face meeting with someone the parent knows or shares commonalities, followed by a phone invitation from someone with whom the parent is familiar. The least effective form of direct communication would be a "cold call", in which the parent is contacted by someone they don't know. All of these methods, however, are more effective than indirect strategies such as posting brochures or circulating flyers (Dumka et al., 1997; Harachi et al., 1997; Oulette & Wilkerson, 2008).

Target Geographically Concentrated Areas

Low-income parents who join community mutual aid organizations report that important reasons for doing so include achieving high levels of weekly interpersonal contact with others, having a safe place to access a positive network of peers, and the opportunity to become friends with other members of the community (Cameron, 2002). These findings are consistent with other studies suggesting that increased connectedness with others is a primary motivating factor for attending PMT programs in low-income, urban communities (Gross et al., 2001). As a result, recruitment efforts for PMT programs have targeted geographically concentrated areas. For example, Harachi et al. (1997) targeted different ethnic communities in a parent training program designed to prevent substance abuse among their children. They offered several different workshops, each housed in a central location (e.g., churches, schools, social service agencies, community recreation centers) within a particular urban ethnic community (i.e., African American, Latino, Native American, and Samoan.) In the TOPS program, all parents in one school community were targeted for inclusion in the program; however, specific "cohorts" of parents who would be taking the training together were targeted based on their proximity to one another. Specifically, parents who lived on the same or adjacent streets were recruited to attend the training at the same time.

In addition to offering the opportunity for parents to increase connectedness with their community in general and neighbors in particular, another advantage of recruiting in geographically concentrated areas is that it capitalizes on naturally existing social networks. People may be more interested in programs, particularly new programs, in which they know other people with whom they can attend. Further, when parents are made aware that everyone in their neighborhood has been invited to the training, it creates another opportunity to potentially influence parents who otherwise were nonresponsive to the community liaison or parent trainer. In the TOPS program, it was a common experience for a parent who had previously refused training to call weeks or months later asking if they could still begin the training sequence because they heard positive reports from their neighbors who attended training sessions.

Provide Structured Follow-up Contacts to Aid in Retention

Even when parents attend initial PMT sessions, the drop-out rate typically exceeds 50% and is highest among low-income, ethnic minority parents (Coatsworth et al., 2006; Oulette & Wilkerson, 2008). The issue of retaining parents in training throughout the training sequence is critical because of lost curriculum content. When parents miss a class, it is difficult to do structured review activities with the group, and it is difficult for parents to acquire new skills that are built on previous course concepts. The most frequent reasons low-income, urban parents provide for dropping out of PMT programs are lack of time, scheduling conflicts, too much stress, and the need for childcare (Gross et al., 2001). As previously discussed, common responses to these barriers include offering training programs in accessible locations, providing childcare, initiating pre-group home visits, offering incentives for participation, and including other parents or community members as resources (Oulette & Wilkerson, 2008).

It is recommended that contacting parents by telephone between group meetings is an effective strategy for increasing retention (Dishion & Kavanaugh, 2003; Oullette & Wilkerson, 2008), and that home visits should be initiated for nonattenders (Dumka et al., 2007). Further, it is recommended that provisions for make-up sessions be made for parents who miss a training session (Harachi et al., 2007). The follow-up procedures in the TOPS program were more structured and intensive than other training programs discussed in the literature. For example, reminder calls were made to parents the day before each training. When a parent missed a scheduled training, they were immediately contacted by phone in an effort to schedule a make-up for that session, and make-ups were offered in a variety of modalities. Specifically, a parent could: (a) attend a group session at a different time (as there were multiple sessions on multiple days offered each week), (b) schedule an individual training session at school, (c) schedule a training session in their home, or (d) participate in an abbreviated training over the phone. If parents could not be reached within three hours of missing their session, liaisons visited the home and a "We Missed You" card was sent home with their child. A total of five contact attempts (including at least two home visits) were required before stopping the make-up effort and mailing the missed materials home. Across the three years of the project, the mean number of contacts was 20 per family (i.e., an average of 5 home visits and 15 calls per family), equating to approximately 102 minutes of direct contact related to recruitment and retention per family. It is the shared belief of the TOPS program directors that the single-most important variable that accounted for high retention rates was this structured and intensive follow-up procedure. Other studies that utilized one reminder call and/or one home visit to nonattenders reported retention rates of less than 50% (e.g., Dumka et al., 1997; Harachi et al., 1997).

At a minimum, it is recommended that reminder calls and make-up sessions be provided. In addition, offering an alternative form or training may increase retention rates. In their training with low-income ethnic minority parents, Harachi et al. (1997) noted that despite making reminder calls, more than half of parents cited time conflicts and changing work schedules as a reason for dropping out of training. Although this was not sufficient to explain overall low retention rates, it was suggested that offering training on a one-time-only basis may be an alternative strategy for families who may not be able to commit to continuing attendance. Finally, some programs have utilized formal, direct interventions for increasing parental participation in PMT. For example, Nock and Kazdin (2005) experimentally evaluated a "Participant Enhancement Intervention" that involved providing parents with information about the importance of attendance, eliciting motivation statements about attending (e.g., "What steps can you take to help change your child's behavior?"), and helping parents to identify and develop plans for overcoming barriers to attendance. The intervention took 5-15 minutes and was administered during several PMT sessions. Compared with parents who didn't receive the Parent Enhancement Intervention, those that did had greater motivation, attended significantly more treatment sessions, and were more likely to implement the strategies they were learning at home.

Provide Training in School and Integrate
PMT with Whole-School Programming

The location of training is as important to parents as the qualities of the recruiter in their decision to participate in prevention programs (Gross et al., 2001). As such, it has been recommended that PMT be extended to community settings in an effort to break down barriers to attendance and create a more familiar and comfortable training climate than might be present in a therapist's office (Kazdin, 1997). Training locations such as a church, community recreational center, private catholic school, housing project center, and public elementary schools have been suggested specifically for PMT programs targeting low-income, ethnic minority families (Harachi et al., 1997). More recently, however, the school has been recommended as a preferred training site for preventive PMT programs in these communities (Howland et al., 2006; Oulette & Wilkerson, 2008; Sanders, 2008).

The primary goal in preventive PMT programs is to build parental skills to enhance the interaction patterns between parents and their children, thereby reducing or offsetting the child's risk for developing antisocial behavior (Eddy, Reid, & Curry, 2002). Research has demonstrated that effective prevention programs for a wide range of childhood problems (i.e., violence, suicide, obesity, substance abuse) address multiple risk factors and consistently involve both home *and* school components (Jason et al., 2002; Jimerson & Furlong, 2006). Two major risk factors for antisocial behavior are ineffective parenting and interaction problems with teachers and peers at school (Eddy et al., 2002). Consequently, it is suggested that preventive PMT programs that integrate parent training of specific skills with programming at the whole-school level will be the most effective at preventing antisocial behavior (Eddy et al., 2002; Eddy, Reid, & Fetrow, 2000; Jimerson & Furlong, 2006; Stoolmiller, Eddy, & Reid, 2000).

Preventive PMT interventions that are delivered in schools and involve whole-school programming are designed to prevent problem behaviors from developing or progressing by simultaneously influencing parents, teachers, and students to: (a) enhance family interactions, (b) increase prosocial and reduce negative peer interactions, and (c) improve the coordination between home and school (Stoolmiller et al., 2000; Eddy et al., 2000). For example, *Linking the Interests of Families and Teachers* (LIFT) is a preventive PMT program that is designed for use in elementary schools, was piloted in low-income neighborhoods, and contains parent and whole-school components. In LIFT, PMT was conducted at the school in groups of 10-15 parents and consisted of six weekly 2.5 hour sessions. All parents of first and fifth graders were invited to attend. Students in these grades participated in classroom-based social skills training sessions involving the general topics of relationship fundamentals (e.g., responding appropriately to others, dealing with anger) and peer group skills (e.g., cooperating within groups, problem-solving). As part of these sessions students engaged in free play on the playground while being actively encouraged, praised and rewarded for positive peer interactions. Although only about a third of parents participated in the group PMT, rates of participation were bolstered by multiple delivery modes (i.e., home visits and mailings). The general outcomes suggested that students exposed to LIFT (as compared with controls) demonstrated less physical aggression toward peers on the playground, improved social skills, and enhanced parent skills during family problem-solving discussions. Further, three years later students who participated in LIFT had fewer deviant peer associations and fewer police arrests - two of the most powerful middle-school predictors of serious and chronic delinquency (Eddy et al., 2000).

In the TOPS program, parents of all students in an elementary school were invited for a 6-week PMT program. All students and staff in the school participated in a climate-change intervention that involved defining and teaching clear expectations in all settings of the school, and praising and rewarding students with tickets who were observed demonstrating appropriate behavior. (At the end of each day, tickets were collected for a prize drawing.) For example, one general expectation was to "Be Kind." Students earned tickets for behaviors such as holding the door for a peer or teacher, picking up an item that someone had dropped, and inviting a new student to enter a playground group. For the expectation of "Be Respectful", behaviors such as throwing away trash in the cafeteria, raising hands and waiting to be called on in the classroom, and walking quietly in the hall earned students praise and tickets.

Unlike project LIFT (Eddy et al., 2000), the TOPS program integrated the home and school components of the intervention. Parents were invited to come to the school on the "kick-off" day of the school program (i.e., the first day that students learned the expectations and started receiving tickets). Parents attended a breakfast and then shadowed their children through teaching stations (i.e., hallway, lunchroom, playground). Parents were provided tickets to give students that they observed following the expectations. This served to educate parents about the school program as well as model specific skills that would be taught during PMT (e.g., rules, praise, token economies). Further efforts to integrate the home and school programs were made by rewarding *students* for their *parents'* participation in PMT. Specifically, each morning the parent trainer or liaison visited classrooms to distribute tickets to students whose parents attended a PMT session the previous day. This practice appeared to also assist with recruitment of parents to the program; several calls were placed to the TOPS hotline early in the process by parents reporting that their child asked them to participate in the program and expressing interest in doing so. The parent graduation was scheduled during a whole-school assembly geared towards further teaching, reinforcement, or recognizing students for following the school expectations.

In the TOPS program, integrating school-based PMT and whole-school programming was associated with high rates of parental attendance during PMT sessions as well as improved student behavior as measured by overall discipline referrals. As previously discussed, it is not uncommon for parents living in low-income, urban, ethnic-minority communities to have negative personal experiences with the school and as a result to engage less with the school at it pertains to their own children (Raffaele & Knoff, 1999). Changing this perception is critical to sustain the long-term partnership between parents and school personnel that is necessary to help build protective factors for children.

Although limited, preliminary data from the TOPS program, as well as anecdotal observations, suggest that parental participation in the program was associated with increased parental involvement in other school activities. For example, the rates of attendance at parent-teacher conferences increased following initiation of the TOPS program, and were higher than control schools in which TOPS was not being implemented. In addition, 57 parents responded to an invitation to return to the school at the end of the third year of the project for a "Meet and Share" luncheon that was offered exclusively to graduates of the TOPS program. The meeting allowed parents from different training cohorts to meet and discuss their experiences, although the primary goal was to invite parents to engage in continued partnership with the school via volunteer activities. Several parents signed up for volunteer positions for the upcoming school year, and two TOPS graduates suggested that the program be expanded to "young/teen" mothers and expressed interest in becoming parent trainers themselves. The combined results suggest that increased levels of parental involvement in school as a function of the preventive PMT program were sustained after the project ended.

Conclusion

Children living in poverty are at risk for a host of negative outcomes, including antisocial behavior. One way to mediate the impact of low SES on social-emotional development is through PMT, a research-based, systematic intervention designed to promote positive interaction patterns between children and their parents. PMT was originally designed and evaluated for use with families with children who have already developed serious disruptive behavior problems. In the last decade, however, researchers and practitioners have recommended that PMT be used as a universal prevention strategy - implemented with all parents in a given community - particularly in low-income neighborhoods.

Recruiting and retaining parents in PMT programs is a significant challenge, and attendance rates are typically lowest for low-income parents. Common barriers include lack of time, logistical issues such as transportation or childcare, mismatches between program goals and parent needs, and income, education, and cultural differences between the trainer and parents. Access to social support is one of the most important reasons that low-income parents are attracted to PMT programs, and the decision to participate is largely dependent upon the way in which the initial invitation is delivered. It is therefore recommended that these factors be carefully considered when attempting to recruit parents for PMT. The use of community liaisons, in-person invitations to training, frequent follow-up with the opportunity to make-up missed training sessions, incentive programming, and partnering with the school all appear to enhance the participation rates of low-income parents.

Comprehensive interventions that target improvements across multiple environmental domains (e.g., family, school, peer group, community) are the most effective in addressing multiple risk factors in children. Based on extensive research reviews of parenting and family strategies for delinquency prevention, the Office of Juvenile Justice and Delinquency Prevention has summarized components of exemplary family programs. Specifically, effective, comprehensive programs (a) are family focused rather than child- or parent-focused only, (b) produce long-term and enduring changes within the family rather than short-term solutions, (c) are culturally sensitive, (d) address developmentally-appropriate risk and protective factors, (e) change ongoing family dynamics, (f) begin in early childhood, (g) reduce barriers to attendance through retention and recruitment efforts, (h) use videos of families demonstrating good and poor parenting skills, and (i) utilize a trainer with high personal efficacy and similar characteristics to the family (OJJDP, 1999). Implementing a universal, school-based PMT program using the strategies described in this chapter will address all of these needs and maximize the likelihood of preventing the development or escalation of antisocial behavior in children living in low-income, urban communities – arguably the children most in need of prevention programming.

Appendix A

Toolbox of Parent Skills (TOPS) Training Curriculum

Module	General Training Topic	Specific Topics/Skills
I.	Following Directions and Giving Attention	Compliance Request-Stress Dilemma Providing Positive Attention Removing Negative Attention
II.	Effective Requests and Praise for Following Directions	Making Effective Requests Premack Principle ("Grandma's Rule") Start-Up Versus Stop Requests Behavior-Specific Praise
III.	Household Rules	Elements of Effective Rules Writing Household Rules
IV.	Reward System for Following Directions	Types of Rewards Home-Based Token Economy
V.	Reducing Negative Behaviors	Using Positive Strategies to Reduce Negative Behaviors Punishment Spiral Logical and Natural Consequences Privilege Removal

Appendix B

Liaison Training Script for Home Visit Recruitment

Training Checklist*

1. Introduce yourself and say you are from the TOPS program at X Elementary School.
2. Invite parent to attend the 5-week TOPS program.
3. Convey that all parents at X Elementary School are being invited to attend the TOPS program over the next several years.
4. Explain that TOPS is a partnership between X Elementary School and Devereux.

5. Tell parent the main goal of TOPS is for parents to show support to their child in school – to be part of the Liftoff Star Program. Children earn tickets when a parent participates.
6. Say: Parents who complete the program graduate in an assembly with their children in attendance.
7. Say: If a parent attends all five sessions they earn a $50 gift certificate.
8. Say: If a parent is unable to attend a session during the scheduled times, they can make an appointment for an individual training at school, in their home, or over the phone.
9. Complete all paperwork documentation (intake, phone log, home visit form)
10. Distribute appropriate tickets, pens, and/or reminder cards to parent.
11. Be responsive to questions.
12. Engage in professional behavior. (Tone of voice is pleasant/calm; "invite" versus "demand"; always go to the door with a co-worker; body language is non-threatening.)

Each step was observed and marked "Met" or "Unmet" by the parent trainer. Liaisons practiced until they met mastery on 10 out of 12 (83%) of the steps three times in a row.

References

Achenbach, T.M., Dumenci, L., & Rescorla, L.A. (2003). Are aAmerican children's problems still getting worse? A 23-year comparison. *Journal of Abnormal Child Psychology, 31*(1), 1-11.

Anastopoulos, A.D., Shelton, T.L., DuPaul, G.J., & Guevremont, D.C. (1993). Parent training for attention-deficit hyperactivity disorder: Its impact on parent functioning. *Journal of Abnormal Child Psychology, 5,* 551-580.

Attar, B.K., Guerra, N.G., & Tolan, P.H. (1994). Neighborhood disadvantage, stressful life events, and adjustment in urban elementary-school children. *Journal of Clinical Child Psychology, 23,* 391-400.

Bank, L, Marlowe, J.H., Reid, J.B., Patterson, G.R., & Weinrott, M.R. (1991). A comparative evaluation of parent-training interventions for families of chronic delinquents. *Journal of Abnormal Child Psychology. 19,* 15-33.

Baker, A. J. (1997). Improving parent involvement programs and practice: A qualitative study of parent perceptions. *School Community Journal, 7*(1), 127-153.

Benner, G.J., Nelson, R.J., & Epstein, M.H. (2002). Language skills of children with EBD: A literature review. *Journal of Emotional and Behavioral Disorders, 10*(1), 43-59.

Bolger, K.E., Patterson, C.J., Thompson, W.W., & Kupersmidt, J.B. (1995). Psychosocial adjustment among children experiencing persistent and intermittent family economic hardship. *Child Development, 66,* 1107-1129.

Boyd, B., & Correa, V. I. (2005). Developing a framework for reducing the cultural clash between African American parents and the special education system. *Multiple Perspectives, 7*(2), 3-9.

Bradley, R.H., & Corwyn, R.F. (2002). Socioeconomic status and child development. *Annual Review of Psychology, 53,* 371-399.

Bradley, R.H., Corwyn, R.F., Burchinal, M., McAdoo, H.P., & Garcia Coll, C. (2001). The home environments of children in the United States. Part 2: relations with behavioral development through age 13. *Child Development,* **72**, 1868-1886.

Bradley, R.H., & Whiteside-Mansell, L. (1997). Children in poverty. In R.T. Ammerman and M. Hersen (Eds.), *Handbook of prevention and treatment with children and adolescents: Intervention in the real world context* (pp. 13-58). New York: John Wiley & Sons, Inc.

Brestan, E.V., & Eyberg, S.M. (1998). Effective psychosocial treatments for children and adolescents with disruptive behavior disorders: 29 years, 82 studies, and 5272 kids. *Journal of Clinical Child Psychology,* **27**, 179-188.

Brinkmeyer, M.Y., & Eyberg, S.M. (2003). Parent-child interaction therapy for oppositional children. In A.E. Kazdin and J.R. Weisz (Eds.), *Evidence-based psychotherapies for children and adolescents* (pp. 204-223). New York: Guilford Press.

Cameron, G. (2002). Motivation to join and benefits from participation in parent mutual aid organization. *Child Welfare,* **31**(1), 33-57.

Caspi, A., Taylor, A., Moffitt, T.E., & Plomin, R. (2000). Neighborhood deprivation affects children's mental health: Environmental risks identified in a genetic design. *Psychological Science,* **11**(4), 338-342.

Coatsworth, D. J., Duncan, L. G., & Pantin, H. (2006). Differential predictors of African American and Hispanic parent retention in a family-focused preventive intervention. *Family Relations,* **55**(2), 240-251.

de Graf, I., Speetjens, P., Smit, F., de Wolff, M., & Tavecchio, L. (2008). Effectiveness of the Triple P Positive Parenting program on behavioral problems in children. *Behavior Modification.* **32**, 714-735.

Dishion, t. J., & Kavanaugh, K. (2003). *Intervening in adolescent problem behavior: A family-centered approach.* New York: Guilford Press.

Dumas, J. E., Moreland, A. D., Gitter, A. H., Pearl, A. M., & Nordstrom, A. H. (2008). Engaging parents in preventive parenting groups: Do ethnic, socioeconomic, and belief match between parents and group leaders matter? *Health Education and Behavior,* **35**(5), 619-633.

Dumka, L. E., Garza, C. A., Roosa, M. W., & Stoerzinger, H. D. (1997). Recruitment and retention of high-risk families into a preventive parent training intervention. *Journal of Primary Prevention,* **18**(1), 25-39.

Eddy, J. M., Reid, J. B., & Curry, V. (2002). The etiology of youth antisocial behavior, delinquency, and violence and a public health approach to prevention. In Shinn, Walker, & Stoner (Eds.), *Interventions for academic and behavior problems II: Preventive and remedial approaches* (pp. 27-52). Bethesda, MD: National Association of School Psychologists.

Eddy, J. M., Reid, J. B., & Fetrow, R. A. (2000). An elementary school-based prevention program targeting modifiable antecedents of youth delinquency and violence: Linking the Interests of Families and Teachers (LIFT). *Journal of Emotional & Behavioral Disorders,* **8**(3), 165-176.

Eyberg, S.M., Funderburk, B.W., Hembree-Kigin, T.L., McNeil, C.B., Querido, J.G., & Hood, K.K. (2001). Parent-child interaction therapy with behavior problem children: One and two year maintenance of treatment effects in the family. *Child & Family Behavior Therapy,* **23**, 1-20.

Forgatch, M., & Patterson, G.R. (1989). *Parents and adolescents living together. Part 2: Family problem solving*. Eugene, OR: Castalia.

Garbarino, J. (1995). *Raising children in socially toxic environments*. San Francisco: Jossey-Bass.

Granic, I., & Patterson, G.R. (2006). Toward a comprehensive model of antisocial development: A dynamic systems approach. *Psychological Review, 113*(1), 101-131.

Gross, D., Julion, W., & Fogg, L. (2001). What motivates participation and dropout among low-income urban families of color in a prevention intervention? *Family Relations, 50,* 246-254

Harachi, T. W., Catalano, R. F., & Hawkins, J. D. (1997). Effective recruitment for parenting programs within ethnic minority communities. *Child and Adolescent social work Journal, 14*(1), 23-39.

Hart, B., & Risley, T.R. (1995). *Meaningful differences in the everyday experience of young American children*. Baltimore, MD: Brookes Publishing Co.

Heinrichs N., Bertram, H., Kuschel, A. & Hahlweg, K. (2005). Parent recruitment and retention in a universal prevention program for child behavior and emotional problems: Barriers to research and program participation. *Prevention Science, 6*(4), 275-286.

Hood, K.K., & Eyberg, S.M. (2003). Outcomes of parent-child interaction therapy: Mother's reports of maintenance three to six years after treatment. *Journal of Clinical Child and Adolescent Psychology, 32*(3), 419-429.

Howell, J.C. (2003). *Preventing and reducing juvenile delinquency: A comprehensive framework*. Thousand Oaks, CA: Sage.

Howland, A., Anderson, J. A., Smiley, A. D., & Abbott, D. J. (2006). School liaisons: Bridging the gap between home and school. *School Community Journal, 16*(2), 47-68.

Jason, L. A., Curie, C.J., Townsend, S. M., Pokorny, S. B., Katz, R.B., & Sherk, J. L. (2002). Health promotion interventions. *Child & Family Behavior Therapy, 24,* 67-82.

Jimerson, S. R., & Furlong, M. J. (2006). Handbook of school violence and school safety: From research to practice. Mahwah, NJ: Lawrence Erlbaum Associates.

Kazdin, A.E. (1995). *Conduct disorders in childhood and adolescence* (2nd ed.). Thousand Oaks, CA: Sage.

Kazdin, A. E. (1997). Parent management training: Evidence, outcomes, and issues. *Journal of the American Academy of Child and Adolescent Psychiatry, 36*(10), 1349-1356.

Kazdin, A.E. (2005). *Parent management training: treatment for oppositional, aggressive, and antisocial behavior in children and adolescents*. New York: Oxford University Press, Inc.

Kazdin, A.E., & Weisz, J.R. (Eds.). (2003). *Evidence-based psychotherapies for children and adolescents*. New York: Guilford Press.

Kern, L., Vorndran, C. M., Hilt, A., Ringdahl, J. E., Adelman, B. E., & Dunlap, G. (1998). Choice as an intervention to improve behavior: A review of the literature. *Journal of Behavioral Education, 8*(2), 151-170.

Levanthal, T., & Brooks-Gunn, J. (2000). The neighborhoods they live in: The effects of neighborhood residence on child and adolescent outcomes. *Psychological Bulletin, 126,* 309-337.

Lippman, L., Burns, S., & McArthur, E. (1996). *Urban schools: The challenge of location and poverty*. Washington, DC: U.S. Department of Education.

Loeber, R., & Stouthamer-Loeber, M (1998). Development of juvenile aggression and violence: Some common misconceptions and controversies. *American Psychologist,* **53**, 242-259.

McCoy, M.G., Frick, P.J., Loney, B.R., & Ellis, M.L. (1999). The potential mediating role of parenting practices in the development of conduct problems in a clinic-referred sample. *Journal of Child and Family Studies,* **8**(4), 477-494.

McLloyd, V.C. (1990). The impact of economic hardship on black families and children: Psychological distress, parenting, and socioemotional development. *Child Development,* **61**, 311-346.

McLloyd, V.C. (1998). Socioeconomic disadvantage and child development. *American Psychologist,* **53**, 185-204.

McMahon, R.J., & Forehand, R.L. (2005). *Helping the noncompliant child: Family-based treatment for oppositional behavior* (2nd ed.). New York: Guilford Press.

McNeil, C.B., Eyberg, S., Eisenstadt, T.H., Newcomb, K., & Funderburk, B. (1991). Parent-child interaction therapy with behavior problem children: Generalization of treatment effects to the school setting. *Journal of Clinical Child Psychology,* **20**, 140-151.

Myers, H., Alvy, K., Arrington, A., Richardson, M., Marigna, M., Huff, R., Main, M., & Newcomb, M. (1992). The impact of a parent training program on inner-city African-American families. *Journal of Community Psychology,* **20**, 132-147.

National Center for Children in Poverty (2008a, October). Who are America's Poor Children: The official story. Retrieved October 24, 2008, from http://www.nccp.org/ publications/index_date_2008.html.

National Center for Children in Poverty (2008b, October). Basic facts about low-income children : Birth to age 18. Retrieved October 24, 2008, from http://www.nccp.org/ publications/index_date_2008.html.

Nock, M. K., & Kazdin, A. E. (2005). Randomized controlled trial of a brief intervention for increasing participation in parent management training. *Journal of Consulting and Clinical Psychology,* **73**(5), 872-879.

Office of Juvenile Justice and Delinquency Prevention (OJJDP) (1999). *Strengthening America's families: Exemplary parenting and family strategies for delinquency prevention.* Retrieved October 6, 2008 from: www.strengtheningfamilies.org

Orell-Valente, J., Pinderhughes, E., Valente, E., Laird, R., & Conduct Problems Presentation Research Group (1999). If it's offered, will they come? Influences on parents' participation in a community-based conduct problems prevention program. *American Journal of Community Psychology,* **27**, 753-783.

Ouelette, P. M., & Wilderson, D. (2008). "They won't come": Increasing parent involvement in parent management training programs for at-risk youths in schools. *School Social Work Journal,* **32**(2), 39-53.

Patterson, G.R. (1975). *Families: Applications of social learning to family life.* Champaign, IL: Research Press.

Patterson, G.R. (1976). *Living with children: New methods for parents and teachers.* Champaign, IL: Research Press.

Patterson, G.R. (1982). *Coercive family process.* Eugene, OR: Castalia.

Patterson, G.R. (2002). The early development of coercive family process. In J.B. Reid, G. R. Patterson and J. Snyder (Eds.), *Antisocial behavior in children and adolescents: A developmental analysis and model for intervention* (pp. 25-44). Washington, DC: American Psychological Association.

Patterson, G.R., & Forgatch, M. (1987). *Parents and adolescents living together. Part 1: The basics.* Eugene, OR: Castalia.

Raffaele, L. M., & Knoff, H. M. (1999). Improving home-school collaboration with disadvantaged families: Organizational principles, perspectives, and approaches. *School Psychology Review, 28*, 448-466.

Reid, J.B. (1993). Prevention of conduct disorder before and after school entry: Relating interventions to developmental findings. *Development and Psychopathology, 5*, 243-262.

Reid, M.J., Webster-Stratton, C., & Hammond, M. (2007). Enhancing a classroom social competence and problem-solving curriculum by offering parent training to families of moderate to high risk elementary school children. *Journal of Clinical Child and Adolescent Psychology. 36*, 605-620.

Rutter, M. (1981). The city and the child. *American Journal of Orthopsychiatry, 51*(4), 610-625.

Sanders, M. G. (2008). How parent liaisons can help bridge the home-school gap. *Journal of Educational Research, 101*(5), 287-296.

Sanders, M.R., Mazzucchelli, T.G., & Studman, L.J. (2004). Stepping stones Triple P: The theoretical basis and development of an evidence-based positive parenting program for families with a child who has a disability. *Journal of Intellectual & Developmental Disability, 29*(3), 265-238.

Scaramella, L.V., Neppl, T.K., Ontai, L.L., & Conger, R.D. (2008). Consequences of socioeconomic disadvantage across three generations: Parenting behavior and child externalizing problems. *Journal of Family Psychology, 22*(5), 725-733.

Schroth, G., Pankake, A., Fullwood, H., & Gates, G. (2001). Rural and urban America. *Rural Special Education Quarterly, 20*(1-2), 13-25.

Snyder, J., & Stoolmiller, M. (2002). Reinforcement and coercion mechanisms in the development of antisocial behavior: The family. In J.B. Reid, G. R. Patterson, and J. Snyder (Eds.), *Antisocial behavior in children and adolescents: A developmental analysis and model for intervention* (pp. 65-100). Washington, DC: American Psychological Association.

Stoolmiller, M., Eddy, J. M., & Reid, J.B. (2000). Detecting and describing preventative intervention effects in a universal school-based randomized trial targeting delinquent and violent behavior. *Journal of Consulting and Clinical Psychology, 68*, 296-306.

U.S. Census Bureau. (n.d.). Table 2. Poverty status of people by family relationship, race, and hispanic origin: 1959 to 2007. Retrieved October 24, 2008, from http://www.census. gov/hhes/ www/poverty/histpov/hstpov2.xls.

Van Acker, R., & Talbott, E. (1999). The school context and risk for aggression: Implications for school-based prevention and intervention efforts. *Preventing School Failure, 44*, 12-20.

Wahler, R.G., & Williams, A.J. (1990). The compliance and predictability hypotheses: Sequential and correlational analyses of coercive mother-child interactions. *Behavioral Assessment, 12*, 391-407.

Walker, H.M., Ramsey, E., & Gresham, F.M. (2004). *Antisocial behavior in school: Evidence-based practices* (2nd ed.). Belmont, CA: Wadsworth.

Webster-Stratton, C. (1992).Individually administered videotape parent training: "Who benefits?" *Cognitive Therapy and Research.* **16**, 31-35.

Webster-Stratton, C. (1997). From parent training to community building. Families in Society: *The Journal of Contemporary Human Services, March/April*, 156-170.

Webster-Stratton, C, & Hammond, M (1997). Treating children with early-onset conduct problems: A comparison of child and parent training interventions. *Journal of Consulting and Clinical Psychology.* **65**, 93-109.

Webster-Stratton, C, Hollinsworth, T, & Kolpacoff, M (1989). The long-term effectiveness and clinical significance of three cost-effective training programs for families with conduct-problem children. *Journal of Consulting and Clinical Psychology.* **57**, 550-553.

Webster-Stratton, C., & Reid, M.J. (2003). The Incredible Years parents, teachers, and children training series: A multifaceted treatment approach for young children with conduct problems. . In A.E. Kazdin and J.R. Weisz (Eds.), *Evidence-based psychotherapies for children and adolescents* (pp. 224-240). New York: Guilford Press.

Webster-Stratton, C, Reid, M.J., & Hammond, M. (2004). Treating children with early-onset conduct problems: Intervention outcomes for parent, child, and teacher training. *Journal of Clinical Child and Adolescent Psychology,* **33**, 105-124.

Wilson, W.J. (1987). *The truly disadvantaged: The inner city, the underclass, and public policy*. Chicago: The University of Chicago Press.

In: Low Incomes: Social, Health and Educational Impacts   ISBN: 978-1-60741-175-8
Editor: Jacob K. Levine, pp. 31-56   © 2009 Nova Science Publishers, Inc.

Chapter 2

A SCHOOL-BASED PREFERENTIAL OPTION FOR THE POOR: CHILD POVERTY, SOCIAL JUSTICE, AND A PUBLIC HEALTH APPROACH TO INTERVENTION

David N. Miller[*][1] *and Kristin D. Sawka-Miller*[2]
[1] University at Albany, State University of New York, USA
[2] Siena College, Loudonville, NY, USA

Abstract

"Making an option for the poor inevitably implies working for social justice, working with poor people as they struggle to change their situation."

– Paul Farmer

Poverty is a significant national problem affecting millions of children in the United States, and it should not and cannot be ignored by schools. To put the problem of child poverty in perspective, in 2007 the U.S. Census Bureau indicated that 18% of children under the age of 18 were living in poverty, up from 17.4% in 2006 (U.S. Census Bureau, 2008). This rate represents approximately 13 million children and is higher than the rate for adults ages 18 to 64 and for senior citizens age 65 and older (Whitehouse, 2006). In addition, data from recent years indicates that about 10% of all American families live in poverty, and that more than a quarter of families headed by single mothers are impoverished (DeNavas-Walt et al., 2005). As such, millions of children in our nation's schools are experiencing poverty, indicating that there is an urgent need to disseminate information to school professionals who work with these children (Whitehouse, 2006).

The purpose of this chapter is to discuss poverty, particularly the many deleterious effects it has on children. A social justice perspective on child poverty will be provided, including the notion of providing a school-based "preferential option" for children living in poverty. Finally, a public health approach to school-based interventions for children in poverty will be

---

[*] Please address all correspondence regarding this manuscript to the first author at: University at Albany, SUNY, 1400 Washington Avenue, ED 215, Albany, NY 12222. Email: dmiller@uamail.albany.edu

described, including a framework for how interventions can be provided across multiple levels. We begin, however, with a brief overview of poverty.

Poverty in Context

"Poverty is so much more than lack of money, lack of food, or lack of decent living quarters. Poverty creates marginal people, people who are separated from the whole network of ideas, services, facilities, and opportunities."

– Henri Nouwen

The concept of poverty can be a vague and ambiguous one (Shipler, 2004). For the purposes of this chapter, poverty may be defined as the "extent to which an individual does without resources" (Payne, 2001, p. 16), of which income is only one example. Other resources that children living in poverty frequently lack include emotional, mental health, and physical resources; adequate support systems; healthy relationships; and appropriate role models. Poverty also marginalizes children, separating and isolating them from other people, resources, and opportunities. Moreover, those living in poverty are frequently labeled in derogatory terms and routinely objectified (Kirylo, 2006). Although Americans continue to offer charitable contributions to those in need and are not unmoved by poverty and the many difficulties it creates, the vast scope of the problem appears to have made many individuals uncertain or even pessimistic about what can and should be done to reduce it (Shipler, 2004).

The problems associated with poverty are "complex, deeply rooted, and value laden" (Whitehouse, 2006, p. 835). For example, poverty is relative and exits only in the context of relationships and expectations; what may seem normal to one child or adult may be quite different from what others experience. Indeed, not all poor children view their situation as atypical, and many may not perceive themselves as living in poverty at all (Payne, 2001; Whitehouse, 2006). The concept of social class is an ambiguous one, as families are placed along a continuum of income levels (Payne, 2001). School professionals also should be aware that poverty occurs in all ethnic groups and in all countries, although it is more prevalent in some than in others (Whitehouse, 2006). For example, in 2003 African-American and Hispanic fourth-grade students were more likely than White fourth-graders to be in high-poverty schools and less likely to be in low-poverty schools (National Center for Education Statistics, 2004).

Whitehouse (2006) suggests that it may be helpful for school personnel to be cognizant of three important concepts when working with children living in poverty, including (1) generational versus situational poverty; (2) cultural rules; and (3) language differences. Each of these concepts is discussed briefly below.

Generational Versus Situational Poverty

Generational poverty exists when a family earns below the poverty line for two or more generations. In contrast, situational poverty is caused by specific circumstances (e.g., divorce; death) and occurs for a shorter period of time (Whitehouse, 2006). Although those living in generational or situational poverty may exhibit many similarities, there are often some important differences between them. For example, individuals "who have experienced poverty for longer periods of time tend to adopt the cultural norms of that group, whereas those in poverty temporarily often bring many resources with them from middle-class culture" (Whitehouse, 2006, p. 836).

Cultural Rules

The notion of "culture" refers to any group of people with shared beliefs, values, and practices. Social class can therefore be considered a culture, as different classes "generate norms that relate to patterns of thought, social interaction, and cognitive strategies" (Whitehouse, 2006, p. 836). The culture of poverty produces rules that govern how individuals act and how they are perceived in terms of intelligence and capability. Like many other institutions, school systems operate under middle-class rules, which are typically "not made explicit and thus may be hidden and confusing to students in poverty" (Whitehouse, 2006, p. 836). Teachers and other school personnel must therefore strive to understand the norms associated with poverty, in the unique context (e.g., urban or rural poverty) in which it exists, as well as teach the rules that will help all students succeed in school (Payne, 2001; Whitehouse, 2006).

Language Differences

Variations in the form and use of language also functions to differentiate social classes (Whitehouse, 2006). In particular, the school system, through both instruction and standardized tests, typically employs what is known as the formal register, or standard sentence syntax. Many children living in poverty, however, are raised using the casual register, or more general word choice supplemented by nonverbal messages. Whitehouse (2006) suggests that the use of formal register is one of the "hidden rules" of middle-class culture, and that it may have little meaning for students living in poverty. For example, middle-class teachers may encourage children to "get to the point" of a story, which may potentially be confusing for children in poverty and be interpreted by them as rude. The use of the formal register rather than a casual one affects story structure as well. For example, children "may struggle academically when they are expected to conform to a standard organizational pattern, because they are more comfortable writing a story that winds around the point before getting there" (Whitehouse, 2006, p. 836).

School personnel should be cognizant of these issues when interacting and working with children living in poverty. To work most effectively with these students, however, requires an understanding of the many deleterious effects poverty has on child development, and this is discussed in greater detail below.

Effects of Poverty on Children

"The inescapable impact of being born into a condition of poverty that this country finds shameful, contemptible, and somehow oddly deserved, has had dominion over me to such an extent that I have spent my life trying to overcome or deny it."

- Dorothy Allison

Living in poverty puts a child inescapably at-risk for a host of negative outcomes related to their educational, physical, psychological, and social well-being (Mash & Wolfe, 2007). Poverty does not directly cause harmful outcomes but rather has a significant indirect effect on children because of its association with stressful influences such as family turmoil, ineffective or harsh parenting, poor nutrition, instability at home and school, less immersion in literacy, exposure to toxins, residential crowding, and parental psychopathology (Evans, 2004). Children growing up in poverty are exposed to more stressors in their environment than children not living in poverty, and these stressful life events occur more frequently and with greater intensity (Whitehouse, 2006). Children who live in extreme poverty or below the poverty line for multiple years are at greatest risk for poor outcomes (Brooks-Gunn, 1997). Further, the earlier that children experience poverty the more harmful the effects on their well-being, suggesting that cumulative risk exposure may be an especially toxic aspect of child poverty (Evans, 2004).

Outcomes related to childhood poverty have been well-documented in many large-scale studies (e.g., Brooks-Gunn, 1997; Chen, Matthews, & Boyce, 2002; Plewis, Smith, Wright, & Cullis, 2002). Although a comprehensive review is beyond the scope of this chapter, the following discussion highlights some major findings related to outcomes of children living in poverty.

Educational

Impairments in learning and achievement occurs significantly more often in children growing up in poverty versus those who are not poor. In fact, the impact of poverty on intellectual growth is greater than its impact on emotional outcomes (Brooks-Gunn & Duncan, 1997). In a longitudinal study, children who experienced poverty early in their life showed diminished vocabularies by the time they were in first grade and lower IQ scores by third grade compared with children in working-class families (Hart & Risley, 1995). More extreme cognitive deficits are observed in children with mild mental retardation, a group that is overrepresented by children from low income households and a condition that has no organic cause in the majority of cases (Mash & Wolfe, 2007).

Children living in poverty demonstrate twice the rate of school problems compared to children living in higher socioeconomic households (Ross, Shillington, & Lochhead, 1995), and the longer a child lives in poverty the larger the deficits in measured academic achievement and intellectual ability (Ackerman, Brown, & Izard, 2004). School dropout is on the rise in the United States, and children from low socio-economic status (SES) households are at particularly high risk, with approximately 21% of students in the bottom 20% of the income distribution not making it to high school graduation (Reschly & Christenson, 2006). Moreover, children who experience poverty in preschool have the highest rates of grade repetition and the lowest rates of school completion among children who are poor (Brooks-Gunn & Duncan, 1997).

Physical

Chronic asthma, lead poisoning, and low birth weight are reported at higher rates for children between 0 and 17 years who are poor, and only 37% of poor children are reported to be in "excellent health" (Brooks-Gunn & Duncan, 1997). In low-income communities where air and water quality are poorer and exposure to environmental toxins is higher, children experience more physical health problems (Evans, 2004). Children in low SES groups also report consuming more fast food and junk food, which puts them at greater risk for childhood obesity, and the rate of chronic illness for children living in poverty is twice as high as children who are not poor (Ross et al., 1995). A particularly concerning connection exists between SES and chronic illness survival rates, with cancer survival being much more difficult for children living in poverty (Mash & Barkley, 2007).

Psychological

Children living in poverty are disproportionately afflicted with mental health problems. Socio-economically disadvantaged children are diagnosed three times more often with externalizing behavior problems such as oppositional defiant disorder (ODD), conduct disorder (CD), and attention-deficit hyperactivity disorder (ADHD) than children who are not poor (Ross et al., 1994). Children of parents who suffer an anxiety disorder are at a much higher risk of developing the disorder if the family is living in poverty, and there is a clear link between low SES and depression, with child poverty being a bigger risk factor than age, gender, race or ethnicity (Mash & Wolfe, 2007). Recent studies have suggested that changes in income are directly related to changes in child mental health. Specifically, if income increases after early childhood, child mental health improves, and a decline in income is associated with increases in depression and conduct problems in children ages 4-14 years (Strohschein, 2005).

Social

Peer rejection is one of the strongest predictors of academic and conduct problems, and children living in poverty often experience rejection from their peers (Whitehouse, 2006). Child maltreatment is more common in low income households, where parental stress and isolation may occur at higher rates (Mash & Barkley, 2007). As a result, children living in poverty are more likely to spend time in foster care or some other out-of-home placement than children who are not poor (Whitehouse, 2006). In adolescence, economic deprivation also appears to put children more at-risk for committing a violent crime, with juvenile arrest rates for homicide increasing as child poverty increases (Messner, Raffalovich, & McMillan, 2006).

Finally, it is important to recognize that most public school districts, where the vast majority of American children are educated, depend largely on local property taxes for funding. As a result, because most Americans live in areas segregated by race as well as class, the financial disparities between school districts are often substantial and serve to perpetuate inequities between children living in poverty and other children (Kozol, 1991). As noted by Shipler (2004): "The schools that have more money provide a superior education, which helps children improve their earning power so they can live in communities that have more to spend on public education" (p. 294). The use of local property taxes as a primary mechanism for funding public school education will inevitably result in inequitable funding streams, particularly for children living with families in highly impoverished areas.

Given the many possible negative side effects that may result from child poverty, as well as the knowledge that children did not cause their poverty and therefore cannot be held responsible for altering it, a social justice perspective provides a potentially useful framework for engaging in what Freire (1990) describes as "reflection and action upon the world in order to transform it" (p. 33).

Social Justice and Poverty

"The poor of the world are not the causal products of human history. No, poverty results from the actions of other human beings."

– Jon Sobrino

Social justice is not easily defined (Shriberg et al., 2008) and may be conceptualized from a number of different perspectives (Sowell, 1987). At its core, however, social justice "is concerned with a just and equitable distribution of resources, advocacy, and empowerment as well as a scrutiny of the processes that lead to inequity" (Robinson-Wood, 2009, p. 284). In the context of education, social justice is associated "with the idea that all individuals and groups must be treated with fairness and respect and that all are entitled to resources and benefits that the school has to offer" (Shriberg et al., 2008, p. 455). As such, a social justice perspective on child poverty would suggest that resources (not simply money) need to be allocated differently than what is currently in place, so that children living in poverty can receive the same benefits and advantages as other, more affluent children in American society.

Although space limitations prevent an exhaustive discussion of social justice, a brief review of several philosophical perspectives may be instructive. First, concepts of liberty and equality form the basis of the major paradigms of social justice (Stevens & Wood, 1992; Vera & Speight, 2003). Early models of social justice, such as the Libertarian Justice model of John Locke, underscored the connection between merit and liberty. In this context, the concept of merit assumes that individuals are free to make decisions and use their differing levels of competencies. From this perspective, one closely associated with a conservative Republican political philosophy, merit is directly linked to individual outcomes. As such, "the acquisition of resources need not be equitable as long as it occurs fairly and reflects what is deserved or entitled" (Vera & Speight, 2003, p. 260). Capitalism and meritocracy both coexist with this approach to social justice. In this model, social, racial, and gender class inequities within society could occur fairly as long as equal opportunity existed, and there would be no requirements that governments or public policy intercede in addressing such inequality.

Instead, assisting those suffering from inequities might occur through philanthropy at the individual level, such as through volunteerism or individual works of charity (Vera & Speight, 2003).

Others, however, suggest that group-based oppression (e.g., poverty, racism, sexism, homophobia) precludes a level playing field, and therefore argued for the need for institutional protection of disenfranchised groups (Vera & Speight, 2003). One such approach to social justice, known as the liberal reformist approach (Rawls, 1971), "builds on the libertarian model but asserts that meritocracy cannot form the basis of justice and that inequity should not become structurally embedded within a society" (Vera & Speight, 2003, p. 260). Under this model of social justice, one closely associated with liberal Democratic political philosophy, the optimal role of government would be to create and enforce laws that prevent gross inequities while promoting liberty and freedom of choice. In theory, public policies would attempt to maintain a level playing field by protecting the basic rights of those who have not benefited from the system in place. Unfortunately, injustice may occur within the confines of the law (e.g., racially segregated educational systems). An extreme extension of this approach is represented by the Socialist approach to social justice, commonly associated with Marx (Vera & Speight, 2003). In a Socialist model, only after a commitment to justice and equity is instilled within the people can freedom of choice be encouraged (Vera & Speight, 2003).

Modern social justice theorists have criticized these models based on their emphasis on outcomes (i.e., the distribution of resources) rather than the processes that guide decisions related to social equality (Young, 1990). This latter approach to social justice has been referred to as a *communitarian* model of justice or *deliberative* justice (Heller, 1987; Young, 1990). In this model, the focus is not simply on equitable distribution but rather on "the process of decision making and interaction that occurs at an individual and systemic level" (Vera & Speight, 2003, p. 260). That is, the processes that facilitate unequal outcomes to begin with must be analyzed and ultimately transformed. According to Young (1990), *marginalization* is typically the main process by which social injustice is maintained. For genuine transformation to occur, traditionally marginalized people (e.g., people living in poverty) must be granted full participation in community life, and from this social justice perspective this cannot occur unless and until structural changes occur in society. Indeed, some benevolent actions by others designed to "help" those living in poverty, such as engaging in charity, are viewed not as solving the problem of poverty but rather perpetuating it, as discussed below.

The Problem of Charity

"True generosity consists precisely of fighting to destroy the causes which nourish false charity."

– Paulo Freire

The notion of providing charity to children in need would seem to be a humane and reasonable response. Many of those committed to social justice principles, however, have argued that charity, despite some short-term benefits to those living in poverty, also serves to perpetuate and reinforce the status quo. For example, in a study of food aid to those living in poverty in the U.S., Poppendieck (1998) links a rise in "kindness" to a decline in justice, suggesting that charity is at once a symptom and a cause of society's failure to address the problem of inequity. Similarly, although providing material goods to poor children through organized charities such as *Toys for Tots* is clearly laudable, it does not impact the environments that brought the child into poverty and that are likely to keep him/her living in it. Indeed, Poppendieck (1998) suggests that the proliferation of charity actually contributes to America's failure to grapple in a meaningful way with poverty, a viewpoint that has been echoed by others (e.g., Freire, 1990; Farmer, 2005).

This perspective should not be interpreted as dismissing the value of charity, which is a significant human virtue and one that is frequently required, particularly in crisis situations. Given the marked tendency toward increasing economic inequity between the rich and poor in America (Greenhouse, 2008), there will be a continuing need to provide charity for children living in poverty. In providing charity, however, there is "the temptation to ignore or hide the causes of excess suffering among the poor" (Farmer, 2005, p. 154). Further, charity will not contribute significantly to the underlying environmental, physical, psychological, or social problems experienced by children living in poverty. To address this issue in a meaningful way therefore requires a different approach to conceptualizing and responding to the problem.

A Radical Alternative: Combining Personal Accountability and Systems Change

"When accountability is spread so broadly and diffused, it seems to cease to exist. The opposite is true. It may look as if nobody is accountable. In fact, everybody is."

– David K. Shipler

Contemporary notions of social justice, particularly the liberal reformist and communitarian approaches described above, are often primarily associated with liberal political philosophy. Some have criticized liberal approaches, however, as being overly dependent and deferential to the workings of government and institutions for change. For example, according to some observers, the problem with traditional liberalism from a social justice perspective is "not only that it is willing to work within the 'system'…but that in doing so it subtly reinforces the power of systems and states. When liberals march on city hall, or on the White House, they contribute to the mistaken belief that city hall and the White House are truly the center of power" (McKanan, 2008, p. 20).

Such approaches have been criticized for not sufficiently taking into account the responsibility of individuals for effectively responding to poverty, and for not sufficiently recognizing that ultimate power resides in individuals serving the collective. In the context of child poverty, what is perhaps needed is an approach to social justice that unites the more broad-based systems approach advocated by political liberals (e.g., institutional intervention) with the promotion of individual efforts (e.g., volunteerism) championed by conservatives. As noted by Hawken (2007): "The world seems to be looking for the big solution, which is itself part of the problem, since the most effective solutions are both local *and* systemic" (p. 20). In other words, there is a need to think locally *and* globally and to act in response to both levels of analysis (Farmer, 2005).

This perspective on social justice can be clearly seen in the example of the Catholic Worker movement (Zwick & Zwick, 2005), a social activist branch of the Roman Catholic church founded by Dorothy Day and Peter Maurin in 1933 (Day, 1952). The Catholic Worker provided – and continues to provide – "houses of hospitality" and "works of mercy" to those in need, particularly those living in poverty. Although widely perceived as a liberal movement, the Catholic Worker is perhaps more accurately viewed as a *radical* movement (McKanan, 2008). Although liberalism and radicalism overlap to some degree, there are some important distinctions between them. Perhaps the most significant difference was concisely stated by Michael Baxter, a prominent figure associated with the Catholic Worker. According to Baxter, "Liberals say, 'The homeless aren't being fed. Let's march on city hall.' Radicals say, 'The homeless aren't being fed. Let's feed them'" (McKanan, 2008, p. 19). The Catholic Worker movement emphasizes a synthesis between the need for structural changes in society as well as the need for individuals to take personal responsibility for helping others living in poverty (Zwick & Zwick, 2005). For example, although Dorothy Day engaged in many actions designed to influence policy-makers at a broader, structural level, she also took personal responsibility for affecting the lives of poor people by individually providing them with food and shelter (Forest, 1986). Her actions on behalf of the poor made Dorothy Day the most influential and inspirational leader in Catholic social service since Saint Francis of Assisi, who also called for a radical redistribution of resources to assist those in need.

This emphasis within the Catholic Worker on a radical approach to social justice, as well as its distrust of charity "as a means of concealing and thus perpetuating social injustices" (McKanan, 2008, p. 8), has much in common with a later religious movement that originated in the 1960s and continues to exert a powerful influence today. Liberation theology developed in Latin America as a school of theology within Christianity, particularly in the Roman Catholic church. Described as a "way of viewing reality from the perspective of the poor and marginalized" (Kirylo, 2006, p. 267), liberation theology (like the Catholic Worker movement) grew out of Catholic social teaching and advocated that a primary duty of the church was to promote economic and social justice (Smith, 1991).

Many theologians in Latin America in the 1960s and 1970s, including Gustavo Gutiérrez (1973), Leonardo and Clodovis Boff (1987), and Oscar Romero (Dennis, Golden, & Wright, 2000), noted the wide disparity between the rich and the poor and called for a greater commitment to social justice through structural changes in society as well as modifications in individual behavior. Some, like Romero, were murdered by oppositional forces for their outspokenness and their actions to benefit the poor. Although liberation theology is not without its critics, including some in the Catholic church as well as on the political right, contemporary religious scholars have noted the strong parallels between the teachings of Christianity and the tenets of liberation theology, particularly in the sense of viewing Jesus as a revolutionary figure (Borg, 2006; Crossan, 1994) who insisted on the obligations of the rich to the poor and marginalized (Borg & Crossan, 2007) and who moved among the poor in an attempt to rebuild society "from the bottom up" (Crossan & Watts, 1996).

Liberation theology has had a powerful influence on many disciplines other than religion, including the practice of medicine (Farmer, 2005; Kidder, 2003), psychology (Martín-Baró, 1994), and education (Freire, 1990; Kirylo, 2006). For example, Farmer (2005) was inspired by the insights he gained from liberation theology to help create Partners in Health, an organization that joined with local community health activists to provide basic medical care and preventive services to the poor in Haiti and other countries. A major component of liberation theology is the notion of making a "preferential option for the poor", and this is discussed in greater detail below.

O for the P

> "Our preferential option for the poor must be as informed as it is wholehearted, as realistic as it is sincere, as oriented to the eradication of poverty as to its relief, and rooted at all times in a vision of the integral dignity of the human person."

> *– Joseph L. Bernardin*

For decades, proponents of liberation theology have argued that we should make a "preferential option" for those living in poverty (Farmer, 2005). The phrase "preferential option for the poor" or "option for the poor" – which Farmer refers to colloquially as "O for the P" (Kidder, 2003) – appears to have first been used by Latin American bishops at Medellin, Columbia in 1968. As a developed principle, however, it was first articulated by Gustavo Gutiérrez in his influential book, *A Theology of Liberation* (1973). Proponents of making a preferential option for the poor suggest that those living in poverty are *more* (rather than equally) deserving of resources than those not living in poverty, and that to effectively respond to poverty requires examining and modifying the social structures that create and maintain it (Farmer, 2005). Making a preferential option for impoverished children is of critical importance for many reasons, not the least of which is the variety of negative educational, psychological, social, and environmental outcomes that confront them.

Although the notion of making a preferential option for the poor grew out of a religious movement, one does not have to subscribe to any particular religious or spiritual doctrine to recognize that making meaningful modifications and accommodations for children living in poverty is essential from a social justice perspective. In the context of schools, making a preferential option for students living in poverty means that school personnel should actively identify these students and provide thoughtful, evidence-based interventions to better promote their academic, social, emotional, and behavioral outcomes. This will require that schools modify their typical manner or structure of providing instruction based on the particular needs of impoverished children. It will also require the individual and sustained efforts of all teachers and school personnel.

Making a school-based preferential option for children living in poverty is not unprecedented. For example, the preschool program known as Head Start was designed specifically for children from impoverished backgrounds (Zigler & Styfko, 2004). Similarly, schools already make a "preferential option" for some students. For example, students who are eligible to receive special education receive additional academic, emotional, and behavioral supports designed to meet their individual needs. Although special education programs vary widely in their effectiveness (Miller & Sawka-Miller, in press), their clear intent is to provide additional services for students most in need of them. The same approach can and should be provided for children living in poverty. One method for accomplishing this goal is to take a school-based public health approach to child poverty, and this is discussed next.

A School-Based Public Health Approach to Child Poverty

"A preferential option for the poor also implies a mode of analyzing health systems."

– Paul Farmer

The concern for public health in the United States essentially began in the 19th century, when physicians and government officials began considering potential environmental and societal variables causing, contributing to, or exacerbating existing health problems (Doll & Cummings, 2008). The first public health programs began as simple policies to clean up communities, with later efforts focusing on medical prevention as we know it today in the form of vaccines and environmental improvements (Strein et al., 2003; Woodside & McClam, 1998). Since the 1970s, the health status of U.S. populations – rather than simply individuals – has been a national priority, and has led to significant changes in research, interventions, and local and federal policy (Peterson & Lupton, 1996; Strein et al., 2003).

More recently, there have been national initiatives to expand the public health model to include mental as well as physical health, particularly among children and youth (Miller, Gilman, & Martens, 2008). The release of the reports of the Surgeon General on Mental Health (1999) and the Surgeon General's National Action Agenda on Children's Mental Health (2000) signaled an important shift in federal health priorities. Specifically, these and later reports "were thematically linked around the premises that (a) mental health was an integral, core, and significant component of the public health system; (b) reducing stigma and increasing early identification of mental health problems was essential to a sound public health system; and (c) strengthening the link between research and practice will achieve the greatest yield for the public" (Hoagwood & Johnson, 2003, p. 3). The impact of this emphasis on mental health promotion has perhaps been strongest in schools, particularly given repeated findings that mental health is critical to academic success (Hoagwood & Johnson, 2003) and that the two are integrally and reciprocally related (Adelman & Taylor, 2006; Doll & Cummings, 2008).

Specific aspects of the public health model that have particular relevance for schools include (a) applying scientifically-derived evidence to the delivery of psychological services; (b) strengthening positive behavior rather than focusing exclusively on decreasing problem behavior; (c) emphasizing community collaboration and linked services; and (d) using appropriate research strategies to improve the knowledge base and effectively evaluate school psychological services (Strein et al., 2003). Public health models may also be useful for enhancing systems capacity in schools through the identification, selection, and implementation of appropriate interventions to address students' diverse needs (Merrell & Buchanan, 2006). The central characteristic of the public health model, however, is its emphasis on prevention (Woodside & McClam; Strein et al., 2003).

A public health approach to prevention can perhaps best be illustrated by Walker et al.'s (1996) three-tiered model. This public health model has often been represented visually through use of a triangle, with three overlapping tiers that "collectively represent a continuum of interventions that increase in intensity (i.e., effort, individualization, specialization) based on the corresponding responsiveness" of individuals (Sugai, 2007, p. 114). The first tier, represented as the base of the triangle, is referred to as the *universal* or *primary* level, because all individuals in a given population (e.g., all the children living in poverty attending a particular school or district) receive a universal set of interventions designed to prevent particular emotional, behavioral, and/or academic problems. The second tier of the triangle, referred to as the *targeted* or *secondary* level, is comprised of more intensive interventions for those students who do not adequately respond to universal interventions. The third and last tier, referred to as the *indicated* or *tertiary* level, is characterized by highly individualized and specialized interventions for those students who do not adequately respond to universal and targeted levels of prevention and intervention (Walker et al., 1996; Sugai, 2007).

The original prevention logic which gave rise to the "triangle model" of public health was developed in the late 1950s as a systematic response for preventing chronic illness. Later, throughout the 1980s and 1990s, the logic of the triangle was refined and applied to other disciplines, including mental health (Sugai, 2007). Most recently, in the late 1990s and early 21st century, the prevention logic of a continuum of interventions to meet individual student needs has focused on the prevention of behavior and academic problems in schools (Doll & Cummings, 2008). For example, the public health approach known as school-wide positive behavior support has been effective in reducing antisocial behavior among students (Horner, Sugai, Todd, & Lewis-Palmer, 2005). For this model to be effective, the intensity of the intervention must be commensurate with the intensity of the problem, and the effectiveness of individualized interventions is highly dependent on the effectiveness of universal interventions (Sugai, 2007).

Although the specific features of the model would differ, this same public health approach can also be potentially useful in the context of providing needed school-based interventions for children living in poverty. Below we provide examples of evidence-based universal, targeted, and indicated interventions that may be used with these children. Both structural changes to traditional educational practices as well as the personal efforts of individual educators will be necessary for these interventions to be effective.

Universal Interventions

From a public health perspective, universal interventions would be applied to *all* students who are living at or below the poverty level in a given school. The goal at this level is to put supportive structures in place to prevent the development of academic, behavioral, and/or mental health problems (Sugai, 2007). Although there are many potential school-based universal interventions, this section will provide recommendations for the identification of students living in poverty and interventions for promoting high rates of praise, effective instruction, and effective parenting. Although there is a large body of literature documenting the importance of early interventions at the preschool level (e.g., Duncan, Ludwig, & Magnuson, 2007; Zigler & Styfco, 2004), this discussion will focus on universal interventions at the K-12 level because it isn't until Kindergarten that all schools have the ability to access each student who is experiencing poverty.

Identification

At the school level, perhaps the most effective and efficient means of identifying children living in poverty is to review the list of students who qualify for free or reduced lunch. This data from National School Lunch Program (NSLP) is the strongest single indicator of student poverty in schools. Children from families with incomes at or below 130% of the poverty level are eligible for free meals (for the 2008-2009 school year this equates to $27,560 for a family of four.) Those with incomes between 130% and 185% of the poverty level (or $39,220 for a family of four for the 2008-2009) are eligible for reduced-priced meals (USDA, 2008). It should be noted that lunch status is likely to be a more valid indicator of student poverty for children in Kindergarten through sixth grade because there is a tendency among students at the junior and senior high school level not to apply for a free or reduced-priced school lunch (NYS Education Department, 2008). Although most universal programming will be applied at the elementary level, this suggests that additional indicators such as parental self-report may be more helpful in identifying students living in poverty at the secondary level.

High Rates of Praise

The demonstrable power of praise in promoting optimal academic and social outcomes for children (and adults) has been clearly established. School-aged students who experience a high rate of teacher praise (as opposed to punishment and reprimands) have higher levels of academic engagement, lower levels of disruptive behavior, higher reading and math achievement, and even higher IQ scores. (Flora, 2000). Providing high rates of praise in schools has been recommended as a universal preventative approach for all students (Sawka-Miller & Miller, 2007). One can argue, however, that it is particularly critical to construct structured opportunities for praise at the elementary level for students living in poverty given their numerous risk factors. Unfortunately, despite decades of research demonstrating its effectiveness, praise is still not routinely used in schools (Flora, 2000; Jenson, Olympia, Farley, & Clark, 2004).

In arguably one of the most powerful demonstrations of the power of praise in affecting outcomes for children in poverty, Hart and Risley (1995) observed families of varying socioeconomic levels with infants in their homes once a month for two and a half years. During the observations, all parent and child language was recorded. Overall, they found that the children living in poverty (classified as "welfare" families) had millions fewer words spoken to them from the ages of 11 to 36 months, and that the quality of those words was demonstrably different, than children living in middle-income homes (classified as "professional" families). Specifically, 80% of feedback given from family members in the impoverished households was negative (e.g., "no", "don't", "stop"), compared with 80% affirmative feedback given in the middle-income family households. Hart and Risley concluded that – irrespective of socioeconomic status – children who made the strongest gains in vocabulary and IQ scores between the ages of 3 and 10 years were more likely to have parents who talked to them more and provided at least six praise and approval statements for every one criticism.

The findings of Hart and Risley (1995) suggest that children living in poverty must be provided a preferential option of increased affirmatives once they reach school-age. The authors asserted that "to keep the confidence building experiences of welfare children equal to those of working class children, the welfare children would need to be given 1,100 more instances of affirmative feedback per week... It would take 26 hours per week of substituted experience for the average welfare child's experience with affirmatives to equal that of the average working-class child (p 188)." Unfortunately, praise rates in schools are typically low, and they are lowest for children who are male, of minority background, developmentally delayed, and living in poverty (Jenson et al., 2004). A universal intervention would involve systematic efforts of teachers to praise children living in poverty at a rate per each child of at least 5 affirmatives to every 1 reprimand or punishing statement. Research suggests it takes the average teacher about three months to achieve this rate of praise when provided supportive assistance to do so (Sawka, McCurdy, & Mannella, 2002). Therefore, beyond a general recommendation for high rates of praise for students living in poverty, it will be necessary at the administrative level to build in mechanisms for creating accountability and monitoring integrity of implementation. Specific guidelines for helping to establish high rates of universal praise can be found in other sources (e.g., Sawka-Miller & Miller, 2007; Sutherland, Copeland, & Wehby, 2001).

Improve Teaching

Perhaps more than any other school variable, quality of instruction is implicated in affecting student achievement rates (Chall, 2000; Murnane 2007). Specifically, a teacher's skill at helping children acquire critical math and reading skills is what often determines a school's overall effectiveness (Chall, 2000; Whitehouse, 2007). Unfortunately, students living in poverty – and particularly urban poverty – are often taught by the most ill-prepared teachers, and parents/caregivers of these students often lack the resources necessary to compensate for poor instruction (Murnane, 2007). The impact of poor teaching is significant and cumulative; for example, fourth graders growing up in low-income communities often are at least three grade levels behind their peers in high-income communities (IES, 2005).

When systematic efforts are made to bring qualified teachers into high-need areas that serve high concentrations of children living in poverty, student academic achievement increases (Murnane, 2007). For example, Teach for America is one program that aims to address educational inequality by recruiting recent graduates from prestigious colleges to teach for two years in urban and rural schools serving high concentrations of children living in poverty. Other efforts to try to attract and retain high-quality staff in schools serving high concentrations of poor children include offering higher pay premiums and changing administrators (Chall, 2002; Murnane, 2007).

In addition to trying to recruit more highly-qualified staff to serve low-income students, one response to the poor skills of teachers in high-poverty schools has been capacity-building in the form of structured professional development aimed at improving teaching skills (Murnane, 2007; Sawka et al., 2002). Unfortunately, professional development activities typically consist of isolated trainings on a particular teaching topic. Research has consistently demonstrated that these "one-shot" approaches are not effective at affecting teacher behavior change in the classroom (Shapiro, Miller, Sawka, Gardill, & Handler, 1999) and that for change to occur there must be some sort of supportive, in-class follow-up to assist teachers in acquiring, demonstrating, and refining newly-learned skills (Sawka et al., 2002; Shapiro et al., 1999). Therefore, when attracting well-qualified teachers to serve children in poverty is not immediately possible, an alternative is to provide a high level of in-class, consultative, technical assistance to build the skills of teachers instructing these students.

Universal Parent Training

Children growing up in poverty are at risk for antisocial behavior, and one of the most promising interventions for offsetting this risk is parent management training (PMT). The goal of PMT is to equip parents with the skills to change their child's problematic behavior and encourage prosocial behavior. PMT focuses on teaching skills such as praise, limit setting, monitoring and supervision, family problem solving, and positive parent involvement (Kazdin, 2005). Typical outcomes related to PMT include improved child compliance, reduced aggressive and antisocial behavior, better parent-child relations (Kazdin, 2005) and improved symptoms related to child depression (Webster-Stratton & Herman, 2008).

Best practice in parent training suggests that families who are at-risk be identified early, before problems develop and in an effort to establish effective parenting patterns (Walker et al., 1996). It has further been suggested that providing parent training to all parents/caregivers in low-income neighborhoods can help prevent the development and escalation of coercive interaction patterns and offset specific risks of children living in poverty. In another chapter in this book, Sawka-Miller and McCurdy (2009) review results from a federally-funded pilot project designed to provide PMT to all parents in a large, low-income, ethnically diverse urban elementary school. In addition to providing incentives such as childcare, transportation, food, door prizes and the opportunity to "graduate" in front of their children, this project utilized community-based "parent liaisons" in recruitment and retention efforts. Outcomes included high parental participation in and satisfaction with the training, improvements in parental knowledge of effective parenting practices, improved child behavior, and increased parental attendance at school-based functions. The overall results suggest that proactively providing PMT was an effective universal intervention. Specific and more detailed suggestions for implementing a school-based universal parent management training program can be found in the chapter by Sawka-Miller and McCurdy (2009) in this volume.

Targeted Interventions

Targeted or selected interventions are applied to students who are beginning to engage in at-risk behavior and need more supportive, structured monitoring and programming than a universal system provides (Sugai, 2007). In essence, students are "targeted" or "selected" for more intensive programming. The goal is to offset risk or reverse any harm that has already occurred, and interventions are typically carried out in a group format. Examples of targeted strategies that are discussed in this section include Check and Connect and mentoring programs for students at-risk for drop-out, peer tutoring and targeted reading and math intervention for students starting to experience academic failure, and increasing family contact for students living in poverty who are displaying disruptive behavior and/or the early signs of mental health problems.

Check and Connect

Students living in poverty are at high risk for school dropout (Reschly & Christenson, 2006). School disengagement is a strong and early indicator that a student may be in need of targeted support. Signs include missing classes, not completing schoolwork, receiving low grades, and expressing disinterest in school (Morse, Anderson, Christenson, & Lehr, 2004). Check and Connect is a comprehensive model to promote student engagement with school, reduce dropout, and increase school completion and is ideally used in conjunction with strong universal prevention efforts. The "Check" component of the program encourages student school engagement by closely monitoring student performance and tracking risk indicators such as attendance, course grades, and behavior referrals. The "Connect" component involves staff giving individualized attention to students. A "monitor", typically a teacher, meets weekly with the student to provide encouragement, problem-solve, coordinate services, and to provide family collaboration and outreach as well as more intensive interventions to meet students' needs (Anderson, Christenson, Sinclair, Lehr, 2004). Outcomes from implementation of the Check and Connect Program in middle and high schools include reduced dropout rates and truancy, increased five-year school completion rates, fewer course failures, and reduced school suspensions (Sinclair, Christenson, Lehr, & Anderson, 2003).

Mentoring Programs

Mentoring programs in which at-risk students are paired with adults attempt to foster positive relationships and are predicated on the notion that some students experiencing poverty and academic failure lack academically successful role models (Whitehouse, 2006). In Twelve Together, one model of mentoring, twelve students starting to experience academic failure are paired with one mentor and meet as a group on a weekly basis. Group discussions are based on student interest and typically focus on personal, family, and peer-related issues, and students agree to not skip classes and attempt to improve their schoolwork as a condition of being in the program. The program also offers assistance with homework, trips to college campuses, and an annual weekend camping outing. Studies have demonstrated that participation in Twelve Together is associated with students staying in school longer (Hershey, Adelman, & Murray, 1995). At the estimated cost of $330 per student per month (Rosenberg & Hershey, 1995), however, less formal mentoring programs might be more feasible. Whitehouse (2006) suggests that programs using volunteer college students or professionals in the community can also serve to help students living in poverty form meaningful connections.

Peer Tutoring

School engagement in the form of attendance and establishing relationships is critical for success. Students living in poverty who are also experiencing academic failure, however, may need other forms of targeted interventions in an effort to improve their necessary core skills to meet curriculum demands. Reciprocal peer tutoring is an academic intervention that can be used across all grade levels and involves thoughtful pairing of students, the use of a structured error correction procedure, and close progress monitoring. In peer tutoring, students should take turns being the "tutor" and the "tutee". In addition to improved academic outcomes (e.g., Greenwood, Terry, Utley, Montagna, & Walker, 1993), the use of peer tutoring has been associated with gains in social skills, self-confidence, and enhancement of career decision-making processes in low-income secondary students (Greenwood, Carta, & Maheady, 1991; Obiuno, 2008). Murnane (2005) suggests that the use of peer tutors with students living in poverty may serve additional functions as well, such as helping teach homework skills that may have not been learned at home. When identifying students in need of more explicit or structured instruction, Murnane (2005) also suggests targeting ninth graders who lack proficiency in reading and math, because although many states have improved the reading and writing skills of elementary students, the number of ninth graders who lack these skills has increased. For a comprehensive online manual to guide planning, implementation, and evaluation of a school-based peer tutoring program, see Wright (2004).

Home-School Collaboration

Increasing contact with families assists in making parents/caregivers and students feel more connected to school and, indirectly, helps facilitate increased attendance and improved student achievement (Murnane, 2005). As a targeted intervention, systematic efforts to communicate and collaborate with parents might take the form of a daily report card (DRC). In a DRC, teachers monitor and record student daily progress toward meeting specific academic, behavioral, and/or social goals deemed necessary for promoting school success. The student brings home the DRC for parents/caregivers to sign, and if the student reaches the criterion for success, rewards are earned at home (Riley-Tillman, Chafouleas, & Briesch, 2007). The key features of the DRC are ongoing monitoring and feedback for the student, and the sharing of positive feedback between home and school. Positive outcomes related to use of the DRC include marked reductions in hyperactive, impulsive, oppositional, and aggressive behavior, as well as improvements in peer relationships, student-teacher relationships, and academic achievement (e.g., Owens, Richerson, Belisten, Crane, Murphy, & Vancouver, 2005). Further, use of the DRC as a targeted intervention has effectively reduced low income students' at-risk status for the development of more serious behavior problems (Cheney, Flower, & Templeton, 2008). A detailed guide describing how to establish a school-home DRC, complete with sample forms and recommended no-cost rewards, can be downloaded from the Center for Children and Families website (http://ccf.buffalo.edu.).

Indicated Interventions

Indicated or tertiary-level interventions are highly individualized, intensive, and typically cross-contextual supports. These interventions are implemented with students who display chronic and severe problem behaviors that are impeding learning or resulting in social or educational exclusion, and for whom universal and targeted interventions have not been successful (Walker et al., 1996). The goal of indicated interventions is to stop further harm and increase the student's adaptive skills and/or opportunities for an enhanced quality of life (Sugai, 2007). These interventions, which typically include multiple elements, usually involve collaboration among and supports from the school, home, and community. Moreover, they involve an in-depth, multidisciplinary analysis of the problems and contexts in which those problems occur, ongoing data collection to monitor progress, and frequent review and modification of the individualized plan.

Indicated interventions are individualized and tailored to the individual needs of the child. Therefore, a comprehensive listing of possible interventions from which to choose is neither available nor advisable. In the case of providing preferential options for students living in poverty, indicated programming in schools would mandate that behavior and instructional teams (typically comprised of a school psychologist, counselor, school social worker, teacher, and administrator) understand and contextualize a student's problems in terms of factors relating to poverty that are potentially placing the student at-risk or in need. That is, teams need to understand that poverty can interfere with school success as much as – and typically more than – an educational disability. Individualized programming needs to directly address factors related to poverty that interfere with school success. The following example from an actual case is offered to illustrate the individualized, cross-contextual nature of indicated interventions and the need to address factors related to poverty in an effort to promote student success.

"Suzie", a high school student experiencing repeated academic failure in her classes, high rates of truancy, and recent fighting at school, was referred to the school support team. In the process of examining the case, the team learned that Suzie's mother – a victim of spousal abuse – left her husband a year earlier and that the family was homeless. The mother had been attempting to find work but this was hindered by her need to frequently move. An assessment with Suzie, an obese teen, indicated that she was experiencing clinical levels of depression. Further assessment revealed that she was being teased in school for her clothes and that her truancy was in part due to her embarrassment about her appearance.

Indicated interventions for Suzie involved (a) a psychoeducational assessment that revealed a previously undiagnosed learning disability, (b) initiation of special education services, (c) assistance from the social worker in helping Suzie's mother find permanent housing and employment, (d) the granting of permission by the school principal for Suzie to be late for school to allow her time to travel from her new home so that she would not have to change schools, (e) assistance in helping the family find community-based mental health counseling services, and (f) the establishment of a behavior plan in which Suzie earned points for attending school and walking laps on the track during her free period. These points were then exchanged for new clothes that the school psychologist and counselor secured through donations from local businesses. Suzie's progress was carefully monitored and additional programming was provided as necessary. This multi-element intervention effectively addressed factors related to the family's homelessness and lack of income, the student's academic and behavioral problems, familial mental health issues, obesity, and barriers to attending school. If the instructional support team had not considered the specific factors related to poverty and only directly addressed the academic failure, it is not likely Suzie's situation would have improved. Although a year behind due to her excessive absences, Suzie stayed in school three more years and graduated.

Finally, it is important to note that the universal, targeted, and indicated interventions discussed in this section are not specific to children living in poverty. The principles of effective instruction and promoting mental health and appropriate student behavior cut across class lines; for example, effective reading interventions for children from privileged backgrounds are essentially no different than reading interventions for children living in poverty. The point of providing and emphasizing these interventions for children living in poverty is simply because they are at risk for a multitude of problems. As such, schools can and should make a preferential option for these students.

Although a public health approach to child poverty can be a useful framework for schools, children living in poverty also need support from their communities. Below we describe one example of how to forge more effective partnerships between schools and communities in serving children in poverty.

Full-Service Schools:
Forging Partnerships between Schools and Communities

"We have to think about health in the broadest possible sense."

– Paul Farmer

There are many ways in which schools and communities can work together to support children living in poverty and to promote and enhance their educational, health, and mental health outcomes. Perhaps the most comprehensive intervention for students and families experiencing poverty is to develop and maintain so-called "full-service" schools (Whitehouse, 2006). Full-service schools (Dryfoos, 1994) provide a variety of services to children and their families in one convenient location. In addition to education, examples of possible services provided in full-service schools include health care, recreation, community events, mental health services, family planning services, drug treatment, adult education, and job preparation (Dryfoos, 1996). Through full-service schools, "families have access to necessary resources and can become more connected to their child's educational environment, and students have access to resources that can improve their social, emotional, physical, and cognitive functioning" (Whitehouse, 2006, p. 843). Full-service schools provide a single point of entry into a system of services, coordinate these services, and can link services to future educational and employment possibilities for children and their families (Park, Turnbull, & Turnbull, 2002).

The implementation of full-service schools is still in its infancy and has not been evaluated fully, although preliminary studies have been promising (e.g., Dryfoos, 1994; Garrison, Roy, & Azar, 1999; McMahon, Ward, Pruett, Davidson, & Griffith, 2000), including demonstrating improvements in student attendance and graduation rates (Park et al., 2002). Full-service schools are increasing in the United States, but substantial resources are needed to maintain them. For example, space must be provided to various professional groups (e.g., psychologists, doctors, nurses, social workers, etc.), often necessitating the use of a separate building on or near school grounds (Whitehouse, 2006). Moreover, for full-service schools to be effective, collaborative relationships between agencies must be developed and various ethical and legal issues addressed (McMahon et al., 2000). Other potential barriers to the successful implementation of full-service schools include local politics, fiscal issues, reimbursement issues, communication and coordination issues, and turf issues (McMahon et al., 2000; Reeder et al., 1997). These barriers can be overcome, however, through careful planning, support, and collaboration (Whitehouse, 2006).

Full-service schools provide an opportunity for more effective and efficient collaboration between schools, communities, and families. For school-based interventions for children living in poverty to be maximally effective, however, there must be greater assistance provided to the parents and caregivers of these children. Although it may seem that schools can have little impact on the economic status of these adults, there is actually much that school personnel can do in terms of advocacy and assistance. Some examples of what this might involve are provided below.

Providing Supports and Advocating for Parents and Caregivers

"Workers at the edge of poverty are essential to America's prosperity, but their well-being is not treated as an integral part of the whole. Instead, the forgotten wage a daily struggle to keep themselves from falling over the cliff. It is time to be ashamed."

– David K. Shipler

For much of its history, Americans have emphasized and internalized the ideal of individualism and personal responsibility. As such, the traditional "bootstrap" theory of poverty, which essentially blames individuals in poverty for their condition and allows that the only way out of it is through individual responsibility and effort (Bageant, 2007), continues to be a popular viewpoint, particularly among those associated with the political right (Beck, 2007). Others, however, have come to the conclusion that poverty is more complex than a simple lack of individual initiative, and that to effectively ameliorate it involves a greater understanding of the environmental and structural variables that both cause and sustain it. For example, it has been widely suggested that stagnating wages, deteriorating health benefits, the loss of manufacturing jobs, and the declining clout of organized labor have all contributed to increased poverty among adults in the United States (Greenhouse, 2008; Shipler, 2004).

What can school personnel do to help support parents and caregivers of children living in poverty? One approach is for school personnel to become cognizant of social justice issues in their communities, and to work to promote the empowerment of marginalized students and their families (Fantuzzo, McWayne, & Bulotsky, 2003; Shriberg et al., 2008). Perhaps most important, school personnel can advocate for parents and caregivers across multiple levels. For example, there is clear evidence that the lower one's income the less likely one is to vote (Shipler, 2004). As such, many adults living in poverty may be sufficiently discouraged by their situation to have developed a sense of learned helplessness regarding the ability of government to improve their lives. Indeed, data from the Census Bureau indicates that the lower one's level of income and education, the less inclined Americans are to believe that voting can make a real difference (Shipler, 2004). Schools are often places where people vote during local and national elections, and school personnel can encourage parents in their district to vote and to assist them in that process. It should be understood, however, that many people do not vote along class lines, and that people living in poverty often vote against their own economic interests, particularly in southern and rural areas (Bageant, 2007).

School personnel can assist parents/caregivers in other ways as well, such as by advocating for an increased minimum wage, affordable housing, job training programs, and universal health care for families of children living in poverty (Ehrenreich, 2001; Shipler, 2004). Moreover, school personnel can ensure that parents/caregivers are aware of and have access to free or affordable educational, medical, and mental health services in their communities that can assist them and their children. Homeless shelters, soup kitchens, and food pantries could also benefit from school personnel willing and able to volunteer their time and energy. Such efforts may be viewed as too small in scope to meet the enormous needs of those in poverty, and they clearly do not impact the structural problems that lead to poverty. Even small changes, however, can have potentially large effects on people and the quality of their lives.

Conclusion

> "I don't think this problem of disparities in wealth is fixable, but there is something to be said for practicing good behavior. The ripples may not be big, but at least we're mussing the surface of complacency. My hope is that all of us who do this work can somehow trigger a chain reaction."

> *– Doctor working with the poor in Haiti*

Like the fields of medicine (Farmer, 2005) and psychology (Hage et al., 1997; Shriberg et al., 2008), education can be viewed as social justice work. Indeed, without school personnel taking a social justice perspective and acting accordingly, children living in poverty are likely to continue to struggle in our nation's schools. Charity may meet some short-term material needs, but it will not be sufficient for altering the environmental structures that both cause and sustain childhood poverty, as well as the many environmental, physical, psychological, and social problems that result from it. Further, although it has been suggested that adults must take some responsibility for their impoverished status (Shipler, 2004), their children are clearly responsible for none of it. Society must therefore make a preferential option for children living in poverty.

The school setting is a place where teachers and other school personnel are in an ideal position to make preferential option decisions when working with children affected by poverty. Although school personnel cannot change the underlying structures that create child poverty, they can modify school environments to address it proactively, as well as take personal responsibility for responding to it in an attempt to potentially reduce its many negative effects. As noted by Kirylo (2006): "The poor and marginalized who come to our schools every day urgently demand our attention, and so we must make preferential choices in our thought processes, actions, and economics; we must be about giving life" (p. 269). In particular, the notion of making a school-based preferential option for the poor provides a useful philosophical and conceptual basis for a public health approach to intervention. For this approach to be effective, changes will need to occur in both systems and in individuals, at both macro and micro levels. There is no better place to begin this process than in our nation's schools, among the school personnel who interact with children of poverty on a daily basis. The responsibility for making a school-based preferential option for the poor is ours.

References

Ackerman, B. P., Brown, e. D., & Izard, C. E. (2004). The relations between persistent poverty and contextual risk and children's behavior in elementary school. *Developmental Psychopathology, 40*, 367-377.

Adelman, H.S., & Taylor, L. (2006). *The school leader's guide to student learning supports: New directions for addressing barriers to learning*. Thousand Oaks, CA: Corwin Press.

Anderson, A. R., Christenson, S. L., Sinclair, M. F., & Lehr, C. A. (2004). Check & Connect: The importance of relationships for promoting engagement with school. *Journal of School Psychology, 42*(2), 95–113.

Bageant, J. (2007). *Deer hunting with Jesus: Dispatches from America's class war*. New York: Crown Publishers.

Beck, G. (2007). *An inconvenient book: Real solutions to the world's biggest problems*. New York: Threshold.

Boff, L., & Boff, C. (1987). *Introducing liberation theology*. Maryknoll, NY: Orbis.

Borg, M.J. (2006). *Jesus: Uncovering the life, teachings, and relevance of a religious revolutionary*. New York: HarperCollins.

Borg, M.J., & Crossan, J.D. (2007). *The first Christmas*. New York: HarperCollins.

Brooks-Gunn, J., & Dunan, G. J. (1997). The effects of poverty on children. *The Future of Children,* 7(2), 55-71.

Chall, J. S. (2000). *The achievement challenge: What really works in the classroom?* New York: Guilford Press.

Chen, E., Matthews, K. A., & Boyce, T. (2002). Socioeconomic status differences in health: what are the implications for children? *Psychological Bulletin,* **128**, 295-329.

Crossan, J.D. (1994). Jesus: A revolutionary biography. New York: HarperCollins.

Crossan, J.D., & Watts, R.G. (1996). *Who is Jesus?* Louisville, KY: Westminster John Knox Press.

Day, D. (1952). *The long loneliness*. New York: HarperCollins.

DeNavas-Walt, C., Proctor, B.D., & Lee, C.H. (2005). Income, poverty, and health insurance coverage in the United States: 2004 (U.S. Census Bureau, Current Population Reports, P60-229). Washington, DC: U.S. Government Printing Office.

Dennis, M., Golden, R., & Wright, S. (2000). *Oscar Romero: Reflections on his life and writings*. Maryknoll, NY: Orbis.

Doll, B., & Cummings, J.A. (2008). (Eds.). *Transforming school mental health services*. Thousand Oaks, CA: Corwin Press.

Dryfoos, J. (1994) *Full-service schools: A revolution in health and social services for children, youth, and families*. San Francisco, CA: Jossey-Bass.

Dryfoos, J. (1996). Adolescents at risk: Shaping programs to fit the need. *Journal of Negro Education,* **65**, 5-18.

Ehrenreich, B. (2001). *Nickel and dimed: On (not) getting by in America*. New York: Metropolitan.

Evans, G.W. (2004). The environment of child poverty. *American Psychologist,* **59**, 77-92.

Fantuzzo, J., McWayne, C., & Bulotsky, R. (2003). Forging strategic partnerships to advance mental health science and practice for vulnerable children. *School Psychology Review,* **32**, 17-37.

Farmer, P. (2005). *Pathologies of power: Health, human rights, and the new war on the poor*. Berkeley, CA: University of California Press.

Flora, S. R. (2000). Praise's magic ratio: Five to one gets the job done. *The Behavior Analyst Today,* **1**(4), 64-69.

Forest, J. (1986). *Love is the measure: A biography of Dorothy Day*. Maryknoll, NY: Orbis.

Freire, P. (1990). *Pedagogy of the oppressed*. New York: Continuum.

Garrison, E.G., Roy, I.S., & Azar, V. (1999). Responding to the mental health needs of Latino children and families through school-based services. *Clinical Psychology Review,* **19**, 199-219.

Greenhouse, S. (2008). *The big squeeze: Tough times for the American worker*. New York: Knopf.

Greenwood, C. R., Carta, J. J., & Maheady, L. 91991). Peer tutoring programs in the regular education classroom. In G. Stoner, M. R. Shinn, & H. M. Walker (Eds), *Interventions for achievement and behavior problems* (pp. 179-200). Silver Spring, MD: National Association of School Psychologists

Greenwood, C. R., Terry, t., Utley, C. A., Montagna, D., & Walker, D. (1992). Achievement, placement, and services: Middle school benefits of classwide peer tutoring used at the elementary level. *School Psychology Review*, **22**(3), 497-516.

Hershey, A., Adelman, N., & Mrray, S. (1995) *Helping kids succeed: Implementation of the School Dropout Demonstration Assistance Program.* Princeton, NJ: Mathematica Policy Research, Inc.

Jenson, W. R., Olympia, D., Farley, M., & Clark, E. (2004). Positive psychology and externalizing students in a sea of negativity. *Psychology in the Schools*, **41**(1), 67-79.

Kazdin, A. E. (2005). *Parent management training: Treatment for oppositional, aggressive, and antisocial behavior in children and adolescents.* New York: Oxford University Press.

Gutiérezz, G. (1973). A theology of liberation: History, politics, and salvation. Maryknoll, NY: Orbis.

Hage, S.M., Romano, J.L., Conyne, R.K., Matthews, Kenny, M., Matthews, C., Schwartz, J.P., & Waldo, M. (1997). Best practices guidelines on prevention practice, research, training, and social advocacy for psychologists. *Counseling Psychologist*, **35**, 493-566.

Hart, B., & Risley, T.R. (1995). *Meaningful differences in the everyday experiences of young American children.* Baltimore, MD: Paul Brookes.

Hawken, P. (2007). *Blessed unrest: How the largest movement in the world came into being and why no one saw it coming.* New York: Viking.

Heller, A. (1987). *Beyond justice.* New York: Basic Books.

Hoagwood, K., & Johnson, J. (2003). School psychology: A public health framework I. From evidence-based practices to evidence-based policies. *Journal of School Psychology*, **41**, 3-21.

Horner, R.H., Sugai, G., Todd, A.W., & Lewis-Palmer, T. (2005). School-wide positive behavior support. In L. Bambara & L. Kern (Eds.), Individualized supports for students with problem behaviors: Designing positive behavior support plans. New York: Guilford.

IES, Institute of Educational Sciences National Center for Educational Statistics (2005). National assessment of educational progress: The nation's report card. Retrieved October 20, 2008 from http://nces.ed.gov/nationsreportcard/

Kidder, T. (2003). *Mountains beyond mountains: The quest of Dr. Paul Farmer, a man who would cure the world.* New York: Random House.

Kirylo, J.D. (2006). Preferential option for the poor: Making a pedagogical choice. *Childhood Education*, **82**(5), 266-270.

Kozol, J. (1991). Savage inequalities: Children in America's schools. New York: HarperCollins.

Martín-Baró, I. (1994). *Writings for a liberation psychology.* Cambridge, MA: Harvard University Press.

Mash, E. J. & Wolfe, D. A. (2007). *Abnormal child psychology* (3rd Edition). Belmont, CA: Thomson/Wadsworth.

McKanan, D. (2008). *The Catholic Worker after Dorothy: Practicing the works of mercy in a new generation.* Collegeville, MN: Liturgical Press.

McMahon, T.J., Ward, N.L., Pruett, M.K., Davidson, L., & Griffith, E.E. (2000). Building full-service schools: Lessons learned in the development of interagency collaboration. *Journal of Educational and Psychological Consultation*, **11**, 65-92.

Merrell, K.W., & Buchanan, R. (2006). Intervention selection in school-based practice: Using public health models to enhance systems capacity of schools. *School Psychology Review,* **35**, 167-180.

Messner, S. F., Raffalovich, L. E., & McMillan, R. (2006). Economic deprivation and changes in homicide arrest rates for white and black youths, 1967-1998: A national time-series analysis. *Criminology*, **39**(3), 591-614.

Miller, D.N., Gilman, R., & Martens, M.P. (2008). Wellness promotion in the schools: Enhancing students' mental and physical health. *Psychology in the Schools*, **45**, 5-15.

Miller, D.N., & Sawka-Miller, K.D. (in press). Beyond unproven trends: Critically evaluating school-wide programs. In T.M. Lionetti, E. Snyder, & R.W. Christner (Eds.), *A practical guide to developing competencies in school psychology*. New York: Springer.

Morse, A. B., Anderson, A. R., Christenson, S. L., & Lehr, C. A. (2004). Promoting school completion. *Principal Leadership Magazine*, **4**(5), 9-13.

Murnane, R. J. (2007). Improving the education of children living in poverty. *Future of Children,* **17**(2). 161-182.

National Center for Education Statistics. (2004). *The condition of education 2004* (NCES 2004-077). Washington, DC: U.S. Government Printing Office.

NYS Education Department (2008). *Kids well-being indicators clearninghouse: Children receiving free or reduced-priced school lunch*. Retrieved October 25, 2008 from http://www.nyskwic.org/

Obiuno, J. J. (2008). The effects of reciprocal peer tutoring on the enhancement of career decision making process among secondary school adolescents. *Educational Research and Reviews*, **3**(7), 236-24.

Owens, J. S., Richerson, L., Beilsten, E. A., Crane, A., Murphy, C. E., & Vancouver, J. B. (2005). School-based mental health programming for children with inattentive and disruptive behavior problems: First-year treatment outcome. *Journal of Attention Disorders*, **9**(1), 261-274.

Park, J., Turnbull, A.P., & Turnbull, III, H.R. (2002). Impacts of poverty on quality of life of children with disabilities. Exceptional Children, 68, 151-170.

Payne, R.K. (2001). *A framework for understanding poverty*. Highlands, TX: aha! Processes.

Peterson, A., & Lupton, D. (1996). *The new public health: Health and self in the age of risk*. London: Sage.

Plewis, I., Smith, G., Wright, G., & Cullis, A. (2002). Linking child poverty and child outcomes: Exploring data and research strategies. ASD Research Branch Working Papers No 1, Department for Work and Pensions. Retrieved October 2, 2008, from http://www.dwp.gov.uk/asd/asd5/WP1.pdf

Poppendieck, J. (1998). *Sweet charity? Emergency food and the end of entitlement*. New York: Viking Press.

Rawls, J. (1971). *A theory of justice*. Cambridge, MA: Harvard University Press.

Reeder, G.D., Maccow, G.C., Shaw, S.R., Swerdlik, M.E., Horton, C.B., & Foster, P. (1997). School psychologists and full-service schools: Partnerships with medical, mental health, and social services. *School Psychology Review*, **26**, 603-621.

Reschley, A. & Christenson, s. L. (2006). *School completion*. In G. G Baer & K. M Minke (Eds.), Children's needs III: Development, prevention, and intervention (pp. 103-113). Bethesda, MD: National Association of School Psychologists.

Riley-Tilman, C. T., Chafouleas, S. M., & Briesch, A. M. (2007). A school practitioner's guide to using daily behavior report cards to monitor student behavior. *Psychology in the Schools*, **44**(1), 77-89.

Robinson-Wood, T.L. (2009). *The convergence of race, ethnicity, and gender*, third edition. Upper Saddle River, NJ: Merrill.

Rosenberg, L., & Hershey, A. (1995). *The cost of dropout prevention programs*. Princeton, NJ: Mathematica Policy Research, Inc.

Ross, D. P., Shillington, E. R., & Lochhead, C. (1994). *The Canadian fact book on poverty*. Ottawa: Canadian council of Social Development.

Sawka-Miller, K.D., & McCurdy, B.L. (in press). Prevention of antisocial behavior: Parent training in low-income urban schools. In F. Columbus (Ed.), *Low incomes: Social, health, and educational impacts*. New York: Nova.

Sawka, K.D., McCurdy, B.L., & Mannella, M.C. (2002). Strengthening emotional support services: An empirically based model for training teachers of students with behavior disorders. *Journal of Emotional and Behavioral Disorders*, **10**, 223-232.

Sawka-Miller, K. D., & Miller, D. N. (2007). The third pillar: Linking positive psychology and school-wide positive behavior support. *School Psychology Forum*, **2**(1), 26-38.

Shapiro, E. S., Miller, D., Sawka, K., Gardill, K., & Handler, M. (1999). Facilitating the inclusion of students with emotional and behavioral disorders into general education classrooms. *Journal of Emotional and Behavioral Disorders*, **7**, 83-93.

Shipler, D.K. (2004). The working poor: Invisible in America. New York: Vintage.

Shriberg, D., Bonner, M., Sarr, B.J., Walker, A.M., Hyland, M., & Chester, C. (2008). Social justice through a school psychology lens: Definition and applications. *School Psychology Review*, **37**, 469-486.

Sinclair, M. F., Christenson, S. L., Lehr, C. A., & Anderson, A. R. (2003). Facilitating student engagement: Lessons learned from Check & Connect longitudinal studies. *The California School Psychologist*, **8**, 29–42.

Sutherland, K. S., Copeland, S., & Wehby, J. H. (2001). Catch them while you can: Monitoring and increasing the use of effective praise. *Beyond Behavior*,11(1), 46-49.

Smith, C. (1991). *The emergence of liberation theology: Radical religion and social movement theory*. Chicago, IL: University of Chicago Press.

Sowell, T. (1987). *A conflict of visions: Ideological origins of political struggles*. New York: William Morrow.

Stevens, E., & Wood, G.H. (1992). *Justice, ideology, and education: An introduction to the social foundations of education*. New York: McGraw-Hill.

Strein, W., Hoagwood, K., & Cohn, A. (2003). School psychology: A public health perspective II. Prevention, populations, and systems change. *Journal of School Psychology,* **41**, 23-38.

Strohschein L. A. (2005). Household income histories and child mental health trajectories. *Journal of Health and Social Behavior*, **64**(4), 359-375.

Sugai, G. (2007). Promoting behavioral competence in schools: A commentary on exemplary practices. *Psychology in the Schools*, **44**, 113-118.

US Census Bureau (2008). Poverty: 2007 highlights. Retrieved September 2, 2008 from http://www.census.gov/hhes/www/poverty/poverty07/pov07hi.html

USDA Food and Nutrition Service (July, 2009). *National school lunch program: Program fact sheet*. Retrieved October 25, 2008 from http://www.fns.usda.gov/CND/Lunch/

US Department of Health and Human Services (1999). *Mental health: A report of the surgeon general.* Rockville, MD: U.S. Department of Health and Human Services, National Institute of Health, National Institute of Mental Health.

US Department of Health and Human Services (1999*). The surgeon general's call to action to prevent suicide.* Washington, DC.

US Public Health Service (2000). *Report of the surgeon general's conference on children's mental health: A national action agenda.* Washington, DC.

Vera, E.M., & Speight, S.L. (2003). Multicultural competence, social justice, and counseling psychology: Expanding our roles. *The Counseling Psychologist*, **31**, 253-272.

Walker, H.M., Horner, R.H., Sugai, G., Bullis, M., Sprague, J.R., Bricker, D., & Kaufman, M.J. (1996). Integrated approaches to preventing antisocial behavior patterns among school-age children and youth. *Journal of Emotional and Behavioral Disorders*, **4,** 193-256.

Webster-Stratton, C., & Herman, K. C. (2008). The impact of parent behavior-management training on child depressive symptoms. *Journal of Counseling Psychology*, **55**(4), 473-484.

Whitehouse, E.M. (2006). Poverty. In G.C. Bear & K.M. Minke (Eds.), *Children's needs III: Development, prevention, and intervention* (pp. 835-845). Bethesda, MD: National Association of School Psychologists.

Woodside, M., & McClam, T. (1998). *An introduction to human services* (3rd edition). Pacific Grove, CA: Brooks/Cole.

Wright, J. (2004). *Kids as reading helpers: A peer tutoring training manual.* Retrieved October 28, 2008 from http://www.interventioncentral.org/

Young, I.M. (1990). *Justice and the politics of difference.* Princeton, NJ: Princeton University Press.

Zigler, E., & Styfko, S.J. (Eds.). (2004). *The head start debates.* Baltimore, MD: Paul Brookes.

Zwick, M. & Zwick, L. (2005). *The Catholic Worker movement: Intellectual and spiritual origins.* New York: Paulist Press.

In: Low Incomes: Social, Health and Educational Impacts   ISBN: 978-1-60741-175-8
Editor: Jacob K. Levine, pp. 57-91   © 2009 Nova Science Publishers, Inc.

Chapter 3

UNDERSTANDING RACIAL ETHNIC SOCIALIZATION IN CHILD CARE PROGRAMS SERVING A LOW-INCOME AFRICAN-AMERICAN AND LATINO IMMIGRANT COMMUNITY

Kay Sanders[a] and Eva Shivers[b]
[a]Whittier College, CA, USA
[b]Indigo Cultural Center, AZ, USA

Abstract

Since the advent of Head Start in the 1960's, preschool interventions targeted children living in poverty. The findings from some of these programs demonstrate some positive results. While teacher education and other features of child care quality have been found to be an important factor in the improvement of childhood outcomes for children in poverty, the relevance of racial ethnic socialization in child care has not been examined as a potentially crucial element toward improving developmental outcomes for African-American and Mexican immigrant children living in urban poverty. Before determining the impact of child care racial ethnic socialization on childhood outcomes, it is necessary to identify what racial ethnic socialization in child care is. This chapter will address this question by presenting original research that describes racial ethnic socialization practices in professional child care programs that serve poor, urban, racial ethnic minority children[1].

Theoretical Background

Racial ethnic socialization, as conceptualized in this paper, is based upon two theoretical assumptions. First, human development is connected to the contexts and histories of the communities in which that development occurs. Secondly, racial ethnic socialization practices of minorities include the socialization of children who will experience at some point in their lives discrimination due to their phenotypic difference. To articulate these assumptions, we

---

[1] The term "racial ethnicity" is adopted in line with Thorne (2005)

rely upon the works of Bronfenbrenner (1979) , Rogoff (2003), Fenton (1999), and Garcia-Coll (1996).

Regarding the first assumption, Bronfenbrenner (1979) proposed a model of development in which the varying levels of interaction between the individual and society are an integral part of a person's development . According to Bronfenbrenner, development of the individual is situated within a web of concentric circles in which historical events, societal changes, institutions and interpersonal connections interact to influence development. Bronfenbrenner described these influences in terms of systems. The overarching macrosystem includes the cultural beliefs, norms and policies of a society. Living in poverty, violence and historical, systemic racism are macrosystem elements of growing up in poor, urban segregated communities, for example. The environments in which the families of this study live are historically the result of economic and racial segregation (Massey & Fischer, 2000; Proctor & Dalaker, 2003).

Within Bronfenbrenner's macrosystem is the exosystem, or the settings that indirectly affect the environments that contain the developing person. In subsidized childcare programs, which many of the childcare programs in urban, poor environments are, there is usually an administrative body that the child does not have direct contact with but whose influence on curricula, hiring/firing of staff, etc., impact the child's experiences in the childcare center.

The third level, the mesosystem, is the interrelations between two or more settings in which the developing person directly participates. Typical and obvious settings are the family and the classroom within the childcare center. Finally, there are the microsystems, which are the ongoing activities and interactions between individuals within a setting. Within the family, interactions between parent and child are a microsystem as are interactions between the childcare teacher and the child at a childcare center.

Layers of environmental context are relevant aspects of development, as are the individuals' perceptions or understandings of those layers of context. What Bronfenbrenner includes under proximal processes, "the inclusion of both beliefs and behaviors in the same research design considerably enhances the explanatory power of analytic models in developmental science" (Bronfenbrenner, 1995). In other words, not only are the contexts important but also the interpretation of those contexts by the individuals experiencing them. The individuals interpret the meaning and influence of racial ethnicity on their lives through their perspectives of the unique cultural and historical position of their community. For example, the childcare teachers in this study are also racial ethnic minorities, many of whom are local residents (Sanders, Deihl, & Kyler, 2007). They hold perceptions of personal experiences regarding the role of race and ethnicity in their lives.

Issues pertaining to race and ethnicity are not a specific focus of Bronfenbrenner's model. Rogoff (2003), however, extended Bronfenbrenner's concentric circle view of development by emphasizing the centrality of culture and social history on human development. Rogoff interpreted culture as the participation of individuals with each other. Culture, in this sense, is not static but a "mutually constituting" (p.51) process in which the individual is not viewed as nested or influenced by cultural processes but as a participant in the creation of cultural communities. Culture transcends ethnic, national and racial boundaries, and an individual participates in more than one cultural community. Take, for example, the hypothetical family of this study. This family belongs to the ethnic communities of their neighborhoods, the family unit and the childcare center community. Each of these communities has a set of histories, values, beliefs and practices. Through participation in these communities, the family creates and maintains the cultural processes of each. Culture is not separate from the individual but created by the individual through practices. Culture, in this sense, is not only your racial or ethnic group but akin to layers of an onion that are interconnected and overlapping to make up the whole.

Although Rogoff's cultural framework is helpful to understand the inter-connectedness of race and ethnicity to cultural processes, it does not account for what Garcia-Coll et al. (1996) referred to as the "social position" (p.1895) of children of color. These social position characteristics (race, gender, ethnicity, for example) become a tool for social stratification mechanisms, such as racism, prejudice, and segregation. Social stratification mechanisms are a central experience most families of color experience at all levels of life (Fenton, 1999). Applying Bronfenbrenner's model specifically to the experiences of the racial ethnic minority, perceptions of social stratification mechanisms by childcare teachers are a proximal process that is part of a child's developmental context. To understand the function of racial ethnic socialization within a poor community of color, it is essential to interpret the practices of this community through its historical experiences; experiences in which exclusion from the mainstream have been pervasive.

Layers of Context

Based on our theoretical framework, racial ethnic socialization is socialization that is embedded within layers of context. We interpret racial ethnic socialization as a process occurring within the regional and cultural contexts of the community. Therefore, we include different yet overlapping layers of context in our model of racial ethnic socialization. Some of these layers are background elements that provide both constraints, as well as depth to our findings.

Racial ethnic socialization is the racial ethnic experiences in the home and out-of-home contexts that children encounter. These experiences help to shape children's views about the self and their views concerning themselves in relation to others. The outermost layer of context, a background layer for this study, is the regional area in which children are reared. In this study, the families live in an urban area of California. This area experiences high levels of community violence and poverty. According to police records, the study area has the highest homicide and aggravated assault levels for its county; much of it due to inter-gang activity.

The study area was historically an African-American community for several decades but it has been as well the first United States' home to many immigrants. Recent census data confirm that the area is still first home to many immigrants from Latin American countries. Approximately 85% of the population located within this region identify as Latino. According to the report by the Economic Roundtable (*The cage of poverty*, 2000), one-million native-born residents left this urban area and "were replaced by one-million immigrants from outside the United States" (p. 23). Not all of these new residents reside in the study area but 46% of the 60,000 residents of this region are foreign born. 79% speak Spanish at home and 50% of those residents speak English less than very well[2].

Overlapping the geographic region are two communities made up of African-American and Latino families. As discussed previously, there are many cultural communities to which

---

[2] Figures derived from U.S. Census Bureau, Census 2000 Summary File 4.

the typical family of this study may belong, and racial ethnic group membership is one of them. We define cultural community as individuals who identify themselves as belonging to the same group through their sharing of a set of practices, history or traditions. One layer of cultural community is the racial ethnic group to which a family identifies itself as belonging. Researchers commonly use race and ethnicity as a proxy for culture (Johnson, Jaeger, Randolph, Cauce, & Ward, 2003), and neither race nor ethnicity are free-floating terms divorced of cultural meaning. Instead, both terms only have meaning when embedded within the cultural milieu of the observed group. The United States, as discussed previously, is a racialized country, and people who share similar skin colors and physical features are grouped into specific categories that are given the label of a racial ethnic group. These groups, when subordinated, share the experiences of discrimination and racism. Our interest in racial ethnic socialization, therefore, is not to examine race as biology but to investigate the practices associated with children of color who belong to subordinated groups. As such, the usage of the term racial ethnicity includes the historical and cultural connectedness to a group in general and to the particular group within the immediate community in which the individual participates.

The final layer is the child care programs, which is the layer of context we place in the foreground. The child care programs introduce a different yet similar community that contains its own unique culture. The child care community, however, also overlaps with the racial ethnic community because the staff who make up the child care community are also members of a racial ethnic group; in this case, African American and Latino. Child care programs have a tradition of caring for children in the community that may or may not match the family practices and beliefs. The programs in this study are unique in that they are traditionally African-American childcare programs that have experienced a shift from having predominantly African-American families in their programs to having both African-American and an increasing number of Latino families. The child care programs become a point of intersection for the African American and Latino communities who reside in the same geographic area.

The child care practices that the African American and Latino children experience in these traditionally African American programs are an integral part of the classroom environment, which are embedded within each child care center. The classroom environment contributes to children's experiences through a set of practices executed by the adults and children therein. Some of the experiences have to do with multiculturalism, such as the level of bias that is tolerated or the degree of African American or Mexican-American cultural elements that the classroom has. Other experiences have to do with the quality of the classroom environment, in terms of the management of the room, the sensitivity toward children or the emotional valence of the environment.

Classrooms are usually divided into age groups with the very youngest children separated physically from the older preschoolers. Teachers order and operate these classrooms according to the mandates of the program, but also according to their own sense of appropriate child rearing practices. The teacher is the one who executes practices associated with aspects of quality and multiculturalism.

In this chapter we provide a brief review of the contexts of the child care programs that took part in the study by discussing research on childhood poverty, child care as an intervention, and racial ethnic socialization. Our premise is that child care programs are also a context for racial ethnic socialization. We describe racial ethnic socialization in child care for poor, urban children through original descriptive research and conclude with suggestions for future inquiry.

Childhood Poverty

Childhood poverty is a prevalent factor in the lives of urban dwelling African American and Mexican immigrant families in the United States. While one in six children in the United States live in poverty, one in four Latino children and one in three African American children experience the effects of poverty in the U.S.[3] The census estimates have been criticized as underestimations of childhood poverty due to an inaccurate computation that does not include real estimates of economic need and cost of living adjustments. Some estimates that adjust for health care costs, child care, and other items not included in official estimates of poverty, reveal that 51 to 66% of African American and Latino immigrant families are experiencing poverty in the United States (Hernandez, Denton, & Macartney, 2007).

Although the nation's poor are not centered in urban America, and whites constitute a substantial number of poor families in the United States (Proctor & Dalaker, 2003), the urban poor is comprised predominantly of African American, and increasingly, Latino families (Alaniz, Cartmill, & Parker, 1998; Massey & Fischer, 2000; Rank & Hirschl, 1999). Children constitute the majority of the poor in America ("America's children: Key national indicators of well-being", 2007; Palmer, Younghwan, & Lu, 2002; Proctor & Dalaker, 2003).

A constellation of hardships is associated with poverty. Poor families lack adequate health care and premature or low-birth weight infants are common (Duncan & Brooks-Gunn, 1997; Gershoff, 2003). Poor environments contain substantially more health risks (Bradley, Corwyn, McAdoo, & Garcia Coll, 2001), including corollaries to adulthood obesity (Olson, Bove, & Miller, 2007), as well as substantial environmental toxins, such as lead, that are deleterious to children's cognitive functioning ("America's children: Key national indicators of well-being", 2007). Poor, urban environments have high levels of violence (Sander-Phillips, 1996) and social support services, such as child care, are of lesser quality (Phillips, 1994).

The effect of poverty on children's outcomes has been well-documented by research (Duncan, Brooks-Gunn, & Klebanov, 1994; Duncan, Yeung, Brooks-Gunn, & Smith, 1998). Poverty is a hindrance to the positive development of children, and it can be particularly harmful when poverty occurs during the early years (Duncan et al., 1998). Poverty has been linked to decreased cognitive outcomes during childhood (Duncan et al., 1994; Farah et al., 2006) and behavior problems from preschool (Dearing, McCartney, & Taylor, 2006; Jackson, Brooks-Gunn, Huang, & Glassman, 2000) into adolescence (Adam & Chase-Lansdale, 2002; McLoyd, Jayaratne, Ceballo, & Borquez, 1994).

Poverty is associated with less than optimal situations in the family environment that are known to impact child development negatively. McLoyd (1990) proposed a model revealing how poverty can negatively affect childhood outcomes indirectly via the stress experienced by the parent. There has been a substantial amount of evidence to support McLoyd's model (Mistry, Vandewater, Huston, & McLoyd, 2002), which includes parental factors, such as,

---

[3] U.S. Census Bureau, Current Population Survey, 2007 Annual Social and Economic Supplement, Detailed Poverty Tables and Historical Poverty Tables.

maternal depression (Petterson & Albers, 2001), marital stress (Conger et al., 2002; Jackson et al., 2000) and punitive or disruptive parenting (Conger et al., 2002; McLoyd, 1990).

While there is substantial documentation to reveal the link between poverty and detrimental childhood outcomes, researchers have questioned the influence of income on children's outcomes by disaggregating income from the conditions of poverty (poorly functioning schools, family factors, etc.). For example, Mayer (2001) concluded that income alone does not account for the adverse childhood outcomes commonly associated with poverty. The outcome in question was educational attainment. In a study that included a wider array of childhood outcomes (i.e. language, positive and problematic social behavior, school readiness), Dearing and colleagues (Dearing, McCartney, & Taylor, 2001) discovered that a change in the income to needs ratio in poor families by 1 standard deviation above the mean change for poor families resulted in childhood outcomes from 1 year to 36 months of age becoming similar to non-poor families. Therefore, although Mayer's analysis does reveal that raising income alone may not alleviate completely negative childhood outcomes, such as educational attainment, it is also clear that conditions both within and outside the family reflect the economic stress associated with poverty (Huston, 2005), and an analysis of income alone provides an incomplete portrait of the lives of families experiencing poverty.

While poverty during early childhood can be harmful, the effect of persistent poverty on childhood outcomes paints an even bleaker picture than transient poverty due to its greater negative effect on IQ and behavior problems in early childhood (Allhusen et al., 2005; Duncan & Brooks-Gunn, 2000; Duncan et al., 1994). The trend of persistent poverty is strongest in African American families than in any other racial or ethnic group (McLoyd, 1990). Although persistent poverty within the African American community is greatest in rural regions (McLoyd, 1990), many African Americans in poor, urban environments may not move in and out of poverty but often remain in poverty for lifetimes (Duncan et al., 1994).

For Latino families, the picture is somewhat similar to that of African American families but poverty levels are associated with immigration status. Children of Latino descent in California experienced the largest increase in poverty rates from 1979 to 2002 (14% increase) (Palmer et al., 2002). Most of these children are immigrants, and may or may not live in urban environments. However, recent immigrants usually "live in racially and ethnically segregated areas characterized by high rates of poverty (…)" and violence (Alaniz et al., 1998), p. 1), which are most likely in urban centers of the United States. If these areas are highly segregated, the risk of poverty for immigrants is even greater (Massey & Fischer, 2000).

Child care programs and parental socialization practices can serve as a buffer against the negative effects of poverty. McLoyd, (1990) identified child care programs, in addition to other social supports, as a potential means through which the stresses of parenting in poverty can be reduced, and thereby disassociate some of the negative socio-emotional outcomes associated with poverty for the urban poor.

Child Care Intervention

There are two strands of research related to child care and its effect on children in poverty. The first includes high quality, targeted interventions with comprehensive services that include early childhood programs as part of an intervention package to alleviate the negative consequences experienced by poor families. Some of the best known of these interventions includes Head Start, Abecedarian Project, and Comprehensive Child Development Program. Another strand of research is not necessarily experimental but focuses on tracking children's progress in community child care programs of varying quality with a diverse array of curricula and services to see how factors, such as teacher education, curricular practices, etc. correlate with or predict childhood outcomes. Quality with these studies is consistently a major player in the relationship between child care program effects on childhood outcomes.

High Quality Child Care Intervention.

Early childhood intervention includes programs that include family/parenting intervention and/or early childhood education. For the purposes of this study, we exclude a review of programs that are solely parent education interventions or home visiting programs. Early childhood education can be a stand alone intervention or it can include some aspect of family intervention, such as home visits or parent education. The majority of proven interventions contain a parent component, and early childhood intervention appears to have the most lasting effects when both childhood education and parent support and training are part of the intervention program (Kağıtçıbaşı, 2007).

Proven outcomes include interventions that contained both an experimental and control or comparison group so that changes in the chosen developmental domain can be tracked and compared between these groups (Abbott-Shim, Lambert, & McCarty, 2003; Garces, Thomas, & Currie, 2002; Hill, Brooks-Gunn, & Waldfogel, 2003; Lally, Mangione, & Honig, 1988; Lazar & Darlington, 1982). Several outcomes have been recorded for the experimental early childhood education programs, including cognitive development (academic achievement, IQ, achievement test scores), and behavioral and emotional development (behavior problems, social competence). One of the most measured developmental outcomes is in the cognitive domain, and several early childhood education interventions, with or without a parental education component, have demonstrated positive results in this area either in terms of academic achievement tests or I.Q. scores (Hill et al., 2003; Lally et al., 1988). Behavioral and emotional outcomes are somewhat more mixed but interventions that measured these outcomes, also demonstrated significantly positive changes ("Making a difference in the lives of infants and toddlers and their families: The impacts of early head start", 2002; Hill et al., 2003).

Findings reveal positive developmental outcomes immediately following the intervention, during the later school years and even into adulthood. Regarding the school years, cognitive developmental domains, such as IQ test and achievement test scores reveal significant differences between the early childhood intervention and the control group. It appears that early childhood intervention does work for poor children, however, there is debate as to whether these significant effects remain strong once the child leaves the program. Effect sizes for the most strongly evaluated programs tend to be small to moderate, which may indicate that the interventions are creating a positive difference but perhaps not strong enough to reverse the negative effects of poverty (Karoly, Kilburn, & Cannon, 2005).

Although fade out, or the slow reduction of developmental benefits from early childhood intervention as the child ages, is a factor in early childhood intervention, adults who experienced early childhood intervention still showed positive gains in comparison to the control group. The gains tended to be in the non-cognitive domains, which has resulted in some policy makers creating the impression that early childhood intervention lacks lasting effects. Rather, the effect of early childhood intervention demonstrates that individuals who were part of the early childhood intervention programs completed more years of schooling, had fewer arrests for violent crimes, held jobs that required skilled labor, and earned higher incomes than the control group participants across several intervention studies (Garces et al., 2002; Reynolds, Temple, Robertson, & Mann, 2001; Schweinhart, 2004). Therefore, early childhood intervention does create positive pathways for individuals across the lifetime, and the early years are a key period to alleviate the stressors of poverty for the long term. These effects, however, are multidimensional, and efforts during these early years that approach intervention through culturally-situated practices, which are sensitive to the unique position of the racial ethnic minority child, is an underdeveloped area that may increase further the positive effects of early childhood intervention for at-risk children.

The Importance of Quality

A factor that contributes substantially to child care's impact on children is the quality of the child care program. Quality is a multidimensional construct that includes structural, process and environmental indicators (Phillips, 1994). Structural indicators of quality are ratios, number of children per group or the education and training of the staff (Howes & Hamilton, 1992). Environmental indicators of quality include ratings of the environment in terms of developmental appropriateness, while process measures include the interactions between the child and caregiver (Phillips, 1994).

All of these aspects of child care quality have positive links to childhood social and cognitive outcomes (Medicine, 2000; National Inst of Child Health & Human Development, 2000; Shonkoff & Phillips, 2000). Structural indicators, such as teacher education levels and low teacher-child ratios, are associated with positive childhood outcomes, such that low child-teacher ratios and higher levels of education positively impact social and cognitive outcomes of children (Dunn, 1993, 1993; Kontos, Hsu, & Dunn, 1994). Similarly, high environmental quality has positive associations with children's short and long-term development (Burchinal, Peisner-Feinberg, Bryant, & Clifford, 2000; Lamb, 1998). Process indicators of quality have the strongest associations with childhood outcomes (Phillips, 1994), and quality, as defined by sensitive teacher-child interactions and a positive emotional classroom climate reveal significant links between quality and the nature of peer interaction and teacher-child relationships (National Inst of Child Health & Human Development, 2001; Shonkoff & Phillips, 2000) .

Conversely, low quality child care, with high turnover, high teacher-child ratios and insensitive caring is associated with less than optimal care and developmental outcomes (Medicine, 2000; Phillips, 1994; Phillips, Howes, & Whitebook, 1992; Shonkoff & Phillips, 2000). According to the National Research Council and Institute of Medicine,

quality of care ultimately boils down to the quality of the relationship between the child care provider or teacher and the child—A beautiful space and an elaborate curriculum—like a beautiful home – can be impressive, but without skilled and stable child care providers, they will not promote positive development" (Shonkoff & Phillips, 2000, p. 315).

For poor children, the impact of child care can be more profound because child care practices can serve as a counterbalancing influence to the negative environmental correlates to poverty. Racial ethnic socialization in the context of childcare, therefore, can cushion the effects of poverty as it is a means through which parents gain assistance in helping their children feel good about themselves and their futures. It is unclear, though, how quality and practices included under our umbrella of racial ethnic socialization relate to each other. Therefore, one goal of this study is to examine the relationship between racial ethnic socialization and child care quality.

Socialization Practices Concerning Racial Ethnicity

Parent/Family Context

The children included in this study are from African-American or Latino, predominantly Mexican immigrant, households. On the surface, both of these groups share a similar "family ecology" (aspects of family functioning that develop in response to the interactions between the family unit and other societal systems) (Harrison, Wilson, Pine, Chan, & Buriel, 1990), of the "caste-like minority" (Ogbu, 1987) (involuntary integration into the United States). African-American families are traditionally descendants of African slaves whereas many Latino families may experience caste-like minority status due to their experiences of conquest and displacement.

Although both groups share a similar family ecology, there can be much variability within each group, and the socialization strategies concerning race exhibited within each community may differ. Within what is commonly referred to as the Latino community, for example, people may herald from several different nations that are dissimilar in history and traditions (Harwood, Leyendecker, Carlson, Asencio, & Miller, 2002). These dissimilarities may make it difficult to group Latinos under one category (Harwood et al., 2002). Similarly, in many urban environments, the "African-American" or Black population contains a substantial number of people who are recent immigrants from Caribbean or African countries. Immigration status and the acculturation process experienced by immigrant families plays a significant role in the racial ethnic socialization of their children (Garcia Coll & Pachter, 2002; Knight, Bernal, Cota, Garza, & Ocampo, 1993). In this study, the sample includes non-Caribbean/African immigrant African-Americans and the Latino sample is majority Mexican-American.

African-Americans and Latinos share the experience of American discrimination and prejudice. Racial ethnic socialization within an immigrant community can be viewed also as a buffer against the effects of discrimination and prejudice. Most often, researchers use the term *ethnic* socialization rather than race socialization for Latino families because Latinos may be of African or other descent and may not fit neatly into the traditional U.S.-based race categories. Studies that focused on the experiences of immigrant populations, primarily in the Latino communities, however, find that their conceptions of their ethnicity in the United States became racialized due to the experiences of discrimination and prejudice from the majority culture (Niemann, Romero, Arredondo, & Rodriguez, 1999). Therefore, a study of racial ethnic socialization is appropriate for Latinos who live in a racialized system, such as the United States. Additionally, the study sample of Latinos does not include Latinos of African descent.

Since the time of the Clark studies (Clark & Clark, 1939), which discovered ambiguous group identification in African-American preschool children from a racially mixed nursery school, scholars have addressed the issue of racial ethnic socialization. Much of this research focused on the African-American child but there is an increasing body of research on the Latino experience (Knight et al., 1993; Knight, Cota, & Bernal, 1993). Much racial ethnic socialization research relied upon interviews and surveys of parents, rather than the examination of non-familial contexts, such as the childcare environments in which the children engage (Johnson et al., 2003). Methodologies used to capture racial ethnic socialization are self-report measures, which require that parents be aware of their behaviors (Hughes & Chen, 2000). Socialization, however, often occurs through the non-verbal modes of transmission that we are unaware of transmitting, and the reliance on self-report by the parent only does not capture the embedded contexts in which racial ethnic socialization occurs.

Racial ethnic socialization is a web of interrelationships in which family background and non-familial institutions influence the socialization processes experienced by the child (Knight et al., 1993). Family background variables include acculturative processes, immigrant status, socioeconomic status and education levels. Acculturation and immigration status are particularly relevant moderators of racial ethnic socialization for immigrant families. In a study by Knight, et al. (1993), family background variables, which captured acculturation to United States or Mexican culture were significantly related to what these Mexican-American families teach their children about being Mexican. Language is commonly a measure of acculturation. In a child care environment, one can imagine that the ability to converse well in English would have a strong influence on the racial ethnic socialization processes that immigrant children experience in child care classrooms. If the child cannot speak in English, the English-speaking children and teachers may perceive her differently. Consequently she may experience a segregated environment that a child of the same group who was facile in English would not experience.

Research into African-Americans' racial ethnic socialization agendas discovered that aspects of the social environment moderate parental agendas. There are many environmental correlates that relate to the nature of African-American parents' race related communications, such as, racial composition of the environment, education levels, parent's age and race-related experiences of the parent's workplace. Findings indicate that families who live in racially diverse environments report socializing their children to racial matters that correspond to Boykin's minority status category (Thornton, Chatters, Taylor, & Allen, 1990).

Boykin and Toms (1985) proposed three modes of racial ethnic socialization: mainstream, black culture and minority status. Although Boykin and Toms focused on African-American families, similar modes may exist in Latino families if they share a similar family ecology as African-Americans of the caste-like minority. Mainstream socialization strategies are communications in which parents articulate mainstream values such as education, religion and hard work. Black culture socialization includes communications that focus on achievements of African-Americans, and other positive aspects of the African-American culture. For the Latino community, these items would include aspects of Latino culture that are a focus of pride. Minority status socialization includes communications that emphasize the low-prestige of Blacks or Latinos in relation to the majority group. One can divide the minority status strategy into preparation for bias and promotion of mistrust (Hughes & Chen, 2000).

Results indicate that many of the findings support Boykin's conceptual framework (Hughes & Chen, 1997; Lesane-Brown, 2006; Marshall, 1995; Spencer, 1983; Thornton et al., 1990). Experiences of discrimination in the workplace, for example, relate to parents' race-related communications that prepare children for bias/mistrust, regardless of the racial composition of the neighborhood (Hughes & Chen, 1997). Spencer (1983) found that African-American parents who communicated Black pride and awareness of discrimination (which falls under preparation for bias) had children with stronger positive orientations toward African-Americans and higher levels of competency than those African-American children who were not socialized similarly.

Given the moderational influence of the environment (Caughy, O'Campo, Nettles, & Lohrfink, 2006), parents' race-related communications are a function of the contexts in which they find themselves. Parents who are more educated and who are older, for example, racially socialize their children more than the converse (Hughes & Chen, 1997). Boykin (1985) proposed that there may be more than one teaching method that parents employ with children of color. The three modes are not mutually exclusive and may be a function of child age and gender. Parents rely upon them to varying degrees and these strategies are dependent upon the child's age, with communications regarding bias and mistrust happening at much later ages.

Although Boykin's framework finds support for the multiple modes of race communication between parent and child, research of African-American parents indicates that the majority do not mention race as a factor when they are asked *generally* about their childrearing practices (Marshall, 1995; Murray & Mandara, 2002; Murry & Brody, 2002; Peters, 1985). Parents tend to discuss the importance of education, love and security, religion, self-esteem and hard work (Peters, 1985; Spencer, 1987; Thomas, 2000). Similarly, Mexican-American parents place much importance on general child rearing values, such as education and a strong work ethic (Niemann et al., 1999). These findings do not appear to be different from what any parent, regardless of race, would want for her child.

However, when researchers asked African-American parents directly about the influence of race on their socialization goals, a large majority of parents reported that it was important (Hughes & Chen, 1997; Marshall, 1995; Peters, 1985, 2002; Richards, 1997; Thornton et al., 1990). Researchers interpreted these findings as evidence of the pervasiveness of racial ethnic agendas in African-American parents' racial ethnic socialization strategies (Peters, 1985; Richards, 1997). It appears that the issue of race is important to many African-American parents but many adhere to what Boykin (1985) referred to as mainstream socialization practices.

Parents of racial ethnic minority children place a culturally specific meaning on the importance of mainstream values, such as education, religion, and hard work. These parents view these items as essential not in spite of their child's racial ethnicity and future encounters with racism but *because of* their child's racial ethnicity and the need to bolster them with the tools and skills to help them thrive in a climate of prejudice (Hughes & Chen, 2000). Peter's (1985) qualitative interviews indicate that the meanings placed on these mainstream socialization goals do have cultural specificity to the African-American parents who participated in her study. Mexican-Americans articulated similar general values (a good education and close family ties) to be a main aspect of their Mexican identities (Niemann et al., 1999). Knight's (1993) report of Mexican-American parents' connection to their home culture and their subsequent emphasis on homeland traditions and values also highlights the importance placed on Mexican heritage and subsequent socialization agendas. Education, in this sense, is not just the education of a child but a shield against the social stratification mechanisms of racism, prejudice and oppression (Harrison et al., 1990).

Child Care Context

Although it has not been a focus of racial ethnic socialization researchers, childcare, as an educational institution, potentially plays a key role in racial ethnic socialization. Practices around race and ethnicity occur within the context of the quality levels of a particular program. However, the emotional features of the caregiving and classroom environment may be distinct from the actual practices of a child care program. In fact, there is evidence that a program's practices have more to do with the community and cultural contexts of the teachers and children than quality standards (Lubeck, 1984; Sanders et al., 2007; Wishard, Shivers, Howes, & Ritchie, 2003). Practices, whether they be academically oriented or child-centered, reflect the groups' cultural values and beliefs concerning what is best for a particular set of children (Howes, in press), and these practices are no less important to the developmental outcomes of children (Kontos, Burchinal, Howes, Wisseh, & Galinsky, 2002).

One goal of this chapter is to identify the aspects of a child care program that fall under the umbrella of racial ethnic socialization. In terms of the environment, previous research demonstrated that simply the racial ethnic compositions of the neighborhood in which a family resides contributes to a parent's racial ethnic socialization practices. Therefore, translating this finding to the child care environment, the racial ethnic composition of the classroom is an important factor to the racial ethnic socialization of the children in child care. Are there only one to two African American children in an all-white environment, for example? For these children, the overall classroom composition of who is "like them" will contribute to the child's racial ethnic understandings.

A second feature of racial ethnic socialization in child care is the type of materials that a program employs. For the programs in this study, which include programs that serve Mexican-American and African-American children only, are there play materials that reflect the cultural practices of these communities? Are the images on the walls reflective of the children and families who are part of the child care program? Are the books and other media consistent with the cultural composition of the children and families?

The materials aspect of racial ethnic socialization is akin to the content approach of the multicultural education rubric presented by Banks (1992). Multicultural education is a curricular approach in terms of "content", "achievement" and "intergroup" relations, which fosters an acceptance of others and a positive attitude of one's culture/race/ethnicity (Banks, 1992; Banks & Banks, 2001). Educational environments that engage in culturally situated practices and multiculturalism contribute to a child's academic success in later years, as well as provide the child with social-emotional competencies that contribute to his overall well-being (Caughy, O'Campo, Randolph, & Nickerson, 2002). Therefore, child care programs provide a socialization context outside of the home for young children, which may provide an additional mediating effect that has not been considered by child care intervention research.

The level of multiculturalism exhibited in content, achievement and inter-group relations is a practical gauge of a program's approach toward racial ethnic socialization. Content approaches apply to efforts to infuse the curriculum with diverse perspectives, such as adding Spanish language and culture books to the library or having dolls of various colors in the dramatic play area. Achievement approaches include aspects of instruction or planning in which the purpose is to improve the learning achievement of minority children. Achievement approaches are most applicable to older students than children in early childhood. The classic example of achievement programs is college entrance affirmative action programs. However, the emphasis on academics that was found in a study on culturally-situated practices in child care programs also exemplifies an achievement approach within early childhood programs' racial ethnic socialization agendas (Sanders et al., 2007). The final approach identified by Banks (1992) is inter-group relations, and it includes actions/methods in which the goal is to foster positive in-group and out-group orientations in children, such as the efforts to create anti-bias environments in child care programs.

In terms of a child care setting, aspects of a program that fall under the umbrella of racial ethnic socialization can include racial ethnic compositions of classrooms, curricula and philosophies of programs, teacher's beliefs regarding child rearing and diversity in child care, caregivers' own experiences with discrimination, and the degree of community building within a classroom. Language usage is also a relevant factor for non-English-speaking children but it will not be included in our analysis due to limitations with the data collection of this information.

Inherent in racial ethnic socialization practices is the caregiver's orientation or attitude toward racial ethnic diversity, as well as their philosophy of parenting. Teacher expectancy research has demonstrated that what teachers believe can have a profound impact on children's academic achievement and self-concept (Kagan, 1992; Rosenthal, 1985). Much of this research has focused on grades beyond preschool (Babad, 1990; Brattesani, Weinstein, & Marshall, 1984; Haller & Davis, 1981; Madon, Jussim, & Eccles, 1997; Weinstein, Marshall, Sharp, & Botkin, 1987). However, there is evidence that even in preschool the beliefs of the teacher permeate his teaching practices (Babad, Bernieri, & Rosenthal, 1989). For example, if a preschool teacher believes that children do not see or understand "race," for example, a curriculum that focuses on children understanding racial differences between each other will not be understood or effectively used by this teacher.

Upon reviewing the components of racial ethnic socialization in child care, what should be apparent is that child care programs engage in racial ethnic socialization of children whether they are aware of it or not. As with parents, programs may have orientations that directly address issues of race and ethnicity, with the intent of changing societal structures (the anti-bias curriculum, for example); or programs may not even think about race and ethnicity at all. Not explicitly addressing it does not mean it is absent. This position is particularly true when the children are racial ethnic minorities within an historically racialized society, such as the United States. It may be that programs that do not explicitly address race and ethnicity engage in practices similar to the mainstream socialization described by Boykin & Toms, for example. Or, perhaps programs that attempt to address racial ethnic socialization in their practices and environment fall more into the socialization category of bias/mistrust or cultural pride.

The main goal of this study is to identify the features of racial ethnic socialization in child care by describing the relationship between child care teacher characteristics and environmental components that comprise racial ethnic socialization in child care. Additionally, a second focus of the study is to determine whether these practices are distinct from the most relevant features of quality, and do variations in the racial ethnic composition of classrooms make a difference in the types of racial ethnic socialization that is discovered. Given that racial ethnic socialization should not be removed from its social historical context, the findings from this study are limited to poor, urban environments in child care programs with a population of racial ethnic minority children.

Method

Participants[4]

Programs

This study reports information based on data collected for another research project, It takes a village (Sanders, 2005). The participants include a total of eight child care programs, seven of which are fully subsidized. Licensed child care in low-income areas, such as the area of this study, is in short supply. Based on the needs assessment of child care for this county, affluent families have a greater range of child care choices than families in low-income areas (Cuthbertson, Burr, Fuller, & Hirshberg, 2000).

The study region is no exception to the paucity of child care options for low-income families. According to the area's Community Care Licensing Department, the licensing body for child care programs, there are 402 licensed child care centers or family child care homes in the study area (Department, 2002). Given that there are approximately 4,416 children under 5 who reside in the areas where the participating child care centers operate, 402 centers and homes do not provide an adequate amount of child care slots. Furthermore, Community Care Licensing figures are inflated and the real number of licensed child care is lower (Cuthbertson et al., 2000). The count includes programs that take children from infancy to school-age. Additionally, umbrella organizations, such as the Urban League or non-profits funded by Head Start or California Department of Education, operate several separately licensed programs within the same facility and the count includes these separate programs as separate facilities.

Child Care Staff

Thirty-six child care workers participated in the study. All but one of the child care staff are female and, as shown in Table 1, the majority of the participants are African-American. Consistent with similar findings concerning child care staff, the teaching staff are disproportionately female and members of a racial minority group (Whitebook, Howes, & Phillips, 1998).

---

[4] For an additional description of the community and programs see: Sanders, et al. 2007

Table 1. Number of Child Care Staff by Occupation, Residence, Education, Birthplace

	African-American N = 23		Latino N = 9	
	N	%	N	%
Occupation				
Director	5	21	1	11
Teacher	11	46	3	33
Assistant	7	29	5	56
Residence				
S. L.A.	19	79	4	44
Not S.L.A.	4	17	5	56
Education				
No degree	9	38	5	56
AA	8	36	1	11
B.A.	3	13	3	33
M.A.	2	8	0	0
Certificate	1	4	0	0
Birthplace				
US born	22	96	5	56
Latin America	0	0	4	44
Other	1	4	0	0

African-American staff have the majority of the college degrees but there is not a large representation of child care staff with college degrees beyond the AA level. Occupationally, the majority of African-American staff hold the higher paying positions of Site Director and Teacher while the Latino staff tend to be concentrated in the lower paying Assistant Teacher positions and the Teacher positions (see Table 1). African-American staff, with the exception of one teacher who was from Nigeria, are U.S. born. The majority of the African-Americans consider the study area to be their home, and 81% have lived there for more than 10 years. In contrast, only 50% of the Latinos consider the study area to be their home and they have lived in the area for over 10 years. Approximately half of the Latino staff were born in Mexico or Central America. The four Latino staff born elsewhere travel to those countries infrequently: 60% visit once per year; 40% visit less than once per year. Although the Latino staff are split evenly between being U.S. born and not U.S. born, all think of the US as their real home, while the Nigerian-born teacher considers Nigeria as her real home.

Child care staff earn a wide range of income levels. The majority of the staff earn salaries that are consistent with the low salary levels of the child care field in general (Whitebook et al., 1998). There is a wide range in adjusted income ranging from a deficit of $-1,200 to a surplus of $5,833 per month. The wide range reflects the disparities in income levels for different child care occupations. In summary, the child care staff in this study reflect national trends in child care staffing. They are predominantly racial ethnic minority females caring for children while receiving little compensation for their education and skill level.

The Children

The study contains a total of 120 children. 65 of the children are African-American (39 female), 54 are Latino (26 female), and one female is identified as mixed (African-American

& Mexican). In the Latino sample all children, excluding two, are of Mexican descent. The children's average age and mode is 4 years. However, the range includes a minimum of 2 years, 5 months (one child) and a maximum of 6 years of age (two children). At the time of data collection, 18% (N=23) of the children were in their first year of attendance but all attended the program for at least five months before data collection occurred. The remaining children attended their child care programs for longer than one to two years, on average. Income levels are homogeneous for this sample due to the fact that the programs mainly accept children who come from families that meet local, state and/or federal poverty levels. In general income eligibility for these child care programs is 75% of the state median income. A majority of the families whose children attend many of these programs fall far below the income ceiling.

Procedure

Classroom Observations

Trained African-American or Latino data collectors observed each child care room with participating children on classroom quality, the environment and children's experiences. Observations occurred during the normal operating hours of the child care center and during the times that children engaged in play with peers or interacted with their teachers. These times occurred during the morning and mid-afternoon periods. Typical observation settings were outdoor activities, unrestricted indoor play and small or large group activities. The observers visited each classroom several times.

Teacher Interviews

The main author interviewed target teachers during individual, one-time meetings that were approximately one hour in duration. Target teachers were the primary teachers and teaching assistants in the classrooms that had participating children. The items included in the interview were: teacher demographics, teachers' perceptions of discrimination, identification with American ideals and the diversity orientation survey. The teacher interviews occurred throughout the data collection period and accommodated the schedule of the teachers.

Measures

Racial Ethnic Socialization

Classroom Racial Ethnic Composition

Table 2 displays the child's group membership by classroom racial ethnic composition. To determine the race composition of each classroom, at the onset of the first observation in classrooms, observers counted the number of Latino and African-American children who were present. There were one to two racial ethnic composition counts per classroom. We then averaged these counts for each classroom and classrooms became classified as, African-American majority (N = 9), Latino majority (N=4) or No Majority (N = 1) racial ethnic group. Of the 120 children, the majority of the African-American children are in classrooms where they constitute the racial majority. Only 10 African-American children are in predominantly Latino classrooms. The Latino children are split evenly between majority Latino classrooms and majority African-American classrooms[5]. Although classrooms had low levels of minority children and they were either strongly majority African-American or majority Latino, none of the children were in classrooms in which there was only a single racial ethnic group present.

Table 2. Child Participants by Ethnicity and Classroom Composition (N=119)

Child Ethnicity	Classroom Composition		Total
	African-American	**Latino**	
African-American	55	10	65
Girls	33	6	39
Boys	22	4	26
Latino	26	28	54
Girls	14	12	26
Boys	12	16	28

Note: Table excludes the 1 African-American girl in a no majority classroom

Community Building

We used a subscale from the Modified Observation Record of the Caregiving Environment (M-ORCE) (Phillips & Ahern, unpublished manuscript) to capture a global rating of the sense of community (expressed community) and efforts made by staff to create community within a classroom (community building). Community building is defined as: respecting human diversity, promoting democracy, in terms of empowering children, and fostering positive interpersonal interaction (Phillips & Ahern, unpublished manuscript). Both positive and negative community building were rated on this scale, as well as a global rating for expressed community, which evaluated whether the setting was "more like a family and/or community or […] like a collection of individual children with little sense of each other's needs or interests" (Phillips & Ahern, unpublished manuscript, p. 46). Ratings were based upon observations of all available caregivers and the general experience of the average child in that setting during the time sampling observations. Scores range from 1 (not at all characteristic) to 4 (highly characteristic).

The M-ORCE (Phillips & Ahern, unpublished manuscript) is an adapted version of the National Institute of Child Health and Human Development Observational Rating of the Caregiving Environment (ORCE) (NICHD). The National Institute of Child Health and

---

[5] The mixed child is in a predominately African-American classroom. Sorters placed her in the ethnicity sort as African-American. She was included in the African-American group and her data are not widely divergent from the rest.

Human Development (NICHD) created the ORCE for their national Study of Early Child Care, one of the most comprehensive longitudinal-designed studies on early child care. The ORCE was derived from well-established child care measures (Abbott-Shim & Sibley, 1987; Harms & Clifford, 1980).

NICHD developed the ORCE to capture the frequencies of children's experiences in child care, the quality of the caregiving environment and structural quality of the classroom. The MORCE, developed for use by the Institute of Child Development, University of Minnesota Family Child Care Research Project (and further adapted by Phillips, Gunnar, Vandell and Howes), expanded or eliminated some of the ORCE coding with the aim to record stress reactions in child care, and to maintain a greater focus on social-emotional development (Phillips & Ahern, unpublished manuscript). The MORCE community building and expressed community scores were highly inter-correlated (Pearson r =.86, p = .01). Therefore, we combined these scores into an overall community score (community).

Africentric Scale

The Africentric Home Environment Inventory (AHEI) (Caughy, Randolph, & Patricia, 2002) is an observational inventory of items in a setting that are culturally specific to African-American culture. The scale provides a level of the degree to which aspects of the African-American culture are present within each classroom. It is a ten-item scale that the authors created by revising items from the well-known HOME-Preschool Inventory (Caldwell & Bradley, 1984). Additionally, the authors included items that, based on the literature, reflected important African-American family values that related to children or adults' social and cognitive aptitudes. Since the scale was developed originally for the home, some items have been changed to reflect the child care context.

The scale has good reliability, predictive validity and goodness of fit (Caughy et al., 2002). For this study, the correlation between African-American observers was .90 (r). Only African-American observers completed the inventory for each classroom due to the finding that the correlation between all observers was low (r =.65).

To complete the scale, observers looked for the ten features in the environment described on the scale, and marked them as being present or not present. If observers did not observe the items, the observer can solicit additional information from the teacher as to whether or not the classroom had such items. The items were averaged to create a single score per classroom, which can range from zero (no items/low Africentricity) to ten (all items/high africentricity).

Latinocentric Scale

To have an equivalent scale to the Africentric Inventory described above for the Latino cultural elements in the child care program, the principal investigator created the Latinocentric Inventory in collaboration with graduate students who study child care in communities of color and through discussions with Mexican-American adults. The measure is identical to the Africentric Inventory except that the examples for each category reference Latino items. Due to the observer problems discovered with the Africentric Inventory, only Latino observers completed the Latinocentric Inventory. The correlation between Latino observers was high (r = .95).

Anti-bias

To provide a comprehensive assessment of the multicultural features of the programs and not only specific cultural elements, the Anti-Bias Curriculum Measure (ABCM) (Howes, unpublished) was used as an observational measure of the quality of cultural sensitivity within classrooms. The ABCM is an adaptation of the National Association for the Education of Young Children's Anti-Bias Curriculum by Derman-Sparks (1989), which provides face validity to the measure. The Anti-Bias Curriculum, developed by Derman–Sparks and the Child Care Task Force is the professional standard of diversity curricula in the early childhood field, and a high score on the ABC measure indicates closer adherence to professionally endorsed diversity practices.

The measure has sixty items corresponding to ten sections that reflect the physical and interpersonal environments of a typical childcare program: visual images, books, dramatic play, language, music, art, dolls, puzzles, interactions, teaching about cultural differences. To complete the measure, observers code whether items described on the scale, such as "caregivers intervene when a child's activity reflects gender stereotyping" or "photos and other pictures of families and staff in the program are displayed in the classroom," was observed (value of 1) or not observed (value of 0) based on the two to three hours of observation in each classroom.

There are three subscales within the ABC: visual/aesthetic environment, material and activities, and interactions. Only the interaction and materials subscale are used in this study.

The measure can be evaluated in terms of the subscale mean scores or by an overall anti-bias mean score. The total Cronbach's alpha for this scale was .90, while Cronbach's alphas were .67 for the interaction and .86 for the materials subscales (Peisner-Feinberg, Jarvis, Ponciano, & Howes, 1999). The ABCM correlated modestly with the ECERS, r(75)=.67, which indicates that while higher quality centers also adhered more closely to anti-bias practices, the ABCM measured aspects of quality that are unique (Howes, unpublished). The correlation between observers was .85 (Pearson).

Teacher Orientation toward Racial Ethnic Diversity

The Diversity Orientation Survey (DOS) (Sanders, unpublished) is a scale that captures an individual's openness and acceptance of a non-majority orientation in early childhood programs. The DOS assesses beliefs that relate to an individual's acceptance of others, and the scale ranges from a non-inclusive to an anti-bias orientation. The researcher developed the scale while observing diversity education in a large, urban childcare program, and participating in discussions with individual teachers about the child care program's practices around diversity education.

Multidimensional scaling (MDS) of the responses of approximately 700 early childhood workers helped to determine the underlying attributes of the scale. MDS provides a visual representation of the similarities or distances among a set of items in a scale. It allows one to flush out the underlying relationships among items by providing a visual representation of the data according to the number of hypothesized dimensions within the scale. To determine whether the dimensions depicted in the visual representation are the best possible fit, MDS provides a stress value, or goodness of fit score. A high stress value indicates poor fit while a low stress value indicates that the data is a good fit to the proposed dimensions. The stress value can range from 0 to 1. Zero to .15 are small stress values, an indication of good fit (Stalans, 1995). For the two dimensions discussed below the stress value was .085, which is within the range for a good fit.

The similarity dimension (α = .91) reflects an individual's orientation to view American culture and European heritage favorably, or as superior to other cultures (items 3, 5, 6, 7, 8, 13, 14, 15). Individuals who have this orientation tend to believe that the discussion of other cultures or the revealing of differences between people is taboo. The difference dimension (α = .83) captures an individual's orientation toward endorsing a broad world-view, and the belief that the discussion or focus on differences in others is beneficial (items 1, 2, 4, 10, 11). The scores for each dimension were calculated by dividing the items for each dimension by the total number of items per dimension.

Teacher Perceptions of Discrimination

The perceived discrimination measure contains 16 statements that the participants rated on a 7-point scale according to how often the statement pertained to her personal experience of discrimination, and one statement, which taps into their perceptions of lifetime discrimination (Contrada et al., 2001). Although Contrada and colleagues derived four subscales of an individual's perceived experiences regarding threat and aggression, verbal rejection, avoidance and disvaluation based on being a member of their racial ethnic group, we used the lifetime perceived discrimination scores only due to the subscale scores having very restricted variability.

Teacher Orientation toward American Values

Identification with American Ideals (IAI) (Phinney, DuPont, Espinosa, Revill, & Sanders, 1994) measures an individual's identification with mainstream notions of what it means to be American rather than cultural, ethnic customs or language use specific to only one ethnic group or country. African Americans and Mexican Americans, as members of a marginal community of color, may or may not identify with mainstream American ideals. Participants rank 12 items as to whether they agree or disagree with the statement through a 7-point Likert scale (1, indicating strongly disagree / 7, indicating strongly agree).

Child Rearing Beliefs

The Modified Child Rearing Practices Report (M-CRPR) (Rickel & Biasatti, 1982) is a 40-item questionnaire created from the 90-item Q-sort Child Rearing Practices Report by Block (1965). The M-CRPR provided an assessment of parent's socialization practices in terms of restrictiveness and nurturance. Unlike the original CRPR, which was time consuming and cumbersome to complete, the M-CRPR contains 40-statements that parents rated on a 7-point Likert scale from very characteristic to most uncharacteristic. The scale contains two subscales: restrictiveness and nurturance. The restrictiveness subscale refers to the aspects of parenting that are control dominated. High scores on this scale indicated a desire to control the child's behavior and feelings. The nurturance subscale is the opposite of restrictiveness. A high score on the nurturance subscale indicated an endorsement of flexible parenting attitudes and practices toward their children. The scale has had good reliability in general and with family child care providers of mixed ethnicity who were not well-educated (Kontos, Howes, Shin, & Galinsky, 1995; Rickel & Biasatti, 1982).

Quality

Quality was assessed through the environmental subscales of the M-ORCE. Specifically, the environmental ratings of emotional climate, chaos and over-control correspond to global environmental quality. The emotional climate scale rated the overall emotional climate of the classroom environment. As with the community building scale, the range of scores was from 1 (not at all characteristic) to 4 (highly characteristic). Observers rated positive and negative emotional climate independently. Positive emotional climate captured the extent to which the caregiver expressed positive regard for the children, as expressed by warmth, physical affection, praise and clear enjoyment of the children. Negative emotional climate coded the extent to which settings were overtly hostile to children. Negative climate was expressions of negative regard toward the children, such as anger and hostility, irritability, punitive controls, and clear disapproval and annoyance. These scores were combined to create an emotional climate composite.

Chaos/Over-Control environmental ratings coded the level of disorganization (chaos) and over-control in the classroom. Both constructs are on a scale from 1 (not at all characteristic) to 4 (highly characteristic). Chaos was defined as a setting in which children are out of control, fighting, behaving inappropriately and teacher control techniques were not successful at bringing about order, regardless of the positive or negative valence of those techniques. Settings in which the caregiver stifled children's actions were over-controlled. In these settings, activities were rigidly structured and spontaneity was discouraged.

The three quality subscales of the MORCE correlated with the Early Childhood Environmental Rating Scale (an increasingly accepted measure of global environmental quality) in a theoretically consistent manner: emotional climate had a strongly positive correlation ($r = .62$, $p < .05$), and the chaos and overcontrol subscales were moderately negatively correlated with the ECERS ($r = -.53$ & $-.19$, nonsignificant) (Sanders, 2005). Additionally, the quality variables were highly inter-correlated (emotional climate with chaos and overcontrol was $-.73$, -75, $p < .01$, respectively). Therefore, we created a simplified version of the quality variables, by placing the three subscales into a single composite. The composite, *quality*, is the difference between emotional control and the sum of the chaos and overcontrol ratings. This variable has a rating scale from -4 to 4. A negative score indicates that the environment contains more chaos and overcontrol than positive emotional climate. While a positive number indicates that the environment is well-managed and organized with more positive emotional regard than negative.

Results

What Are the Racial Ethnic Socialization Practices & Environments of Urban Child-Care Programs for Poor Racial Ethnic Minority Children?

Table 3 displays the central tendencies for the racial ethnic socialization variables. The average scores on the cultural items scales indicate that Africentric items are more prevalent than Latinocentric items in these classrooms. However, the frequencies of cultural items are not equally shared among classrooms. The classrooms either have a fairly equal amount of cultural items representative of both ethnic groups or a majority of African-American cultural items.

Table 3. Central Tendencies of Modified Observational Record of Caregiving Environment (MORCE) Community, Emotional Climate, Chaos and Over-Control, Atmosphere, Antibias, Africentric and Latinocentric Scales, and Teacher Atttiudes

Measure	Minimum	Maximum	Mean	Standard Deviation
M-ORCE				
Community	1.00	4.00	2.00	0.89
Emotional Climate	-2.67	3.00	0.90	1.62
Chaos	1.00	3.50	1.75	0.59
Over control	1.00	4.00	2.04	0.72
Atmosphere Composite	-4.25	1.14	-1.11	1.77
Antibias	1.53	2.92	2.20	0.40
Interaction	1.75	3.15	2.26	0.32
Materials	1.23	2.80	2.17	0.50
Africentric	3.00	9.00	6.64	2.21
Latinocentric	1.00	4.00	2.64	1.08
Perceived Discrimination	1.00	5.00	2.80	1.37
Identification American Ideals	2.67	7.00	5.50	1.03
Diversity Orientation				
Difference	2.60	5.00	4.55	0.56
Similarity	2.25	5.00	3.84	0.62
Modified Childrearing Practices Report				
Restrict	2.27	5.95	3.90	0.89
Nurture	1.22	7.00	6.17	1.08

Given that some classrooms contain a preponderance of children from a single racial ethnic group, racial ethnic composition may be a significant contributing factor to the amount of African-American or Latino cultural items within a classroom. However, subsequent analysis revealed that racial ethnic composition in classrooms did not affect significantly the amount of African-American or Latino cultural items. Regardless of racial ethnic composition, the African-American cultural items are the only cultural items that are present in frequencies greater than 5. For example, two of these classrooms, which have more African-American cultural items than Latino cultural items, contain a racial ethnic composition that is majority Latino. Therefore, for the Latino children in these traditionally African American programs, cultural items reflective of their familial experiences are under-represented.

In terms of the levels of anti-bias in the classroom overall, anti-bias practices are low. The classrooms are fairly equal in terms of their anti-bias materials and interactions. Anti-bias interaction and anti-bias materials are significantly related. Not surprisingly, the more frequent interactions concerning anti-bias occur, the greater the number of materials associated with anti-bias (Pearson r = .54, p = .05).

Although programs with greater numbers of anti-bias materials are more likely to engage in anti-bias interaction or vice versa, this interaction does not seem to manifest itself in terms of an orientation toward community. The classroom environments reflected minimal community atmosphere. Characteristically minimal levels mean that there is a low emphasis on facilitating children's efforts to solve their own conflicts, there are frequent instances of laughing at or teasing between children and there is minimal expression of empathy between children. Based on the anti-bias averages and the community averages, it appears that when interaction concerning anti-bias does occur, that interaction may take the form of attending to the individual but not necessarily creating a group synergy that places the values of the classroom community at the forefront.

In addition to environmental features, child care staff characteristics are an important contributor to the racial ethnic socialization practices of a program. As shown in Table 3, child care staff in this study reflected fairly low levels of perceived discrimination but relatively high levels of identification with American ideals. During the lifetime, perceived discrimination is higher, on average, for African-American child care workers than Latino child care workers. However, a univariate analysis of variance with race as the grouping variable and PDS lifetime as the dependent variable revealed that there were no significant differences between African American and Latino child care staff when it came to perceived discrimination across the lifetime.

Our next step was to determine whether these racial ethnic socialization features could be combined to create portraits of environmental and child care staff racial ethnic socialization, as well as to simplify these multiple variables for subsequent analysis. We computed two exploratory factor analyses (principal components analysis with varimax rotation). One factor analysis focused on the environmental variables, and the second included the child care staff characteristics.

The racial ethnic socialization environment factor analysis included the M-ORCE community composite, the ABC anti-bias subscales and the cultural items scores. Based on the initial eigen values that were over 1 and an examination of the scree plot, two factors were the best solution statistically and conceptually. The two factors accounted for 71% of the variance. The first factor, entitled *multicultural materials*, took up 46% of the variance. The variables Africentric (.652), Latinocentric (.858) and the ABC materials subscale (.728) loaded onto this factor. Classroom that score highly on this factor are ones in which multiculturalism is reflected in the materials available for the children, such as dolls of different ethnicity and children's books that reflect a variety of experiences. The second factor, *anti-bias community*, accounted for 25% of the variance and it included the variables, ABC interaction (.889) and M-ORCE community (.858). Classrooms that score highly on this factor tend to work toward creating a community environment and engage in interactions with children that counter bias.

Based on the relationships among the child care staff scales, we included the IAI, the M-CRPR parenting attitudes subscales, and the diversity orientation subscales in the second principal components factor analysis. The scree test and initial eigenvalues over 1 indicated that a two-factor solution was the best fit. After various iterations, the final solution resulted in the diversity orientation *difference* subscale dropping out. The final factor solution was a two-factor solution that accounted for 71% of the variance. The first factor is entitled

Restrictive Americanism and it included the identification with American Ideals (factor load = .793), M-CRPR restrictive parenting (factor load = .619) and the DOS similarity diversity orientation (factor load = .866). Restrictive Americanism accounted for 45% of the variance. Teachers who score high on this factor are ones who identify strongly with the basic principles of the United States, for example, America is a land of opportunity. They believe more strongly that early childhood practices mainly need to focus on our similarities and they tend to endorse restrictive parenting practices, such as, believing that children should be seen and not heard, believing that children should not try things if there is chance of failing or that scolding and criticism of a child will make him/her improve. The second factor, *Nurture* includes only one loading: nurturant parenting (factor load = .897). The nurturance factor accounted for 26% of the variance. Teachers who score highly on this factor are ones who endorse very strongly the beliefs connected to nurturant parenting, such as, having respect for children's opinions and believing that a child should be given comfort when scared and upset, expressing affection with hugs or encouraging children to wonder and think about life.

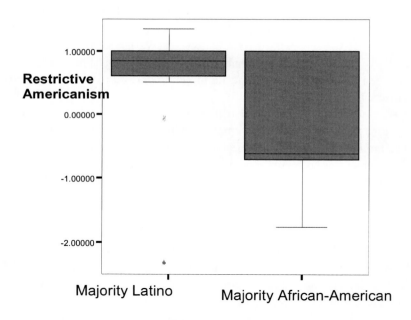

Figure 1. Boxplot of Restrictive Americanism by Classroom Child Ethnic Composition.

The Role of Lifetime Perceived Discrimination

There is tentative support of racial ethnic socialization practices in child care being associated with the caregiver's own experiences with discrimination (see Table 4). Correlations disclose that teachers' perceived discrimination during their lifetimes is correlated positively with anti-bias community but negatively related to multicultural materials. This orientation is similar to findings in parental racial ethnic socialization, and is analogous to the preparation for bias orientation.

Although perceived discrimination is not very high, an increase in perceived discrimination relates to a decrease in an identification with American ideals (r = -.38, $p<$ .05). Similarly, child care workers who endorse mainly cultural similarity (DOS similarity subscale) in their orientation toward diversity, also tend to perceive less discrimination across their lifetimes (r = -.46, p <.01). Therefore, although discrimination is weakly perceived in this sample of child care workers, there is an inverse relationship between their personal perceptions of discriminatory experiences and their perceptions of their roles as child care workers. An adherence to mainstream values coincides with relatively weaker beliefs regarding the importance of anti-bias practices or multiculturalism.

Table 4. Correlations between Quality, Discrimination, Teacher Characteristics and Multicultural Materials and Anti-bias Interactions

	American Restrict.[a]	Nurture[a]	Discrimination	Quality
Multicul. Materials[a]	.54**	-.05	-.30*	-.002
Anti-bias Community[a]	-.41**	.43**	.29*	.67**
Quality	-.01	.25*	.06	n/a

**p=.01; *p = .05

[a]Composite scores from factor solutions (Multicultural Materials: Howes anti-bias material subscale, africentric & latinocentric subscales; Anti-bias Interaction: Howes anti-bias interaction subscale and M-ORCE community subscale; American Restrictiveness: M-RCPR restrictiveness subscale, IAI; Nurture: M-RCPR subscale)

It appears that childcare teachers do more work around issues of diversity when they perceive that they have experienced higher levels of discrimination in their lifetimes. Within child care for racial ethnic minority children, the personal experiences of discrimination contribute to a caregiver's perspectives regarding racial ethnic socialization.

Relations between Quality and Racial Ethnic Socialization

The second question we addressed was whether the constructs articulated as racial ethnic socialization are consistent with process features of child care quality or distinct from it. To answer this question, we computed a series of correlations between the racial ethnic socialization classifications and the composite quality scores. Some aspects of racial ethnic socialization do correspond with global child care quality. The factor anti-bias community has a significantly positive relationship with child care quality. Conversely, multicultural material (which included cultural items and anti-bias materials) does not have a significant relationship with the quality indicator. In other words, having the materials does not reflect quality but the ability to use them constructively with children does. This relationship is further reinforced by the significant finding that teacher orientations that adhere to nurturance and less to American restrictiveness are related positively to anti-bias community and quality.

In summary, it appears that racial ethnic socialization is both related and not related to child care quality. The cultural materials within a classroom are distinct from child care quality. The interactions that occur between caregivers and children are when child care quality is most important for children, and perhaps, most conducive to racial ethnic socialization in child care. An important feature to anti-bias community is the anti-bias component. Interaction, in this sense, is not only positive engagement with children but a proactive effort by the staff to counteract bias. In a classroom that includes only racial ethnic minority children, much of this counter-bias work took a form similar to the parental racial ethnic minority socialization of preparation *for* bias (Sanders et al., 2007). Therefore, quality counts in these child care programs because it contributes to the teacher's ability to create an environment that attempts to prepare children of color for bias. For those classrooms where quality was not as high, the type of racial ethnic socialization that occurred may be more akin to the Boykin & Toms category of cultural socialization, and this type of racial ethnic socialization did not relate to quality.

Classroom Racial Ethnic Composition as a Factor of Racial Ethnic Socialization

Our final question addressed whether there are significant differences in racial ethnic socialization orientations when there are varying racial ethnic compositions within classrooms. Due to the significant relationship between anti-bias interaction and quality, we restricted this portion of the analysis to addressing whether teacher beliefs of restrictive Americanism are more or less prominent in classrooms with differing racial ethnic compositions. We conducted a Mann-Whitney U Test to evaluate whether orientations toward American restrictiveness were equal to or more prevalent within classrooms that had an African American child majority versus classrooms that were majority Latino. The results of the test reveal a significant distinction between teacher's propensity to endorse beliefs consistent with restrictive Americanism and the classroom ethnic composition, $z = -2.60$, $p = .009$. African American classrooms had a lower average rank of 30.43, while predominantly Latino classrooms had an average rank of 43.19. The belief of restrictive Americanism, which is an adherence to more mainstream American values and traditional child rearing practices, lacks endorsement when the child ethnic majority is African American in this context. Rather, teachers who tend to endorse restrictive Americanism are in classrooms that contain a majority of Latino immigrant children.

Conclusion

Racial ethnic socialization in child care is made up of environmental features, such as the materials in a classroom, or the number of children who are the same in ethnicity; and the teacher's attitudes toward diversity and child rearing.

Racial ethnic socialization in child care demonstrates parallels between previous racial ethnic socialization research on families of color. Some teachers of color who work with children of color endorse and work in classrooms that engage in preparation for bias, while other teachers who have not experienced discrimination as strongly, and who endorse traditional mainstream American ideals work in classrooms that engage in more cultural socialization. As mentioned in the introduction, preparation for bias and cultural socialization has positive connections to older children's academic achievement. Unlike earlier race socialization research, which found preparation for bias to be a socialization strategy parents tend to use at later stages than cultural socialization, both orientations are present in these childcare programs. However, rather than the measurement relying solely on the statements parents make to children, there is evidence from this study that racial ethnic socialization practices that may become more explicit during the later years take root during the child's early years in nonverbal forms.

In terms of cultural socialization for the Latino children, there is a disjoint reflective of the cultural historical practices of these traditional African-American programs. A rudimentary analysis of ethnic composition reveals a significant finding that Latino children are experiencing higher levels of restrictive Americanism than nurturing anti-bias communities. The significant finding between ethnic composition and teacher orientations highlights how important it is to promote high quality childcare programs in poor urban areas. Quality and preparation for bias may not be mutually exclusive. Having high quality programs most likely assists teachers who are oriented toward nurturing children in all its forms to provide the type of care for children of color that fit the social and historical contexts in which these programs operate. These teachers are also African American and Latino. Their patterns of caring reflect the context (Sanders et al. 2007).

Future Research

This study has limited generalizability due to the sample. It would be useful to reproduce it in a larger context that would allow for greater sophistication in analysis. Additionally, it is unclear from this study how the findings impact childhood development specifically since a childhood outcome was not included. For example, a study with a larger sample may be able to parcel out the contributions childcare racial ethnic socialization provides to childhood developmental outcomes, such as preliminary racial/ethnic identity milestones or the developing self-concept.

The answer as to how the findings in child care relate to parental/familial racial ethnic socialization was not a focus of this study but it would be useful to determine the relationship between these two constructs. Does childcare racial ethnic socialization contribute significantly to the family's socialization practices regardless of the type, or does childcare racial ethnic socialization only impact childhood outcomes in terms of the degree of continuity with familial racial ethnic socialization practices?

Teacher characteristics were relevant features of racial ethnic socialization, and a productive extension of the findings from this study is to determine whether other teacher demographics, such as education or the years of training or working in early childhood, play into these preliminary racial ethnic socialization descriptions. Given that teacher education does relate to childcare quality, the relationships that we found concerning quality and anti-bias community may be confounded with teacher education, for example.

This study was not an exhaustive examination of racial ethnic socialization in child care. There are other features that could be part of childcare racial ethnic socialization that we did not included in our definition or analysis. For instance, previous racial ethnic socialization has found relationships between parental socialization practices or children's awareness of racial differences and the racial ethnic demographics of the neighborhood. Similarly, neighborhood racial ethnic demographics may influence or relate to teacher diversity practices in child care. We did not include peer groupings or language usage. In interracial settings, for example, is it important to consider who is playing with whom when teachers engage in anti-bias techniques, such as intervening and re-directing a child who may be acting in a biased manner toward another child, or to consider ways in which teacher practices and peer-peer engagement in multilingual childcare classrooms impact racial ethnic socialization strategies and effects?

One may ask what all of this means for children in poverty. Children are not only poor but also part of a social, historical and cultural milieu that impacts the way in which adults interact with them as well as the way in which the children may interact with the world. For African-American and Latino children in the United States, race and ethnicity are main features that will be a part of their identity always; and the manner in which teachers engage in practices, create environments, and enact their personal beliefs regarding racial and ethnic diversity is crucial to understand so that we may create better programs that have the potential to contribute to poor children's positive developmental pathways.

References

Chapter 2: Industry restructuring, migration and the working poor in Los Angeles. (2000).). Los Angeles: *Economic Roundtable.*

Making a difference in the lives of infants and toddlers and their families: The impacts of early head start. (2002). In U. S. D. o. H. a. H. Services (Ed.) (Vol. 1): *Administration for Children, Youth and Families.*

America's children: Key national indicators of well-being. (2007). *Federal Interagency Forum on Child and Family Statistics.* Washington, D.C.: US Government Printing Office.

Abbott-Shim, M., Lambert, R., & McCarty, F. (2003). A comparison of school readiness outcomes for children randomly assigned to a head start program and the program's waitlist. *Journal of Education for Students Placed at Risk*, 8(2), 191-214.

Abbott-Shim, M., & Sibley, A. (1987). Assessment profile for early childhood programs.Atlanta, GA: *Quality Assist.*

Adam, E., & Chase-Lansdale, L. (2002). Home sweet home(s): Parental spearations, residential moves, and adjustment problems in low-income adolescent girls. *Developmental Psychology,* 38(5), 792-805.

Alaniz, M., Cartmill, R., & Parker, R. (1998). Immigrants and violence: The importance of neighborhood context. *Hispanic Journal of Behavioral Sciences*, 20(2).

Allhusen, V., Belsky, J., Booth-LaForce, C., Bradley, R., Brownell, C., Burchinal, M., et al. (2005). Duration and developmental timing of poverty and children's cognitive and social development from birth through third grade. *Child Development,* 76(4), 795-810.

Babad, E. (1990). Measuring and changing teachers' differential behavior as perceived by students and teachers. *Journal of Educational Psychology,* 82, 683-690.

Babad, E., Bernieri, F., & Rosenthal, R. (1989). Nonverbal communication and leakage in the behavior of biased and unbiased teachers. *Journal of Personality and Social Psychology,* **56**(1), 89-94.

Banks, J. (1992). Multicultural education for young children: Racial and ethnic attitudes and their modification. *In In Handbook of Research on the Education of Young Children,* edited by Bernard Spodek. New York: Macmillan, 1993, pp. 236-250.

Banks, J., & Banks, C. M. (2001). *Handbook of research on multicultural education.* San Francisco: Jossey-Bass.

Block, J. (1965). The child rearing practices report. Berkeley: University of California, *Institute of Human Development.*

Boykin, A. W., & Toms, F. D. (1985). Black child socialization: A conceptual framework. In H. P. McAdoo (Ed.), *Black children: Social, educational, and parental* environments. (pp. 33-51). Thousand Oaks, CA, US: Sage Publications, Inc.

Bradley, R., Corwyn, R., McAdoo, H. P., & Garcia Coll, C. (2001). The home environments of children in the united states part 1: Variations by age, ethnicity and poverty status. *Child Development,* **72**(6), 1844-1867.

Brattesani, K. A., Weinstein, R. S., & Marshall, H. H. (1984). Student perceptions of differential teacher treatment as moderators of teacher expectation effects. *Journal of Educational Psychology,* **76**(2), 236-247.

Bronfenbrenner, U. (1979). *The ecology of human development.* Cambridge: Harvard University Press.

Bronfenbrenner, U. (1995). Developmental ecology through space and time: A future perspective. In P. Moen, G. Elder & K. Luscher (Eds.), *Examining lives in context: Perspectives on the ecology of human development* (pp. 619-647). Washington, D.C.: American Psychological Association.

Burchinal, M., Peisner-Feinberg, E., Bryant, D., & Clifford, R. (2000). Children's social and cognitive development and child-care quality: Testing for differential associations related to poverty, gender, or ethnicity. *Applied Developmental Science,* **4**(3), 149-165.

Caldwell, B., & Bradley, R. (1984). *Home observation for measurement of the environment--* revised edition.Little Rock: University of Arkansas at Little Rock.

Caughy, M., O'Campo, P., Nettles, S., & Lohrfink, K. (2006). Neighborhood matters: Racial socialization of african american children. *Child Development,* **77**(5), 1220-1236.

Caughy, M., O'Campo, P., Randolph, S., & Nickerson, K. (2002). The influence of racial socialization practices on the cognitive and behavioral competence of African American preschoolers. *Child Development,* **73**(5), 1611-1625.

Caughy, M., Randolph, S., & Patricia, O. C. (2002). The africentric home environment inventory: An observational measure of the racial socialization features of the home environment for African-American preschool children. *Journal of Black Psychology,* **28**(1), 37-52.

Clark, K. B., & Clark, M. P. (1939). Segregation as a factor in the racial identification of negro preschool children. *Journal of Experimental Education,* **11**, 161-163.

Conger, R., McCloyd, V., Brody, G. H., Wallace, L., Sun, Y., & Simons, R. (2002). Economic pressure in African-American families: A replication and extension of the family stress model. *Developmental Psychology,* **38**(2), 179-193.

Contrada, R., Ashmore, R., Gary, M., Coups, E., Egeth, J., Sewell, A., et al. (2001). Measures of ethnicity-related stress: Psychometric properties, ethnic group differences and associations with well-being. *Journal of Applied Social Psychology, 31*(9), 1775-1820.

Cuthbertson, B. B., Burr, E., Fuller, B., & Hirshberg, D. (2000). *Policy analysis for california education*: Los Angeles county needs assessment.Berkeley: University of California & Stanford University.

Dearing, E., McCartney, K., & Taylor, B. (2001). Change in family income-to-needs matters more for children with less. *Child Development, 72*(6), 1779-1793.

Dearing, E., McCartney, K., & Taylor, B. (2006). Within-child associations between family income and externalizing and internalizing problems. *Developmental-Psychology, 42*(2), 237-252.

Department, S. S. L. A. C. (2002, 10/02/02). Los angeles county child care directory. from *http://childcare.co.la.ca.us*

Derman-Sparks, L. (1989). The anti-bias curriculum.Washington, D.C.: *The National Association for the Education of Young Children.*

Duncan, G., & Brooks-Gunn, J. (1997). *Consequences of growing up poor.New York:* Russell Sage Foundation.

Duncan, G., & Brooks-Gunn, J. (2000). Family poverty, welfare reform, and child development. *Child Development, 71*(1), 188-196.

Duncan, G., Brooks-Gunn, J., & Klebanov, P. (1994). Economic deprivation and early childhood development. *Child Development, 65*, 296-318.

Duncan, G., Yeung, W. J., Brooks-Gunn, J., & Smith, J. (1998). How much does childhood poverty affect the life chances of children? *American Sociological Review, 63*, 406-423.

Dunn, L. (1993). Proximal and distal features of day care quality and children's development. *Early Childhood Research Quarterly, 8*(2), 167-192.

Dunn, L. (1993). Ratio and group size in day care programs. *Child & Youth Care Forum.22*(3), 193-226.

Farah, M., Shera, D., Savage, J., Betancourt, L., Giannetta, J., Brodsky, N., et al. (2006). Childhood poverty: Specific associations with neurocognitive development. *Brain Research, 1110*, 166-174.

Fenton, S. (1999). *Ethnicity: Racism, class and culture.Lanham:* Rowman & Littlefield Publishers, Inc.

Garces, E., Thomas, D., & Currie, J. (2002). Longer term effects of head start. *American Economic Review, 92*(4), 999-1012.

Garcia Coll, C., Crinic, K., Lamberty, G., Wasik, B., Jenkins, R., Garcia Vazquez, H., et al. (1996). An integrative model for the study of developmental competencies in minority children. *Child Development, 67*, 1891-1914.

Garcia Coll, C., & Pachter, L. M. (2002). Ethnic and minority parenting. In M. H. Bornstein (Ed.), *Handbook of parenting: Social conditions and applied parenting* (2 ed., Vol. 4, pp. 1-20). Mahwah, NJ: Lawrence Erlbaum Associates.

Gershoff, E. (2003). Low income and hardship among America's kindergarteners (No. 3). New York: *National Center for Children in Poverty,* Mailman School of Public Health, Columbia University.

Haller, E., & Davis, S. (1981). Teacher perceptions, parental social status and grouping for reading instruction. *Sociology of Education, 54*, 162-174.

Harms, T., & Clifford, R. M. (1980). *Early childhood environment rating scale.*New York: Teachers College Press.

Harrison, A. O., Wilson, M., Pine, C., Chan, S., & Buriel, R. (1990). Family ecologies of ethnic minority children. *Child Development,* 61, 347-362.

Harwood, R., Leyendecker, B., Carlson, V., Asencio, M., & Miller, A. (2002). Parenting among Latino families in the U.S. In M. H. Bornstein (Ed.), *Handbook of parenting: Social conditions and applied parenting* (2 ed., Vol. 4, pp. 21-46). Mahwah, JN: Lawrence Erlbaum Associates.

Hernandez, D., Denton, N., & Macartney, S. (2007). Demographic trends and the transition years. In R. Pianta, M. Cox & K. Snow (Eds.), *School readiness and the transition to kindergarten in the era of accountability* (pp. 217-281). Baltimore: Paul H. Brookes Publishing.

Hill, J., Brooks-Gunn, J., & Waldfogel, J. (2003). Sustained effects of high participation in an early intervention for low-birth weight premature infants. *Developmental Psychology,* **39**(4), 730-744.

Howes, C. (in press). *Early childhood education programs as a way to understand culture as an integrated constellation of community practices.*New York: Oxford Press.

Howes, C. (unpublished). *Antibias curriculum scale,* revised 1998.

Howes, C., & Hamilton, C. (1992). Child care for young children. In B. Spodek (Ed.), *Handbook of research on the education of young children* (pp. 322-336). New York: MacMillan.

Hughes, D., & Chen, L. (1997). When and what parents tell children about race: An examination of race-related socialization among african american families. *Applied Developmental Science,* **1**(4), 200-214.

Hughes, D., & Chen, L. (2000). The nature of parent's race-related communications to children: A developmental perspective. In L. Balter & C. S. Tamis-Lemonda (Eds.), *Child psychology: A handbook of contemporary issues* (pp. 467-490). New York: Taylor & Francis.

Huston, A. (2005). The effects of welfare reform and poverty policies on children and families. In D. Pillemer & S. White (Eds.), *Developmental psychology and social change:* Research, history & policy (pp. 83-103). Cambridge: Cambridge University Press.

Jackson, A., Brooks-Gunn, J., Huang, C.-C., & Glassman, M. (2000). Single mothers in low-wage jobs: Financial strain, parenting and preschoolers' outcomes. *Child Development,* **71**(5), 1409-1423.

Johnson, D., Jaeger, E., Randolph, S., Cauce, A. M., & Ward, J. (2003). Studying the effects of early child care experiences on the development of children of color in the united states: Toward a more inclusive research agenda. *Child Development,* **74**(5), 1227-1244.

Kagan, D. M. (1992). Professional growth among preservice and beginning teachers. *Review of Educational Research,* **62**(2), 129-169.

Kağıtçıbaşı, Ç. (2007). *Family, self and human development across cultures: Theory and applications* (Revised Second ed.). Hillsdale, NJ: Lawrence Erlbaum.

Karoly, L., Kilburn, R., & Cannon, J. (2005). *Early childhood interventions: Proven results, future promise.* Santa Monica: RAND Corporation.

Knight, G., Bernal, M., Cota, M., Garza, C., & O'Campo, K. (1993). Chapter 7: Family socialization and mexican-american identity and behavior. In M. Bernal & G. Knight

(Eds.), *Ethnic identity: Formation and transmission among hispanics and other minorities* (pp. 105-129). Albany, NY: State University of New York Press.

Knight, G., Cota, M., & Bernal, M. (1993). The socialization of cooperative, competitive, and individualistic preferences among mexican american children: The mediating role of ethnic identity. *Hispanic Journal of Behavioral Sciences*, **15**(3), 291-309.

Kontos, S., Burchinal, M., Howes, C., Wisseh, S., & Galinsky, E. (2002). An eco-behavioral approach to examining the contextual effects of early childhood classrooms. *Early childhood Research Quarterly*, **17**, 239-258.

Kontos, S., Howes, C., Shin, M., & Galinsky, E. (1995). *Quality in family child care and relative care*.New York: Teachers College Press.

Kontos, S., Hsu, H.-C., & Dunn, L. (1994). Children's cognitive and social competence in child care centers and family day-care homes. *Journal of Applied Developmental Psychology,* **15**(3), 387-411.

Lally, R., Mangione, P., & Honig, A. (1988). The Syracuse University family development research program: Long-range impact of an early intervention with low-income children and their families. In D. Powell & I. Sigel (Eds.), *Parent education as early childhood intervention: Emerging directions in theory, research and practice* (pp. 79-104). Norwood, N.J.: Ablex Publishing Corporation.

Lamb, M. (1998). Nonparental child care: Context, quality and correlates. In Handbook of Child Psychology: Volume 4. *Child Psychology in Practice* (pp. 73-133). New York, NY: Wiley.

Lazar, I., & Darlington, R. (1982). Lasting effects of early education: A report from the consortium for longitudinal studies. *Monographs of the Society for Research in Child Development*, **47**(2-4).

Lesane-Brown, C. (2006). A review of race socialization within Black families. *Developmental Review*, **26**, 400-426.

Lubeck, S. (1984). Kinship and classrooms: An ethnographic perspective on education as cultural transmission. *Sociology of Education,* **57**(4), 219-232.

Madon, S., Jussim, L., & Eccles, J. (1997). In search of the powerful self-fulfilling prophecy. *Journal of Personality and Social Psychology,* **72**(4), 791-809.

Marshall, S. (1995). Ethnic socialization of African American children: Implications for parenting, identity development, and academic achievement. *Journal of Youth & Adolescence*, **24**(4), 377-396.

Massey, D., & Fischer, M. (2000). How segregation concentrates poverty. *Ethnic and Racial Studies*, **23**(4), 670-691.

Mayer, S. (2001). How did the increase in economic inequality between 1970 and 1990 affect children's educational attainment? *American Journal of Sociology*, **107**(1), 1-32.

McLoyd, V. (1990). The impact of economic hardship on Black families and children: Psychological distress, parenting, and socioemotional development. *Child Development,* **61**, 311-346.

McLoyd, V., Jayaratne, T. E., Ceballo, R., & Borquez, J. (1994). Unemployment and work interruptions among African American single mothers: Effects on parenting and adolescent socioemotional functioning. *Child Development,* **65**, 562-589.

Medicine, N. R. C. a. I. o. (2000). Growing up in child care. In J. P. Shonkoff & D. A. Phillips (Eds.), From Neurons to Neighborhoods: *The Science of Early Childhood Development* (pp. 297-327). Washington, DC: National Academy Press.

Mistry, R., Vandewater, Huston, A., & McLoyd, V. (2002). Economic well-being and children's social adjustment: The role of family process in an ethnically diverse low-income sample. *Child Development*, **73**, 935-951.

Murray, C., & Mandara, J. (2002). Racial identity development in african-american children. In H. P. McAdoo (Ed.), *Black children: Social, educational & parental environments* (pp. 73-95). Thousand Oaks, CA: Sage Publications.

Murry, V. M., & Brody, G. H. (2002). Racial socialization processes in single-mother families: Linking maternal racial identity, parenting, and racial socialization in rural, single-mother families with child self-worth and self-regulation ii: Racial messages. In H. P. McAdoo (Ed.), *Black children: Social, educational and parental environments* (2 ed., pp. 97-115). Thousand Oaks, CA, US: Sage Publications, Inc.

National Inst of Child Health & Human Development, E. C. C. R. N. (2000). The relation of child care to cognitive and language development. *Child Development,* **71**(4), 958-978.

National Inst of Child Health & Human Development, E. C. C. R. N. (2001). Child care and children's peer interaction at 24 and 36 months: The nichd study of early child care. *Child Development*, **72**(5), 1478 - 1501.

NICHD. (October 20, 1999). NICHD study of early child care: Phase 1 instrument document. from *http://public.rti.org/secc*

Niemann, Y. F., Romero, A. J., Arredondo, J., & Rodriguez, V. (1999). What does it mean to be "Mexican"? Social construction of an ethnic identity. *Hispanic Journal of Behavioral Sciences,* **21**(1), 47-60.

Ogbu, J. (1987). Variability in minority responses to schooling: Nonimigrant vs. Immigrants. In G. Spindler & L. Spindler (Eds.), *Interpretative ethnography of education: At home and abroad* (pp. 255-280). Hillsdale, NJ: Erlbaum.

Olson, C., Bove, C., & Miller, E. (2007). Growing up poor: Long-term implications for eating patterns and body weight. *Appetite,* **49**(1), 198-207.

Palmer, J., Younghwan, S., & Lu, H.-H. (2002). The changing face of poverty in California.New York: *National Center for Children in Poverty*, Mailman School of Public Health, Columbia University.

Peisner-Feinberg, E., Jarvis, V., Ponciano, L., & Howes, C. (1999). Measuring a multicultural and antibias curriculum. Paper presented at the AERA Symposium: Perspectives on quality in early childhood settings: *Findings from the National Center for Early Development and Learning.*

Peters, M. F. (1985). Racial socialization of young black children. In H. P. McAdoo (Ed.), *Black children: Social, educational, and parental environments.* (pp. 159-173). Thousand Oaks, CA, US: Sage Publications, Inc.

Peters, M. F. (2002). Racial socialization of young black children. In H. P. McAdoo (Ed.), *Black children: Social, educational, and parental environments.* (pp. 57-72). Thousand Oaks, CA, US: Sage Publications, Inc.

Petterson, S., & Albers, A. B. (2001). Effects of maternal depression on early child development. *Child Development,* **72**(6), 1794-1813.

Phillips, D. A. (1994). Child care for children in poverty: Opportunity or inequity? *Child Development*, **65**, 472-492.

Phillips, D. A., & Ahern, E. (unpublished manuscript). *Modified observational ratings of caregiver environmnet* (m-orce).Unpublished manuscript.

Phillips, D. A., Howes, C., & Whitebook, M. (1992). The social policy context of child care: Effects on quality. *American Journal of Community Psychology*, **20**(1), 25-51.

Phinney, J. S., DuPont, S., Espinosa, C., Revill, J., & Sanders, K. (1994). Ethnic identity and american identification among ethnic minority youths. In A.-M. Bouvy, F. van de Vijver, P. Boski & P. Schmitz (Eds.), *Journeys into cross-cultural psychology* (pp. 167-183). Lisse: Swets & Zeitlinger.

Proctor, B., & Dalaker, J. (2003). *Poverty in the United States:* 2002 (No. p60-222). Washington, D.C.: U.S. Census Bureau, current population reports.

Rank, M., & Hirschl, T. (1999). The economic risk of childhood in America: Estimating the probability of poverty across the formative years. *Journal of Marriage and Family*, **61**, 1058-1067.

Reynolds, A., Temple, J., Robertson, D., & Mann, E. (2001). Long-term effects of an early childhood intervention on educational achievement and juvenile arrest: A 15-year follow-up of low-income children in public schools. *Journal of American Medical Association*, **285**(18), 2339-2346.

Richards, H. (1997). The teaching of afrocentric values by African American parents. *Western Journal of Black Studies*, **21**(1), 42-50.

Rickel, A., & Biasatti, L. (1982). Modification of the Block child rearing practices report. *Journal of Clinical Psychology*, **38**(1), 129-134.

Rogoff, B. (2003). *The cultural nature of human development*. Oxford: Oxford University Press.

Rosenthal, R. (1985). From bias to expectancy effects. In J. Dusek (Ed.), *Teacher expectancies* (pp. 37-66). Hillsdale, NJ: Lawrence Erlbaum Associates.

Sander-Phillips, K. (1996). The ecology of human violence: Its relationship to health promotion behaviors in low-income black and latino communities. *American Journal of Health Promotion*, **10**, 308-317.

Sanders, K. (2005). *It takes a village: Early race socialization of African-American and Latino children in child care*. Unpublished Dissertation, University of California, Los Angeles.

Sanders, K. (unpublished). Beliefs regarding multicultural education in child care: *The meaning of diversity to early childhood educators*.

Sanders, K., Deihl, A., & Kyler, A. (2007). D.A.P. In the 'hood: Perceptions of child care practices by African American child care directors caring for children of color. *Early Childhood Research Quarterly*, **22**, 394-406.

Schweinhart, L. (2004). *The High / Scope Perry preschool study through age 40: Summary, conclusions, and frequently asked questions.*Ypsilanti, MI: High/Scope Educational Research Foundation.

Shonkoff, J. P., & Phillips, D. A. (Eds.). (2000). *From neurons to neighborhoods: The science of early childhood development.*Washington, D.C.: National Academy Press.

Spencer, M. B. (1983). Children's cultural values and parental child rearing strategies. *Developmental Review*, **4**, 351-370.

Spencer, M. B. (1987). Black children's ethnic identity formation: Risk and resilience of caste-like minorities. In J. S. Phinney & M. J. Rotheram (Eds.), *Children's ethnic socialization: Pluralism and development* (pp. 103-116). Newbury Park: Sage Publications.

Stalans, L. (1995). Multidimensional scaling. In L. G. Grimm & P. Yarnold (Eds.), *Reading and understanding multivariate statistics* (pp. 137-168). Washington, D.C.: American Psychological Association.

Thomas, A. J. (2000). Impact of racial identity on African-American child-rearing beliefs. *Journal of Black Psychology, 26*(3), 317-329.

Thorne, B. (2005). Unpacking school lunchtime: Structure, practice, and the negotiation of differences. In C. Cooper, C. Garcia-Coll, T. Bartko, H. Davis & C. Chatman (Eds.), *Developmental pathways through middle childhood: Rethinking contexts and diversity as resources* (pp. 63–88). Mahwah, NJ: Erlbaum.

Thornton, M., Chatters, L., Taylor, R., & Allen, W. (1990). Sociodemographic and environmental correlates of racial socialization by Black parents. *Child Development, 61*, 401-409.

Weinstein, R. S., Marshall, H. H., Sharp, L., & Botkin, M. (1987). Pygmalion and the student: Age and classroom differences in children's awareness of teacher expectations. *Child Development, 58*(4), 1079-1093.

Whitebook, M., Howes, C., & Phillips, D. A. (1998). *Who cares? Child care teachers and the quality of care in America: Final report, national child care staffing study.*Washington, D.C.: The Center for the Child Care Workforce.

Wishard, A., Shivers, E., Howes, C., & Ritchie, S. (2003). Child care program and teacher practices: Associations with quality and children's experiences. *Early Childhood Research Quarterly, 18*, 65-103.

In: Low Incomes: Social, Health and Educational Impacts   ISBN: 978-1-60741-175-8
Editor: Jacob K. Levine, pp. 93-107   © 2009 Nova Science Publishers, Inc.

Chapter 4

HEALTH SATISFACTION AND INCOME IN KOREA

Seunghun Joh[*1] *and Youngmin Kim*[2]

[1] Happiness Economics Institute, 201-701 Worldcup Apt.
Sangamdong Mapogu Seoul, South Korea
[2] Graduate School of Environmental Studies,
Seoul National University, Seoul, South Korea

Abstract

The primary goal of the present study is to empirically investigate the association among income, health promotion behaviors, and health satisfaction in Korea. The findings obtained in the current study support a clear relationship between self-assessed health status and income in the context of health promotion behaviors. The results confirm that income matters in the health context in that it is associated with health promotion behaviors. However, by income level, the mechanism of income in health differs. Health satisfaction among the rich is higher than that of the poor, and participation in health checkups and regular exercise shows a proportional association with income levels except in the richest group. As for the low income group, the primary reason for poor health stems from low levels of health management in seeking health checkups and engaging in regular exercise, which are associated with income level. For the low income group, the problem of low health satisfaction is mainly due to health management resources, while for the richest, making money appears to be the first priority. This idiosyncratic nature of the two types sheds an informative light on implementing health policy. In order to increase health satisfaction for the low income groups, the appropriate policy focuses on providing them with financial assistance for health checkups. Regarding a health promotion policy for the richest people, there seems to be little government attention. The action that the richest people need to take is to free themselves from a money-oriented mindset. They should recognize that there might be a trade-off between the amount of money earned and level of health satisfaction.

---

[*] E-mail address: happy@happykorea.info

1. Introduction

Health status is a consequence of a series of processes stemming from various factors. The World Health Organization (WHO) addresses the determinants of health, which include the social and economic environment, the physical environment, and the person's individual characteristics and behaviors. Health status is strongly associated with the context of people's lives. Individuals are unlikely to be able to directly control many of the determinants of health. Socioeconomic status is significantly pertinent to health inequality. Higher income and social status are linked to better health. The greater the gap between the richest and poorest, the greater the difference in health status. Low education levels are linked with poor health, more stress and lower self-confidence. Education level is in part correlated with socioeconomic status. Social support from family, friends and community is linked to better health. Customs and traditions, and the beliefs of the family and community, all affect health. Physical environment, employment, and working conditions all impact health satisfaction. Genetic inheritance plays an important role in determining lifespan, health, and the likelihood of developing certain illnesses. Personal behavior and coping skills—balanced eating, staying active, smoking, drinking, and mechanisms for coping with life's stresses and challenges—all affect health. The availability of health services is an important factor in health condition. Men and women suffer from different types of diseases at different ages.

Among the various factors mentioned above, this chapter deals with the relationship between socioeconomic and demographic variables and health satisfaction with a focus on income levels. Socioeconomic status is regarded as an important determinant of health status. The scientific study of the relationship between socioeconomic status and health dates back at least as far as the 19th century (Cutler, 2008). Evidence shows that most of the global burden of disease and the bulk of health inequalities are caused by social determinants (McGinnis. et al., 2002; Tarlov, 1996). One of the most heavily-researched topics in economics and other social sciences is the relationship between income and health (Frijters et al., 2005). There is general agreement that low income is a risk factor for disease and poor health (Syme, 1998).

The literature regarding the causal inquiry of income and health is much more recent. The causal effect of income on health as a more step-forward analysis in the area of health economics has been carried out to date without arriving at a unified consensus (Adams et al., 2003; Benzeval et al., 2000; Benzeval and Judge, 2001; Case et al., 2002; Meer et al., 2003; Smith, 1999). The appropriate understanding of the direction is important, in that the causality between income and health is vital for policy design aimed at improving general health or narrowing health inequalities in society.

The reason for the confusion surrounding causality implies that the nature of causality is case-specific. In this vein, we are not focusing on the causality per se. Instead, the primary effort is made to empirically investigate the association among income, health promotion behaviors, and health satisfaction. Mean value, correlation, and regression are the main tools utilized in the present study. The association between income and health-promotion behaviors is investigated with adopting a binary logit model controlling for age, education, sickness experience, and smoking.

We proceed as follows: In section 2, we offer a brief overview of the relationships among health, socioeconomic status, and health-promotion behaviors. Section 3 describes our statistical analysis, including the data used in the empirical study and econometric approach, followed by the results. Section 4 concludes.

2. Health, Health-Promotion Behaviors, and Socioeconomic Status

Heath status is strongly associated with socioeconomic status. There is a substantial body of evidence regarding a well-known positive association with socioeconmic status, such as household income, education, occupation, race, and health (Cutler et al., 2008; Chan et al., 2008; Contoyannis et al., 1999).

Figure 1 shows the relationship between gross domestic product (GDP) per person and life expectancy, the most objective measure of physical health. Average life expectancy is proportional to GDP level. Figure 2 shows the relationship between individual income and self-reported health. Not surprisingly, these show that individual income is strongly related to individual differences in health—the lower the income, the poorer the health.

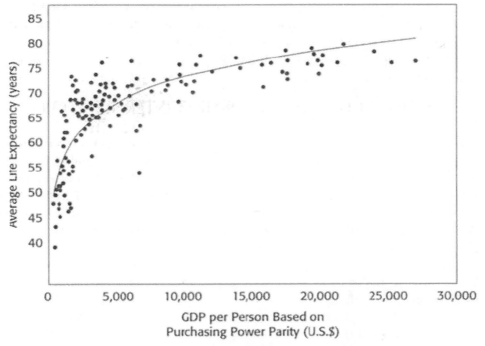

Source: World Bank, 1997; World Organization, 1999; Hofrichter, 2003, re-citation.

Figure 1. Gross Domestic Product per Person and Life Expectancy in 155 Countries, c. 1993.

Although all segments of the population are getting healthier, income-related inequalities in health, favouring the higher income groups, is getting worse, and is particularly high in the United States (Doorslaer et al., 1997).

Education and occupation can widen health inequality. As shown in figure 3, the more educated, the better the health status in adults over the age of 25.

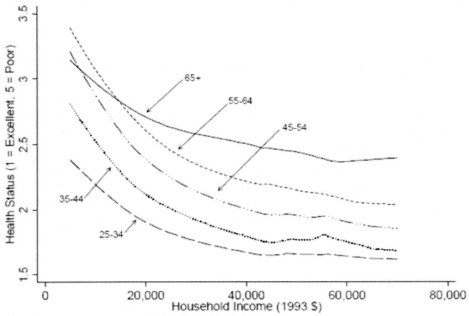

Notes: The curves are local linear regression estimates. The regressions are weighted using the survey weights provided by the NHIS (National Health Interview Surveys). Household income is reported in income brackets in the NHIS; it is imputed here from the March CPS (Current Population Survey) of the same year as the mean income in the income bracket and education cell of the household head.
Source: Cutler et al., 2008, p49.

Figure 2. Income and Self-Reported Health, U.S. Adults over Age 25, NHIS 1986–1995.

On the other hand, socioeconomic status affects lifestyle behavior, especially health promotion behavior which is crucial to good health. For example, regular physical activity (PA) is essential for disease prevention and health promotion. Regular PA reduces the risk of diabetes, colon cancer, hypertension, and obesity. Physical inactivity is an independent heart disease risk factor of similar magnitude (relative risk of 1.9) to smoking, hypertension, and hypercholesterolemia. PA promotes psychological well-being, and builds and maintains healthy bones, muscles, and joints, thus reducing the risk of falls in the elderly and increasing functional independence (Glasgow et al., 2001).

However, people with lower income may have no time or money to exercise regularly. Furthermore, earlier studies have found lower income individuals and those with little education or on Medicaid to be less likely to receive a physician's advice to exercise (Friedman et al., 1994; Glasgow et al., 2001; Kreuter MW et al., 1997). Women especially are not physically active enough to gain the health benefits of physical activity. A common key barrier to participation in physical activity among women is lack of time due to work. Also, having a mastery motivational style and a higher income were strong predictors of physical activity participation in middle-aged women in China (Sit et al., 2008).

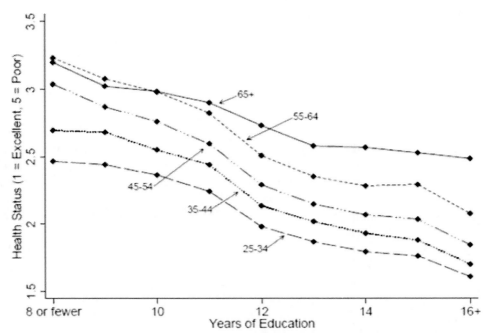

Notes: The means are weighted using the survey weights provided by the NHIS (National Health Interview Surveys).
Source: Cutler et al., 2008, p48.

Figure 3. Education and Self-Reported Health, U.S. Adults over the age of 25, NHIS 1986–1995.

Tobacco use, alcohol consumption and diet as well as PA are major risks of morbidity and mortality. Berrigan et al. (2003) analyzed patterns of health behavior by characterizing adherence to public health recommendations for behavior related to exercise, tobacco, alcohol, dietary fat intake, and fruit and vegetable consumption by using data from the Third National Health and Nutrition Examination Survey (NHANES III) of the U.S. As a result, adherence to recommendations concerning five aspects of health behavior increased with age, income, and education level, was more common in women than men, and varied by race/ethnicity. Non-adherence to all five recommendations decreased with age and education, and was more prevalent in men than women.

The impact of socioeconomic factors on health promotion behavior also is greater in patients. For example, Raymond et al. (2008) reported that socioeconomically disadvantaged patients were more ill at baseline and less behaviorally responsive to embarking on healthy lifestyle changes after acute myocardial infarction (AMI) than those of higher socioeconomic status.

Associations between health-related behaviors are important for two reasons. First, disease prevention and health promotion depend on understanding both prevalence of health behaviors and associations among such behaviors. Second, behaviors may have synergistic effects on disease risk (Berrigan et al., 2003). And socioeconomic status, like household income, education, employment, health promotion behaviors and race, is an important determinant of health-promotion behaviors, like exercise, dietary behavior, smoking cessation and health checkups. Therefore, understanding the effect of socioeconomic status on health and health-promotion behaviors may be useful for health-promotion strategies.

3. Empirical Study

3.1. Data

We address the linkages between health satisfaction and household income using the Korea General Social Survey 2006 carried out by the National Statistical Office. This survey was conducted to investigate levels of quality of life and current changes of the society by individual consciousness related to the quality of life. The data are utilized as basic materials for making social development policies. The areas of the survey include health, family, social participation, and labor. The nationwide survey was done by person-to-person interview in July, 2006. The survey covers all persons aged 15 and over who usually reside in 33,000 sample households. Important for the purposes of the present study, the survey provides information regarding individuals' health satisfaction, household income, and various activities regarding health promotion. The data set used for the current study is for people over the age of 19, with a sample size of 30,501.

Level of health satisfaction is measured from self-reported survey answers: "How much are you satisfied with your health status?" with answers of 1 meaning poorest through 5 meaning best. The variable education indicates total years of education. The household income is defined as before-tax yearly total household income. Table 1 displays the definition and means of the variables used in the empirical analysis.

Table 1. Definition and Means of Variables for the Sample Data (N=30,501)

Variables	Unit	Mean	Standard Deviation	Minimum	Maximum
Sex	male=1 female=2	1.26	0.44	1	2
Age	years	49.63	14.07	20	94
Education	years of education	11.07	4.42	0	18
Household Income	USD10,000/year	2.64	2.16	0.3	14.4
Health Satisfaction	1=poorest 5=best	3.25	0.90	1	5

3.2. Health Satisfaction

Of particular concern in this study is whether there exists any consistency between income levels and health satisfaction. We first derive mean values of health satisfaction, years of education and age by nine income levels (table 2).

Table 2. Mean Values of Health Satisfaction,
Years of Education and Age by Income Level

Household Income		Sample Size		Health Satisfaction		Years of Education		Age	
Level	USD 10,000/ year	Person	%	Mean	Standard Deviation	Mean	Standard Deviation	Mean	Standard Deviation
1	0.3	3387	11.10	2.54	0.99	5.90	5.09	64.46	15.51
2	0.9	4879	16.00	2.96	0.94	8.90	4.45	55.62	15.09
3	1.8	8419	27.60	3.30	0.83	11.28	3.48	46.65	13.19
4	3	6970	22.85	3.45	0.78	12.37	3.16	45.25	10.60
5	4.2	3718	12.19	3.50	0.77	13.12	3.19	45.74	9.87
6	6	2132	6.99	3.60	0.78	14.01	3.14	46.27	9.57
7	8.4	518	1.70	3.60	0.78	14.87	3.05	46.36	8.88
8	10.8	190	0.62	3.64	0.84	14.54	3.38	47.45	9.46
9	14.4	288	0.94	3.49	0.84	13.18	3.68	48.66	10.68

As we expected, health satisfactions are generally proportional to income level. The degree of the proportion, however, appears somewhat different. In the lower income levels of 1st through 3rd, we can see stronger relationships between health satisfaction and income than that of the middle income levels of 4th through 6th (figure 4). Up to the 8th income level, we can find a trend of diminishing marginal satisfaction of health.

We find some intriguing phenomena in the top income level. The level takes account of about 1% total sample size with a mean annual household income of USD 144,000. The value of health satisfaction almost equals that of the 5th income level, which is 29% of the 9th income level.

The second approach, which aims to figure out the relationship between health and income, is to deal with how health-promotion activities differ by income level. We analyze five activities that are pertinent to individual behaviors that impact health. They include how many people have regular breakfast, have good sleep in terms of appropriate hours of 6 to 8, engage in regular exercise, have regular health checkups, and smoke.

The result of correlation coefficient indicate that health satisfaction is most closely associated with income level (table 3). It is interesting that smoking shows a negative association with health-promotion behaviors, but the smoking has a positive relationship with health satisfaction and income level.

The coefficient signs are negative with significant p values for breakfast, sleep, exercise, and health checkups. These results imply that smoking possesses a mixed nature of both input to and consequence of health status. We can see no clear evidence of such a hybrid causal relationship from other four behaviors.

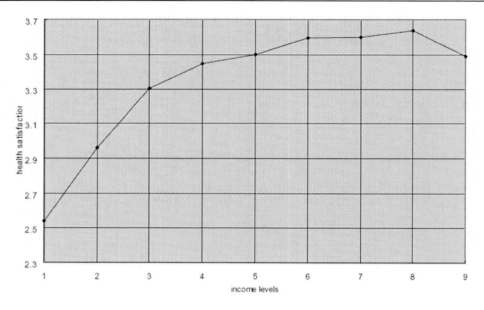

Figure 4. Health Satisfaction by Income.

**Table 3. Pearson Correlation for Health Satisfaction,
Income and Health-Related Behaviors**

Pearson Correlation Coefficients, N = 30501 Prob > |r| under H0: Rho=0							
	Health Satisfaction	Income	Breakfast	Sleep	Exercise	Check	Smoking
Health Satisfaction	1.00	0.24	0.01	0.11	0.15	0.08	0.07
		<.0001	0.23	<.0001	<.0001	<.0001	<.0001
Income	0.24	1.00	0.02	0.02	0.11	0.18	0.06
	<.0001		<.0001	0.00	<.0001	<.0001	<.0001
Breakfast	0.01	0.02	1.00	0.26	0.14	0.16	-0.12
	0.23	<.0001		<.0001	<.0001	<.0001	<.0001
Sleep	0.11	0.02	0.26	1.00	0.13	0.12	-0.07
	<.0001	0.00	<.0001		<.0001	<.0001	<.0001
Exercise	0.15	0.11	0.14	0.13	1.00	0.26	-0.12
	<.0001	<.0001	<.0001	<.0001		<.0001	<.0001
Health Check	0.08	0.18	0.16	0.12	0.26	1.00	-0.09
	<.0001	<.0001	<.0001	<.0001	<.0001		<.0001
Smoking	0.07	0.06	-0.12	-0.07	-0.12	-0.09	1.00
	<.0001	<.0001	<.0001	<.0001	<.0001	<.0001	

Table 4 shows the mean values for the activities by nine income levels as figure 2 illustrates the corresponding graph. The mean values indicate the rate of fulfilling the activity of concern. For instance, 82% lowest income level has breakfast, as 83% of the richest level does. It seems that breakfast, sleep and smoking play no significant role in explaining the gap in health status vis-à-vis health satisfaction by income level. As we see in figures 4 and 5, exercise, health checkups, and health satisfaction display consistent trend in terms of household income. The correlation is greater for exercise and health checkups than other behaviors.

Based on the previous analyses, we argue as follows: First, regular behaviors of exercise and health checkups are good indicators for health satisfaction. Second, the two are consistently associated with income levels, showing that a gap of health satisfaction by income level could be in part explained by the two indicators.

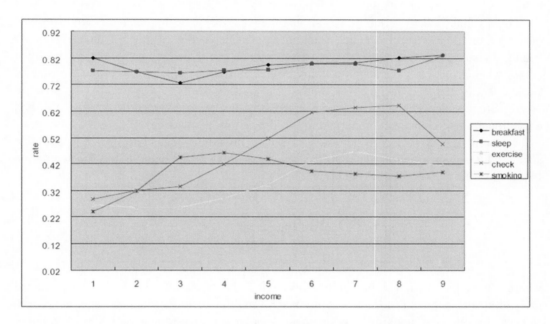

Figure 5. The Fulfillment Rates of Health-Related Behaviors by Income Level.

Table 4. Mean Values of Health-Related Behaviors (0=don't, 1=do)

Household Income	Breakfast		Sleep		Exercise		Health Check		Smoking	
	Mean	Standard Deviation	Mean	Standard Deviation	Mean	Standard Deviation	Mean	Standard Deviation	Mean	Standard Deviation
1	0.82	0.39	0.77	0.42	0.27	0.44	0.29	0.45	0.24	0.43
2	0.77	0.42	0.77	0.42	0.26	0.44	0.32	0.47	0.32	0.47
3	0.73	0.45	0.76	0.42	0.26	0.44	0.33	0.47	0.44	0.50
4	0.77	0.42	0.77	0.42	0.29	0.45	0.42	0.49	0.46	0.50
5	0.79	0.40	0.78	0.42	0.34	0.47	0.52	0.50	0.44	0.50
6	0.80	0.40	0.80	0.40	0.43	0.50	0.62	0.49	0.39	0.49
7	0.80	0.40	0.80	0.40	0.47	0.50	0.64	0.48	0.38	0.49
8	0.82	0.38	0.77	0.42	0.44	0.50	0.64	0.48	0.37	0.49
9	0.83	0.37	0.83	0.38	0.41	0.49	0.50	0.50	0.39	0.49
Total	0.77	0.42	0.77	0.42	0.30	0.46	0.40	0.49	0.40	0.49

* **Note**: For Household Income 1 is the poorest and 9 is the richest.

3.3. Binary Logit Analysis for Health Behaviors

Next, we take in-depth steps to investigate the relationship between health behaviors and income level. It is possible that many conditions have an influence on health behaviors, such as income, education, age, culture, and so forth. To avoid such a problem, we control for factors that could influence health behaviors. Without controlling them, any correlation between health status, or health satisfaction, with health-related behaviors could be spurious. We run regression to control this problem. A binary logit model is applied with health behaviors as dependent variable and income, age, education, sickness experience, and smoking as independent variables. Recall that the data for the health behaviors are expressed only 'do' or 'don't'. In this model, smoking is considered not so much a direct factor on health satisfaction as a condition that has an impact on health behaviors. Sickness experience means whether people have developed any disease during the past two weeks at the time of survey. The variable is included to control for short-term effect of a negative episode on health satisfaction. Generally, as income increases, health status becomes better. Age and education are also considered important in fulfilling some health behaviors.

The binary logit model is represented as the probability calculated using cumulative standard logistic distribution function. The regression predicts the logit, that is, the natural log of the odds of, for example, having breakfast or not. That is,

$$\ln(ODDS) = \ln\left(\frac{\hat{Y}}{1-\hat{Y}}\right) = a + bX$$

where $\hat{Y}$ is the predicted probability of having the breakfast, $1-\hat{Y}$ is the predicted probability of no breakfast, and X is predictor variables including income, age, education, sickness history, and smoking, a is intercept, b is parameter estimate, and X is a vector of predictors.

In all regressions presented in tables 5 through 8, results for the effect of independent variables on each health behavior are robust and in line with intuition. For instance, a positive sign for income indicates that the household income is positively associated with having a regular breakfast. This relationship holds true for years of education, age, no-sickness experience and no-smoking.

A variable age seems the most important determinant for health promotion behaviors. The magnitudes of standardized estimate are largest except for the case of exercise, in which the largest one is for years of education (0.28) followed by the age (0.23). If information about the relative importance of variables is necessary, standardized estimates are typically needed (Cortina and DeShon, 1998). Because the variables adopted themselves vary in terms of units, it is not possible to directly compare the relative magnitude of effects among variables. We find the sickness experience to be the least important variable with a criterion of standardized estimate.

As the primary goal of the present analysis is to explore how income level affects health, we focus on the income variables in association with the health behaviors. We have shown that regular exercise and health checkups are strongly pertinent to income level (figure 5).

After controlling for other factors, income still plays a significant role in fulfilling health behaviors.

In the binary logit model, the point estimate is odds ratio and there exist diminishing magnitudes of partial effects. Take the breakfast example. The point estimate for income is equal to 1.10, meaning that with controlling for age, sickness experience, education and smoking, one more household income of USD 1,000 is going to increase by 10% the probability of having breakfast in average condition.

We compare odds ratios of household income variable in four health behaviors. The largest point estimate for the income is the case of health checkup with 1.18, followed by 1.10 for breakfast, 1.06 for regular exercise, and 1.04 for appropriate sleeping hours. Insofar as income is concerned, it is not against intuition that the health checkup out of four health promotion behaviors is the most relevant one, and the least relevant for sleeping hours.

Table 5. Regression Results (dependent variable= breakfast with binary logit N=30501, Max-rescaled R-square 0.1591)

Parameter	Estimate	Standard Error	Wald Chi-Square	Pr > ChiSq	Standardized Estimate	Point Estimate	95% Wald Confidence Limits	
Intercept	-3.30	0.14	576.56	<.0001	N.A	N.A	N.A	N.A
Household Income	0.09	0.01	129.50	<.0001	0.11	1.10	1.08	1.12
Years of Education	0.03	0.01	31.27	<.0001	0.07	1.03	1.02	1.04
Age	0.07	0.00	1886.14	<.0001	0.51	1.07	1.07	1.07
Sickness Experience	0.16	0.04	19.38	<.0001	0.04	1.18	1.10	1.27
Smoking	0.35	0.03	143.39	<.0001	0.09	1.42	1.34	1.50

Table 6. Regression Results (dependent variable= sleep with binary logit N=30501, Max-rescaled R-square 0.0261)

Parameter	Estimate	Standard Error	Wald Chi-Square	Pr > ChiSq	Standardized Estimate	Point Estimate	95% Wald Confidence Limits	
Intercept	-1.02	0.12	67.72	<.0001	N.A	N.A	N.A.	N.A
Household Income	0.04	0.01	30.32	<.0001	0.05	1.04	1.03	1.06
Years of Education	0.01	0.00	8.68	0.0032	0.03	1.01	1.00	1.02
Age	0.02	0.00	279.02	<.0001	0.17	1.02	1.02	1.03
Sickness Experience	0.30	0.03	78.16	<.0001	0.07	1.35	1.26	1.44
Smoking	0.25	0.03	79.42	<.0001	0.07	1.29	1.22	1.36

Table 7. Regression Results (dependent variable= exercise with binary logit N=30501, Max-rescaled R-square 0.0820)

Parameter	Estimate	Standard Error	Wald Chi-Square	Pr > ChiSq	Standardized Estimate	Point Estimate	95% Wald Confidence Limits	
Intercept	-4.87	0.12	1631.57	<.0001	N.A	N.A	N.A	N.A
Household Income	0.06	0.01	100.29	<.0001	0.07	1.06	1.05	1.08
Years of Education	0.12	0.00	828.66	<.0001	0.28	1.12	1.12	1.13
Age	0.03	0.00	634.38	<.0001	0.23	1.03	1.03	1.03
Sickness Experience	0.06	0.03	3.86	0.0495	0.01	1.07	1.00	1.14
Smoking	0.54	0.03	383.75	<0.0001	0.15	1.72	1.63	1.82

Table 8. Regression results (dependent variable= health check with binary logit N=30501, Max-rescaled R-square 0.0965)

Parameter	Estimate	Standard Error	Wald Chi-Square	Pr > ChiSq	Standardized Estimate	Point Estimate	95% Wald Confidence Limits	
Intercept	-3.85	0.11	1182.13	<.0001	N.A	N.A	N.A.	N.A
Household Income	0.17	0.01	637.64	<.0001	0.20	1.18	1.17	1.20
Years of Education	0.09	0.00	523.79	<.0001	0.21	1.09	1.08	1.10
Age	0.03	0.00	829.98	<.0001	0.26	1.03	1.03	1.04
Sickness Experience	-0.11	0.03	13.80	0.0002	-0.03	0.90	0.84	0.95
Smoking	0.34	0.03	180.94	<.0001	0.09	1.41	1.34	1.48

4. Conclusion

Before going to the conclusion, we discuss the methodological appropriateness of employing self-assessed health satisfaction as a proxy variable for health condition. Someone may place in doubt the subjective evaluation of health status. They might point out whether self-rated health is meaningful in that there is a relationship between how an individual subjectively perceives his or her health and any objective measure of health status or health outcome. Regarding subjectivity regarding health status, there exist some arguments supporting the superiority of self-assessed evaluation (Idler and Benyamini, 1997; Joh, 2007; Lopez, 2004). Lopez defends that health status is more than just the absence of disease. It includes a whole set of factors that relate to how an individual feels and how well that individual can function in society and the environment. As far as subjectivity matters in health status, Joh asserts that the objective data which are determined by medical criteria might not be more appropriate than subjective data. Note that health status is judged in a subjective way at the moment of survey. It means that if the respondents know anything about diseases or symptoms medically defined, the fact known may bring about a negative cognitive evaluation. The problem to clearly address is how to understand the case of medically poor health status but subjectively good happiness. Idler and Benyamini (1997) addressed the reasons for preferring subjective assessment over a medical approach. First, self-rated health is by nature a more valid assessment of health status than alternative measures. Second, it is more likely to include undiagnosed or early-stage illness that might be missed by a physician. Third, it is based on an individual's complex assessment of their total health status. Fourth, it includes an individual's understanding of his or her social and familial history. Fifth, it does not rely on current health status but incorporates an individual's assessment of the trajectory of his or her health status. Individuals may base their health-related behaviors at least in part on how they perceive their health status. Sixth, it reflects the availability of resources and the quality of environmental factors that may ultimately affect health.

The findings obtained from the current study support a clear relationship between self-assessed health status and income. The results confirm that income matters in the context of health in that it is associated with health-promotion behaviors. However, by income level, the mechanism of income in health differs. The health satisfaction of the rich is higher than that of the poor, and the fulfillment of health checkups and participation in regular exercise shows a proportional association with income level except in richest group. We are concerned regarding why such a phenomenon takes place for the richest. Our best guess involves 'optimal endeavor for health'. Generally speaking, high income comes from multiple consequences of a high magnitude of work hours and high physical and mental work intensity, resulting in a negative impact on health status and satisfaction. Because the richest 9th group has fewer health checkups and less participation in regular exercise than the 5th or 6th through 8th income groups, it seems that the problem is pertinent not to the economic costs for checkups and exercise, but their circumstances, mostly time constraints. Some might say that it takes 3 ~ 4 hours for a health checkup, therefore it is an exaggeration to link the amount of checkup time to time constraints. It should be recognized that for the richest the health checkup behavior represents a sort of symbolic criteria to focus on prioritizing making money. It seems that the rules for the richest are heavily money oriented—that is, they are not optimal behavior in terms of a strategy for maximizing health satisfaction. Health satisfaction can be improved through either health-promotion behaviors, such as health checkups and exercise, or making more money to be used for obtaining, for instance, a healthful diet and various health instruments. Another explanation for the rich-but-unhealthy phenomenon has something to do with the framework of expectation. As their income is high, their expectation level for health is proportionally increasing. However, this seems to secure no strong recognition. It means that a more acceptable argument is that the work-intensive life-pattern makes the richest feel stressed, fatigued, and ill.

As for the low income group, the primary reason for poor health stems from low levels of health management in seeking health checkups and engaging in regular exercise, which are associated with income level. For the low income group, the problem of low health satisfaction is mainly due to health management resources, while for the richest, making money appears to be the first priority. This idiosyncratic nature of the two types sheds an informative light on implementing health policy. In order to increase health satisfaction for the low income groups, the appropriate policy focuses on providing them with financial assistance for health checkups. Regarding a health promotion policy for the richest people, there seems to be little government attention. The action that the richest people need to take is to free themselves from a money-oriented mindset. They should recognize that there might be a trade-off between the amount of money earned and level of health satisfaction.

References

Articles in Journals

Adams, P., Hurd, M., McFadden, D., Merrill, A., & Ribeiro, T. (2003). Healthy, wealthy, and wise Tests for direct causal paths between health and socioeconomic status. *Journal of Econometrics,* **112**, 3–56.

Benzeval, M., Taylor, J., & Judge, K. (2000). Evidence on the relationship between low income and poor health: is the government doing enough? *Fiscal Studies,* **21**, 375–399.

Benzeval, M., & Judge, K. (2001). Income and health: the time dimension. *Social Science and Medicine,* **52**, 1371–1390.

Cortina, J. M., & R.P. DeShon. (1998). Determining relative importance of predictors with the observational design. *Journal of Applied Psychology,* **83**(5), 798-804.

Case, A., Lubotsky, D., & Paxson, C. (2002). Economic status and health in childhood: The origins of the gradient. *American Economic Review,* **92**, 1308–1334.

Berrigan, D., Dodd, K., Troiano R.P., Krebs-Smith, S.M.., & Barbash R.B. (2003). Patterns of health behavior in U.S. adults. *Preventive Medicine,* **36**, 615–623.

Chan, R. H.M., Gordon, N.F., Chong, A., & Alter, D.A.(2008). Influence of Socioeconomic Status on Lifestyle Behavior Modifications Among Survivors of Acute Myocardial Infarction. *The American Journal of Cardiology,* In Press, Corrected Proof, Available online 9 October 2008.

Contoyannis, P., & Forster, M., (1999). The distribution of health and income: a theoretical framework, *Journal of Health Economics,* **18**, 605–622.

Doorslar, E., Wagstaff, A., & Bleichrodt, H. (1997). Income-related inequalities in health: some international comparisons, *Journal of Health Economics,* **16**, 93-112.

Friedman, C., Brownson, R.C., Peterson DE., & Wilkerson JC. (1994). Physician advice to reduce chronic disease risk factors. *Am J Prev Med ,* **10**, 367–371.

Frijters, P., Haisken-DeNew, J.P., & Shields, M.A. (2005). The causal effect of income on health: Evidence from German reunification. *Journal of Health Economics,* **24**, 997–1017.

Glasgow, R.E., Eakin, E.G., Fisher, E.B., Bacak, S.J., & Brownson, R.C. (2001). Physician Advice and Support for Physical Activity Results from a National Survey, *American Journal of Preventive Medicine,* **21**(3), 189-196.

Idler, E., & Benyamini, Y. (1997). Self-rated health and mortality: A review of twenty-seven community studies. *Journal of Health and Social Behavior,* **38**, 21–37.

Kreuter, M.W., Scharff, D.P., Brennan, L.K., & Lukwago, S.N. (1997). Physician advice for diet and physical activity. *Prev Med ,* **26**, 825–33.

Lopez, R. (2004). Income inequality and self-rated health in US metropolitan areas: A multi-level analysis. *Social Science & Medicine,* **59**, 2409–2419.

McGinnis, J.M., Williams-Russo P., & Knickman J. (2002). The case for more active policy attention to health promotion. *Health Affairs,* **21**(2), 78-93.

Meer. J., Miller, D., & Rosen, H., (2003). Exploring the health-wealth nexus. *Journal of Health Economics,* **22**, 713–730.

Sit, Cindy H.P., Kerr, J.H., & Wong, I.T.F. (2008). Motives for and barriers to physical activity participation in middle-aged Chinese women. *Psychology of Sport and Exercise,* **9**, 266–283.

Smith, J. (1999). Healthy bodies and thick wallets: the dual relation between health and economic status. *Journal of Economic Perspectives* **13**, 145–166.

Syme, L. (1998). Social and economic disparities in health: Thoughts about intervention. *The Milbank Quarterly*, **76**, 493–505.

Books

Cutler, D.M., Lleras-Muney, A., & Vogl, T. (2008). Socioeconomic Status and Health: Dimensions and Mechanisms *NBER Working Paper*. No. 14333 September 2008

Hofrichter, R. (2003). *Health and social justice*. San Francisco: Jossy-Bass

Joh, S. (2007). A happiness approach to air pollution policy in Korea, In Sergio P. Balduino (Ed.), *Progress in Air Pollution Research* (pp.273-285). NewYork: Nova Publishers.

Tarlov A. (1996). Social determinants of health: the sociobiological translation. In Blane D, Brunner E, & Wilkinson R (Eds). *Health and social organization* (pp. 71-93). London: Routledge.

In: Low Incomes: Social, Health and Educational Impacts   ISBN: 978-1-60741-175-8
Editor: Jacob K. Levine, pp. 109-140   © 2009 Nova Science Publishers, Inc.

Chapter 5

CYCLERS, LEAVERS AND STAYERS IN WELFARE DYNAMICS: WHY DO UNEMPLOYMENT EFFECTS DECREASE WITH TIME?

Luis Ayala[a,1] and Magdalena Rodríguez[b,2]
[1] Universidad Rey Juan Carlos, Madrid, Spain
[2] Instituto de Estudios Fiscales, Madrid, Spain

Abstract

The main aim of this paper is to analyse the contribution of unemployment and individual characteristics to welfare durations taking into account different ways of modelling unemployment and including heterogeneity according to participation sequences. The programme studied in this paper is the Minimum Income Integration programme (*IMI*) of the Madrid Government. Administrative records are available from more than eleven years and the number of households and spells is larger than in other studies (over 50,000 spells). We estimate different discrete time duration models with alternative ways of controlling unobserved heterogeneity. Our results show that there are clearly differentiated types of recipients depending on the recurrence and duration of welfare participation. The unemployment rate at the moment of entering the programme seems to be a relevant factor for the probability of leaving, but having less weight than that exerted by the recipients' socio-demographic characteristics. There is also a certain degree of duration dependence and the effects of macroeconomic conditions drastically differ depending on the length of the welfare spell.

Keywords: welfare, poverty, discrete time duration models, multiple spells, unobserved heterogeneity.
JEL: I30, I38, C41

[a] E-mail address: luis.ayala@urjc.es. Facultad de Ciencias Jurídicas y Sociales, Universidad Rey Juan Carlos, Paseo Artilleros s/n, 28032 Madrid, SPAIN.
[b] E-mail address: magdalena.rodriguez@ief.minhac.es. Instituto de Estudios Fiscales, Cardenal Herrera Oria, 378, 28035 Madrid, SPAIN.

1. Introduction[1]

Welfare policies have come under increasing strains in many countries. In order to prevent long-term participation, most social assistance schemes have undergone reforms attempting to incorporate active measures to the programmes. Compared to the traditional passive nature of these policies, which were focused almost exclusively on providing cash benefits to low-income households, the new initiatives make an effort to foster the transitions from welfare to work.

Various questions arise related to both the necessity as well as the results of the reforms. The question of whether the problem of prolonged welfare spells is a result of the recipients' characteristics and attitudes or whether, on the other hand, entries and exits are essentially due to changes in the economic cycle has attracted great attention. There is an extensive body of literature attempting to identify which of these two factors has more influence. Studies analysing long time-series or panel data have shown that macroeconomic conditions play a decisive role[2]. Microeconomic analysis of welfare participation decisions has also served to find a set of household characteristics associated with a lower probability of leaving welfare[3]. The utility of either taking part or leaving these programmes differs considerably depending on the recipients' characteristics. The effects of macroeconomic conditions, in general, and unemployment in particular, although significant, vary widely among the various demographic groups.

Most studies that focus on the contribution made by individual characteristics and unemployment to welfare dynamics are usually constrained by two limitative factors. The first one is related to the modelling of unemployment effects. In the standard model of welfare participation unemployment plays a decisive role in the duration of the spells. A worsening of labour market conditions should reduce employment and earnings opportunities. The foreseeable result should be longer spells. However, as opposed to studies that impose straightforward linear relationships the effect that entries into the programmes have during periods of economic expansion might be very different from the one they have in a recession. It can be expected that spells of households entering welfare in periods of strong economic growth will be longer than those that do so during recessions. Using the safety net even when the labour market offers ample opportunities seems to be limited to households suffering from very serious structural problems. Therefore, it seems necessary to test alternative specifications of unemployment considering both the rate when entering into the programme as well as its changes over time.

A second difficulty arises from the existence of a considerable degree of heterogeneity among recipients, identified by the variety of welfare spells sequences and durations. A growing literature focusing on welfare dynamics has concentrated on recidivism and multiple

[1] The authors would like to thank the Instituto de Estudios Fiscales and the Ministry of Science and Technology (grant SEJ2004-07373-c03-03) for research support. The authors are also grateful to Rebecca Blank for useful suggestions.
[2] The literature on welfare caseloads is extensive. Most of the studies coincide in pointing out the importance of macroeconomic conditions. In most cases, the economic cycle is approached through changes in the unemployment rate. See Moffitt (1992), Stapleton *et al.* (1997), Mayer (2000), Bell (2001), Blank (2001, 2002), and Grogger (2005), among others.
[3] For a comprehensive review of the empirical evidence, see Moffitt (2001), Green and Warburton (2001), Blank (2002) and Grogger *et al.* (2005).

spells[4]. Considering durations from this context is crucial for an adequate measurement and interpretation of welfare dependency. There are different kinds of welfare recipients according to the number of spells and the probability of recidivism. This diversity may introduce some biases when measuring the effects of unemployment on durations. Changes in macroeconomic conditions should in principle be more significant in the case of short-term than in long-term claimants. Nonetheless, some studies have found no evidence for the existence of significant differences in the characteristics of the two types of recipients (Miller, 2002, and Moffitt, 2001).

The main aim of this paper is to analyse the contribution of macroeconomic conditions to welfare duration taking into account different ways of modelling unemployment, in addition to including heterogeneity due to participation sequences. We estimate different duration models including unobserved heterogeneity and duration dependence. We use data from the Minimum Income program of the Madrid Regional Government (IMI). Social Assistance in Spain is completely decentralized and the IMI can be considered an 'average' program within the complex set of regional schemes. IMI is also a standard program within the variety of schemes existing in Southern Europe. In some of these countries, like France or Spain, new welfare designs were introduced some years before reforms were implemented in other OECD countries.

This programme's administrative records have many advantages over other sources, like the longer time period covered and the high number of households and spells included. The dataset offers important advantages over other sources commonly used in the U.S. welfare literature. First, we have the complete history of the programme, avoiding left-censoring problems and allowing for a more precise analysis of multiple spells. Second, there is a longer time period covered by the records (eleven years) and the inclusion of a much higher number of households and spells than in other studies (over 50,000 spells).

Previous studies have found that macroeconomic conditions have significant effects in the programme's caseloads. Applying different time series techniques, Ayala and Pérez (2005) examined variations in the IMI caseloads on the basis of four different factors: macroeconomic conditions, interactions with other income maintenance programmes, changes in the programme's parameters and changes in the demographic structure. Their results showed that institutional factors carry more weight than macroeconomic factors concerning changes in the welfare caseloads. The effects, however, vary considerably among the different demographic groups. Ayala and Rodríguez (2007) also found that barriers to employment seem also strongly associated with the probability of leaving welfare.

The paper is structured as follows. First, we provide a general background about the relationship between unemployment and welfare dynamics within a context of recipients' heterogeneity. The programme's characteristics and participation sequences, and the way the administrative records are processed are described in the third section. The effects of macroeconomic conditions and individual characteristics on durations are then estimated. The paper ends with a brief list of conclusions.

---

[4] See Weeks (1991), Blank and Ruggles (1994), Cao (1996), Meyer and Cancian (1996), Sandefur and Cook (1997), Brandon (1995), Harris (2000), Keng et al. (2000), Carrington et al. (2002), and Ayala and Rodríguez (2004).

2. Background

The literature on welfare dynamics has traditionally been based on search theories and take-up models. It is easy to interpret durations in these programmes as the result of entry and exit decisions. These decisions can be specified combining the equations used by labour supply models with non-linear budget constraints and the cost functions of job search models. The key question resides in the utility (U) provided by the different combinations of income and leisure resulting from welfare benefits and labour opportunities. The latter are affected by the socio-demographic characteristics of each household. Following Moffitt (2001), a general system of entry and exit equations containing the previous arguments can be defined. If we focus on the probability of leaving welfare, the exit function (E_t) for households taking part in the programme will be determined by:

$$E_t{}^* = U(w_t, y_t) - U\{w_t(1-\tau), y_t(1-\tau)+G\} - C_V - C_S \tag{1}$$

where w_t represents earnings, y_t is unearned income, τ is the implicit marginal tax rate for income other than welfare and G is the guarantee level. The costs associated with the decision of leaving the programme may consist of variable costs (C_V), including processing costs, time costs, the obligation to participate in training activities and the social stigma involved, and fixed costs associated with the decision of leaving welfare (C_S). It can be easily deduced that $E_t=1$ if $E_t{}^* > 0$, and $E_t = 0$ if $E_t{}^* \leq 0$. There is a greater probability of leaving the programme if benefits are reduced. This probability is higher if the tax burden on other non-benefit income is increased or if employment and earnings opportunities decrease:

$$\frac{\partial E_t^*}{\partial G} < 0, \quad \frac{\partial E_t^*}{\partial \tau} > 0, \quad \frac{\partial E_t^*}{\partial w} > 0 \tag{2}$$

If we accept G and τ as given, then exits would be determined by changes in macroeconomic conditions, which are assumed to follow some kind of stochastic process. The effects of macroeconomic conditions on welfare can be approached by a variety of ways. To the extent that general declines in unemployment would be probably mirrored in declines in wage rates, the previous assumption for wages also holds in the case of unemployment. Under a linear specification of the relationship between wages and unemployment, it should be expected that increases in unemployment (D) reduce exits and boost entries:

$$\frac{\partial E_t^*}{\partial D} < 0.$$

A reasonable assumption can then be made that the current unemployment rate is a key variable explaining welfare spells. This conclusion also holds up under a dynamic specification of welfare duration. As Moffitt (2002) points out, the net result of these models in the life cycle labour supply literature is that there is little if any alteration in the basic effects found in the standard static model. Uncertainty and time limits, however, could make labour participation the preferred choice. With time limits and low unemployment rates recipients could choose to work today and go onto welfare in the future. In this context, the effect on welfare entries may not change.

More doubts arise over the effects of unemployment in contexts where uncertainty is related to the returns of training or other specific human capital measures usually embedded in welfare programmes. In periods of strong economic growth with high earnings and low unemployment levels, the opportunity cost of participation could be too high increasing thereby the probability of leaving welfare[5]. Following Moffitt's (2002) analysis for a two-period model, the individual's participation decision will depend on the net present value of the investment (NPV):

$$NPV = -w_1(1-t)I + \frac{1}{1+r} \{P_2[(w_2-w_1)(1-t)H_2] + (1-P_2) [(w_2-w_1)H_2 - (G - tw_1H_2)]\} \quad (3)$$

where w_1 represents the wage if the individual were not to undergo the training program, w_2 is the wage in the period two if she/he does, I is the time devoted to investment in period one, H_2 is the number of hours worked in period two, P_2 is a dummy in period two reflecting whether the individual undergoes the program, and G is the benefit amount. If the net present value is positive, a reasonable assumption can be made that prolonged participation will increase the recipient's utility. A foreseeable result should be that the duration of the first welfare spell would be longer, with lower exit rates even if unemployment rates fall.

The hypothesis that unemployment has a strong and significant effect on welfare exits has not always found support in the empirical literature. On one side, some authors have pointed out that the effects are not constant over time within a spell: employment and wages opportunities for unemployed individuals decrease with time (Mortensen, 1977). The hypothesis of linearity in the specifications taking changes in the unemployment rate obviates the existence of the very different effects unemployment has at the moment of either entering or leaving the programme. An opposite effect of macroeconomic conditions from what is commonly forecasted by conventional models can occur if the unemployment rate at the moment of entering the programme is taken as reference. First, a drastic fall in the unemployment rate or an improvement in earnings, for instance, may not result in exits if the lengthening of welfare participation leads to a worsening of recipients' skills. As Ashenfelter (1984), Layard et al. (1991) and Machin and Manning (1999) all pointed out, there is a striking serial correlation or persistence of unemployment in most OECD countries. This phenomenon would give rise to a process of duration dependence, reducing the probability of abandoning the programme as durations lengthen[6]. In this case both the level of benefits received as well as macroeconomic conditions might be expected to have almost no effect on the probability of leaving the programmes (Nickell, 1979; Narendranathan and Stewart, 1993). Second, only households suffering from serious structural problems and with low levels of employability enter welfare during periods of economic expansion.

---

[5] It must be noted that opportunity costs could also be altered by increasing reservation wages with employment growth (Bover et al., 2002).

[6] *Some authors have tried to find the delayed effects of the economic cycle on welfare participation by developing autoregressive models (Bartik and Eberts, 1999; Figlio and Ziliak, 1999; Ziliak et al., 2000; and Klerman and Haider, 2000).*

If we focus on unemployment rates at entry in addition to a dynamic consideration of macroeconomic conditions, an alternative assumption of non symmetrical effects of unemployment rates could also be tested. A high unemployment rate at entry could be associated with short spells if the recession does not last long (the number of temporary spells would rise). Low unemployment rates would lead to the opposite (the weight of recipients having long-term spells would increase). The key question is whether or not unemployment effects are different according to the different duration of each welfare spell. In our empirical exercises, a first specification will try to test the effects of the unemployment rate at the beginning of welfare participation. A second specification will focus on a dynamic characterization of unemployment effects.

On the other side, common heterogeneity problems are especially outstanding in the case of welfare populations. Numerous studies have revealed that heterogeneity across recipients has a very varied influence on the dynamics of welfare participation, making the effects of unemployment largely dependent on certain characteristics which are hard to be observed[7]. If unobserved heterogeneity exists, it is possible that the inferences on the reasons for leaving the programmes are subject to error. This is particularly important when analyzing duration dependence. The argument that duration dependence exists has inspired most of recent reforms of welfare programs. A prolonged spell could lead to a worsening of an individual's skills, therefore making access to the job market difficult in spite of employment and earnings improvements.

One potential source of heterogeneity is the variety of participation sequences among welfare recipients. In practice, a significant proportion of households go through multiple participation spells. If individual spells are seen as independent, an incomplete picture of the programmes' dynamics could be obtained, with duration estimates that are biased downwards. There is abundant empirical evidence differentiating long-term (stayers), short-term (leavers) and recurrent recipients (cyclers). If the effects of unemployment differ among these three groups, the estimated durations for the whole set of recipients could be biased.

It seems reasonable to expect that the effects of unemployment would be much more significant for recipients who enter these programmes temporarily. The elasticity of long-term participants to changes in macroeconomic conditions would be relatively low:

$$\frac{\partial E_c^*}{\partial D} < 0, \ \frac{\partial E_l^*}{\partial D} < 0, \ \frac{\partial E_s^*}{\partial D} \approx 0 \qquad (4)$$

where the sub-indices c, l and s denote, respectively, cyclers (recipients with recurrent participation spells), leavers (temporary recipients), and stayers (long-term recipients). It is easy to broaden the aforementioned non-linear hypothesis if unemployment at entry is considered as one of the exogenous factors. High unemployment rates at the beginning of the spell could be related to short spells for cyclers and leavers.

---

[7] See O'Neill et al. (1987), Blank (1989), Hoynes and MaCurdy (1994), Sandefur and Cook (1997), Fortin et al. (1999) and Gottschalk (1997).

3. The IMI Programme

3.1. Characteristics of the IMI Programme

The programme studied in this paper is the Minimum Income Integration programme (*IMI*) of the Madrid Government. We focus on a regional programme due to the fact that welfare programmes are completely decentralized in Spain. The lack of homogenous information for all the Spanish territorial governments has made it necessary to concentrate on a specific experience. The IMI was chosen instead of other programmes due to the fact that its basic parameters are close to the national average, such as per capita costs or the percentage of the population covered by the programme, along with the availability of a database of administrative records that is more complete than those of other regional programmes. To some extent, some conclusions could be extrapolated to other regional schemes.

The IMI programme was implemented in the last quarter of 1990. Based on the French *Revenu minimum d'insertion* and in line with developments in other South European countries and Spanish regions, an attempt was made to combine within a single social welfare instrument the two-fold function of providing an economic safety net and developing "insertion measures" in order to favor transitions into the labour market more quickly than through traditional welfare programmes. The eligibility requirements are similar to those of other European programmes. IMI has an upper age limit (65 years of age, at which claimants can benefit from the national non-contributory pension scheme) and a lower age limit (25 years, except for claimants with dependent children). It also has requirements regarding the prior setting up of a household in an attempt to avoid household units being artificially created to becoming eligible for the programme. Another legal requirement is having a registered residence in the region, which is compatible with the fact that non-Spaniards are entitled to receive benefits.

The benefit is calculated as the difference between the scales set for each type of household and other incomes received. Nominal benefits for single-person households were 354 euros in 2008. This amount is far below the minimum wage. Additionally, real benefits decreased over the period studied because there was no updating of the amounts in some of the years considered. Most welfare programmes in Spain tax 100% of other social benefits and earned income. However, the IMI introduced some exceptions to encourage labour market participation. Once benefits have been approved by the program's managers, recipients must sign an 'insertion contract' with the welfare agencies. Initially, these contracts are intended to improve the recipients' self-sufficiency through an individualized design of 'insertion' measures adjusted both to individual and households' characteristics.

There have not been great regulatory changes during the time the IMI has been in place, allowing us to focus our attention on the main objective of assessing the effects of both individual characteristics and the unemployment rate on the programme's durations. Prior time-series studies have revealed that the programme's evolution has been marked by both the economic cycle as well as institutional specific factors, like changes in the national unemployment benefit scheme (Ayala and Pérez, 2005). Nonetheless, these studies have also shown the important contribution made by demographic factors, such as changes in household structure and the increasing weight of single-parent households and single individuals within the programme.

3.2. The Data

The processing of the programme's administrative records has made over 50,000 spells in the programme available for that period. These records contain a rich array of information on the characteristics of each household. These spells correspond to slightly more than 39,200 households. Of these, 8,500 have left and re-entered the programme at least once. Having administrative records available to study welfare durations provides many advantages. These include very detailed and precise data, a larger number of observations and fewer biases than in surveys. We also have the complete history of the programme, avoiding thereby the usual left-censoring problem[8]. The time period covered by the study is from October 1990 to December 2001. This time period (135 months) is longer than in most studies analyzing multiple welfare spells.

However, the fact that the records have been essentially designed with the needs of administrative management in mind has obliged us to cleaning up and reorganising the data. Different administrative files have been merged, original variables have been cleaned by cross-checking fields, control variables have been added and new variables have been created to adapt the information to the study's goals[9]. Furthermore, in order to construct a suitable file to analyse durations, it was necessary to undertake different types of imputations and adopt alternative decisions regarding how to define programme entries and exits as well as on quarterly IMI participation sequences[10].

Regional unemployment rates from the Labour Force Survey (EPA) have been added as a variable. The data from the Labour Force Survey (*EPA*) for the Madrid region were used to this end. This data is released on a quarterly basis and provides information on the percentage of the unemployed in the labor force. The available information shows the existence of two clearly differentiated sub-periods (Figure 1). Unemployment rose drastically until the mid 1990s due to a dramatic fall in economic activity. The trend then changed and the rate of unemployment gradually declined until it reached its lowest level at the end of the period under study.

A descriptive analysis of the IMI data allows us to give a preliminary assessment of the characteristics of recipients. Table 1 differentiates between the households that completed a spell in the program at some time between 1990 and 2001 and the households that were receiving benefits at the time data were collected. The data on age show a larger presence of middle-aged individuals among household heads. Concerning the differences between completed and ongoing spells, the lower proportion of young people and the greater presence

---

[8] Prior to the beginning of the program there were no general cash assistance schemes in Madrid. Therefore, there were no possibilities of people transferring from other programs to IMI. This fact makes the claim of no left-censoring more persuasive.

[9] The number of observations eliminated is relatively low (10 per cent).

[10] After eliminating inconsistencies in the dates registered, the moment the benefit was first received was considered as the entry date. The exit date was considered as the date when the recipient file was filled in for the last time. A time sequence of twenty-three semesters was defined (from the second half of 1990 to the second half of 2001) to check for possible inconsistencies in trajectories within the programme that could be inferred from the records.

of individuals over 55 in the former stand out[11]. Frequencies of recipients' gender suggest that the program has been increasingly used by women. Regarding household size and type, small households stand out in general. People living alone make up a third of total households and have gained in relative weight over time. The presence of single-parent households is also striking. As expected, educational levels are low as shown by the huge percentage of recipients whose highest attainment is primary education. However, no straight inferences should be made regarding the possibilities for finding a job. Employability frequencies reveal that a non-negligible segment of recipients could access employment now[12].

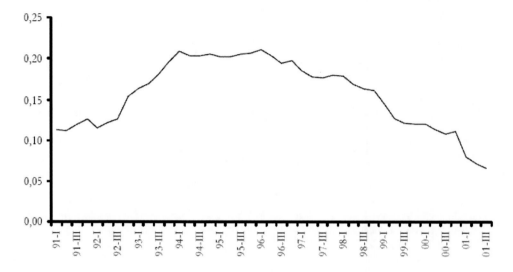

Figure 1. Unemployment Rate.

Table 1. Socio-Economic Characteristics of IMI Recipients (frequency distribution)

	Completed spells, 1990-2001	Ongoing spells, 2001
AGE		
<26	6.7	11.4
26–35	30.9	29.5
36–45	28.7	26.5
46–55	18.0	19.6
56–65	15.7	12.9
GENDER		
Male	40.3	34.2
Female	59.7	65.6

---

[11] This is because of the transfer of recipients to the national non-contributory pension scheme.
[12] Employability is a variable defined by social workers the first time future clients apply for benefits. It takes the lowest level if there are no possibilities of working and a maximum level if recipients could already be in the labour market.

Table 1. Continued

	Completed spells, 1990-2001	Ongoing spells, 2001
HOUSEHOLD SIZE		
1 person	25.8	33.4
2 people	20.6	21.1
3 people	20.2	18.6
4 people	15.5	12.1
5 people	8.9	7.6
6 people	4.7	3.9
7 people	2.2	1.9
8 or more people	2.0	1.3
HOUSEHOLD TYPE		
Single person	25.8	33.4
Lone-parent household	31.6	37.6
Other households with children	20.1	12.0
Other households without children	22.5	17.0
EDUCATION		
Does not read or write	10.3	13.6
No academic qualifications	20.6	21.6
Primary Education	36.7	35.5
Middle School Education	18.1	15.8
Secondary Education	6.6	6.6
Level 1 Vocational Training	2.9	2.3
Level 2 Vocational Training	1.7	1.4
University Degree	1.3	1.3
Post-Graduate Degree	1.5	1.8
LABOUR FORCE STATUS		
Employed	18.0	13.5
Unemployed	59.1	69.0
Inactive	22.9	17.5
EMPLOYABILITY		
Totally unfit for normal work	9.6	8.0
Needs process of social / health	23.8	37.3
recuperation	21.1	25.4
Unemployed needing training /	32.4	21.3
education	8.3	7.0
Could access employment now	4.8	1.1
Does work on hidden economy or		
equivalent		
Does normal work or equivalent		
activity		
Number of observations	(41,996)	(7,568)

3.3. Participation Sequences and Dynamics of the Programme

In addition to observed heterogeneity for all households, differences in participation patterns could give rise to potential unobserved heterogeneity among IMI recipients. As abovementioned, there may be different kinds of welfare recipients according to the number of spells and the probability of recidivism. The characteristics of the different groups are not homogenous and the effects of unemployment and other covariates on the probability of leaving the programme could be affected by the former.

A first and necessary step to address this question is to characterize the dynamics of the programme and the different types of recipients. The debate on welfare reform and dependency problems has been largely associated to the duration of welfare participation. Prolonged welfare spells and low probabilities of leaving the programme could justify the introduction of new measures aimed at reducing durations in the IMI. Table 2 shows the differences in the average durations of spells both for ongoing (censored) and completed spells. In the case of spells that have come to an end, the data reveals a notable concentration of recipients in shorter time intervals. The distribution of ongoing spells shows a profile that is relatively similar, although there are some differences. Though the percentages are higher in the first two intervals the figures are lower than those of the first column, while just the opposite happens with longer-term spells. These results seem lower than the ones estimated for other countries. Nevertheless, any inferences should take into account the few years the program has been in operation, and the IMI's low benefits and replacement rates.

Table 2. Distribution of Spells

	Completed spells	Ongoing spells
< 1 year	6.1	16.6
1 to 2 years	60.8	37.5
3 to 4 years	16.2	13.0
5 to 6 years	8.6	11.3
7 to 8 years	3.9	6.9
9 to 10 years	2.0	5.6
> 10 years	2.3	9.3
TOTAL	100.0	100.0

As discussed above, there could be different types of recipients depending on participation sequences and durations. To examine the effects of unemployment and individual socio-economic characteristics on welfare duration, it seems necessary to verify whether or not there are different types of recipients depending on their temporary, chronic or intermittent spells. Some studies, like Miller's (2002), have attempted to define three types of recipients: *stayers* (households who remain in the programme for a long time), *leavers* (households who leave the programme and remain outside it at least for a minimum period) and *cyclers* (households who enter and leave the programme on a recurrent basis)[13].

---

[13] The definitions for "*leavers*" vary considerably in the different studies that have broached the issue. For instance, "*leavers*" are considered in some studies as recipients who leave the programmes and remain outside them for a period of at least a year (Moffitt and Roff, 2000). Other authors typify them as recipients who leave the programme for at least two consecutive months within a specific time interval (Miller, 2002).

In this paper we divide recipients into three different groups according to the IMI's data. *Cyclers* are defined as those recipients whose information appears more than once, including those censored when data gathering was completed. *Leavers* are those who only registered one spell in the programme that lasted less than 24 months. Finally, *stayers* are recipients who only registered one spell in the programme that lasted 24 months or more (this group may include censored recipients who have spent at least 24 months in the programme). In addition, there would also be another group covering censored observations that cannot be classified as either *cyclers* or *stayers*.

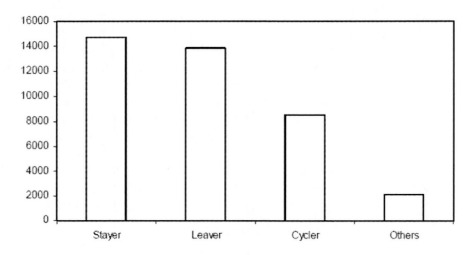

Figure 2. Types of Recipients.

As can be observed in Figure 2, the percentage of households that re-enter the programme is somewhat more than a fifth of the total. According to some of the studies mentioned above, the incidence of recidivism is apparently lower than in the United States or Canada. More than a third of the households that entered the IMI left it and did never return again, at least during the observation period. Benefits helped to maintain these households' incomes during a transitory period. A similar percentage of recipients had long-term spells, concentrating a large part of the programme's resources. In keeping with the previous result, the proportion of households with more than two spells is low (Table 3). Only a seven percent of the recipients have more than two spells.

Table 3. Number of Spells

Spells	Frequency	Percentage	Cumulative Percentage
1	29075	74.10	74.10
2	7347	18.72	92.82
3	2020	5.15	97.97
4	596	1.52	99.49
5	153	0.39	99.88
6	34	0.09	99.97
7	11	0.03	99.99
8	2	0.01	100.00

A central question in the analysis of welfare dynamics is assessing to what extent the probability of leaving the programme increases or decreases with time. An intuitive way to estimate the conditional probability of leaving the IMI resides in using non-parametric methods like the Kaplan-Meier estimator (1958). Recipients may leave the programme in different time periods, $t_1 < t_2 < ... < t_k$. In each period t_j, there are n_j households that remain in the programme and d_j households that leave it. The Kaplan-Meier (KM) estimator is defined as follows:

$$\hat{S}(t) = \prod_{j|t_j \leq t} \left(\frac{n_j - d_j}{n_j} \right)$$

(5)

In order to represent the programme's hazard functions resulting from the application of the estimator, we chose to apply a kernel smoothing procedure. The algorithm put forward by Ramlau-Hansen (1983) was used because of its properties to estimate hazard functions[14].

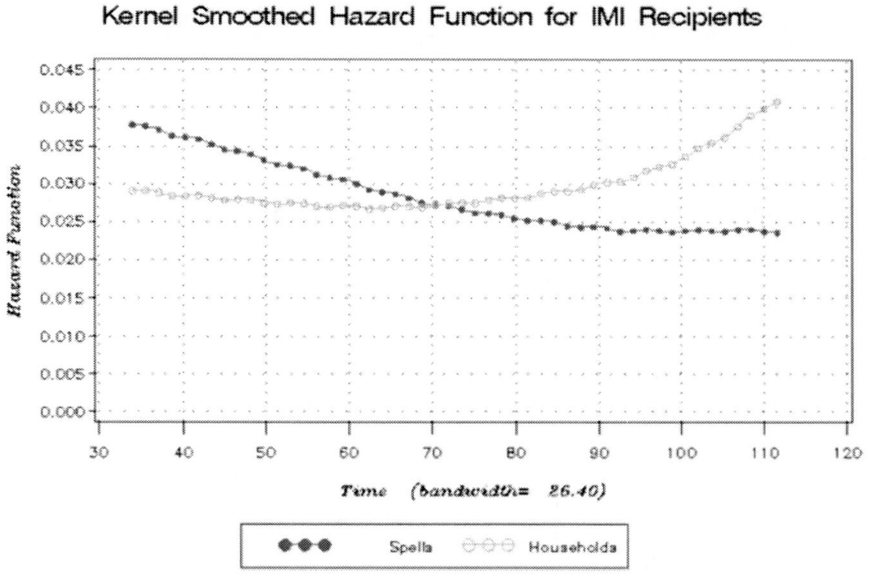

Kernel Smoothed Hazard Function for IMI Recipients

Figure 3. Kaplan-Meier Estimates of the Hazard Function.

As discussed above, two alternative duration distributions can be used to estimate the hazard function. On the one hand, there is an original distribution in which each spell is considered independently. On the other, an alternative distribution can be defined in which households are the unit of reference and their respective durations are constructed by aggregating the length of each spell. Figure 3 shows the profile of the programme's hazard function considering the two distributions. An optimum smoothing parameter was introduced after the different estimates with alternative parameters were studied. The contrast between

---

[14] The filter is defined as $\hat{\lambda}(t) = \frac{1}{b} \int_0^t K\left(\frac{t-s}{b}\right) d\hat{\beta}(s)$, when $b > 0$.

the two functions is striking and clearly differentiated conclusions can be drawn from them. The data corresponding to the spells taken independently indicate the existence of decreasing hazards as duration increases. From this point of view, the programmes would be affected by a certain degree of negative duration dependence. The profile is just the opposite when total time spent in the programme is considered by aggregating the different spells. The probability of leaving the programme rises considerably once recipients have spent between sixty and seventy months in the programme.

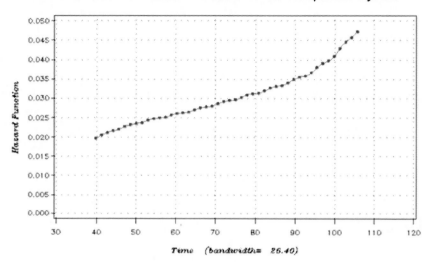

Figure 4. Kaplan-Meier Estimates of the Hazard Function: Cyclers.

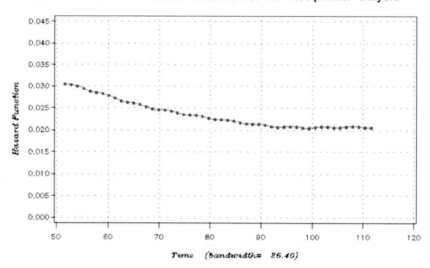

Figure 5. Kaplan-Meier Estimates of the Hazard Function: Stayers.

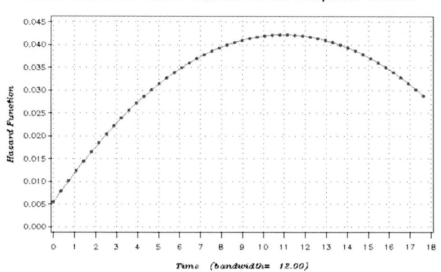

Figure 6. Kaplan-Meier Estimates of the Hazard Function: Leavers.

The asymmetry mentioned above when spells are considered on an independent basis instead of aggregating them gives room for remarkable differences. The existence of a great deal of heterogeneity among recipients with regard to the way they take part in the programme leads to a decreasing probability of leaving the programme over time when spells instead of households are considered. Furthermore, this generalisation disregards the fact that each of the aforementioned groups has its own hazard function. Figures 4, 5 and 6 show the existence of profound divergences in the programme's hazard functions for cyclers and stayers. For the former, it increases monotonously while it decreases in a parabolic way for the latter, without there being any indications of convergence at all with the curve for leavers.

4. Determinants of the Probability of Leaving Welfare

4.1. A Discrete Time Duration Model for the IMI Programme

The previous picture has very different implications concerning the design of welfare policies. First, different results arise when welfare spells are considered as independent observations instead of aggregating them into a single measure of duration. Second, the analysis of aggregate durations could be biased due to substantial differences among stayers, leavers and cyclers. In order to address this issue, we develop a two-step empirical strategy. First, we estimate a discrete time duration model for the probability of leaving the programme[15]. This approach allows us to reinterpret the dynamics of the IMI programme from a perspective of total time on welfare. In keeping with the above discussion, we first test

---

[15] The data is organized so that for each household there are as many data rows as there are time intervals at risk of leaving the programme (one observation for each semester receiving benefits).

the effects of macroeconomic conditions at entry. Second, we estimate an alternative model considering unobserved heterogeneity and a dynamic specification of unemployment.

The use of semi-parametric models has become generalised to study unemployment duration as well as time spent on welfare. These models do not impose forms to the probability distributions of durations. However, due to the specific nature of the administrative records –registered each semester– discrete time regression models could work better for the analysis of the IMI programme. Discrete time duration models can also address the aforementioned questions in a very flexible way. Furthermore, discrete time duration models have the advantage over continuous time models of combining time varying and constant covariates and very flexible specifications of duration dependence (Jenkins, 1995).

Among the different options for discrete time duration models we use here the *log-log* complementary function (Jenkins, 2002). The hazard rate in discrete time of leaving the programme for household *i* in period *j* can be specified as:

$$h_j(X_{ij}) = 1 - \exp\left[-\exp(\beta X_{ij} + \theta(t))\right] \tag{6}$$

where X_{ij} represents the set of explanatory variables (constant or time varying), β represents the coefficients to be estimated and $\theta(t)$ is the functional form of duration dependence. The dependent variable in this model is a logarithmic transformation (the complementary *log-log*) of the hazard rate. The $\theta(t)$ function is specified on the basis of a set of dummies corresponding to each semester of the programme's history. Following Jenkins (2002), if an indicator variable is defined $y_{it}=1$ if household *i* exits the programme during the interval (*t-1,t*) and $y_{it}=0$ otherwise, the likelihood function can be expressed in sequential binary response form:

$$\log L = \sum_{i=1}^{n} \sum_{j=1}^{t_i} \left\{ y_{ijl} \log h_j(X_{ij}) + (1 - y_{ij}) \log\left[1 - h_j(X_{ij})\right] \right\} \tag{7}$$

We estimate this model including in the regression two types of explanatory variables. A first type of variables provides information on the probability of leaving the IMI programme as the welfare spells lengthen over time. Under the idea of introducing more flexibility in the shape of the baseline hazard function we use a non-parametric specification for the baseline hazard with dummy variables for each duration interval. The second kind of variables includes unemployment rates at entry, the age of the household head, employability, the number of concurrent social problems, educational attainment, the household size, along with four dummy variables indicating the head sex, single-parenthood, whether or not it is a single-person household and ethnicity.

The results for the whole set of households reveal that most variables are highly significant (Table 4). The effects exerted by macroeconomic conditions and the various characteristics chosen on the probability of leaving the programme can be differentiated. The variables related to the labour environment highly contribute to the probability of leaving the programme. The coefficient for the unemployment rate at entry reveals that adverse macroeconomic conditions are associated with higher exit rates. Recessions tend to push into these programmes not only individuals suffering from structural problems but also a large proportion of recipients very vulnerable to changes in the economic cycle. The latter enter the programme on a temporary basis and then leave it when economic conditions improve. Some of the supply variables, such as employability or educational attainment, also seem to have a positive and significant effect on the probability of leaving the programme.

Table 4. Results of the Discrete Time Duration Model

	No frailty	Frailty
Unemployment rate at entry	0.025***	0.039***
Age	-0.034***	-0.073***
Employability	0.162***	0.317***
Number of social problems	-0.054***	-0.095***
Educational attainment	0.092***	0.124***
Gender (female=1)	-0.122***	-0.263***
Lone parents	-0.290***	-0.483***
Single person	-0.269***	-0.374***
Ethnic minority	-0.665***	-1.026***
Household size	0.025	0.050
Number of children	-0.011	-0.016
S1	-4.273***	-4.556***
S2	-2.235***	-2.347***
S3	-1.931***	-1.760***
S4	-1.915***	-1.470***
S5	-1.901***	-1.204***
S6	-1.881***	-0.942***
S7	-1.769***	-0.576***
S8	-1.967***	-0.542**
S9	-2.053***	-0.411**
S10	-2.085***	-0.248
S11	-2.102***	-0.080
S12	-2.194***	0.004
S13	-2.022***	0.354
S14	-2.311***	0.224
S15	-1.849***	0.858**
S16	-2.172***	0.710**
S17	-2.075***	0.948**
S18	-2.326***	0.821**
S19	-2.205***	1.055**
S20	-1.844***	1.551***
S21	-1.792***	1.812***
S22	-2.100***	1.634**
S23	-1.953*	1.925*
Gamma variance		1.082***
N	114611	114611
Log L	-44044	-43883

Standard errors in brackets. ***Significant at 99%, **Significant at 95%, *Significant at 90%.

Various socio-demographic characteristics cause longer welfare spells. Among these, belonging to an ethnic minority undoubtedly stands out. Living in a single-parent or a single-person household also increases expected durations, although to a lesser degree. The fact of longer spells for the former type of households is in keeping with the results obtained for the gender variable. These findings therefore confirm the hypotheses previously set out. Unemployment, employability, the type of household and a set of specific socio-demographic characteristics, such as belonging to an ethnic minority, constitute the main determining factors of the probability of leaving welfare.

The coefficients for each semester show that the probability of leaving the programme increases non-monotonically with duration. On the contrary, the size and statistical significance of these coefficients seem to draw a log-normal profile of duration dependence. The probability of leaving the programme increases rapidly for short spells, its pace of increase slows down afterwards and remains more or less constant from then on. To some extent, this profile suggests that the probability of leaving the programme is not too sensitive to cyclical changes, including those related to macroeconomic conditions.

Therefore, to a certain extent taking part in the programme at a given moment in time could not affect too much to preferences or opportunities. Longer spells might not alter income and leisure effects by displacing the utility curve. On the contrary of the general belief of negative duration dependence, potential scarring effects associated to IMI participation would be very small. This result, however, could be affected by relevant information that has not been taken into account in the model's specification. Recipients could have different skills or motivations making the exit from these programs easier for a group of recipients. In fact, we have previously found that individual hazards can be very different according to participation sequences. The possibility of taking recipients' unobserved differences into account is, therefore, necessary in order to assess any possible duration dependence. If these are important, duration dependence in the IMI programme could turn out to be a spurious result.

As it is widely known, neglected heterogeneity can be regarded as omitted variables which can be represented by a random disturbance term. A standard procedure to include unobserved heterogeneity in the previous model is incorporating a gamma distributed random variable (ε_i):

$$h_j\left(X_{ij}\right) = 1 - \exp\left[-\exp\left(\beta X_{ij} + \theta(t) + \log(\varepsilon_i)\right)\right] \qquad (8)$$

The results of the discrete time duration model including unobserved heterogeneity are shown in the second column of Table 4. Results for the gamma variance suggest that unobserved heterogeneity is significant. Comparing both models, it can be appreciated that the profile of dependence derived from duration coefficients does not change too much when unobserved heterogeneity is taken into account. Duration dependence does not seem, therefore, to be related only to omitted information. The fact that there is a strong and significant relationship between the time spent on the programme and the probability of leaving it should be a key question for a better design of welfare reforms.

The estimated coefficients of the covariates in this second model are remarkably larger and they all have the expected signs. It appears that non accounting for unobserved heterogeneity not only induces an under-estimate of the extent to which the hazard rate changes with duration, but also reduces the magnitude of the effects of covariates on the probability of leaving the programme. This change is especially remarkable in the case of employability –with a rather larger impact on exits from the programme when the problem of unobserved heterogeneity is taken into account– and belonging to an ethnic minority, with the opposite sign.

However, new doubts arise about the specification of macroeconomic conditions. Our initial hypotheses suggested that the effects of unemployment might considerably differ for the different types of recipients. This could also mean that the impact of unemployment on the probability of leaving the programme could change for the same household during different stages of a prolonged spell. In this sense, an extended version of the discrete time model relaxing the hypothesis of constant effects of unemployment could yield more relevant policy insights. We can also test the effects of macroeconomic conditions considering changes in the unemployment rate instead of the rates at the beginning of welfare participation.

Table 5. Results of the Discrete Time Duration Model with Interactions (current unemployment rate)

	No frailty	Frailty	No frailty	Frailty
S1	-7.456^{***}	-8.332^{***}	-8.365^{***}	-8.369^{***}
S2	-2.471^{***}	-3.397^{***}	-3.377^{***}	-3.432^{***}
S3	-1.018^{***}	-1.927^{***}	-1.923^{***}	-1.963^{***}
S4	-0.470^{***}	-1.254^{***}	-1.374^{***}	-1.295^{***}
S5	-0.501^{***}	-1.094^{***}	-1.406^{***}	-1.144^{***}
S6	-0.638^{***}	-1.009^{***}	-1.542^{***}	-1.068^{***}
S7	-0.707^{***}	-0.864^{***}	-1.608^{***}	-0.931^{***}
S8	-0.887^{***}	-0.882^{***}	-1.786^{***}	-0.956^{***}
S9	-1.047^{***}	-0.897^{***}	-1.940^{***}	-0.976^{***}
S10	-0.705^{***}	-0.439^{**}	-1.601^{***}	-0.522^{*}
S11	-0.685^{***}	-0.284	-1.583^{***}	-0.372
S12	-0.658^{**}	-0.076	-1.553^{***}	-0.172
S13	-0.526^{**}	0.229	-1.419^{***}	0.128
S14	-0.458	0.432	-1.343^{***}	0.326
S15	-0.661^{**}	0.358	-1.543^{***}	0.248
S16	-0.961^{**}	0.157	-1.848^{***}	0.044
S17	-1.007^{*}	0.156	-1.891^{**}	0.044
Unemployment rate			-1.190^{***}	-0.016
Age	-0.075^{***}	-0.054^{***}	-0.033^{***}	-0.052^{***}
Employability	0.134^{***}	0.254^{***}	0.152^{***}	0.250^{***}
Number of social problems	-0.077^{***}	-0.082^{***}	-0.055^{***}	-0.080^{***}
Educational attainment	0.038^{***}	0.116^{***}	0.086^{***}	0.116^{***}
Gender (female=1)	-0.203^{***}	-0.196^{***}	-0.117^{***}	-0.189^{***}
Lone parents	-0.329^{***}	-0.328^{***}	-0.281^{***}	-0.398^{***}
Single person	-0.509^{***}	-0.328^{***}	-0.267^{***}	-0.317^{***}
Ethnic minority	-0.710^{***}	-0.891^{***}	-0.655^{***}	-0.881^{***}
Household size	-0.167^{***}	0.045	0.015	0.048
Number of children	0.005	-0.023	-0.012	-0.023

Table 5. Continued

	No frailty	Frailty	No frailty	Frailty
(S1*unemployment rate)	0.252***	0.246***	0.443***	0.262***
(S2*unemployment rate)	0.094***	0.097***	0.284***	0.112***
(S3*unemployment rate)	0.026***	0.038***	0.216***	0.053**
(S4*unemployment rate)	-0.008*	0.006	0.182***	0.021
(S5*unemployment rate)	-0.005	0.007	0.185***	0.022
(S6*unemployment rate)	0.005	0.012*	0.195***	0.027
(S7*unemployment rate)	0.017**	0.020**	0.206***	0.035*
(S8*unemployment rate)	0.014*	0.017**	0.204***	0.032
(S9*unemployment rate)	0.019**	0.020**	0.209***	0.036
(S10*unemployment rate)	-0.006	-0.006	0.184***	0.010
(S11*unemployment rate)	-0.010	-0.012	0.180***	0.004
(S12*unemployment rate)	-0.019	-0.027	0.171***	-0.011
(S13*unemployment rate)	-0.017	-0.032*	0.172***	-0.016
(S14*unemployment rate)	-0.048**	-0.067**	0.140***	-0.052
(S15*unemployment rate)	0.004	-0.019	0.193***	-0.003
(S16*unemployment rate)	0.001	-0.026	0.190***	-0.010
(S17*unemployment rate)	0.012	-0.017	0.201***	-0.002
Gamma variance		0.652***		0.622***
N	114611	114611	114611	114611
Log L	-43926	-43691	-43783	-43690

Standard errors in brackets. ***Significant at 99%, **Significant at 95%, *Significant at 90%.

A natural approach for a dynamic specification of unemployment considering the time spent on welfare consists of including interactions between the semesters' dummies and the unemployment rate. Table 5 shows the results of these new estimates with and without variables representing unobserved heterogeneity and the current unemployment rate[16]. In general terms, introducing these interactions produces similar coefficients and signs of the relevant covariates. The main change can be observed in duration dependence results and in the interactions between macroeconomic conditions and duration of welfare participation. The specification of duration dependence yields a clearer picture than the one previously tested, with coefficients rather larger. Figure 7 shows that in the short-term the probability of leaving the programme substantially increases, coming to a halt when recipients spend two years in the programme. This at least suggests that targeted intensive actions for improving the labour and social opportunities of new recipients might be important to reduce potential problems of welfare dependency.

---

[16] We consider the possible number of interactions allowed by multicollinearity and significance constraints.

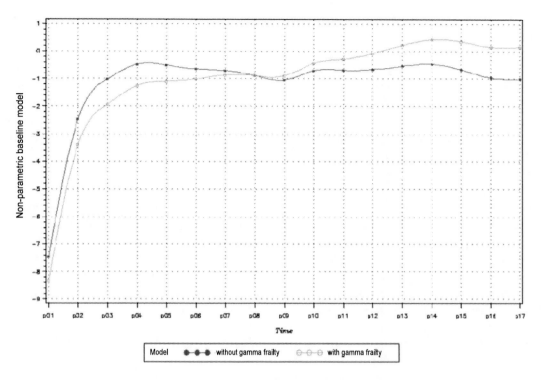

Figure 7. Duration dependence coefficients.

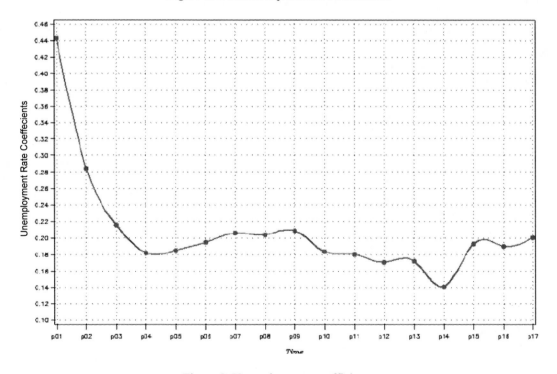

Figure 8. Unemployment coefficients.

Regarding unemployment, there seems to be a strong and significant relationship between unemployment and the probability of leaving the programme. High current unemployment rates reduce the probability of leaving welfare. This result is also in keeping with the one forecasted by the standard model of welfare participation. However, when unobserved heterogeneity is taken into account we find that current unemployment rates are not significant. This result may be due to a potential multicollinearity problem related to the interactions with time. In practice, the effects of these interactions are much better defined for the first semesters than for longer durations. In keeping with the previous hypothesis of strong effects of unemployment at entry these coefficients are positive and high in the case of the first three semesters. It can also be observed that the impact of unemployment clearly diminishes with time. These coefficients are depicted in Figure 8. In contrasting evidence with the results for short spells, the effects of macroeconomic conditions are very modest when recipients remain in the programme for long time periods. In short, our results give general support to the notion that, to a high degree of statistical confidence, the effects of unemployment clearly decrease with time.

In general terms, results appear to be consistent with the preliminary hypotheses and earlier research. This allows us to simulate changes in the hazards given a fixed vector of characteristics. Figure 9 uses the coefficients resulting from the discrete time model to simulate the effects of changes in employability and unemployment on the probability of leaving the programme. For each one of these variables we consider the highest, the average and the lowest values in the dataset, holding constant the values of the other variables. We use as reference categories women, with low educational level, aged 26-35, no single-parent household, no single person, in a household with 2-4 members, and not belonging to an ethnic minority. For each case we consider the mean and median values of the distribution of estimated hazards.

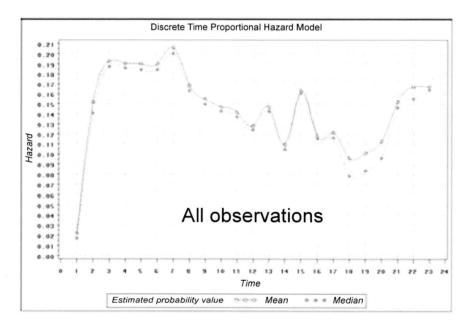

Figure 9. Continued on next page.

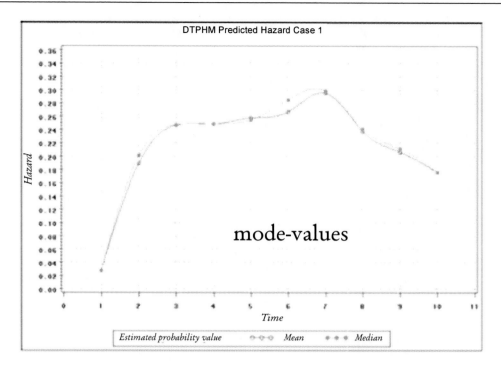

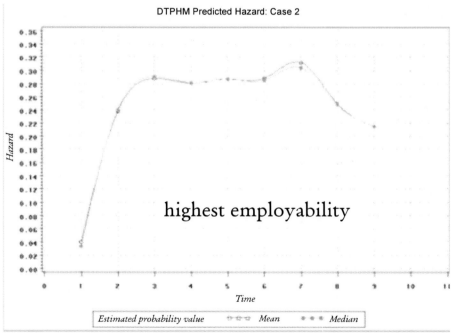

Figure 9. Continued on next page.

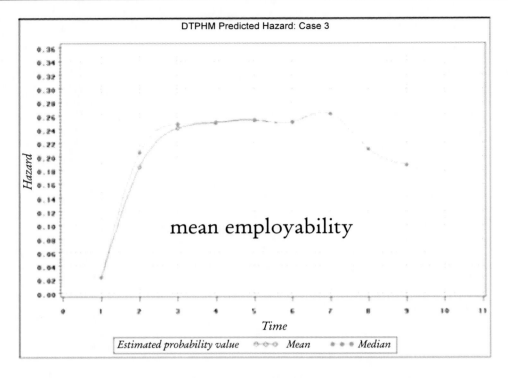

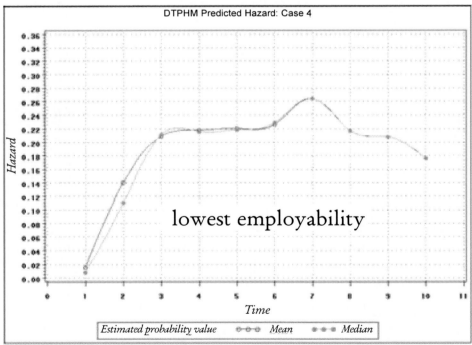

Figure 9. Continued on next page.

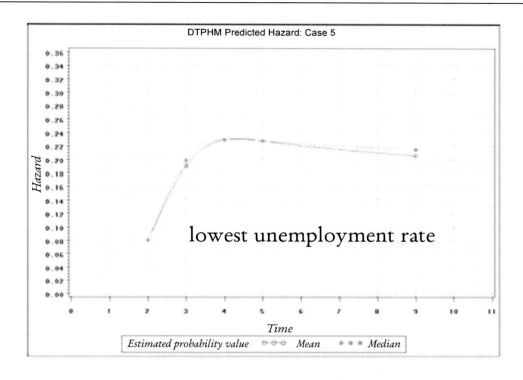

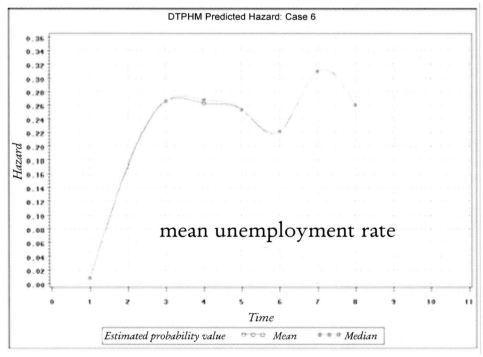

Figure 9. Continued on next page.

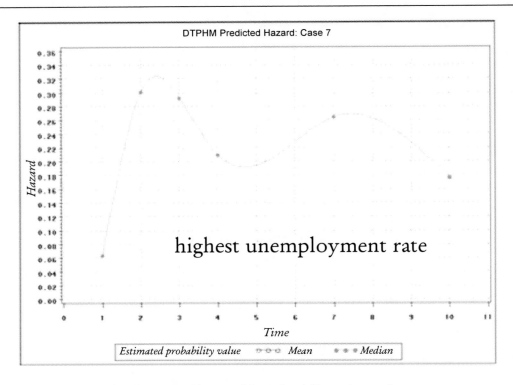

Figure 9. Variations in expected hazars with employability and unemployment at entry.

The first two figures show the hazards for the estimated model with all the observations and with the mode-values, respectively. As pointed out before, the hazard presents a log-normal profile, rapidly increasing the probability of leaving the programme for short spells, slowing down afterwards and remaining more or less constant from then on. Simulations show that employability seems important in determining how quickly households will leave welfare. Moving from a situation of low to high employability gives rise to around a 15 percent increase of the probability of leaving the IMI programme[17]. The hazards are systematically higher for the highest levels of employability. The estimated hazards for different rates of unemployment at the beginning of the spells show more different patterns. Both for short and long-term durations, entering into the programme with higher unemployment rates is associated with a higher probability of leaving it. As stated before, many recipients enter the programme on a temporary basis and then leave it when economic conditions improve.

4.2. Multiple Spells and Unobserved Heterogeneity

One of the key assumptions in our basic model is that all the inter-individual heterogeneity is due to observed variables. It is this assumption which enables us to write the likelihood function as a product of independent binary probabilities. As outlined by different authors in the analysis of unemployment duration, on the presence of unobserved

[17] These estimates correspond to durations of seven semesters.

characteristics correlated over time this independence assumption would be violated, resulting in inconsistent parameter estimates (Narendranathan and Stewart, 1993). Given the results of the estimated models, neglecting unobserved heterogeneity seems to cause a bias in the duration dependence estimation. Such heterogeneity is also likely to bias downwards the effects of unemployment and individual characteristics on the probability of leaving the programme.

There is considerable evidence showing that the results of frailty models using gamma distributions are largely subject to possible misleading estimates in discrete time duration models[18]. One way to address this problem is by exploring the multiple spells nature of IMI data. Our previous results showed that the hazard functions for leavers, stayers and cyclers considerably differ from each other. An advantage of the availability of different spells for the same individuals resides in the possibility of considering different methods for addressing the problem of unobserved heterogeneity. When events are repeatable, it is relatively easy to separate the true hazard function from unobserved heterogeneity. However, there could be a problem of dependence among observations amplifying the difficulties caused by unobserved heterogeneity (Allison, 1995). This dependence will add the problem of biased standard errors to those of artificiality declining hazard functions and attenuated coefficients. Some of the effects previously found for unemployment and individual characteristics could be distorted if both problems are not taken into account.

Table 6. Results of the Models with Multiple Spells

	Pooled model	Second spell model	WLW model	FEPL model
Unemployment rate at entry	0.024***	0.044***	0.030***	0.124***
Age	-0.027**	0.014*	-0.034**	-0.027**
Employability	0.132***	-0.001	0.140***	0.348***
Number of social problems	-0.052***	-0.029**	-0.059***	-0.052***
Educational attainment	0.074***	0.002	0.078***	0.074***
Gender (female=1)	-0.106***	-0.013	-0.110***	-0.106***
Lone parents	-0.227***	-0.043*	-0.227***	-0.227***
Single person	-0.227***	-0.034	-0.295***	-0.227***
Ethnic minority	-0.625***	-0.294***	-0.643***	-0.625***
Household size	0.027	0.008	0.038	0.027
Number of children	-0.004	-0.002	0.008	-0.004
Duration of the first spell		-0.002***		
N	21351	17368	21351	21351

Standard errors in brackets. ***Significant at 99%, **Significant at 95%, *Significant at 90%.

There are different ways to address the problems of serial dependence and unobserved heterogeneity in a multiple spells framework. A very ad-hoc procedure to detect dependence among the individual spells is pooling them together and estimating a single model. Then it

---

[18] Nicoletti and Rondinelli (2006) explored the effects of misspecifying the random effects distribution in discrete time duration models finding few biases for duration dependence and the covariate coefficients estimation. The biases were larger when the error distribution was misspecified, assuming a normal or an extreme value distribution instead of a logistic one.

can be estimated a model for the second spell with the duration of the first spell as a covariate. A significant relationship could be interpreted as a sign of serial dependence. Following this procedure, the general model of the previous section including unemployment rates at entry and different individual covariates can be estimated again by treating each spell as a distinct observation.

The results of the pooled model are presented in the first column of Table 6. The overall magnitude and signs of the coefficients are consistent with the previous results. These new findings confirm again the initial hypotheses: high rates of unemployment at the beginning of the spells and high employability levels appear to be determinants of a higher probability of leaving welfare. However, as stated above, pooling the spells without taking the dependence among them into account can give rise to biased estimates (Allison, 1995). To the extent that dependence among spells can be thought of as arising from unobserved heterogeneity it seems necessary to detect its magnitude.

The second column of table 6 presents the result of a model for the second spell using the duration of the first spell as a covariate. There are two noteworthy results. First, the duration of the first spell has a highly significant negative coefficient, indicating that prolonged initial spells are associated with low hazards in future spells. Therefore, there is dependence that must be corrected. Second, the coefficients for the other covariates have changed substantially from the values in the pooled model, despite unemployment at entry still has a positive and significant effect. This is a further indication that dependence may be influencing the results in some way.

In any case, the model for the second spell including the duration of the first spell is only a tool for detecting serial dependence. The coefficients are not necessarily any better than those estimated in the previous models. It shows us that the pooled estimations must be corrected taking into account unobserved heterogeneity. There are several methods to deal with this problem in situations where individuals experience repeated welfare spells. Most of them impose specific structures of dependence among spells. Wei *et al.* (1989) proposed a method for getting robust variance estimates allowing for dependence among multiple event times that avoids making assumptions about the structure of the dependence (WLW method). However, there is no correction for biases arising from unobserved heterogeneity. In this approach, we can model the marginal distribution of the duration of each spell and the model's parameters are estimated by maximizing the failure-specific partial likelihoods.

The results of the WLW method for the first four spells are presented in the third column of Table 6. These results can be compared with the pooled estimates of the first column. There are no big differences, with the coefficients remaining about the same. Their values are slightly higher in the WLW method. Therefore, the general conclusions concerning the role of unemployment at entry and employability and other individual characteristics still hold in a pooled model when the problem of dependence among the multiple spells is addressed.

There are other ways to correct the problem of serial dependence, focusing not only on standard errors and test statistics but also on the bias caused by unobserved heterogeneity. Chamberlain (1984) proposed a model of multiple spells that explicitly introduces a disturbance term representing unobserved heterogeneity. We follow this approach opting by a fixed-effects model assuming that this term is a set of fixed effects constants rather than a random variable (FEPL method). This disturbance term is allowed to be correlated with any of the covariates.

One drawback of the FEPL method is that it can only estimate coefficients for covariates varying across the successive spells for each individual. The two variables that vary over time in our data are employability and unemployment. A fixed-effects analysis for these variables yields similar results to those of the initial pooled model. The results of the FEPL method for the first four spells are presented in the fourth column of Table 6. The coefficient for unemployment is positive and highly significant and a similar result is found for employability. These coefficients are rather larger than those of the uncorrected pooled and the WLW models. Nevertheless, they confirm again that unemployment and employability largely contribute to the probability of leaving the program.

5. Summary and Conclusions

The reforms implemented to welfare programmes in recent years have led to a growing interest in their dynamic aspects. The two-fold critique of growing spending and work disincentives has given rise to an intense debate concerning the design of traditional programmes and the possibilities opened up by the recent reforms. Their outcomes, however, can only be assessed properly if there is good knowledge about entry and exit processes, as well as about the determining factors that shorten or lengthen welfare spells. In this sense, an adequate assessment of macroeconomic conditions seems to be crucial in order to properly understand the possibilities and constraints of public intervention.

The main aim of this study has been to offer an accurate description of these processes by using an analytical model in which welfare duration is dependent on both macroeconomic conditions and recipients' individual characteristics. In order to do so, the Madrid Government's minimum income programme was taken as reference and an alternative model was put forward. The main components of this procedure consist of taking into consideration both a large set of socio-demographic characteristics as well as the unemployment rate upon entry into the programme and a dynamic specification of unemployment effects.

First, we find that there are clearly differentiated types of recipients depending on the recurrence and duration of welfare participation. Second, the unemployment rate at the moment of entering the programme seems to be a relevant factor, but having less weight than that exerted by the recipients' socio-demographic characteristics. However, the combination of macroeconomic and individual factors could differ notably among the three groups defined in the study according to participation sequences. Neglecting this source of heterogeneity could give rise to misleading inferences. Third, the broadening of the analytical model by taking into account different specifications and unobserved heterogeneity reinforces the general conclusions. The probability of leaving the programme is systematically higher for the highest levels of employability and the effects of unemployment clearly decrease with time.

References

Allison, P.D. (1995): *Survival Analysis Using the SAS System: A Practical Guide,* Cary, NC: SAS Institute Inc.

Ashenfelter, O. (1983): "Determining Participation in Income-Tested Social Programmes", *Journal of the American Statistical Association,* **78**, 517-526.

Ayala, L. and Pérez, C. (2005): "Macroeconomic Conditions, Institutional Factors and Demographic Structure: What Causes Welfare Caseloads?". *Journal of Population Economics,* **3/05,** 563-581.

Ayala, L. and Rodríguez, M (2004): "Multiple Ocurrence of Welfare Recipiency: Determinants and Policy Implications", Instituto de Estudios Fiscales, *Working Paper* **13/2004**.

Ayala, L. and Rodríguez, M (2007): "Barriers to employment and welfare duration", *Journal of Policy Modeling.* **29,** 237-257.

Bartik, T. and Eberts, R. (1999): "Examining the Effect of Industry Trends and Structure on Welfare Caseloads". In Danziger, S.H. (ed.) (1999): *Economic Conditions and Welfare Reform.* Michigan: Upjohn Institute for Employment Research.

Blank, R. (1989): "Analyzing the Length of Welfare Spells", *Journal of Public Economics*, **39,** 245-273.

Blank, R.M. (2001): "What Causes Public Assistance Caseloads to Grow?", *Journal of Human Resources*, **36,** 85-118.

Blank, R.M. (2002): "Evaluating Welfare Reform in the United States", *Journal of Economic Literature,* **40**: 1105-1166

Blank, R. and Ruggles, P. (1994): "Sort-Term Recidivism among Public Assistance Recipients", *American Economic Review,* **84,** 49-53.

Bell, S.H. (2001): "Why Are Welfare Caseloads Falling?", *The Urban Institute, Assessing the New Federalism Discussion Papers.* no. **01-02**.

Bover, O., Arellano, M. and Bentolila, S. (2002): "Unemployment Duration, Benefit Duration and the Business Cycle", *Economic Journal,* **112,** 223-265.

Brandon, P. (1995): "Vulnerability to Future Dependence Among Former AFDC Mothers", Institute for Research on Poverty, *Discussion Paper* no. **1055-95**.

Cao, J. (1996): "Welfare Recipiency and Welfare Recidivism", Institute for Research on Poverty, *Discussion. Paper* no. **1081-96**.

Carrington, W.J., Mueser, R. and Troske, K.R. (2002): "The Impact of Welfare Reform on Leaver Characteristics, Employment and Recidivism". *IZA Discussion. Paper* n° **561**, Bonn.

Chamberlain, G. (1984): "Heterogeneity, Omitted Variable Bias and Duration Dependence". En Heckman, J. and Singer, B. (eds.): *Longitudinal Analyses of Labor Market Data.* New York: Academic Press.

Figlio, D.N. and Ziliak, J.P. (1999): "Welfare Reform, the Business Cycle and the Decline in AFDC Caseloads". In Danziger, S.H. (ed.): *Economic Conditions and Welfare Reform.* Michigan: Upjohn Institute for Employment Research.

Fortin, B.; Lacroix, G. and Thibault, J.F. (1999): "The Interaction of UI and Welfare, and the Dynamics of Welfare Participation of Single Parents", *Canadian Public Policy,* **25**: 115-132.

Frederikseny, A., Honoré, B.E., and Hu, L. (2006): "Discrete Time Duration Models with Group-level Heterogeneity", *SIEPR Policy.* paper No. **05-008**.

Gottschalk, P. (1997): "Has 'Welfare Dependency' Increased?", *Institute for Research on Poverty*, n°**1147-97**.

Green, D.A. and Warburton, W.P. (2001): "Tightening a Welfare System: The Effects of Benefit Denial on Future Welfare Receipt", University of British Columbia, WP n°02-07.

Grogger, J. (2005): "Markov Forecasting Methods for Welfare Caseloads", *NBER Working Paper* n°**11682**.

Grogger, J. and Karoly, L.A. (2005): Welfare Reform: effects of a Decade of Change, Cambridge, M.A.: Harvard University Press.

Harris, K.M. (2000): "Life after Welfare: Women, Work and Repeat Dependency", *American Sociological Review,* **61**, 407-426.

Hoynes, H. and MaCurdy, T. (1994): "Has the Decline in Benefits Shortened Welfare Spells?", *American Economic Review,* **84**: 43-48.

Jenkins, S.P. (1995): "Easy Estimation Methods for Discrete-Time Duration Models", *Oxford Bulletin of Economics and Statistics,* **57**, 129-138.

Jenkins, S.P. (2002): "Estimation of Discrete Time (Grouped Duration Data) Proportional Models: pgmhaz". ESRC Research Centre on Micro-Social Change, University of Essex (mimeo).

Kaplan, E.L. and Meier, P. (1958): "Nonparametric Estimation from Incomplete Observations", *Journal of the American Statistical Association,* **53**, 457-481.

Keng, S.H.; Garasky, S. and Jensen, H.H. (2000): "Welfare Dependence, Recidivism and the Future for Recipients of Temporary Assistance for Needy Families", Center for Agricultural and Rural Development, Iowa State University, Working Paper 00-WP 242.

Klerman, J. and Haider, S. (2000): "A Stock-Flow Analysis of the Welfare Caseload: Insights from California Economic Conditions". RAND, Santa Monica, CA.

Layard, R., Nickell, S. and Jackman, R. (1991): *Unemployment. Macroeconomic Performance and the Labour Market.* Oxford University Press.

Machin, S. and Manning, A. (1999): "The Causes and Consequences of Longterm Unemployment in Europe". In Ashenfelter, O. and Card, D. (eds.): *Handbook of Labor Economics,* vol. 3. Elsevier, Amsterdam.

Mayer, S.E. (2000): "Why Welfare Caseloads Fluctuate: A Review of Research on AFDC, SSI and the Food Stamps Program". The New Zealand Treasury Working Paper 00/7.

Meyer, D.R. and Cancian, M. (2000): "Life after Welfare", *Public Welfare,* **54**, 25-29.

Miller, C. (2002): *Leavers, Stayers and Cyclers: An Analysis of the Welfare Caseload,* Manpower Demonstration Research Corporation.

Moffitt, R. (1992): "Incentive Effects of the U.S. Welfare System: A Review", *Journal of Economic Literature,* **30**, 1-61.

Moffitt, R. (2001): "The Temporary Assistance for Needy Families Program". In Moffitt, R. (ed.): *Means-Tested Programs in the United States.* Chicago: NBER and University of Chicago Press.

Moffitt, R.,(2002): "Welfare Programs and Labor Supply". In: Auerbach, J.M. and M. Feldstein (Eds.): *Handbook of Public Economics*, vol.4. Ámsterdam: North-Holland.

Moffitt, R. and Roff, J. (2000): "The Diversity of Welfare Leavers". Policy Brief 00-2. Baltimore: John Hopkins University.

Moffitt, R. and Stevens, J. (2001): "Changing Caseloads: Macro Influences and Micro Composition", *Federal Reserve Bank of New York Economic Policy,* September 2001, 37-51.

Mortensen, D. (1977): "Unemployment insurance and job search decisions", *Industrial and Labor Relations Review,* **30**, 505-17.

Narendranathan, W. and Stewart, M.B. (1993): "How Does the Benefit Effect Vary as Unemployment Spells Lengthen?", *Journal of Applied Econometrics,* **8**, 361-381.

Nickel, S. (1979): ""The Effect of Unemployment and Related Benefits on the Duration of Unemployment," *Economic Journal,* **89**, 34-49.

Nicoletti, C. and Rondinelli, C. (2006): "The (mis)specification of discrete time duration models with unobserved heterogeneity: a Monte Carlo study", *ISER Working Paper* **2006-53**.

O'Neill, J.A.; Bassie, L.J. and Wolf, D.A. (1987): "The Duration of Welfare Spells", *The Review of Economics and Statistics,* **69**, 241-248.

Ramlau-Hansen, H. (1983): "Smoothing Counting Process Intensities by Means of Kernel Functions", *The Annals of Statistics,* **11**, 453-466.

Sandefur, G.D. and Cook, S.T. (1997): "Duration of Public Assistance Receipt: Is Welfare a Trap?". Institute for Research on Poverty, *Discussion Paper* no. **1129-97.**

Stapleton, D.; Livermore, G. and Tucker, A. (1997): *Determinants of AFDC Caseload Growth.* Department of Health and Human Services, Washington.

Ziliak, J., Figlio D.N., Davis E.E. and Connolly, L. (2000): "Accounting for the Decline in AFDC Caseloads: Welfare Reform or the Economy?" *Journal of Human Resources.* **35**(3): 570–586.

Weeks, G. (1991): "Leaving Public Assistance in Washington State", Washington State Institute for Public Policy.

Wei, L.J.; Lin, D.Y. and Weissfeld, L. (1989): "Regression Analysis of Multivariate Incomplete Failure Time Data by Modeling Marginal Distributions", *Journal of the American Statistical Association,* **84**, 1065-1073.

In: Low Incomes: Social, Health and Educational Impacts   ISBN: 978-1-60741-175-8
Editor: Jacob K. Levine, pp. 141-159   © 2009 Nova Science Publishers, Inc.

Chapter 6

SOCIETAL CHALLENGES IN LOW-INCOME HOUSING: LEARNING FROM THE SRI LANKAN EXPERIENCE

Ranjith Dayaratne
Department of Civil Engineering and Architecture
University of Bahrain; Bahrain

Abstract

This paper looks at the housing experiences of Sri Lanka over the past four decades during which it has adopted both 'top-down', regulated approaches to 'bottom-up' flexible practices to address the issues of low–income housing. It focuses on the issues of social perceptions, engagements, expectations, values and mechanisms of interactions between people and the state that are at the core of the housing problem which often lead to the construction of impoverished and improvised shelter. While the strategies most governments adopt such as low-cost building technologies, enabling the acquisition of land, infra-structure and finance and offering support to resolve the construction issues are useful and important, addressing the underlying social challenges are key to unlocking the potentials that exist in the low-income communities to house themselves well. The paper offers insights into how the complexities of these social challenges have been confronted in Sri Lanka through support housing and will suggest the way forward in dealing with them in order to devise more meaningful and positive interventions n low-income housing.

Introduction

For decades, many governments around the world have been struggling to house their low-income communities in socially acceptable settlements. Starting with the 'provision' approach that dominated the 1970s, housing practices shifted to 'supporting' in the 1990s reversing the top-down methods to bottom-up ones while accepting that the people themselves are the main actors of the housing process. Despite these enlightened and community-based strategies to engage the low-income communities and set-up holistic programs to provide alternatives to the slums, the shanties and the improvised shelters of the poor, majority of the world's low-income communities continue to live in structures that are unacceptable as living accommodation in the contemporary societies. Although Sri Lanka innovated the support approach to housing and persuaded the United Nations to declare 1987 as the International Year of Shelter for example, 51% of the capital Colombo's housing stock is still constituted of slums, old settlements and shanties. Undeniably, huge challenges exist in transforming such low-income settlements to decent acceptable housing and in ensuring their continuity into the future.

Housing as a Problem

A small island nation off the southern tip of India, Sri Lanka had not seen housing as a problem during its long civilized history during which a number of well-planned cities and human settlements had existed up until the late 19th century subsequent to colonization. Undeniably, this has been the case in many countries where the question of providing accommodation to increasing populations and the new families were taken care of by the communities themselves through traditions, cultural norms and social and societal practices. Extended families and shared living or multi-habitations were the main mechanisms of the traditional communities and the responsibility of housing the new families were shouldered by the families themselves. In the traditional communities in Sri Lanka, extended living safeguarded against land and house sub-divisions and ensured shared consumption of these resources. Moreover, as having been comprised largely of peasant communities, families hardly abandoned their ancestral places of residence to re-locate elsewhere either for want of employment or otherwise. Villages grew and expanded slowly for which purpose ample land was available around the villages themselves. New house constructions employed village labor and material such as mud for bricks and tiles and timber came from the surrounding forest reserves.

It was only at the beginning of the 19th century that the state got involved in the provision of housing when the British government whose occupation of the island began in 1855, took over administration from the largest to the smallest entity and began employing people for state service and locating them away from their places of residence. Thus the school teachers, railway workers and other government servants had to be provided with accommodation in the form of 'government quarters' as a standard practice. Government service offered stable employment, housing accommodation and pensions and the expectations among the ordinary people shifted from working in agriculture to securing government jobs in order to acquire wealth and stability of income that could lead to own modern houses and properties.

At the same time, much of vacant land in villages were confiscated as state land and the traditional practice of village expansions were curtailed and material resources for building became limited. The World War II aggravated the situation when all resources were channeled away from welfare to war efforts and restrictions on resources became the norm. State control of land and vegetation therein, coupled with a social system that replaced self-employment as peasants who owned land with government employment created a society of land-less families whose children could not house themselves unless they found government employment, became entrepreneurs or inherited property from the parents. The poor, the peasants and the low-paid state workers therefore were increasingly left in the dark unable to become property owners.

Moreover, much of state land in the hill country were transformed into tea estates and led the industrialization process. Colombo to which the railways brought the tea for export evolved as a commercial and industrial capital attracting factory workers whose accommodation needs had to be met. In the absence of affordable rented accommodations, many occupied state lands and erected temporary shelters in the city while urban residents also quickly erected substandard huts for rent in order to gain from the demand for cheap housing.

There is no evidence however that during the colonial rule, housing the poor has been seen as a problem and a government responsibility, except those of the state workers. Indeed it is only a generation later, particularly since independence in 1948, what began as a way of providing accommodation for state workers transformed itself into a housing problem that transferred the provision of accommodating large populations in both the city and the village as a government responsibility. Although the provision of 'government quarters' was still the responsibility of the respective ministry assisted by the Public Works Department (PWD), in 1952, a ministry of housing was also established to tackle the problems that arose from a multitude of situations such as the middle-income, homeless and the squatters.

Early Housing Solutions

The earliest of the solutions to the shortage of housing in Sri Lanka has been thus driven by the notion that the government must 'provide'; lands and houses built upon them; the model having evolved from government quarters. At the same time, the municipality system and the practice of professions had evolved particularly with regard to the government service. Land surveyors, engineers and architects were attached mainly to the state sector and became the main actors of development. Thus state allocated land, employed architects to design and engaged contractors to build. Limited by resources and the need to build as many houses as possible, the underlying forces demanded that the houses were small, comprised of basic facilities and the costs were minimal. 'Low-cost' emerged as the principle approach particularly where the recovery of the costs involved were perceived to be in question. A number of housing strategies were adopted to reach out to the people in different situations; the low-cost, low-income and middle income housing projects and the walk-up-flats.

Low cost housing was constructed in the peripheral disadvantaged sites of Colombo to which the squatters were re-located often without their expressed consent, while middle-class housing projects in more affluent suburbs were distributed through the mechanism of mortgages; the government financing the initial project costs and distributing them through the state mortgage bank set up primarily as a lending institution to facilitate housing. Flats and housing schemes as they were popularly known proliferated in and around the capital city Colombo and its suburbs and these became the outstanding achievements of the state intervention in housing. [1]

However, these efforts to provide housing for the needy were continuously constrained by many intrinsic historic and social factors. One of the most significant among them was that people were considerably poor and had very limited levels of affordability, economy being

---

[1] The most well-known middle income housing schemes among them were the Narahenpita flats, Bambalapitiya flats, Maligawatte flats, police flats at Thimbirigasyaya, and government flats in Havelock town.

driven by agriculture and small-scale industries. Unlike in the traditional communities where collective labor of the village was available to build the houses, it was no more the case with the emergence of government-employed, state-dependant, nuclear-family based new communities. Government failed to provide as expected and the housing short-fall began to increase.

The shortfall of housing however cannot be seen as a simple housing issue alone. In fact, the breakdown of the traditional systems and the emergence of a society driven by the rising bourgeois class had a devastating impact on the communities; particularly the youth. Having shifted from agriculture and having abandoned farming as a vocation, the educated youth found unemployment on the increase which had a reciprocal effect on housing. The frustrations among the youth discontent about the dominance of the rich and the powerful political middle class led to a government that was centre-left but was constituted also of extreme left parties. State moved for social reform, distribution of resources and equity among the haves and have-nots. Indeed, import was restricted with the hope of promoting local industry and products and engaging in luxury was considered vice and therefore banned. So extreme was the socialist approach that controlled the transport of rice and other products from one region to another, food and materials became scarce. Almost everything required a government permit, including a marriage ceremony where the number of guests had a ceiling imposed by the government. In this context of 'ceilings' imposed by the government, a Ceiling on Housing and Property Law nationalized land in excess of 50 acres and houses in excess of one property to be owned by any individual. Understandably, house construction for rent came to a standstill, and property owners themselves sometimes became homeless, because the law enabled those who were on rent over a long period of time to claim the properties in preference to the owners. Given the favor received in the law, the tenants took advantage of the situation and claimed ownership to the properties often involving long drawn-out court cases in which house owners and renters were locked in, paralyzing the entire housing market.

Interestingly however, despite these socialist state policies aimed at the distribution of wealth, an extreme socialist movement led by the youth revolted against the government and the society itself. An armed rebellious movement rose from the grassroots determined to oust the government and take over power with the hope of setting up a communist state. The have-nots were pitted against the haves and the landless and homeless were agitated against the land owners and home owners. Although the insurgency by the youth and the peasants had grievances mainly on unemployment, education, economic disadvantage and political disempowerment, it was also invariably connected to property, land ownership and housing.

Amog the numerous social, political and cultural situations that led to the conditions which created such social unrest, it is undeniable that the housing policies which have been adopted since independence had a significant role to play in their makng. The major events of the housing policy development within the provision approach could be outlined as follows.

1945   1950   1960   1970

■Independence (1948)
  ■First Ministry of Housing(1952)
  ■National Housing Department established (1952)

        ■Peoples United Front government radical welfare reforms (1956)

                        ■Insurgency by peasants and youth (1971)

                    ■Ceiling on Housing Property law (1973)

Although the insurgency was ruthlessly put down in 1971, the socialist government itself faced a major revolt of the average public at the 1977 elections in preference for a party that advocated free market economy and liberalism opposing the practice of limited land and house ownership and state control of social affairs.

A Major Institutional Change

With the centre-right United National Party (UNP) government in power, 1977 saw a major shift in policy that moved to open-economy and engagement of the private sector in development. Major structural changes took place in the state sector, particularly in the area of development and housing. According to Economic Review (1980), one of the new agencies formed in early 1979 was the National Housing Development Authority (NHDA) with powers and functions included, the formulation of schemes to establish housing development projects in order to alleviate the housing shortage and to cause the clearance of slum and shanty areas and the re-development of such areas. At the same time, the newly set up Urban Development Authority (UDA) was also empowered with the same "to formulate the clearance of slum and shanty areas and to undertake the development of such areas". In addition, both NHDA and UDA had the powers of compulsory acquisitions under the Land Acquisition Act of July 1977. Continuing the provision approach aggressively, the NHDA was entrusted with the task of constructing some 36,000 houses and flats during the period of 1978 and 1983, mostly in Colombo. NHDA was thus not just a major user of land for housing but also of crucial importance in determining the nature and extent of Colombo's development.

Housing having been high on the political agenda of the government, the prime minister himself was assigned (under a presidential system) the housing portfolio among other ministries related to development. Moreover, the prime minister who had ascended to this position having struggled up from the grassroot levels himself had the support of and the responsibility to the ordinary masses who by and large were the poor both in the urban and rural areas. In fact, not only did he have the responsibility as the minister, but had known the housing problems by experience, having grown up in a low-income community himself.

At the outset, the minister declared his intentions to 'construct' 100,000 houses within the five years (1978-1983) to alleviate the housing issue altogether. Ambitious and hard-hearted yet service-oriented, the minister mobilized his ministry officials to be innovative and deliver on his promises. The Ministry of Housing was put into action with all the state powers directed to address the housing issue aggressively and decisively. Under the circumstances, the program known as the Hundred Thousand Housing Program (HTHP) articulated three strategies to achieve its objectives; direct construction, employing aided self-help, and offering housing loans.

The HTHP is noteworthy for its ambitiousness and boldness in addressing housing as the focused activity of the government. Given the fact that the previous government with socialist welfare policies had constructed only 4700 units over the period of seven years from 1970-1977, it was unimaginable that a hundred thousand houses could be achieved within such a short period of time. Even the Ministry of Housing itself was baffled by the tasks and goals set for it in the HTHP that was announced at a political rally without any professional involvement in its decision. However, major shifts underlined the commitment and seriousness of the efforts and the tasks had to be accomplished without fail. These were,

1. Creation of new institutional structures for Housing and Urban Development. (NHDA and UDA).
2. Engagement of housing as a major sector of development to promote economic growth in comparison to treating it as a social welfare activity.
3. Increase in public spending for housing. From 35 million Rupees in 1976, to 1000 million in 1980.
4. Engagement of the private sector as a major engine of the delivery process.
5. Introduction of a new legal framework together with the relaxation of the socially restrictive legislation on housing.

Understandably, HTHP suffered immensely from an absence of any new vision but ambitions and desires. Its delivery system was the same as before and led to the new housing projects to cost overruns and delays. Many housing schemes intended for the low-income thus became unaffordable for the poor. *Rukmalgama, Raddolugama* and *Hantane* housing schemes for example eventually served the middle income groups and provided no major increase in the housing stock available to the low-income. They consumed heavy subsidies but did not reciprocate further developments elsewhere and thus failed to become the engine of growth. Despite the allocation of funds, government resources were limited in terms of finance, man-power and even materials. Most significantly, the ministry officials failed to see beyond the conventional approach of 'provision'; defined by type plan houses which led to uniform, stereo-typed settlements lacking in the qualities for creating healthy communities. Moreover, when the statistics were compiled, it was discovered that the actual increase of the housing stock in the country far exceeded the numerical achievements of the state; people were still building by themselves in numbers far more than the state. However, housing shortage was also on the increase despite the fact that both the government and the people were involved in building houses. Weerapana notes that "a study which was undertaken in 1982 has shown that the annual deficiency of housing in the country is around 140,000 units.... This deficit though small in numbers is significantly large when compared with the size of the population of the country or when taken as a percentage of the available units" (1986:50).

An Ambitious Shift

Since 1983, a change of emphasis of this approach took place resulting from both policy changes as well as economic and other constraints faced by the government. For instance, the evolution of the support approach was forced mainly by the circumstances of the housing practices of provision that preceded it. Gunatilake (1987) attributes a number of reasons for the shift and suggests that they were mainly economic and social pressures. On the one hand, despite the increased attention on housing during the 1970s, housing shortage was on the increase resulting from the increasing demand prompted by increased owner occupation and encouragement for new households. The traditional extended family systems were on the decline and apparent availability of housing and the increased spending power resulting from improved economic conditions within the free market system made new demands for housing. At the same time, housing provided did not relate to the socio-cultural needs of the communities. For instance, storied housing or low-cost housing did not provide for the traditional, culturally deep-rooted habits and behaviors nor did they allow for growth and change in and around the dwellings.

The provision approach was not favored by either the economists or the donor agencies whose interests were largely in measured economic expenditure and gain. For instance, the cost of housing and public expenditure on housing had escalated heavily during the period when HTHP was in operation. Ganesan (1982) had reported that the unit cost of Aided Self-Help housing had gone up by 250% while that of direct construction had gone up by 450% within the five year period from 1978 to 1981. Public sector investment on housing had been 12% in 1979 and 1980 and as per the World Bank reports, the public investment in urban housing alone amounted to 375 million Rupees in 1979 and exceeded 1000 million in 1980 (Gunatilake, 1987). Thus there were mounting pressures both from outside donor agencies (such as the World Bank) as well as the internal financial institutions to seek an alternative approach to housing which would employ more cost-effective ways.

Evaluation of the achievements of the HTHP also revealed the inefficiency of the state sector programs. In terms of statistics, of the total addition of houses to the housing stock between 1971 and 1981, 185,000 had been constructed by the people themselves while the state had managed to build only 75,000, despite the heavy expenditure.

By 1980s, ideas that housing is a process and that housing by the people was a more wholesome practice than those of the developers and the state was well-known and had also been accepted worldwide among housing professionals. Indeed, Turner (1976) Habraken (1972) and Alexander (1977) had been advocating the need to transfer the power of decision making in housing to the people, in three different contexts that represented the major situations of housing. As such, the paradigm shift in Sri Lanka coincided with the international development and both learned from and contributed to its articulation across the world. However, the Sri Lankan paradigm shift is claimed to have been based on first hand experiences in Sri Lanka, although similar interpretations could be found in other different contexts. For example, Sirivardane writes that "distinguished writers like Charles Abrahams, Otto Koenigsberger and John Turner have made erudite expositions of it. But our own perception and conceptualization is primarily form internal Sri Lankan sources" (1987:10)

The Paradigm Shift: From Provision to Support

Thus in 1984, an even more ambitious program, the Million Housing Program (MHP) was launched as a second phase of the HTHP, despite the fact that HTHP had not fully achieved its objectives. Politically however, HTHP made a huge impact, given the fact that it aimed at housing the poor and seemed to make a greater effort than ever before. Six years of experience had shown to the people that housing indeed could be a catalyst for accelerated development and creation of wealth at the grassroots levels.

MHP however deviated conceptually from the very beginning and was founded on the insights gained in HTHP. At the end of HTHP, the government took serious note of the discovery that the major builders of the houses were the people themselves and what the governments achieved and could achieve was very limited. It also realized that the people's process of building could be accelerated if the government took the role of the facilitator, and worked towards removing the obstacles to people's processes of building. Thus, MHP was conceived not on the basis of provision and state-centered delivery, but as a mechanism to recognize what the people did for themselves and to support their efforts whereby the state could with little financial commitment get involved in improving the housing conditions of the poor. Undeniably, it was also thus possible for the government to claim to have been involved in a larger number of houses than by direct construction, which was politically important to substantiate the promises of 'million houses' made at the political platforms, and keep the financial agencies, both internal and external, content.

The major premises of this approach could be summarized as follows.

1. Recognition that housing is a process rather than houses as products.
2. Recognition that house building among people is an incremental activity.
3. Recognition that people worked towards house building as a matter of every day living, which was the main stream of housing.
4. Accepting that the role of the state was not in providing houses/lands.
5. Accepting that the role of the professional must not be deterministic but interventionist.
6. Understanding that previous approaches were top-down; treating people as mere recipients of houses.
7. Understanding that community had far more resources than the state.
8. Recognition that the vernacular, cultural practices had a central role to play in housing.
9. Accepting that 'standards' defined by the state hindered rather than facilitated the process.

What is also noteworthy of the MHP is that it reached every low-income family of the 25,000 or so rural villages and all urban centers of Sri Lanka. Coupled also with a program known as 'Gam Udawa' meaning 'awakening of villages', poor felt that the state was both interested and active in solving one of the burning issues of everyday life. Gam Udawa however was both a development as well as a political program that ensured to keep the state machinery tirelessly working to achieve the objectives set by the state and to keep the people engaged in the processes. Gam Udawa had monthly exhibitions of its activities in the form of an entertaining celebration running for a week in a chosen remote corner of the island and this attracted both infrastructure development as well as investment to a region that had hitherto not seen any large scale government functions. In this way, *Gam Udawa* simultaneously inter-twined infrastructure development, private sector, community, entertainment, social welfare and politics to promote housing development and social progress.

Generating Theory from Practice

Thus MHP was not just another housing program. It was radically different in its theoretical and conceptual postulates and its modes of operation were politically highly visible and had a significant impact upon the entire population. However, its unfolding should not be seen as a 'grand plan' conceived by housing professionals and planners out of theoretical analysis. On the contrary, support approach was a practical, mundane shift that was forced by sheer necessity and circumstances where the housing professionals were forced to deliver on a political promise, although eventually, a sophisticated and convincing theoretical position was discovered, articulated and celebrated. Sirivardana outlines the process of evolution of this approach.

"The task force discussions were based on working papers prepared by the activists in it. They were rapidly written analysis of singe issues. One of the most fascinating and intractable issues related to costs. On one side, the scale had been determined (The politicians had committed for the construction of a million houses as an electoral promise). On the other, the ministry of finance indicated that only 04% of public investment would be available for housing... The inquiry drove to us a quite unfamiliar truth – that the affordability levels totally excluded even the most minimalist efforts at building houses... We learnt another truism, namely that for every single house produced by the state, the private sector had produced seven. If that was the case, the choice before us in relation to the million, was quite simple... we decided against having a state sub stream at all. Instead, we opted to put all the limited resources we had, at the command of the mainstream".

1988: 9-10

Moreover, the right conditions prevailed for such a shift. As Weerapana (1986) points out, the Sri Lankan situation was unique in a number of ways which helped the realization of a more people-based approach and a strategy. On the one hand, there was a highly motivated political leadership which favored people-based, bottom-up approaches rather than an institutionalized process. On the other hand, there were constant evaluations of experiences, a willingness to learn and a sincere exchange of views between the political leadership and the professionals.

The essential conceptual position of this approach is now recognized as 'supporting and enabling the peoples' process of shelter'. Although comprised of three major facets, the economic, the environmental and the social, understanding of the socio-psychological processes of the people can be seen as the most enlightening and revealing facet of this approach.

The Social and Societal Processes of Housing

In Sri Lanka, the low-income people are constantly involved in generating and allotting resources either in terms of financial savings, jewelry holdings or building materials to be eventually utilized in building a house. Most such buildings are also built with self-help, although there is a general reluctance to initiate the building process for fear of uncertainties of land ownership and unreliability of continuous income. Nevertheless, one could also discover social networks and processes which support individuals or families to acquire accommodation, ownership of land and dwelling for sheltering purposes. In both rural and urban communities, social ties still remain strongly focused towards the welfare of the family where housing takes a predominant concern and therefore self-help processes are mobilized to achieve them.

At the same time, people are constantly involved in locating possibilities, making or modifying some kind of shelter for purposes of living, generating income, leisure, and all such domestic activities. From the very impermanent illegal dwellings such as the slums and shanties to more permanent and affluent ones, people's own housing processes are a part of everyday life of most people, complexly interwoven with work, living and social interactions. Support approaches recognized that supporting peoples' processes means to understand the ways in which such practices take place and to provide support in whatever means it is required, and this is not necessarily limited to financial aid. As Sirivardana (1988) notes "supporting is also to support the people morally and psychologically" Thus at a methodological level, this meant that the processes people employed in acquiring shelter were to be recognized and legitimized. They were to be strengthened where they were found to be weak. They were to be initiated where they were lacking. They were to be facilitated to overcome the hurdles where they were encountering problems.

Thus support involved a wide range of facilitating activities and has been categorized into two kinds: Hardware and software supports (Sirivardana and Lankatilake 1987). Hardware involved tangible entities such as land, infrastructure, and materials while software involved information, training, credit and community organizations.

The fundamental slogan of the MHP thus was,

"Minimal intervention and maximum support by the state: Maximum involvement of the user families".

Sirivardana, 1987:13

Within the program, support took different shapes and they could be related to the varying opportunities made available to the people for making shelter and to the varying activities of the state and the professionals. On the one hand, the state offered Housing Options Loan Packages (HOLP) and on the other, there were the enabling activities of the state professionals intended to support people's existing processes. The offer of housing options which was the response to the variety of individual and family needs were the key to supporting. Four key options were offered with variations extending to 19 choices of which 16 were meant for the poor and 3 were meant for the middle income people.

Table 1. A Comparison between Support and Provision

Support	Provision
• Central theme is user control.	• Opportunity for user control is peripheral and token.
• Housing needs and priorities are perceived in users terms.	• Needs are perceived in state's terms.
• Decentralized and based in the local setting.	• Process is centrally controlled and managed.
• Progressive, housing unfolds overtime.	• Instant and short term: aims at the production of completed houses.
• Flexible through a wide range of options.	• Options are rigid and limited to a few choices.
• The emphasis of the state is on the delivery of resources.	• Emphasis is on the delivery of standard houses.
• Standards are minimal, users could adopt standards incrementally.	• Standards are rigid and unnecessarily high. Housing do not reach the poor.
• Financial support is based on affordability and willingness to pay.	• Based on subsidies. Cost is rigid and abstractly determined.
• Performance is judged by the variations in the products.	• Performance is judged by the numbers of units completed.
• Building activity takes on a very informal character.	• Building activity takes on a very formal character.

Table 2. Matching needs with options

Needs	Options
• Upgrading repairing improving or extensions	• Upgrading package • Dwellings+ Toilets
• Land is available and a new house is needed	• New Housing Package • Core House + increments
• Services needed for existing dwellings	• Utilities Package • Acquisition or Improvement
• Land and a new house needed	• Sites and services package

Upgrading

Upgrading option was mainly aimed at the rural poor who already had a dwelling constructed in land privately owned. Nevertheless, needs for services or improvements to existing services needed state support. In this, state loans were made available to improve housing and other services. These ranged from replacing a roof, adding another room or improving water supply or sanitary facilities. Usually, this option catered to needs of scattered individual houses.

New Building

In this, optional loan packages were available to individual families for the construction of new dwellings. Evidence of intention was an essential pre-condition in obtaining these supports and generally, building materials collected and ownership of land provided this evidence. However, those who were without land could obtain these loans provided their ability to repay could be substantiated. Such support was expected to motivate people to pool financial and other support from relatives and friends.

Utilities Package

Utilities package was similar to the upgrading in that small financial loans were issued for the upgrading of existing service facilities. The distinction here was that the improvements or upgrading of dwellings was not required but the services were. These included improvements to wells, obtaining electricity, installation of water pumps etc.

Sites and Services

Most urban housing in support housing employed sites-and-services approach because they involved either upgrading of existing squatter settlements or new constructions for displaced people. In the new settlements, people received serviced sites and housing loans and other supportive services such as community centers nurseries etc. The community was organized or existing community organizations were revitalized in such a way that they became the major actors in the development process.

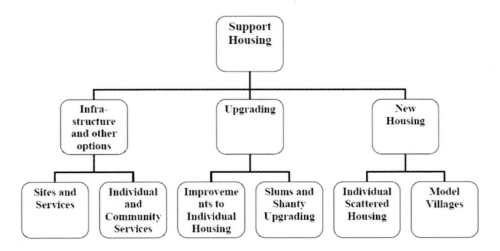

Figure 1. The support Approach and its sub programs.

As can be seen, the Sri Lankan support approach differs markedly from that of support and infill approach of Habraken (1985) and transfer of power to people to build (Turner, 1976). In fact, it goes beyond and evolves into a more effective and meaningful approach which employs the otherwise disadvantaged but resourceful situations of low-income settlers positively and skillfully. The Sri Lankan support approach is directly related to the specific experiences and processes of situations and places of interventions. As Sirivardana wrote "our understanding of the theory of housing is a direct outcome of this distinctively internal experience" (1987:1)

The uniqueness of the practice was that it employed the resources and the existing processes of the people towards the improvement of housing particularly for the low-income. Its methodology enabled the involvement of the individuals and communities themselves in the making of dwellings and settlements. Decision making had become more social and outside intervention had become directive rather than authoritative. Its many practices were place-specific and place-conscious and offered opportunities for people to make their own places. In fact, it had brought about a variety of dwellings and settlements, each unique in their own right. Compared with the provision approach that produced uniform houses based on type plans and equally similar settlements created on grid plans by the architects, the support could be said to support 'people's own place making practices' where the individual and community conceptualizations of places had a significant impact on the nature of those places.

However, this did not mean that the architects and planners had to abandon their involvement in housing development or settlements. To the contrary, The new insights helped the planners and architects to realize and recognize their roles more meaningfully and they re-evolved their roles to suit the support approach. The idea of planning and plans underwent a dramatic change. For example, Benjamin wrote that physical plans must be considered as negotiation tools between users and authorities about appropriate interventions; recognizing the users need to transform their dwellings according to individual or group priorities (1985). Thus in the support approach, there was an understanding that what plans and designs do is to provide the framework and the baseline upon which the users own personalizations will take place. People were expected to transform the settings; the forms, shapes and activities based on private and public demands and their compromises.

Design and Planning

In fact, planning has been perceived as an intervention in the process rather than as an initiation as is usually the case. Interventions were not decisive but complimentary and this led to the more positive support rather than what actual physical interventions would have done. For instance, there is hardly any professional intervention in the design of traditional dwellings in rural areas where people's processes of making home environments have remained healthy. On the one had, outside regulations and rules do not apply and thus the forces on form, arrangement and details have always been derived mainly from the traditions and conventions or the contemporary versions of the traditional practices which have absorbed and responded to changing aspirations and needs of the communities (Senanayake,1991). On the other, images of 'types' of dwellings were still shared as in the traditional communities and the village artisans were mainly instrumental in advising the forms of such buildings. At the same time, land was less constrained and enabled its configurations to be considered less restrictive. In the rural program therefore, intervention had taken a neutral position in the realm of the physical environment.

In the urban areas however, this took a different dimension. For instance, there were building regulations applicable to construction in most of the urban areas. Tradition and conventions were no longer considered valid because they have been subject to varying influences and modifications resulting from exposure to other cultures. Artisans no longer relied on or related to images of 'types' of dwellings in determining the forms of the houses. Above all, sites were critically small and imposed highly demanding and exacting conditions which required individual and specific dwelling forms to be developed. For these reasons and particularly in order to enable house construction in smaller plots where general building regulations could not be observed, the state took steps to declare these areas as special project areas.

Within this approach, one of the major methods of planning the settlements has been that of grouping dwellings to small clusters; a method identified as the '*Navagamgoda*' meaning a new group of villages. In these clusters, generally, there has been a central compound around which a number of plots have been organized to both facilitate their serving as well as to suggest a small community group, re-formation of traditional cultural patterns, and to enable the emergence of spatial identities. A guideline provided a comprehensive check-list and interpretations of issues and aspects which ought to be used only as a route to new settlement planning (Hamdi, & Goethard,: 1984). However, it has been stressed that the grouping have to be interpreted in the context of geographical and physical sites, and the specific characteristics of the places such as the street patterns, block arrangements and open spaces. In this, the sensitivity and the perceptions of the designers involved were seen as crucial in making meaningful settlement forms.

Support housing mobilized the community in numerous ways to influence the design and planning of their own places. Among them, the Community Development Councils, Community Development Guidelines, and Community Planning Workshops were the main instruments of change. Community Development Councils (CDC) were often community-based grass root organizations that had existed in many settlements. Most often, there were thrift societies or committees set up to assist and organize social events. When such formations were not present in a given place, the professionals helped the people to organize themselves into new ones, which were recognized as the legitimate grass root mobilizers of community strength. They were democratically elected and were entrusted with the task of enabling their social and societal formations to manifest in the design of the settlements and their houses.

In order to engage the communities in the process of development, the CDCs held forums that involved representatives of people, professionals, government officials, local authority members and others who were considered to be important to the development practice. The CDCs had meetings often and usually formed sub groups to discuss the issues that were relevant to them. These included issues such as allocation of space in the front and rear areas and surroundings to the settlements, public spaces, provision of infrastructure, heath and building standards and other specific issues. Guidelines were prepared, rules to be followed by the community were established and enforcement mechanisms and sanctions to be imposed in the event of non-adherence to those rules were also established by the CDCs assisted by the professionals and community leaders. In this way, the community's perceptions, rules and values were made to play a significant role in the development process whereby traditions and conventions could be easily accommodated.

One of the most important outcomes of these workshops were the community building guidelines which adopted, from the common building regulations that were in force in the area, and modified those which were found to be inappropriate. A household file that contained the community rules and guidelines and other information pertaining to procedures and ways of developing house plans were shared among the community, which at later meetings became the source upon which the professionals and individuals worked in developing the individual building designs (Lankatilaka, Jayarathne, & Boyd,1988).

This practice known as the Community Action Planning in fact introduced a process of development later to be called the participatory urban development by which the social and societal facets of the communities of concern to development programs were given an opportunity to influence the planning outcomes. Although there were numerous problems arising from, conflicts within community groups and sometimes from lack of will or lack of understanding of the CAP, on the whole, this has been one of the most effective development practices that enabled the community empowerment and unleash the potentials they possessed in housing themselves. The ceiling on Property law having been repealed in 1990, the program evolved into a more holistic development practice of the island.

These transformations can be outlined as follows.

1977 -
- UNP government (center right) came into power
- National Housing Development Authority
- Urban Development Authority
- Greater Colombo Economic Commission
- Mahaveli Development Authority

- Hundred Thousand Housing Program
  Self-help
  Direct Construction

1979 -
- Unicef Urban Basic Services Program

1983 -
- Million Houses Program
  Devolving power to people
  Enabling Strategy

1985 -
- Community Action Planning
- Participatory Urban Development
- Grass roots program
- Local Government Regeneration Program
- Urban Projects Unit established

1990 -
- Ceiling on Property law repelled

Since the change of government subsequently however, the program lost its main drivers; the minister with the vision and commitment and the housing experts who both articulated and evolved program with the people. Unfortunately, only the residues of the practices continue now, with marginal references and application of support policies under different names. Nevertheless, the lessons that were learnt from the Sri Lankan experiences have remained an underlying force in all housing interventions.

Lessons to Be Learnt

The Sri Lankan experience in low-income housing clearly shows that successful interventions for low-income housing may come about only when the three participant groups of the housing process; the people, the professionals and the state acquire a realistic and common understanding of the tasks at hand and how to face the multitude of challenges under the given circumstances. It also shows that the key to understanding and unlocking the enormous potentials that exist within the low-income communities has to come from a visionary yet practical political leadership whose interest and engagement with the issue has to be deeply rooted in the community itself. This must be complimented by committed and insightful professionals who are willing to learn from the experiences and unlearn the inhibitive theoretical postulates that are often repeated in housing literature. In fact, it is to be acknowledged that the communities and people are resourceful but those resources can hardly be harnessed without the intervening mechanisms being receptive to the nuances of the social and societal facets of those communities.

Asserting this, Weerapana writes

"Sri Lanka is an extraordinary example of a country where a highly motivated political leadership impacts heavily on shelter decisions. Her unique achievements in transforming a very conventional delivery program within a relatively short space of time can therefore be attributed to these 'right' conditions."

Weerapana, 1986:89

In the case of the Sri Lankan Million Housing Program and the support housing that it evolved, this was primarily inspired by the minister of housing who had a deep-seated conviction that low-income housing has to be at the centre of development in a developing country like Sri Lanka, and that there were enormous opportunities there to bring about fundamental change. The minister was also fearlessly forceful in demanding the state sector mechanisms to deliver and provided all the structural, financial and motivational incentives needed to make that change. Secondly, it was the presence of visionary and ideologically creative professional leadership at the National Housing Development Authority that was able to translate the unprecedented vision and demand made politically by the minister into a practical program that was effective, meaningful and implementable. Theory was necessary but theory was generated from practice rather than *vice versa*, and theorizing was left to follow the process that was unfolding and unfolded thorough inferences, actions and reflections. Most significantly, it was the poor, the low-income and the marginalized who were instrumental in taking the process forward despite the fact that state and the professionals were strategizing at the tail end of the process.

Sirivardana pointed out

"We need a theory of the home which will build from the base up. It will not discriminate against the poor, but will consider them as a resource for strengthening and enriching the productivity of the village and the city. We as practitioners of theory have to radically relearn from their self-help ideology and practice" (1987:18)

The foremost unique societal condition that prevailed in the Sri Lankan situation was that people practiced self-help as a major social mechanism in everyday life; in meeting economic hardships, in dealing with educational issues, in dealing with life events such as marriages, funerals as well as in dealing with housing and accommodation. The practice was deeply rooted in tradition, particularly in the rural communities and given the fact that many of the urban poor had migrated from the rural did continue the practice as a natural accompaniment to everyday living. Although this may or may not be the case in other communities across the world where it is a given by tradition, most often the sheer necessity itself seems to push low-income people to depend on help from others with similar needs. The Million Housing Program and the support approach harnessed the full potential of this social practice by understanding its nature and thereby articulating it as a strategy to be engaged by the state and by recognizing the possibility that existed in organizing and directing it towards achieving common social goals.

The second unique social practice that prevailed in Sri Lanka was that people were collecting building materials on an every day basis with the intention of putting up a socially-accepted dwelling. Although poverty and low-income were the visible signs of the communities, there existed wealth - particularly in either having such materials already at hand or in the ability to gather them without major financial costs. This was a principal resource particularly in the rural areas where actual costs involved in constructing dwellings were in purchasing those that were not readily available in the rural areas. Ironworks, such as nails, door locks, hinges, electric accessories and plumbing accessories had to be purchased from the market place and labor for specialized works such as plumbing required hard currency, which most were unable to afford, while the basic building materials were available. Provision approach hardly recognized these resources and went on the assumption that development had to commence from a zero position. Instead, the support approach mobilized those resources as the base upon which to build. This not only eased the financial burden upon the people and the state but also sustained this cultural practice leading often to recycling materials from old houses that were demolished. In fact, a whole industry of small scale entrepreneurs cashing in on the demand for used materials evolved which undeniably has contributed immensely to sustainable practices in building.

The most innovative social practice of the support housing was that it engaged the community in planning, design and setting standards for their own developments. This practice hinged to the healthy self-help basis of the community led to the "questioning" of sweeping local authority standards that were neither people-specific nor place-specific. Thus the communities were allowed to develop their own building and development guidelines, guided by the professionals and the state, which undeniably led to the healthy re-definitions of new standards and practices that responded to community concerns and specifities of their own conditions. Moreover, it enabled the incremental nature of development to progress at a phase amenable and affordable to the people which otherwise would have been discouraged given the usually alien and irrelevant building regulations that prevailed in Sri Lanka. These place-specific and community-generated guidelines were sensitive to the nuances of the ground realities of the places in which they resided and drew emphasis to particular issues confronting different communities in different places.

This brings us to the critical lesson to be leant from the experiences of low-income housing in Sri Lanka. In fact, the point must be made that what has been done in Sri Lanka may not be applicable *en-masse*, in any other country or a place, given the unique social facets of the communities and given the involvement of the political and professional leadership it had received which underlined its success. Moreover, it is important to recognize that successful housing interventions in low-income communities may be devised only on the understanding of the people and the places in which they live. In other words, the programs have to be people-specific and place-specific although in a given culture, society or a country, commonalities may prevail which could be engaged to create the frameworks for large scale programs. While low-income suggests a common characteristic of being economically less able, this by no means is a good enough definition to apply a common analysis, standards or programs of housing.

Understanding people and places however is no easy task. It is most difficult when outsiders are involved, but at the same time, outside intervention is a healthy intrusion to the communities. This is partly because, the outsiders are not accustomed to seeing things as the communities see and also are unlikely to take things for granted. These new perceptions could bring new insights and help the communities to discover potentials that they posses but have not recognized. Because the poor often have self-imposed negative perceptions of themselves and their conditions, an outsider's view may help transform them positively provided that the outsiders have broader understanding and are willing to and able to observe, listen, unlearn and learn. Outside intrusion is also healthy because the poor have the tendency to trust the 'others' who are believed to 'have'; financially, emotionally and intellectually. They are organisable by the outsiders often whose independence may be trusted more than some insiders whose motivations may be often mistrusted. In fact, there is no question that those communities and its members; particularly representatives are not necessarily often 'innocent'; politically neutral, intentionally unbiased or strategically non-manipulative. Nevertheless, the outsiders interventions must always be based on a common understanding of the situations; often generated after deeply engaging involvements with the community and recognizing that at the end, it is the community that will live in the place and it is their perceptions that matter and it is their actions that will transform a place to a healthy or an unhealthy one.

Such an approach which may be called a 'place-based approach' to housing and development however does not mean to be based only on the support paradigm, although in this paper the support paradigm was hailed as the way forward as the Sri Lankan experiences unfolded. Instead, in facing the challenges of the low-income housing, all approaches, both provision and support and their numerous forms should be engaged depending on the specificity of the people and the places.

As Hamdi, wrote "Building houses for lots of *people* and *places* one does not know is no good design practice' (1992).

References

Alexander, C. (1977) *A Pattern language*. New York: Oxfrod University Press.
Benjamin, S. (1985) Towards responsive projects and programmes – Lessons from a sites and services project MIT/NHDA.

Ganesan, (1986) *The construction industry in Sri Lanka.* ILO, World Employment Program, Research Working Paper.

Gunatilaka, V. (1987) *From provision to support.* An unpublished M.Phil thesis University of Newcastle upon Tyne. U.K.

Habraken, N. (1972) *Supports, an alternative to mass housing.* London: Architectural press.

Habraken, N. (1985) *who is participating.* Key note speech at the international design participating conference at Eindhoven.

Hamdi, N. and Goethard R. (1984) *Guidelines for Navagamgoda project planning and design- An options oriented approach.* Ministry of Local government Housing and Construction. Sri Lanka.

Hamdi, N. (1992) *Housing without houses.* New York:Van Nostrand Reinhold

Lankatilaka, L. Jayarathne, K. and Boyd, G. (1988) *Community Building Guidelines and Rules,* Colombo: NHDA.

Senanayaka, D (1991) *Architect's contribution to People's process.* An unpublished M.A dissertation submitted to the Institute of Advanced Architectural Studies, University of York. U.K.

Sirivaradna, S. (1986) *Reflections on the implementation of the Million Housing Programme, in Habitat International* Vol. 10. No.3. pp. 91-108

Sirivaradna, S. (1987) *Process initiatives and support. A search for fundamentals.* A revised version of the key note paper presented at the session on THE HOME at the Union of International Architects XVI congress on 'Shelter and Cities'; Building Tomorrows World, Brighton, England.

Sirivaradna, S. (1988) *Housing mainstreams: A case study in learning.* The Sri Lanka case study prepared for presentation at the Washington senior level shelter policy seminar, Washington, November 6-9 Colombo: NHDA.

Sirivaradna, S. and lankatilaka L. (1987) *Some key issues in the participatory planning and management of the urban low-income housing process.* A paper presented at the second congress of local authorities for development of human settlements in Asia and Pacific. Colombo Urban Development in Economic Review, April 1980.

Turner, J (1976) *Housing by people, towards autonomy in building environments,* London: Maryan Boyers.

Weerapana, D. (1986) Evolution of a support policy of shelter – The experience of Sri Lanka, *Habitat International,* Vol.10. No. 3 pp. 79-89

In: Low Incomes: Social, Health and Educational Impacts   ISBN: 978-1-60741-175-8
Editor: Jacob K. Levine, pp. 161-172   © 2009 Nova Science Publishers, Inc.

Chapter 7

UNEQUAL IMPACT OF DISEASE AND SOCIAL DISADVANTAGES IN OLDER AGE: EMPIRICAL EVIDENCE ON THE ITALIAN CASE

Maria Lucchetti, Giovanni Lamura and Andrea Corsonello[*]

INRCA; National Institute of Research and Care for the Elderly,
Ancona; Cosenza, Italy

Abstract

This paper deals with health inequalities attributable to economic, social, and cultural factors. It first analyses how social inequalities have increased in many developed countries in the last decade, following a lengthy period of decline since the early 20th century. Secondly, and narrowing its focus to older Italians, it investigates how a low Socio-Economic Status (SES) can be an independent predictor of further risks in terms of health status. Furthermore, the paper tries to explain key aspects of this phenomenon and their impact on older people's needs within society. Finally, the paper attempts to identify policy options for relevant actors, reviewing the current debate on the topic, including recent advances and future research needs.

Introduction

In the EU27 the share of people aged 65 years or over in the total population is projected to increase from 17,1% in 2008 to 30% in 2060. Similarly, the number of people aged 80 years and over will almost triple in the same period, while the old age dependency ratio is expected to increase substantially from current 25,4% to 53,5% [1-2].

Some authors react to these projections with concern and fear of increased social risks; others, on the contrary, emphasize the aspect of successful ageing, neglecting new problems emerging from mass ageing. A correct interpretation of these phenomena needs a

[*] We thank Pietro Alessandrini for comments and suggestions.

supplementary investigation of the associations existing between older people's SES, health and inequality of income, as shown by different European studies [3-4].

The understanding of these relations is imposed also by the recognition that the economic growth and the development of social protection systems have led to remarkable improvements in social conditions in most OECD countries, but are far from having solved all social problems. Older people, in particular, continue to face great risks in terms of isolation and limited autonomy, as "from the mid-1970s to the mid 1990s labour and capital incomes have become more unequally distributed among the population in every OECD country" [5].

Cross-National Trends in Income Inequalities

Recent cross-national trends in income inequality, both at international [6] and European level (1), show that this has risen significantly since 2000 in Canada, Germany, Norway United States and Italy, whereas has declined in the United Kingdom, Mexico, Greece and Australia (see figure 1 and figure 2). Although the OECD reports a decreasing poverty among older people, poverty among young adults and families with several children being instead on the increase, this apparently positive trend in the aged population must consider the fact that most older people live either with their children or with other younger adults [7].

As far as Italy is concerned, income inequality in this country has risen in the last 20 years. As a result, in 2008 the level of income inequality and poverty, measured by the Gini coefficient[1], is 0,33, one of the highest in the EU and well above the OECD average (which is 0,12).

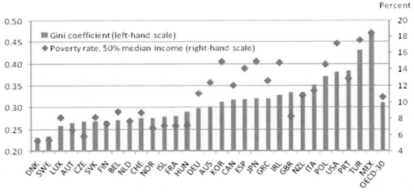

Note: Countries are ranked in increasing order of the Gini coefficient of income inequality. Data refer to the distribution of household disposable income in cash across people, with each person being attributed the income of the household where they live adjusted for household size.
Source: OECD.

Figure 1. Levels of income inequality and poverty in the mid 2000s.

---

[1] The Gini coefficient standardizes from 0 to1 the distance between observed income distribution and one income equi-distribution .

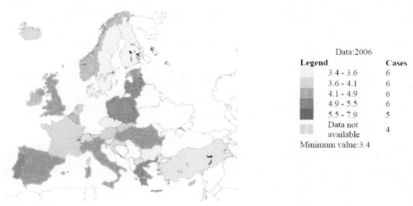

Source: EUROSTAT 2007.

Figure 2. Inequality of income distribution - Income quintile share ratio.

As a result, about 15 millions of Italian people are considered to be today at risk of poverty. The most disadvantaged groups are represented by disabled people, in particular if in old age and living alone – the income of over 65 year old Italians living alone is less than half of the median income of all families (table 1) – and by households with a large number of children [8-10]. The regional distribution of income is also differentiated [11], showing a higher inequality in the Southern regions (figure 3), where the percentage of poor families is four times higher than in the North-Central ones (table 2).

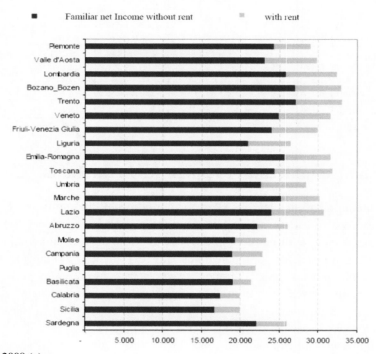

Source: ISTAT 2008 (a).

Figure 3. Regional distribution of income inequality in Italian Region. Median in Euro. 2005.

Table 1. Incidence and intensity of poverty by household in Italy. 2006. %

	Incidence*	Intensity**
	%	%
Nord	5,2	17,8
Centre	6,9	16,9
South	22,6	22,5
Italy	11,1	20,8

*Incidence of poverty is the ratio between poor families and the total of families.
** Intensity of poverty measure how much the media expense of families is lower than poverty line.
Source: ours processing of ISTAT, 2007.

**Table 2. Poor households by household characteristic –
Net household Income. Years 2004-2006. Euro**

FAMILY DISTINCTIONS	MEDIAN INCOME			
	North	Center	South	ITALY
Household				
1) by age				
Total> 65 years	15017	16323	12924	14430
of which: Alone	11005	11206	10092	10735
2) by gender				
male	28164	26867	20435	25111
female	18040	18577	13545	16781
3) by education				
primary	15378	15138	12723	14094
degree	38257	39652	38939	38558
Families with elderly people	15051	16968	12582	14423
Total families	24887	24410	18406	22353

Source: ours processing of ISTAT 2008.

Socio-economic and Health Inequalities in the Italian Context

Socio-economic status is clearly linked to morbidity and mortality [4, 12-16], but the *mechanisms responsible* for the association are not yet completely understood [17-18]. The existence of strong regional differences in Italy are confirmed by a synthetic health indicator that considers five aspects: demographic rates (life expectancy, mortality), lifestyles, self perception of health, prevention and chronic diseases [12].

The relationship between morbidity/life expectancy and income/social class has been often explored in the literature, whose main findings indicate, on the whole, that the poor have a lower chance of survival than those who are more well-off [19-22]. The direction of causality is however not immediately obvious, since adults might be economically disadvantaged because they are in poor health (and subsequently end up dying/being ill) or because being poor might make them more likely to die/being ill.

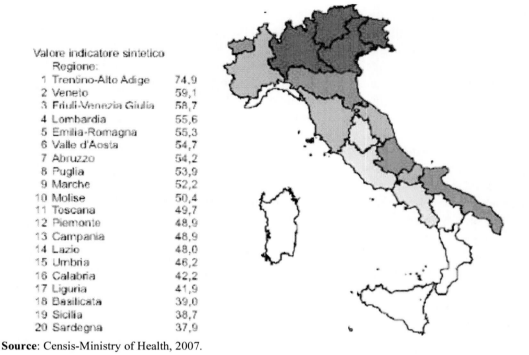

Valore indicatore sintetico Regione:	
1 Trentino-Alto Adige	74,9
2 Veneto	59,1
3 Friuli-Venezia Giulia	58,7
4 Lombardia	55,6
5 Emilia-Romagna	55,3
6 Valle d'Aosta	54,7
7 Abruzzo	54,2
8 Puglia	53,9
9 Marche	52,2
10 Molise	50,4
11 Toscana	49,7
12 Piemonte	48,9
13 Campania	48,9
14 Lazio	48,0
15 Umbria	46,2
16 Calabria	42,2
17 Liguria	41,9
18 Basilicata	39,0
19 Sicilia	38,7
20 Sardegna	37,9

Source: Censis-Ministry of Health, 2007.

Figure 4. Health and territorial diversity. Synthetic Indicator for Italians Regions.

Socio-economic inequality and its impact on health is a growing concern also in the European debate on public health [23], and in many countries the issue is moving away from the "description" towards the "identification" of the determinants of inequalities, and to the development of policies explicitly aimed at reducing inequalities in health.

Italian data from national and local studies show that mortality increases linearly with social disadvantage for a wide range of indicators at both individual (education, social class, income, quality of housing) and geographical level (deprivation indexes computed at different levels of aggregation). This positive correlation, which is very strong among adults of working age, persists also among the elderly. According to Caiazzo et al. [24], the causes of death result highly correlated with social inequality. Moreover, the increasing inequality recorded over the last decade is correlated with more harmful lifestyles (such as smoking, heavy drinking, drug use, unhealthy diet, obesity and physical inactivity). The same study also highlights the existence of a "contextual" effect on health (i.e. related to the social environment in which the subject live), as opposed to the "compositional" effect (given solely by the aggregation of individual processes). Another recent study confirms that quantitative measures of frailty are significantly influenced by social and environmental factors [25]. According to these hypotheses, characteristics of the infrastructure and of the physical and socio-economic environment of an area might have an impact on individual health, independently from the cultural and economic resources personally available to people living in that area [26].

Recent studies conduct in Southern Italy show that ecological and environmental factors may indeed be involved in preventing or compensating cognitive decline, at least in persons coming from homogeneous rural areas [27], since low social demands in a protective family environment do not stimulate high intellectual performance, and signs of dementia may not be recognized by persons living in this context until the patient reaches a relatively severe stage of disease.

With respect to the health care system, various Italian investigations show that poor and less educated people have inadequate access both to primary prevention and early diagnosis, as well as to early and appropriate care and drug use [28-33]. Several studies also show that perceived health status is associated both with mortality [34] and with unequal use of health services [35].

In Italy, the relationship between income inequality and health is mixed and not universal. A positive association was observed only in provinces with lower absolute income. Elderly persons living in Southern Italy represent the population subgroup that is most vulnerable to unequal income distribution. Moreover, income inequality can, in part, explain the historically higher mortality among women in Southern Italy compared to the North [36, 37].

Ours studies in the Region Calabria, in Southern Italy, demonstrate the role played by social, environmental and economic factors in determining subjective perception of aging in older people. They confirm the strong association between social and environmental characteristics of older Italian subjects, as well as the clear differentiation between residents in metropolitan areas and residents in rural areas [38-39]. According to these findings, main potential predictors of high social and health risk are poor education, low-income, female gender, widowhood, unsatisfactory health perception, high functional perceived disability and living arrangements.

Inequalities within the Elder Care Sector and the Italian Welfare State

Since the late 1970s, the Italian welfare regime has organised care provision by distinguishing health from social care. This has sometimes resulted in difficulties with access and usage of elder care services, not only because the imperfect financial and organisational integration of the relevant authorities (the Regions for health, the Municipalities for social care), but also because of the traditional preference of the Italian welfare system for providing monetary payments (i.e. allowances), rather than direct services. In these circumstances, care recipients enjoy not only the freedom but also the burden of deciding how to use the allowances received. This arrangement has indirectly promoted the development of a wide private care market, mainly on an undeclared basis, in the form of foreign migrants employed as live-in home care workers directly by the families of older people. This solution, which can without exaggeration now be considered as standard in Italy for the provision of long term care to an older person affected by a disability or chronic illness, has been facilitated also by a series of other factors.

One of these is represented by the fact that, traditionally, the most relevant means of providing support to dependent persons in Italy is by monetary transfers, whose amount can vary between 2000 and 11,300 Euros/year [40]. Over time the percentage of the older population receiving these allowances almost has strongly increased, reaching 7.7% of the population over age 65 in 2005. The explanation of this trend might be found in the long standing phenomenon of misuse of these allowances as a hidden form of income supplementation, allocated irrespective of real care needs. This is especially common in some Central and Southern regions of the country, where in 2005 recipients of this allowance reach 7.3% and 8.4% respectively, compared to 6.4% in the North of the country [41]. In the last decade further means-tested care payments have been introduced by several regions and municipalities, with the aim of supporting home care for (mostly older) dependent persons, and these are estimated to add up to a monthly average of 300-350 Euros per recipient [41].

Another factor to be taken into account is that Italy has a strong regional inequalities in both the extent and the types of municipal social services, per capita expenditure by regions and municipalities on social care in the North of the country being often double that recorded in the South [42]. These geographical differentiation is so remarkable in terms of care delivery mechanisms that some observers have distinguished Italian regions into different "welfare regimes", identifying four main types – "munificent", "efficient", "under pressure" and "fragile familist", confirming the existence of a negative association between levels of formal and informal care, i.e. *in areas with lower public social care the family's contribution is often higher* [42-43]. According to this classification, the demand for private care services is higher in those regions with regimes of the "efficient" and "under pressure" welfare types, where the higher impact of population ageing is not compensated for by the resources made available for public care services.

A further factor impacting on the amount of potential family support in Italy is represented by the growing female employment rate, increased between 1994 and 2005 from 42.4% to 50.7%, and from 13.6% to 20.8% in the 55-64 age group [44]. This indirectly reduces the availability of the core contributors to elder care, traditionally women in the age of 45-64 [34]. EUROFAMCARE data show that, not unlike reports of family caregivers in other European countries, Italian family carers of older people experience a variety of restrictions on work due to their caregiving involvement [45]. The most widespread is a reduction in working hours - affecting 14% of all employed family carers – followed by difficulties experienced in developing one's career (5%) and the need to work on an occasional basis (5%). In almost all circumstances women are more frequently affected by restrictions than men, confirming that the rigidity of the Italian labour market has a negative impact on women's ability to balance professional and caring responsibilities.

All this clarifies why more and more Italian families employ migrants, often on a live-in basis, as home care workers to assist their older relatives. In 2005, over 13% of households in Italy with a dependent older person employed such a migrant carer [46]. This "ethnification" of the elder care work in Italy has reached the point of overshadowing its traditional feminisation, as reflected by data on the gender composition of migrant carers, still overwhelmingly women. A further reason for the trend has been a historical shortage of nursing staff compared to a relative abundance of medical staff [40], so that some nursing functions have been reduced to a minimum in health care services (including hospital care), resulting in an inappropriate delegation of these responsibilities to older people's families.

Discussion and Policy Recommendations

In Italy two dimensions of change can be currently considered central in the debate on the relation between income and health inequalities: 1) the increased prevalence of chronic diseases and disability in older age; 2) the increase in the size of groups of people characterised by low SES. In this respect, a key problem affecting older Italians is the demand of a public protection for long term care. Furthermore, it should be considered that income inequalities interact with social exclusion, diseases and disabilities. Older people can adapt to and find an equilibrium with illnesses or disabilities, but if they fall in so called "trap" conditions, as exemplified in figure 5, they need the support of social care services to receive prompt and personalized interventions.

> To be
> To have
> - poor education
> - poor social relations
> - poor health information
> To live
> - in a Region non yet developed
> - in a problematical City
> - in a territory which supply
>   few accessible ed efficient services

Figure 5. The "traps" for no self government in old age.

The identification of these mechanisms provides more options for policy remedies. Given the pervasive effects of socio-economic status, there is no single policy nor even one domain of policy that, alone, can eliminate health disparities. The Acheson Commission in the United Kingdom identified thirty-nine recommendations for reducing health disparities in that country [47], organized by key-groups (such as children, older people, and ethnic minorities) and domains (such as income and tax benefits, education, and employment) and suggesting that, for older people, prevention of morbidity and disability rather than mortality may be a relevant focus. Policy relevant recommendations concerned:

- promoting material well-being, the maintenance of mobility, independence, and social contacts;
- improving the quality of homes in which older people live;
- meliorating accessibility of health and social services for older people and distribution according to need;
- monitoring inequalities in health and their determinants at a national and local level.

These recommendations can be still considered valid today, not only for the UK, but to a great extent also for the Italian context.

Conclusions

This article has presented some evidence concerning the impact on older Italians of socio-economic transformations. Even though these processes are widespread throughout Europe, their knowledge is largely forgotten in the daily experience. This is much more worrying as, contrary to the expectation of falling inequalities, in Italy these have increased in the last decade, similarly to what has happened in other countries of the world. The evolution of income and health inequalities, in general, and the emergence of new significant forms of inequality for frail elder people, in particular, must therefore become of primary interest for researchers and policy makers, who should address the social, cultural and political impacts of this increase in inequalities and disaggregate them at different territorial levels [48, 5, 6].

Policy interventions to reduce inequalities in the use of health and social services need to be fully developed in next decade [49-50]. To this purpose, more research is needed to ascertain the effectiveness of such interventions in relation to the SES of the persons, according to an ideal agenda ordered as follows:

- monitor social groups living in conditions of exclusion and suffering (often including older people) to prepare adequate support;
- convert interventions based on monetary transfers in favour of in-kind interventions supplying quality services; improve access to long term care through policies supporting informal carers;
- increase availability of formal home care services to frail elderly;
- implement more integrated residential care facilities in the community;
- monitor systematically the quality of care provided, by adopting appropriate assessment processes involving both care providers and care users;
- adopt a life course approach both at individual and social group level, in order to acknowledge the relevance of past events and processes on present life conditions as a basis for planning future service characteristics.

Reducing the health disadvantage of lower socio-economic group is a very difficult goal, requiring an active commitment not only in public health sector but, transversally, in many other policy areas, such as education, social security, working life and city planning. Notwithstanding, the adoption of such an approach based on mainstreaming the reduction of health inequalities represents a crucial, inevitable strategy to ensure a sustainable, long-term impact of current health and social care policies for the older population.

References

[1]   EUROSTAT 2007-EUROPOP2008, convergence scenario: http://epp.eurostat.ec.europa.eu/ portal/page?_pageid=1996,39140985&_dad=portal&_schema=PORTAL&screen=detailref &language=en&product=REF_TB_living_conditions_welfare&root=REF_TB_living_condi tions_welfare/t_livcon/t_ilc/t_ilc_ip/tsisc010;

[2]   Calzabini, P., Turcio, S., Scientific supervisors, (2004), *Activage Project*, Deliverable D1: WP1- Country Report Italy, p. 5.

[3]   Wagstaff, A., and van Doorslaer E.,. (2000). Measuring and testing for Inequity in the Delivery of Health Care. *Journal of Human Resources* **35**(4):716-733.

[4]   Mackenbach, J., Meerdling, W., Kunst, A. *Economic implications of socio-economic inequalities in health in the European Union*, European Commission, July 2007.

[5]   OECD (2005). *Extending opportunities: how active Social Policy can benefit us all*. http://www.oecd.org/dataoecd/39/12/34607634.pdf, p.5.

[6]   OECD Publishing 2008. Growing Unequal? Income Distribution and Poverty in OECD Countries.

[7]   Banerjee, A. V., Duflo, E., (2007). The Economic Lives of the poor, *Journal of Economic Prospectives,* American Economic Association , Vol. 21 (1), pages 141-168.

[8]   Caritas Italiana, *Rapporto 2008 su povertà ed esclusione sociale in Italia.*Fondazione E. Cancan. Edizioni Il Mulino, Ottobre 2008.

[9]   ISTAT (2007), *La povertà relativa in Italia nel 2006,* Rome, p. 9.

[10] ISTAT (2008), *Indicatori socio-sanitari regionali Occupazione e povertà,* http://www.istat.it/sanita/sociosan/

[11] ISTAT (2008 a), *Distribuzione del reddito e condizioni di vita in Italia (2004-2006),* Rome p. 8.

[12] Censis (2007), *Rapporto sulla situazione sociale del Paese.* Franco Angeli.41:251

[13] Cesaroni, G., Agabiti, N., Forestiere, F., Ancona, C., Peducci, C. A., Socio-economic differentials in premature mortality in Rome: changes from 1990 to 2001. (2006). *BMC Public Health, 6:270* http://www.biomedcentral.com/1471-2458/6/270

[14] Devaux, M., Jusot, F., Trannoy, A., Tubeuf, S., (2008b). *La santé des seniors selon leur origine sociale et la longévité de leurs parents*, IDEP, Documents de travail, n. 0809.

[15] Hansen, DG., Sondergaard, J., Vach, W., Gram, LF., Rosholm, JU., Mortensen, PB., et al. Socio-economic inequalities in first-time use of antidepressants - a population-based study. (2004). *Eur. J. Clin. Pharmaco.; 60*. 51-5.

[16] Morris, JN., et al.(2000), A minimum income for healthy living. *Journal of Epidemiology and Community health, 54*: 885-889

[17] Adler, N. E.; Newman, K.. Socioeconomic Disparities In Health: Pathways And Policies *Health Aff.(2002). Millwood; 21,* 60-76.

[18] Goldberg, M., Melchior, M., Leclerc, A., Lert, F. (2002). Les déterminants sociaux de la santé: apports récents de l'épidémiologie sociale et des sciences sociales de la santé. *Sciences Sociales et santé. 20*. 75-128.

[19] Donnon, A., Goldblatt, P., Lynch, K. Inequalities in life expectancy by social class 1972-1999. (2002). *Health Statistics Quaterly, 15*.5-15.

[20] Adler, N.E., Boyce, W.T., Chesney, M.A., Folkman, S., Syme, S. L.). Socioeconomic inequalities in health. No easy solutions. (1993). *JAMA,* Vol 269 N°.24, June 23, 269:3140-3145.

[21] Mini, G. K. (2008). Socioeconomic and demographic diversity in the health status of elderly people in a transitional society, Kerala, India. *Journal of Biosocial Science* Cambridge University Press.

[22] WHO, Word Health Statistics 2008, http://www.who.int/whosis/whostat/ EN_WHS08_Table5_Inequities.pdf

[23] Woodward, A., Kawachi, I. Why reduce health inequalities?. (2000). *J. Epidemiol. Community Health;54*. 923-929.

[24] Caiazzo, A., Cardano, M., Cois, E., Costa, G., Marinaci, C., Spadea, T., Vannoni, F., Venturini. L.,Inequalities in health in Italy. (2004*) Epidemiol. Prev. May-Jun;28*(3 Suppl):i-ix, 1-161.

[25] Zhang, JX., Woo, J. Assessing mental health and its association with income old-old Chinese in Hong Kong. *AM. J. Geriatr. Psychiatr.* (2005). 13 (3). 236-243.

[26] Stjärne, M. K., Ponce de Leon, A., Hallqvist, J. and the SHEEP Study Group. Contextual effects of social fragmentation and material deprivation on risk of myocardial infarction—results from the Stockholm Heart Epidemiology Program (SHEEP). (2004). *International Journal of Epidemiology* 33(4).732-741.

[27] Milan, G., Iavarone, A., Vargas, NF., Vargas, NM., Fiorillo, F., Galeone, F., Gallotta, G., Postiglione, A. (2004). Effects of demographic and environmental variables on cognitive performance in a rural community sample of elderly people living in Southern Italy. *Aging Clin. Exp. Res.* **16**, 398-402.

[28] Borrell, C., Rue, M.,Pasarin, MI., Rohlfs, I., Ferrando, J., Fernandez, E.. Trends in social class inequalities in health status, health-related behaviors, and health services utilization in a Southern European urban area (1983-1994). (2000) *Preventive Medicine,* Vol. 31, Issue 6,

[29] Gebo, K.A., Keruly, J., Moore, R.D. (2003) Association of Social Stress, Illicit Drug Use, and Health Beliefs with Nonadherence to Antiretroviral *Therapy J Gen Intern Med.* February; **18**(2). 104–111.

[30] Kasper JA., Wilson R.. Use of prescribed medicines: a proxy indicator of access and health status (1983). *Int. J. Health Serv;* **13**, 433-42.

[31] Mortensen, J.T., Olesen, A. V., Bøggild, H., Olsen, J., Westergård-Nielsen, N. C., Socioeconomic correlates of drug use based on prescription data: A population-based cross-sectional register study in Denmark 1999. (2007). *Danish Medical Bulletin* - No. **1**. February. Vol. 54. 62-65.

[32] Scott, A., Shiell, A., King, M. Is general practitioner decision making associated with patients' socio-economic status? (1996). *Soc. Sci. Med.* **42**. 35-46.

[33] Thomsen, RW., Johnsen, SP., Olesen, AV., Mortensen, JT., Boggild, H., Olsen, J., et al. Socioeconomic gradient in use of statins among Danish patients: population-based cross-sectional study. (2005). *Br. J. Clin. Pharmacol.* Nov. 60(5).534-42.

[34] Wolinsky, FD., Johnson , RJ. Perceived health status and mortality among older men and women. (1992). *Journal Of Gerontology: Social Sciences,* Nov;47(6): S304-12.

[35] De La Hoz, F., Leon, D. A. (1996). Self-Perceived Health Status And Inequalities In Use Of Health Services In Spain. *Int. J. Epidemiol.* **25** (3) 593-603.

[36] Materia, E., Cacciani, L., Bagarini, G., Cesaroni, G., Davoli M., Mirale, MP., Vergine, L., Baglio, G., Simeone, G., Peducci, CA. (2005). Income inequality and mortality in Italy. *Eur. J. Public Health.* **15**, 411-417.

[37] Costa, G., Marinacci, C., Caiazzo, A., Spadea, T. (2003). Individual and contextual determinants of inequalities in health: the Italian case. *Int. J. Health Serv.* **33**, 635-667.

[38] Lucchetti, M.,Gattaceca, R., Mazzoni , E., Corsonello, A. (2006). Percezione dell'invecchiamento e determinanti socioambientali in aree differenziate (metropolitana e rurale) della Regione Calabria. *Giornale di Gerontologia.* **54**, 204-216.

[39] Lucchetti, M., Corsonello, A., Gattaceca, R. (2008). Environmental and social determinants of aging perception in metropolitan and rural areas of Southern Italy. *Arch Gerontol Geriatr.* May-Jun;46(3), 349-57. Epub 2007 Jun 27.

[40] Principi A (2005). I trasferimenti monetari nazionali. In: Lamura G, Gori C, Hanau C, Polverini F, Principi A, Tomassini C (eds) *L'informazione statistica sull'assistenza agli anziani in Italia.* pp. 175-195. Roma, Commissione per la Garanzia dell'Informazione Statistica presso la Presidenza del Consiglio dei Ministri.

[41] Mesini D, Gambino A (2006). La spesa per l'assistenza continuativa in Italia. In C. Gori (ed.) *La riforma dell''assistenza ai non autosufficienti. Ipotesi e proposte,* pp. 45-82. Bologna: Il Mulino.

[42] Caltabiano C., (2004). *Il prisma del welfare: analisi dei regimi socio-assistenziali nelle regioni italiane.* Roma, IREF.

[43] Van Groenou, M. B.,Glaser, K., Tomassini, C., Jacobs, T. Socio-economic status differences in older people's use of informal and formal help: a comparison of four European countries. (2006). *Ageing & Society* **26**. 745-766.

[44] EUROSTAT, (2006). Data on Population. Luxembourg.

[45] Quattrini S (2006). Main characteristics of the Italian family carers' and older people's sample. In: Quattrini S., Melchiorre M.G., Balducci C., Spazzafumo L., Lamura G. (eds.) *EUROFAMCARE: The National Survey Report for Italy,* pp. 67-81. Ancona: INRCA.

[46] Lamura G, Ferring D, Mnich E (2006). *Loneliness and economic resources of older people in Europe: recent empirical evidence and policy implications.* Paper presented at the Technical Meeting for the Madrid Implementation Plan of Action on Ageing, Segovia (Spain), November 26.

[47] Acheson, D., (1998). *Indipendent Inquiry into Inequalities in Health Report* http://www.archive.official-documents.co.uk/document/doh/ih/part2g.htm.

[48] De Yeatts., T Crow., E Folts. (1992).Service use among low-income minority elderly: strategies for overcoming barriers. *The Gerontologist,* Vol 32, Issue 1 24-32, The Gerontological Society of America.

[49] Syme, S. L., Lefkowitz, B., Kivimae Krimgold, B. Incorporating Socioeconomic Factors Into U.S. Health Policy: Addressing The Barriers, *Health Aff.* **21** (2): 113-119.

[50] Programme Committee on Socio-economic inequalities in health (SEGV-II). *Reducing socio-economic inequalities in health.* The Hague, Ministry of Health, Welfare and Sport, 2001.

In: Low Incomes: Social, Health and Educational Impacts   ISBN: 978-1-60741-175-8
Editor: Jacob K. Levine, pp. 173-205   © 2009 Nova Science Publishers, Inc.

Chapter 8

ZOOTHERAPY AS ALTERNATIVE THERAPEUTIC IN SOUTH AMERICA

Rômulo Romeu da Nóbrega Alves[1],
Carla Calixto da Silva[2], Raynner Rilke Duarte Barboza[3]
and Wedson de Medeiros Silva Souto[4]

[1] Departamento de Biologia, Universidade Estadual da Paraíba,
Avenida das Baraúnas, Campina Grande, Paraíba 58109-753, Brasil
[2] Programa de Pós-Graduação em Economia, Universidade Federal de Pernambuco,
Centro de Ciências Sociais Aplicadas, Departamento de Economia,
Cidade Universitária 50670-901, Recife, Pernambuco, Brasil.
[3] Mestrado em Ciência e Tecnologia Ambiental, Universidade Estadual da Paraíba,
Avenida das Baraúnas, Campina Grande, Paraíba 58109-753, Brasil
[4] Programa Regional de Pós-Graduação em Desenvolvimento e Meio
Ambiente (PRODEMA), Universidade Estadual da Paraíba,
Avenida das Baraúnas, Campina Grande,
Paraíba 58109-753, Brasil

Abstract

The healing of human ailments by using therapeutics based on medicines obtained from animals or ultimately derived from them is known as zootherapy. The use of animal-derived medicines as an alternative therapeutic has also been recorded in different parts of the globe, yet little attention has been paid to the cultural, medical, or ecological significance of zootherapeutic practices, even in countries where the use of medicinal animals is well established. Despite their importance, studies on the therapeutic use of animals and animal parts have been neglected, when compared to plants. This chapter paper discusses some related aspects of the use of animals or parts thereof as medicines in South America, and their implications for public health, ecology and economy. Our review revealed that at least 322 species of animals belonging to 157 families are used in traditional folk medicine in South America. The use of medicinal animals is a fundamental component within traditional health systems and medical practice in South America. Besides being influenced by cultural aspects, the relations between humans and biodiversity in the form of zootherapeutic practices are conditioned by the social and economic relations.

Keywords: Zootherapy, traditional medicine, public health.

Introduction

Although recent advances in molecular biology and physiological chemistry have greatly enhanced our understanding and treatment of diseases, a large segment of the population still relies on traditional medicine or so-called alternative medicine as the preferred form of health care [1]. The World Health Organization (WHO) estimates that as many as 80% of the world's more than six billion people rely primarily on animal and plant-based medicines [2, 3].

Medicinal plants and animals, since times immemorial, have been used in virtually all cultures as a source of medicine [2, 4-9]. Traditional human populations have a broad natural pharmacopoeia consisting of wild plant and animal species. Ingredients sourced from wild plants and animals are not only used in traditional medicines, but are also increasingly valued as raw materials in the preparation of modern medicines and herbal preparations [10].

Due to the extensive use of plant materials, traditional medicine is associated with herbalism. However, animal-based medicines also play a significant role in healing practices of many societies. Several authors (e.g. Alves et al. [5], Alakbarli [4], Lev [11], Adeola [12], Alves et al. [13], Unnikrishnan [14]; Vázquez et al [15]; Mahawar and Jaroli [16], Van and Tap [17]; Ashwell and Walston [18]) have showed that animals and products derived from different organs of their bodies have constituted part of the inventory of medicinal substances used in various cultures since ancient times.

The healing of human ailments by using therapeutics based on medicines obtained from animals or ultimately derived from them is known as zootherapy [2, 19]. As Marques [20] states, "all human culture which presents a structured medical system will utilize animals as medicines". The phenomenon of zootherapy is marked both by a broad geographical distribution and very deep historical origins. In modern societies, zootherapy constitutes an important alternative among many other known therapies practiced worldwide [2].

The use of biological resources for various therapies has been documented in many different parts of the world - but largely in remote regions, where traditional medicines provide a *de facto* alternative to "modern" health care systems [5, 21-24]. It is well established that traditional medicine plays a crucial role in health care for a large part of the population living in developing countries. In fact, for centuries, traditional medicine was the only health care system available to the prevention and treatment of diseases in different cultures. The interfaces among public health, traditional medicine and biodiversity encompass a number of relevant and contemporary issues, which are seldom dealt with in an integrated fashion by policy makers [25].

The South America region is remarkably heterogeneous in terms of climate, ecosystems, human population distribution, and cultural traditions. South America's rich biological and cultural diversity makes it an exceptional location in which to examine and increase our knowledge of faunistic resources used as in traditional folk medicine, and to draw attention to the need to their importance for public health, protect traditional knowledge and biodiversity.

In that context, the aim of this work was to provide an overview of the use of medicinal animals in South America, identify those species used as folk remedies, and discuss the implications of public health.

Methods

In order to examine the diversity of animals used in traditional medicine in South America, all available references or reports of folk remedies based on animal sources were examined. Only taxa that could be identified to species level were included in the database. Scientific names provided in publications were updated according to the ITIS Catalogue of Life: 2007 Annual Checklist [26]. The sources analyzed were: Alves et al. [5], Alves and Rosa [24, 25], Almeida [27], Almeida and Albuquerque [28], Alves [29], Alves and Pereira-Filho [30], Alves and Rosa [31, 32], Alves et al. [33], Andrade and Costa-Neto [34], Apaza et al. [35], Barbarán [36], Begossi [37], Begossi and Braga [38], Begossi et al. [39], Branch and Silva [40], Campos [41], Costa-Neto [19, 42-51], Costa-Neto and Oliveira [52], Costa-Neto and Pacheco [53], Costa-Neto et al. [54], Figueiredo [55], Freire [56], Lenko and Papavero [57], Mallmann [58], Marques [59], Moura and Marques [60], Pinto and Maduro [61], Seixas and Begossi [62], Silva et al. [63], Souto et al. [64], Vargas [65].

Results and Discussion

The medicinal fauna South America has been the focus of some ethnozoological research over the last two decades, mainly in countries such as Brazil and Bolívia. These studies have been showed the importance of zootherapy to traditional communities in various socio-cultural environments (e.g. Alves et al. [5], Alves and Rosa [31], Apaza et al. [35]). This is not surprise, considering the rich biological resources and cultural of the region, that generated invaluable local knowledge systems that include extensive information on animal uses in general and medicinally useful species in particular [5, 66].

Our review revealed that at least 322 species of animals belonging to 157 families are used in traditional folk medicine in South America. The taxonomic group with the largest number of animal species fishes (with 85 species), followed by mammals (73), birds (44), reptiles (43) and insects (36). Other groups mentioned by the interviewees were crustaceans (16), molluscs (13), echinoderms (7), amphibians (3) and cnidarians (2) (see Table 1 and figure 1). Similarly to the results obtained in previous studies (Alves and Rosa [24], Almeida and Albuquerque [28], Apaza et al. [35], Begossi [37], Branch and Silva [40], Seixas and Begossi [62], Silva et al. [63], Sodeinde and Soewu [67], El-Kamali [68], Kakati and Doulo [69]), in our review the taxonomic groups with the largest number of medicinal species documented were vertebrates.

The high taxonomic diversity of animal species used in traditional medicine is not surprising, as numerous workers have pointed out that animals are among the resources frequently used in folk medicine worldwide. However, considering the relatively small number of published studies on the subject in many countries of South America, we presume that the true number of medicinal animal species used is greater than that recorded here.

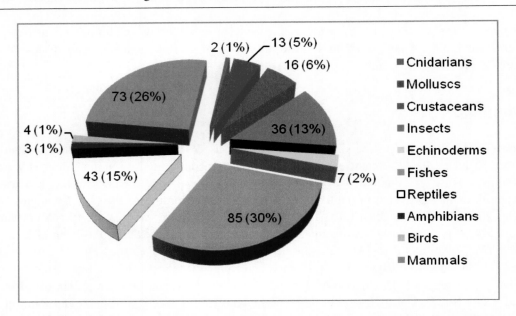

Figure 1. Representativeness of animals taxonomic groups used in South America Traditional Medicine.

Some widespread species are used in different countries, such as *Tupinambis* spp. (in Argentina and Brazil), and *Tapirus terrestris* (in Brazil and Bolivia) [35, 70]. A given reptile often has multiple medicinal uses and can be employed to treat more than one ailment, while different reptiles can likewise be used to treat the same illnesses. Products derived from *Tupinambis merianae* and *T. teguixin*, for instance, were indicated for treating 14 and 29 conditions, respectively, in Brazil; in Bolivia, products derived from the *Agouti paca* (Linnaeus, 1766) have been documented as remedies for general body pain, leishmaniasis, snakebite, rheumatism, heart pain, pain in bones, liver pain, fever, and pain during childbirth [35].

Animals were used for treating 249 diseases, asthma, rheumatism, wounds, thrombosis and bronchitis being the most usual ones. Most animals (n=181, 56.21%) were prescribed for treating different diseases. For geographically widespread species, similar uses were found in different countries. Some examples are: *H. reidi* and *C. durissus* for treating asthma and *Apis mellifera* (Linnaeus, 1758) (Apidae) and *Mellita sexiesperforata* (Leske, 1778) for treating flu and cough [16-18, 24, 25, 28, 31, 40, 58, 63, 68].

Despite their importance, the use of animals and their body parts in medicine have been neglected, when compared to plants [24]. Traditional drugs and traditional medicine in general represent a still poorly explored field of research in terms of therapeutic potential or clinical evaluation. There is a current preoccupation about this, since it is well-established that all sorts of vegetable, animal and mineral remedies used in a traditional setting are capable of producing serious adverse reactions. It is essential, however, that traditional drug therapies be submitted to an appropriate benefit/risk analysis. Numerous infectious diseases can be transmitted from animals to humans (i.e. zoonoses). In this context, the possibility of transmitting infections or ailments from animal preparations to the patient should be seriously considered [71]. Several organs and tissues including bones and bile can be a source of *Salmonella* infection causing chronic diarrhoea and endotoxic shock. The possibility of transmission of other serious and widespread zoonoses such as tuberculosis or rabies should be considered whenever animal tissues from unknown sources are handled and used as remedies [72]. The possibility of toxic or allergic reactions to animal products should also be considered [73]. As pointed out by Pieroni et al. [74], the chemical constituents and pharmacological actions of some animal products are already known to some extent and ethnopharmacological studies focused on animal remedies could be very important in order to clarify the eventual therapeutic usefulness of this class of biological remedies.

Traditional medicine still makes use of animals and products derived from animal organs such in rural areas as in many urban and semi-urban localities. For instance, biological remedies are openly commercialized in essentially all of the towns and cities in Brazil, principally in public markets. It is common to find specific places in these markets where plants and animals are sold for medicinal purposes - locations that serve to unite, maintain, and diffuse empirical knowledge from different regions and of different origins [5, 28, 30-32, 43, 63, 75-79]. This reflect the widespread usage of animal-based remedies, and the resilience of zootherapeutic practices, which have come to co-exist with allopathic medicine in urban and semi-urban environments [31]. As pointed by Athais [80] and Sanchez [81], even in many Indigenous communities, traditional medicine is still practiced, with a link to allopathic medicine use [80]. In addition to the use of traditional healers, known as Shamans (more formally Opygua, Pai, and other denominations), many families have their own knowledge and access to medicinal plants and animals for use in emergencies.

Besides their role in healing, natural products often have magical-religious significance, reflecting the different views of health and disease that exist within different cultures. In this context, animal parts are used to prepare clinical remedies as well as to make amulets or charms used in magical/religious diagnoses. Popular beliefs usually affect the way species are used in zootherapy [24]. One form of spiritual treatment involves the use of amulets containing reptile parts to protect the user from the "evil-eye" or from diseases [30]. An example is caiman teeth (*C. latirostris*, *M. niger*, and *P. palpebrosus*) used as protection against snake bites [5].

In addition to the belief systems, the socioeconomics aspects also influence the zootherapeutic practices [5]. Latin America has one of the greatest disparities in income distribution in the world. Overall, the health profile of the Latin American population can be classified as undergoing a slow epidemiological transition. At one extreme of the spectrum there is a high incidence of (and mortality from) chronic noninfectious diseases such as cardiovascular problems and cancer, which predominate in large metropolitan areas. On the other hand, infectious diseases still impose a heavy burden on the poverty-stricken parts of the population. The reasons for this dichotomy are two-fold: uneven socioeconomic development within countries and the extreme diversity of regional environments [82]. Brazil, for example, is a highly heterogeneous socially and regionally marked by profound internal inequalities in distribution of income [83]. For the majority of population, access medical-hospital care is available within the public sector and the organization of health care system reflects the schisms within Brazilian society. High technology private care is available to the rich and inadequate public care to the poor [84; 85]. Studies suggest that Indigenous peoples of Latin America still have inadequate access to mainstream health services, and health prevention and promotion programmes, and that services that do exist are often culturally inappropriate [80, 81]. Some of the barriers to health care access are structural and economic factors (distance and location of health care facilities, isolation of Indigenous communities, scarcity of health insurance or funds to pay for services, or time factors) and poor cultural sensitivity and appropriateness of health care systems (disregard of health personnel towards Indigenous peoples or their culture, disrespect for traditional healing practices, language and religious barriers, or uncomfortable and impersonal environment of hospitals and clinics) [86-89]. Hence, resorting to the use of medicinal animals and plants, which were easily accessible and relatively cheap is an important component to health care. Nevertheless, it has been documented that people sometimes resort to traditional home remedies as a means of resisting urban modern medicine [90] and of asserting their traditional culture [91].It is important to note that behind the perceived efficacy by users, the popularity of animal-based remedies is influenced by cultural aspects, the relations between humans and biodiversity in the form of zootherapeutic practices are conditioned by the social and economic relations between humans themselves [24].

The traditional medicine is widely available and affordable, yet in remote areas, and generally accessible to most people. In many developing countries, a large part of the population, especially in rural areas, depends mainly on traditional medicine for their primary health care, because it is cheaper and more accessible than orthodox medicine [5, 92-94]. Traditional medicine is also more acceptable because it blends readily into the peoples' socio-cultural life [95]. Nazarea et al. [96] highlight that social, economic and cultural factors play a large role in determining how individuals and communities use natural resources.

The use of medicinal animals and plants is a fundamental component within traditional health systems and medical practice in South America. Recently, concern about the ethics of exploiting indigenous knowledge and resources from tropical countries, without sharing the benefits with those who are the traditional custodians of the knowledge and land, has gained attention through the convention on biological diversity (CBD), which requires that such knowledge be protected, respected and preserved [97]. Traditional knowledge related to traditional medicine may be protected and conserved through the development of intellectual property rights (IPRs) and/or through benefit sharing [98, 99]. Intellectual property rights are rights over intangible information that provides incentives for future innovations [98]. The compensation of indigenous people can validate their knowledge of the biodiversity they manage and also provide them with an equitable reward for sharing it, thereby compensating biological stewardship and encouraging conservation (see Moran et al. [98], Svarstad [100]). In fact, as pointed out by Smith et al. [101], the explanations for difficulties in access to essential drugs in the poor countries relate not only to the population precarious socio-economic conditions, but also to lack of organization health services, inadequate supply system management and irrational prescription.

Many countries (including Argentina, Bolivia, Venezuela, Colombia, Ecuador, Mexico, Nicaragua, and Paraguay) have revised their Constitutions to legally recognize the rights of Indigenous people to maintain and promote their specific cultural, linguistic, and territorial integrity. In 2003, the Unit of Indigenous Communities and Community Development analysed the constitutions and legislation of 21 Latin American countries according to eight variables of best legislative practice.

In several countries, the importance of plants (and animals) and medication systems has led to the creation of national bodies to protect them. The main threat to such natural resources in Latin America is the rapid destruction of ecosystems, and the loss of biodiversity, both exacerbated by climate change. Between 1975 and 1988, nearly 500 000 km² of tropical rainforest was deforested in Amazonia, 10·1% of the total surface [102, 103]. In the presente work, we verified that is common the medicinal use of threatened species as remedies. From the perspective both of the faunistic resources and of traditional knowledge holders, habitat loss and landscape alterations are potential treats to the survival of many potential valuable medicinal animals and the cultural aspects associated to them. As discussed by Anyinam [104], environmental degradation also affects users of traditional medicine, both by limiting their access to the resources traditionally used and by extirpating from their community the knowledge base upon which traditional medicine is constructed.

If the need for conservation is to be accepted by people who make their livelihoods from wildlife or use wildlife as food and/or medicine, then care should be taken to avoid approaches with little or no social resonance (i.e., that may be perceived as ideological or culturally imperialistic) [25]. Sustainability of harvesting of medicinal animals is challenged by many factors, from both social and ecological perspectives. It is important to respect differing views of the value of wildlife, while, at the same time, conserving biodiversity.

Table 1. Animal Taxa Recorded as Having Medicinal Properties

Family / Species / local name	Conditions to which remedies are prescribed
CNIDARIANS	
Mussidae	
Mussismilia harttii (Verril, 1868) – "Coral"	Vaginal discharge, diarrhoea
Physaliidae	
Physalia physalia (Linnaeus, 1758) - Portuguese-man-of-war, "jellyfish"	Asthma
MOLLUSCS	
Ampullariidae	
Pomacea lineata (Spix, 1827) - Snail, "Clam"	Asthma, sprains, boils, ulcer
Cassidae	
Cassis tuberosa (Linnaeus, 1758) - "Conch"	Asthma
Littorinidae	
Littorina angulifera (Lamarck, 1822) - Periwinkle snail	Chesty cough, shortness of breath
Lucinidae	
Lucina pectinata (Gmelin, 1791) – "Shellfish"	Sexual impotence
Melongenidae	
Pugilina morio (Linnaeus, 1758) – "Conch"	Sexual impotence
Mytilidae	
Mytella charruana (Orbigny, 1842) – Mussel, "Shellfish"	Ophthalmological problems
Mytella guyanensis Lamarck (1819) - Mussel, "Shellfish"	Weakness
Ostreidae	
Crassostrea rhizophorae (Guilding, 1828) "Mangrove oyster"	Osteoporosis, pneumonia, stomach ache, cancer, flu, weakness, pain relief in injuries caused by the dorsal fin spine of a species of catfish, anaemia, tuberculosis
Strombidae	

Table 1. Continued

Family / Species / local name	Conditions to which remedies are prescribed
Strombus pugilis Linnaeus, 1758 – "West Indian fighting conch"	Sexual impotence
Teredinidae	
Neoteredo reynei (Bartsch, 1920) "Shipworm"	Anaemia, tuberculosis
Teredo pedicellata Quatrefages, 1849	Tuberculosis
Vasidae	
Turbinella laevigata (Anton, 1839) – "Conch"	Sexual impotence
Veneridae	
Anomalocardia brasiliana (Gmelin, 1791) – Clam, "shellfish"	Asthma, flu, stomach ache
CRUSTACEANS	
Calappidae	
Calappa ocellata Holthuis, 1958 – "Ocellate box crab"	Asthma, osteoporosis
Gecarcinidae	
Cardisoma guanhumi Latreille, 1825 – "Blue land crab"	Asthma, bronchitis, wounds, boils
Grapsidae	
Goniopsis cruentata (Latreille, 1802) – "Mangrove root crab"	Epilepsy, venereal disease
Plagusia depressa (Fabricius, 1775) - "Tidal spray crab"	Epilepsy
Hippidae	
Emerita portoricensis Schmitt, 1935 - "Puerto Rican sand crab"	Earache
Ocypodidae	
Ocypode quadrata (JC Fabricius, 1787) – "Ghost crab"	Asthma, haemorrhage in women, flu, to alleviate the symptoms of intoxication with poison of 'niquim' (Pisces, Batrachoididae)
Ucides cordatus (Linnaeus, 1763) – "Swamp Land crab"	Hemorrhage in women, incontinence, osteoporosis, cough, asthma, tuberculosis, womb disorders, arthrosis, bronchitis
Uca maracoani (Latreille, 1802) – "Fiddler crab"	Asthma, whooping cough
Palaemonidae	
Macrobrachium carcinus (Linnaeus, 1758) – "Bigclaw river shrimp", "Painted river prawn"	Amnesia
Macrobrachium acanthurus (Wiegmann, 1836) – "Cinnamon river shrimp"	Irritation when milk teeth are erupting
Macrobrachium borellii (Nobili, 1896) – "Freshwater shrimp"	Irritation when milk teeth are erupting
Penaeidae	
Family / Species / local name	Conditions to which remedies are prescribed

Table 1. Continued

Family / Species / local name	Conditions to which remedies are prescribed
Xiphopenaeus schmitti (Burkenroad, 1936) – "Southern white shrimp"	Irritation when milk teeth are erupting, skin spots
Xiphopenaeus kroyeri (Heller, 1862) – "Atlantic seabob"	Irritation when milk teeth are erupting, skin spots
Pseudosquillidae	
Cloridopsis dúbia (H. M. Edwards, 1837) – "Mantis shrimp"	Asthma
Armadillidiidae	
Armadillidium vulgare (Latreille, 1804) – "Pillbug"	Asthma
Sesarmidae	
Aratus pisoni (H. Milne Edwards, 1837) – "Mangrove crab"	Epilepsy, to alleviate the symptoms of intoxication with poison of *Colomesus psittacus* (a species of pufferfish)
INSECTS	
Apidae	
Apis mellifera (Linnaeus, 1758) – "Africanised honey bee"	Cough, flu, rheumatism, tuberculosis, bronchitis, hoarseness, ulcer, diabetes, verminosis, headache, giddiness, backache, wounds, burns, mumps, varicose veins, arthrosis, cellulitis, amoebiasis, sore throat, ashma, anaemia
Cephalotrigona capitata (Smith, 1854) - "Bee"	Snake bite (antidote)
Frieseomelitta silvestrii (Friese, 1902) - "Stingless bee"	Flu
Melipona compressipes (Fabricius, 1804) – "Stingless bee"	Asthma, cough
Melipona mandacaia Smith, 1863 – "Stingless bee"	Wounds
Melipona quadrifasciata Lepeletier, 1836 "Neotropical stingless bee"	Snake bite
Melipona scutellaris (Latreille, 1811) – "Stingless bee"	Headache, migraine, stroke, verminosis, stomach ache, tuberculosis, haemorrhage, cataracts, mycosis in the mouth, flu, cancer, asthma, bronchitis, intestinal disorders, cough, sexual impotence, ophthalmological problems, weakness, thrombosis, amoebiasis, snake bite (antidote), rabies, sinusitis
Melipona subnitida (Ducke, 1910) - "Honey bee"	Flu, sore throat
Partamona Cupira (Smith, 1863) – "Stingless bee"	Sore throat, swelling, headache, thrombosis, stroke
Plebeia cf. *emerina* Friese, 1900 – "Mosquito"	Mycosis in the mouth area
Tetragonisca angustula Latreille, 1811 – "Bee"	Cataracts, sinusitis, cough, flu, ophthalmological problems, sore throat, leucoma
Trigona mosquito Lutz, 1931 – "Stingless bee"	Cough

Table 1. Continued

Family / Species / local name	Conditions to which remedies are prescribed
Trigona spinipes (Fabricius, 1793) – "Stingless bee"	Asthma, cough, flu, bronchits, acne, diabetes, strokes, thrombosis, migraine, itching, sore throat, giddiness, weakness, scabies, nasal congestion, to induce abortion, whooping cough, irritation when milk teeth are erupting, earache, epilepsy, shortness of breath, late menstruation
Blattidae	
Periplaneta americana (Linnaeus, 1758) – "American cockroach"	Heartburn, asthma, stomach ache, intestinal colic, earache, alchoolism, epilepsy, vomit, boil, haemorrhage, bronchits, diarrhea, gonorrhea, panaris, cancer, stroke, burns, menstrual cramps, wounds, to suck a splinter out of skin or flesh, detoxification (alcohol abuse)
Chrysomelidae	
Coraliomela brunnea Thumberg, 1821 – "Fake cockroach"	Epilepsy
Pachymerus cf. *nucleorum* (Fabricius, 1792) – "Caterpillar"	Earache, stroke, swelling, wounds, seborrheic dermatitis, inflammation, thrombosis
Curculionidae	
Rhynchophorus palmarum Linnaeus, 1758 – "Pest of coconut palm"	Fever, headache, boils
Rhinostomus barbirostris Fabricius, 1775 – "Pest of coconut palm"	Fever, headache, boils
Formicidae	
Atta cephalotes (Linnaeus, 1758) - "Leaf-cutter ant"	Sore throat
Atta serdens (Linnaeus, 1758) – "Leaf-cutting"	Stomach ache, heart diseases, chest palpations
Dinoponera quadriceps (Santschi, 1921) - "Bullet ant"	Asthma
Solenopsis saevissima (Smith, 1855) – "Ant"	Wart
Gryllidae	
Acheta domesticus (Linnaeus, 1758) - "House cricket"	Scabies, asthma, eczema, lithiasis, earache, oliguresis, rheumatism, urine retention, children that urinate in bed and speak with lateness, incontinence urinary, ophthalmological problems
Paragryllus temulentus Saussure 1878 - "Cricket"	Rheumatism
Meloidae	
Palembus dermestoides (Fairmaire, 1893) – "Peanut beeatle"	Sexual impotence, ophthalmological problems, rheumatism, weakness
Muscidae	
Musca domestica (Linnaeus, 1758) - "House fly"	Boil, baldness, eyesore, external sebaceus lamps, stye, spots in the face, ophthalmological problems, dermatosis, cysties
Pediculidae	

Table 1. Continued

Family / Species / local name	Conditions to which remedies are prescribed
Pediculus humanus Linnaeus, 1758 - "Body louse", "Head louse"	Tootache
Psychidae	
Eurycotis manni Rehn, 1916 – "Beetle"	Headache
Oiketicus kirbyi Guilding, 1827 – "Case moth"	Asthma, earache, haemorrhage
Termitidae	
Microcerotermes exignus (Hagen, 1858), - "Termite"	Asthma, bronchitis, flu, whopping cough
Vespidae	
Family / Species / local name	Conditions to which remedies are prescribed
Apoica pallens (Oliv., 1791) – "Paper wasp"	Thrombosis, ashtma, giddiness, nasal haemorrhage, haemorrhage, stroke, disorders after parturition (to accelerate recovery after parturition), ophthalmological problems, mumps, late menstruation
Brachygastra lecheguana (Latreille, 1824) – "Dark paper wasp"	Cough, asthma
Polistes canadensis (Linnaeus, 1758) – "Wasp"	Cough, whooping cough
Polybia sericea (Olivier, 1791) - "Wasp"	Thrombosis
Protopolybia exigua (Saussure, 1854) – "Wasp"	Evil eye, tobaccoism, ophthalmological problems
Synoeca surinama (Linnaeus, 1767) – "Paper wasp"	Asthma, shortness of breath
ECHINODERMS	
Echinasteridae	
Echinaster brasiliensis Müller & Troschel, 1842 – "Starfish"	Asthma
Echinaster echinophorus Lamarck, 1816 – "Starfish"	Asthma
Echinometridae	
Echinometra lucunter (Linnaeus, 1758) – "Rock boring urchin"	Asthma
Luidiidae	
Luidia senegalensis Lamarck, 1916 - "Starfish"	Asthma, cough, metrorrhagia
Mellitidae	
Mellita sexiesperforata (Leske, 1778) – "Six holed keyhole urchin"	Asthma, cough
Oreasteridae	
Oreaster reticulatus (Linnaeus, 1758) – "Starfish"	Asthma
Toxopneustidae	
Lytechinus variegatus (Lamarck, 1816) – "Green sea urchin"	Snake bite

Table 1. Continued

Family / Species / local name	Conditions to which remedies are prescribed
FISHES	
Auchenipteridae	
Trachelyopterus galeatus (Linnaeus, 1766) - "Driftwood Cat"	Umbilical hernia, asthma, sexual impotence
Anostomidae	
Leporinus friderici (Bloch, 1794) – "Frederici's leporinus"	Earache
Leporinus piau Fowler, 1941 "Black piau"	Rheumatism
Schizodon knerii (Steindachner, 1875) - "White piau"	Leucoma, edema
Ariidae	
Bagre bagre (Linnaeus, 1766) – "Coco sea catfish"	Injuries caused by itself
Genidens barbus (Lacepède, 1803) – "White sea catfish"	Pain relief caused in injuries by the species' sting
Genidens genidens (Cuvier, 1829) – "catfish"	Injuries caused by itself
Sciadeichthys luniscutis (Valenciennes, 1837) – "Catfish"	Pain relief caused in injuries by the species' sting
Aspredinidae	
Aspredo aspredo (Linnaeus, 1758) – "Banjo, catfish"	Asthma
Aspredinichthys tibicen (Valenciennes, 1840) – "Tenbarbed banjo"	Asthma
Balistidae	
Balistes capriscus Gronow, 1854 – "Grey triggerfish"	Bronchitis
Balistes vetula (Linnaeus, 1758)[VU] – "Queen triggerfish"	Stroke, asthma, thrombosis, earache, pain relief caused in injuries by the species' sting, haemorrhage, ascites, schistosomiasis, appendicitis, menstrual cramps, gastritis
Batrachoididae	
Thalassophryne nattereri (Steindachner, 1876) – "Venomous toadfish"	Pain relief caused in injuries by the species' sting
Callichthyidae	
Callichthys callichthys (Linnaeus, 1758) – "Armoured catfish"	Asthma, umbilical hernia
Carcharhinidae	
Carcharhinus limbatus (Müller & Henle, 1839)[LR] – "Blackfin shark"	Osteoporosis
Carcharhinus porosus (Ranzani, 1840) – "Smalltail shark"	Asthma, rheumatism, wounds, inflammations, osteoporosis, anaemia
Galeocerdo cuvier (Péron & Lesueur, 1822)[LR] – "Tiger shark"	Osteoporosis
Rhizoprionodon lalandii (Müller & Henle, 1839) – "Brazilian sharpnose shark"	Rheumatism

Table 1. Continued

Family / Species / local name	Conditions to which remedies are prescribed
Rhizoprionodon porosus (Poey, 1861) – "Sharpnose shark"	Rheumatism
Sphyrna lewini (Griffith & Smith, 1834) – "Scalloped hammerhead"	Asthma, wounds, rheumatism, inflammation
Salmonidae	
Oncorhynchus mykiss (Walbaum, 1792) – "redband trout"	Rheumatism, used with Borax to eliminate the bad smell of feet
Centropomidae	
Centropomus parallelus Poey, 1860 - "Smallscale fat snook"	Nephritis
Centropomus undecimalis (Bloch, 1792) – "Common snook"	Edema in the legs
Characidae	
Astyanax bimaculatus (Linnaeus, 1758) – "Twospot astyanax"	Alcoholism, leishmaniosis, skin burns, wounds, rheumatism
Brycon nattereri Günther, 1864 – "Pirapitinga"	Flu
Colossoma macropomum (Cuvier, 1818) – "Black-finned colossoma"	Paralysis of arms and legs
Hydrolycus scomberoides (Cuvier, 1816) – "Vampire characin"	Earache
Clupeidae	
Opisthonema oglinum (Lesueur, 1818) – "Atlantic thread herring"	Alcoholism
Dasyatidae	
Dasyatis guttata (Bloch & Schneider, 1801) – "Longnose stingray"	Asthma, pain relief caused in injuries by the species' sting, burns
Dasyatis marianae (Gomes, Rosa & Gadig, 2000) – "Brazilian large-eyed stingray"	Asthma, pain relief caused in injuries by the species' sting, burns
Doradidae	
Franciscodoras marmoratus (Reinhardt, 1874) – "Urutu"	Injuries caused by itself
Lithodoras dorsalis (Valenciennes, 1840) "Bacu Pedra"	Swelling
Megalodoras uranoscopus (Eigenmann & Eigenmann, 1888) – "Catfish"	Rheumatism
Platydoras costatus (Linnaeus, 1758) - "Catfish"	Rheumatism
Pterodoras granulosus (Valenciennes, 1821) - "Catfish"	Rheumatism
Oxydoras niger (Valenciennes, 1821) - "Catfish"	Rheumatism
Echeneidae	
Echeneis naucrates Linnaeus, 1758 - "Live sharksucker"	Asthma, bronchitis
Electrophoridae	

Table 1. Continued

Family / Species / local name	Conditions to which remedies are prescribed
Electrophorus electricus (Linnaeus, 1766) – "Electric eel"	Sprains, bruises, insect bites, snake bite, asthma, flu, pain in general, muscle strain, rheumatism, osteoporosis, deafness, pneumonia, itching, tuberculosis, earache, toothache
Erythrinidae	
Erythrinus erythrinus (Bloch & Schneider, 1801) – "Red (hi-fin) Wolf fish"	Asthma
Hoplias malabaricus (Bloch, 1794) - "Trahira"	Ophthalmological problems, rheumatism, cataracts, wounds, snake bite, conjunctivitis, stroke, thrombosis, asthma, toothache, fever, earache, diarrhoea, deafness, boils, bleedings, alcoholism, tetanus, sore throat, itching, sprains, leucoma
Hoplias lacerdae Miranda Ribeiro, 1908 "Giant trahira"	Leucoma
Gadidae	
Gadus morhua Linnaeus, 1758 – "Atlantic cod"	Boils
Ginglymostomatidae	
Ginglymostoma cirratum (Bonnaterre, 1788) – "Nurse shark"	Rheumatism
Heptapteridae	
Pimelodella brasiliensis (Steindachner, 1876) – "Mandim"	Injuries caused by that fish species
Rhamdia quelen (Quoy & Gaimard, 1824) – "Catfish"	Tonic
Holocentridae	
Holocentrus adscensionis (Osbeck, 1765) – "Squirrelfish"	Wounds
Megalopidae	
Megalops atlanticus (Valenciennes, 1847) – "Tarpon"	Stroke, headache, asthma, shortness of breath, thrombosis, chest pain, injuries caused by bang
Muraenidae	
Gymnothorax funebris Ranzani, 1840 – "Green moray"	Bleeding (wounds)
Gymnothorax moringa (Cuvier, 1829) – "Spotted moray"	Bleeding (wounds)
Gymnothorax vicinus (Castelnau, 1855) – "Purplemouth moray"	Bleeding (wounds)
Myliobatidae	
Aetobatus narinari (Euphrasen, 1790) – "Spotted eagle ray"	Asthma, pain relief caused in injuries by the species' sting, burns, haemorrhage
Narcinidae	
Narcine brasiliensis (Olfers, 1831) - "Brazilian electric Ray"	Toothache
Ogcocephalidae	

Table 1. Continued

Family / Species / local name	Conditions to which remedies are prescribed
Ogcocephalus vespertilio (Linnaeus, 1758) – "Batfish"	Asthma, bronchitis
Osteoglossidae	
Arapaima gigas (Schinz, 1822) – "Giant arapaima"	Asthma, pneumonia
Pimelodidae	
Phractocephalus hemioliopterus (Bloch & Schneider, 1801) – "Redtail catfish"	Asthma, wounds, hernia, burns in the skin, rheumatism, flu, cough, pneumonia
Pseudoplatystoma corruscans (Spix & Agassiz, 1829) – "Spotted sorubim"	Flu
Pseudoplatystoma fasciatum (Lunnaeus, 1776) – "Tiger catfish"	Cold
Sorubimichthys planiceps (Spix & Agassiz, 1829) – "Sorubim"	Leishmaniosis, tuberculosis
Zungaro zungaro((Humboldt, 1821) – "Black manguruyu"	Asthma, toothache, earache, wounds, athlete's foot, burns in the skin, rheumatism, flu
Potamotrygonidae	
Paratrygon aiereba (Müller & Henle, 1841) – Discus ray, "Arraia"	Asthma, hernia, flu, pneumonia, cough, earache, burns
Potamotrygon hystrix (Müller & Henle, 1834) - Porcupine river stingray arraia	Asthma, hernia, flu, pneumonia, cough, earache, burns
Potamotrygon motoro (Müller & Henle, 1841) - Ocellate river stingray arraia	Asthma, hernia, flu, pneumonia, cough, earache, burns
Potamotrygon orbignyi (Castelnau, 1855)	Pain relief caused in injuries by that species' sting
Plesiotrygon iwamae Rosa, Castello & Thorson, 1987	Pain relief caused in injuries by the species' sting, wounds, cracks in the sole of the feet
Pristidae	
Pristis pectinata Latham, 1794 – Smalltooth sawfish, "espadarte", "peixe-serra"	Asthma, rheumatism, arthritis
Pristis perotteti Müller & Henle, 1841 – Largetooth sawfish, "espadarte"	Asthma, rheumatism and arthritis
Prochilodontidae	
Family / Species / local name	Conditions to which remedies are prescribed
Prochilodus argenteus Spix & Agassiz, 1829 – "curimatá-pacú", "curimatá"	To avoid swelling of the breast feeding, mycosis
Prochilodus nigricans Spix & Agassiz, 1829 - Black prochilodus, "curimatã"	Chilblain, skin burns, wounds, rheumatism, eye pains
Rajidae	
Atlantoraja cyclophora Regan, 1903 - Eyespot skate	Haemorrhage after delivery
Serrasalmidae	
Mylossoma duriventre (Cuvier, 1818) – Pacupeba, "pacu-manteiga"	Venereal disease
Serrasalmus brandtii (Lütken, 1875) - White piranha, "pirambeba"	Inflammations, sexual impotence
Sciaenidae	

Table 1. Continued

Family / Species / local name	Conditions to which remedies are prescribed
Cynoscion acoupa (Lacepède, 1801) - Acoupa weakfish, "pescada amarela"	Renal failure
Cynoscion leiarchus (Cuvier, 1830) - Smooth weakfish, "pescada branca"	Renal failure
Micropogonias furnieri (Desmarest, 1823) – Whitemouth croaker, "corvina"	Pain relief caused in injuries by the species' sting, cough, asthma, bronchitis
Pachyurus francisci (Cuvier, 1830) - San Francisco croaker, "cruvina-de-bico"	Asthma, urinary incontinence, backache
Plagioscion surinamensis (Bleeker, 1873) – Bashaw, "pacora", "Curvina"	Urinary disorders, haemorrhage, snake bites
Plagioscion squamosissimus (Heckel, 1840) - South american silver croaker, "curvina'	Urinary disorders, haemorrhage, snake bites
Sparidae	
Calamus penna (Valenciennes, 1830) - Sheepshead porgy, "peixe-pena"	Asthma
Synbranchidae	
Synbranchus marmoratus Bloch, 1795 - Marbled swamp eel, "muçum"	Bronchitis
Syngnathidae	
Hippocampus erectus Perry, 1810 – Horsefish, "cavalo-marinho"	Asthma
Hippocampus reidi (Ginsburg, 1933) - Longsnout seahorse, "cavalo-marinho"	Asthma, edema, bronchitis, haemorrhage, haemorrhage in women, disorders after parturition (to accelerate recovery after parturition), gastritis, tuberculosis, to prevent abortion
Tetraodontidae	
Colomesus psittacus (Bloch & Schneider, 1801) - Banded puffer, "baiacu"	Breast cancer, backache, warts
Sphoeroides testudineus (Linnaeus, 1758) - Checkered puffer, "baiacu"	Rheumatism
Trichiuridae	
Trichiurus lepturus Linnaeus, 1758 - Largehead hairtail	Asthma
Urolophidae	
Urotrygon microphthalmum (Delsman, 1941) - Smalleyed round stingray, "raia"	Asthma, pain relief caused in injuries by the species' sting, burns
AMPHIBIANS	
Bufonidae	
Chaunus schneideri (Werner, 1894) – Cururu toad, "sapo cururu"	Urinary incontinence, dental caries, cancer, wounds, boils, erysipelas acne, to induce abortion
Chaunus marinus (Linnaeus, 1758) – Marine toad, "sapo-cururu"	Scorpion sting (antidote)
Leptodactylidae	
Leptodactylus cf. *labyrinthicus* (Spix, 1824) – South american pepper frog, "jia-de-peito", "rã-pimenta"	Earache, rheumatism, joint pain, cancer, sore throat

Table 1. Continued

Family / Species / local name	Conditions to which remedies are prescribed
REPTILES	
Gekkonidae	
Hemidactylus mabouia (Moreau de Jonnes, 1818) - Afro-American house gecko, "lagartixa", "briba"	Sore throat
Iguanidae	
Iguana iguana (Linnaeus, 1758) - Common iguana, "camaleão"	Earache, erysipelas, asthma, rheumatism, edema, abscesses, joint pain, wounds, acne, athlete's foot, sore throat, swelling, burn, tumour, to suck a splinter out of skin or flesh, boil, injuries caused by the spines of the 'arraia' and others fishes, inflammation, hernia
Teiidae	
Ameiva ameiva (Linnaeus, 1758) – Lizard, "sardão grande"	Inflammation, dermatitis, venereal diseases, snake bites
Cnemidophorus gr. *ocellifer* (Spix, 1825) – Lizard, "sardão pequeno"	Inflammation, dermatitis, venereal diseases, snake bites
Tupinambis merianae (Duméril & Bibron, 1839) – Lizard, "tegu", "tejuaçú"	Earache, deafness, rheumatism, erysipelas, skin thorns and wounds, respiratory diseases, sore throat, snake bite, asthma, tumour, swelling, infection, bronchitis
Tupinambis teguixin (Linnaeus 1758) – Lizard, "tegu", "tejuaçú"	Sexual impotence, rheumatism, erysipelas, dermatitis, snake bites, asthma, tetanus, earache, thrombosis, wounds, panaris, swelling, herpes zoster, irritation when milk teeth are erupting, jaundice, inflammation, tumour, sore throat, infection, bronchitis, injuries caused by the spines of the 'arraia', pain relief in injuries caused by snake bites, toothache, suck a splinter out of skin or fresh, headache, cough, stroke, coarse throat
Tropiduridae	
Tropidurus hispidus (Spix, 1825) - Lizard, "lagartixa", "catenga"	Alchoolism, dermatomycosis, warts, abscesses, boils, sore throat, erysipelas, healing of umbilical cord of newborn baby
Tropidurus semitaeniatus (Spix, 1825) – Lizard, "lagartixa-de-lajedo"	Measles, asthma, alcoholism, dermatomycosis, warts
Tropidurus torquatus (Wied, 1820) – Lizard, "lagartixa"	Chicken pox
Uranoscodon superciliosus (Linnaeus, 1758), "tamaquaré"	As a sedative
Boidae	
Boa constrictor (Linnaeus, 1758) - Boa,"jibóia"	Rheumatism, lung disease, thrombosis, boils, tuberculosis, stomach ache, edema, snake bite, cancer, ache, swelling, to prevent abort, pain in the body, inflammation, athlete's foot, calluses, tumours, cracks in the sole of the feets, goitre, sore throat, arthrosis, insect sting, dog bite, erysipelas, thrombosis, asthma, neck strain, strain muscle, back ache

Table 1. Continued

Family / Species / local name	Conditions to which remedies are prescribed
Corallus caninus (Linnaeus, 1758) - American emerald tree boa, "cobra papagaio"	Pain relief caused by sting of animals
Corallus hortolanus (Linnaeus, 1758) – Snake	To assist in removing spines or other sharp structures from the skin, rheumatism
Eunectes murinus (Linnaeus, 1758) - Anaconda, "sucurujú", "sucuri"	Wounds, skin problems, bruises, sprains, arthrosis, rheumatism, boils, sexual impotence, headache, sore throat, thrombosis, swelling, tumour, asthma, muscle strain, numbness, syphilis, to reduce pain, luxation
Epicrates cenchria (Linnaeus, 1758) – Brazilian rainbow boa, "salamanta"	Rheumatism, pain in articulations, injuries caused by itself, sore throat
Colubridae	
Leptophis ahetula (Linnaeus, 1758) - Parrot snake, "cobra cipó"	Pain relief caused by sting of animals
Mastigodryas bifossatus (Raddi, 1820) – Rio tropical racer, "jaracuçú"	Snake bites
Oxyrhopus trigeminus Duméril, Bibron & Duméril, 1854 – "Coral falsa"	Rheumatism
Spilotes pullatus (Linnaeus, 1758) - Tiger snake	Pain relief in injuries caused by sting of insects and snake bite
Tachymenis peruviana Wiegmann, 1835	Pain in the bones, Pain in kidneys and to treat inflamations, tootache and scare
Crotalidae	
Crotalus durissus (Linnaeus, 1758) - Neotropical rattlesnake, "cascavel"	Asthma, snake bite, thrombosis, wounds, luxation, rheumatism, pain in the legs, erysipelas, deafness, epilepsy, skin diseases, tuberculosis, hanseniasis, backache, tumour, boil, headache, earache, osteoporosis, sore throat, toothache, pain relief in injuries caused by sting of insects and snake bite, irritation when milk teeth are erupting,
Elapidae	
Micrurus ibiboboca (Merrem, 1820) - "Cobra-coral"	Rheumatism, snake bite
Viperidae	
Bothrops leucurus Wagler, 1824 - Lance head, "jararaca"	Tumour, boils
Lachesis muta (Linnaeus, 1766) - Bushmaster,"surucucu pico-de-jaca"	Rheumatism, swelling, tumour, boil, pain relief in injuries caused by sting of insects and snake bite
Chelidae	
Phrynops geoffroanus (Schweigger, 1812) - Geoffroy's side-necked turtle, "cágado"	Asthma, sore throat, swelling, earache, rheumatism, arthrosis, healing of umbilical cord of newborn baby, mumps
Mesoclemmys tuberculata (Luederwaldt, 1926) – Tuberculate toadhead turtle, "cágado", "cágado-d'água"	Rheumatism, discharge, thrombosis, bronchitis, diarrhoea, haemorrhag, asthma, sore throat, hoarseness
Cheloniidae	

Table 1. Continued

Family / Species / local name	Conditions to which remedies are prescribed
Caretta caretta (Linnaeus, 1758) - Loggerhead turtle, "tartaruga cabeçuda"	Injuries caused by bang, toothache, diabetes, headache, backache, wounds, cough, bronchitis, asthma, thrombosis, rheumatism, stroke, hoarseness, flu, backache, earache, sore throat, swelling
Chelonia mydas (Linnaeus, 1758) - Green sea turtle, "tartaruga verde", "aruanã"	Injuries caused by bang, toothache, diabetes, headache, backache, wounds, cough, bronchitis, asthma, flu, thrombosis, rheumatism, toothache, stroke, hoarseness, earache, sore throat, swelling, whooping cough, arthritis, erysipelas, boil, wounds, arthrosis, inflammation
Eretmochelys imbricata (Linnaeus, 1766) - Atlantic hawksbill, "tartaruga de pente"	Injuries caused by bang, toothache, diabetes, headache, backache, wounds, cough, bronchitis, asthma, thrombosis, stroke, hoarseness, flu, rheumatism, earache, sore throat, swelling
Lepidochelys olivacea (Eschscholtz, 1829)	Injuries caused by bang, toothache, diabetes, headache, backache, wounds, cough, flu, bronchitis, asthma, thrombosis, rheumatism, stroke, hoarseness
Dermochelyidae	
Dermochelys coriacea (Vandelli, 1761) - Leatherback turtle, "tartaruga de couro"	Rheumatism, earache, sore throat, swelling
Geoemydidae	
Rhinoclemmys punctularia (Daudin, 1802) - Spot-legged turtle	Wounds, tumour, erysipelas, earache, rheumatism
Podocnemididae	
Podocnemis expansa (Schweiger,1812) - Amazon river turtle, "tartaruga da amazônia"	Inflammation, acne, tumour, boil, rheumatism, pterygium, skin spots, backache, earache, arthrosis, arthritis, swelling, wrinkle
Podocnemis unifilis (Troschel, 1848) – Yellow-spotted river turtle, "tracajá"	Wounds, tumour, erysipelas, earache, rheumatism
Podocnemis sextuberculata Cornalia, 1849 - Six-tubercled Amazon River turtle	Blackhead; acne
Peltocephalus dumeriliana Schweigger 1812 – "Cabeçuda"	Blackhead; acne
Testudinidae	
Geochelone carbonaria (Spix, 1824) - Red-footed tortoise, "jabuti"	Catarrh, erysipelas, bronchitis, to stop the sensation to getting thirsty, asthma
Geochelone denticulata (Linnaeus, 1766) – Yellow-footed tortoise, "jabuti"	Sore throat, rheumatism, hernia, wounds, leishmaniosis, varicocele, earache, part of woman's body
Alligatoridae	
Caiman crocodilus (Linnaeus, 1758) - Common cayman, "jacaré tinga"	Asthma, stroke, bronchitis, backache, earache, rheumatism, thrombosis, sexual impotence, snake bites (antidote), evil eye, irritation when milk teeth are erupting, discharge, swelling, scratch, athlete's foot, ophthalmological problems, sore throat, amulet used as a protection against snake bite, hernia, prostate problems, infection, inflammation

Table 1. Continued

Family / Species / local name	Conditions to which remedies are prescribed
Caiman latirostris (Daudin, 1801) – Cayman, "jacaré-do-papo-amarelo"	Asthma, sore throat, amulet used as a protection against snake bite, rheumatism, irritation when milk teeth are erupting, hernia, prostate problems
Melanosuchus niger (Spix, 1825) - Black cayman, "jacare açú"	Thrombosis, infection, swelling, asthma, amulet used as a protection against snake bite, injuries caused by spines of the 'arraia', pain relief in injuries caused by snake bites
Paleosuchus palpebrosus (Cuvier, 1807) - Cayman, "jacaré coroa", "jacaré", "jacaré-preto", "crocodilo"	Snake bite, asthma, stroke, rheumatism, thrombosis, backache, sexual impotence, edema, mycosis, evil eye, irritation when milk teeth are erupting, discharge, sore throat, amulet used as a protection against snake bite, hernia, prostate problems
Paleosuchus trigonatus (Schneider, 1801) - , "Jacaré coroa"	Rheumatism
BIRDS	
Accipitridae	
Geranoaetus melanoleucus (Vieillot, 1819) - Black-chested Buzzard-Eagle	The feathers are used as inensing and to makemasks. The meat used to avoid the wrinkles.
Anatidae	
Anser anser (Linnaeus, 1758) – Greylag goose, "ganso"	Laryngitis, pharyngitis, tonsillitis
Anhimidae	
Anhima cornuta (Linnaeus, 1766) – Horned screamer, "anuhma"	Intoxication from poisonous animals
Ardeidae	
Ardea cocoi (Linnaeus, 1766) – White-necked Heron	Swelling, inflammation, injuries caused by the spines of the 'arraia' and others fishes, asthma, boil, tumour, rheumatism, earache
Ardea alba Linnaeus, 1758 – Galça	Bronquithis and pneumonia
Ardeidae	
Tigrisoma lineatum (Boddaert, 1783) – socó, Rufescent Tiger-Heron	Bronquithis and pneumonia
Caprimulgidae	
Nyctidromus albicollis (Gmelin, 1789) – Pauraque, "bacurau"	Amulets, snake bite
Cathartidae	
Coragyps atratus (Bechstein, 1793) - Black vulture, "urubu", "urubu-preto"	Deafness, bronchitis, anaemia, alcoholism, asthma, flu (catarrh), earache, rheumatism
Cracidae	
Penelope jacucaca (Spix, 1825) – White-browed guan, "jacu"	Insomnia
Penelope superciliaris Temminck, 1815	Asthma
Phoenicopteridae	
Phoenicopterus andinus Philippi, 1854	To alliviate labor pain, sprains and distend

Table 1. Continued

Family / Species / local name	Conditions to which remedies are prescribed
Phoenicopterus chilensis Molina, 1782	To alliviate labor pain, sprains and distend
Phoenicopterus jamesi Sclater, 1886	To alliviate labor pain, sprains and distend
Ciconiidae	
Vultur gryphus Linnaeus, 1758	Not mentioned
Ciconia maguari (Gmelin, 1789) - Maguari stork	Injuries caused by the spines of the 'arraia' and others fishes, thrombosis
Columbidae	
Leptotila rufaxilla (Richard & Bernard, 1792) – Gray-fronted dove, 'juriti"	Thrombosis
Columba livia (Gmelin, 1789) – Rock pigeon, "pombo"	Asthma, laryngitis, pharyngitis, tonsilite
Family / Species / local name	Conditions to which remedies are prescribed
Corvidae	
Cyanocorax cyanopogon (Wied, 1821) – White-naped jay, "can-can"	Asthma, neurological problems
Cotingidae	
Procnias nudicollis (Vieillot, 1817) - araponga , Bare-throated Bellbird	Tuberculosis
Cuculidae	
Crotophaga ani Linnaeus, 1758 – Smooth-billed ani	Bronchitis, thrombosis, asthma, whooping cough, rheumatism
Guira guira (Gmelin, 1788) – Guira cuckoo, "anum branco"	Asthma
Charadriidae	
Vanellus chilensis (Molina, 1782) – Southern lapwing, "quero-quero"	To stay awake
Emberezidae	
Coereba flaveola (Linnaeus, 1758)– Banana quit, "caga-sebo"	Thrombosis
Falconidae	
Herpetotheres cachinnans (Linnaeus, 1758) - Laughing falcon, "acauã"	Snake bite
Caracara plancus (Miller, 1777) - Southern caracara, "caracará"	Snake bite
Falco rufigularis Daudin, 1800 - Bat falcon, "cauré"	Snake bite
Furnaridae	
Furnarius rufus (Gmelin, 1788)- Rufous hornero, "maria-barreira"	Mumps
Meleagrididae	
Meleagris gallopavo Linnaeus, 1758 – turkey, "peru"	Asthma
Phasianidae	

Table 1. Continued

Family / Species / local name	Conditions to which remedies are prescribed
Gallus gallus (Linnaeus, 1758) - Domestic chicken, "galinha"	Catarrh, fever, warts, haemorrhage, bronchitis, nasal congestion, flu, skin thorns and wounds, asthma, sore throat, tumour, poor digestion, healing of umbilical cord of newborn baby, swelling, cough, tuberculosis, earache, tonsillitis, rheumatism, diarrhea, inflammation, pneumonia
Picidae	
Dryocopus lineatus (Linnaeus, 1766) - Lineated woodpecker, "pica-pau-de-banda-branca"	Sexual impotence
Pavo cristatus Linnaeus, 1758 - Indian peafowl	Thrombosis, epilepsy
Rallidae	
Aramides cajanea (Statius Muller, 1776) – Grey-necked wood-rail, "saracura"	Evil eye
Ramphastidae	
Ramphastos tucanus Linnaeus, 1758 - Red-billed Toucan, "tucano"	Thrombosis, Sexual impotence
Family / Species / local name	Conditions to which remedies are prescribed
Ramphastos vitellinus Lichtenstein, 1823 - Channel-billed toucan, "tucano-de-bico-preto"	Sexual impotence
Pteroglossus aracari (Linnaeus, 1758) - Black-necked aracari, "araçari-de-bico-branco"	Sexual impotence
Pteroglossus inscriptus - Swainson, 1822, Lettered aracari, "araçari-miudinho-de-bico-riscado"	Sexual impotence
Rheidae	
Rhea americana (Linnaeus, 1758) – Greater rhea, "ema"	General aches, rheumatism, thrombosis, strokes
Pterocnemia pennata (Orbigny, 1834)	Not mentioned
Tinamidae	
Crypturellus noctivagus (Wied, 1820) - Yellow-legged tinamou, "zabele"	Thrombosis, stroke, snake bites, tuberculosis, deafness
Nothura boraquira (Spix, 1825) – White-bellied nothura, 'codorna"	Thrombosis, stroke, tootache
Rhynchotus rufescens (Temminck, 1815) – Red-winged tinamou, "perdiz"	Snake bite, thrombosis, tuberculosis
Trochilidae	
Eupetomena macroura (Gmelin, 1788) – Swallow-tailed hummingbird, "beijola", "beija-flor"	Cardiopathies, asthma, flu, ache
Tyrannidae	
Fluvicola nengeta (Linnaeus, 1766) - Masked water-tyrant, "lavandeira"	Boils
Pitangus sulphuratus (Linnaeus, 1766)	Earache
MAMMALS	
Agoutidae	

Table 1. Continued

Family / Species / local name	Conditions to which remedies are prescribed
Agouti paca (Linnaeus, 1766) – Spotted paca, "paca"	Wound in the breast caused by suckling, ophthalmological problems, stomach disorders, pterygium, to suck a splinter out of skin or flesh, injuries caused by the spines of 'arraia', control cholesterol level, thrombosis, General body pain, leishmaniasis, snake bite, rheumatism, heart pain, pain in bones, liver pain, urinary, fever, child birth, ant bite
Balaenopteridae	
Balaenoptera acutorostrata Lacépède, 1804 – Minke whale, "baleia minke"	Rheumatism, sore throat, wounds
Bovidae	
Bos taurus Linnaeus, 1758 – Cow, "vaca"	Thrombosis, evil eye, amulet used as a protection against snake bite, baldness, sexual impotence, measles, varicella, anaemia, whooping cough, alcoholism, rheumatism, inflammation, asthma, cough, sore throat, wounds, cracks in the sole of the feet, bronchitis, dizziness, anemia, bladder problems, chickenpox
Bubalus bubalis (Linnaeus, 1758) – Water buffalo (feral), "búfalo"	Rheumatism, osteoporosis, thrombosis
Ovis aries (Linnaeus, 1758) – Sheep, "carneiro"	Edema, fractures, erysipelas, herpes zoster, backache, swelling, to assist children who take longer than usual to start walking, arthritis, arthrosis, rheumatism, muscle strain, inflammation, luxation, cracks in the sole of the feet, joint pain
Capra hircus Linnaeus, 1758 – Domestic goat, "bode"	Evil eye, snake bite, muscle strain
Bradypodidae	
Bradypus variegatus Shinz, 1825 – Brown-throated three-toed sloth, "Preguiça pequena"	Thrombosis
Bradypus tridactylus Linnaeus, 1758 – Pale-throated three-toed sloth, "Preguiça"	Thrombosis, insects bite, scorpions bite
Canidae	
Lycalopex culpaeus (Molina, 1782)	Scare
Lycalopex gymnocercus (G. Fischer, 1814)	Air loss, asthma, backache, disorders after parturition, pain in the bones, rheumatism, scare, sprains, ulcer.
Canis lupus (Linnaeus, 1758) – Domestic dog, "cachorro"	Chicken pox, mumps, smallpox, asthma, varicella, measles, menstrual cramps
Cerdocyon thous (Linnaeus, 1766) – Crab-eating fox, "raposa"	Rheumatism, flu, haemorrhoids, disorders after parturition (to accelerate recovery after parturition), diabetes, Thrombosis, backache
Chrysocyon brachyurus (Illiger, 1815) – Maned wolf, "lobo-guará"	Epilepsy
Dusicyon thous – Linnaeus, 1766 – Crab-eating fox, "raposa"	Alcoholism, thrombosis, rheumatism, ophthalmological problems, diabetes, urinary infection
Speothos venaticus (Lund, 1842) – Bush dog, "cachorro-do-mato"	Haemorrhoids

Table 1. Continued

Family / Species / local name	Conditions to which remedies are prescribed
Caviidae	
Cavia aperea Erxleben, 1777 – "Preá"	Inflammation
Kerodon rupestris (Wied-Neuwied, 1820) – "Mocó"	Constipation
Cebidae	
Alouatta belzebul (Linnaeus, 1766) – Red-handed howler monkey, "guariba", "macaco"	Whooping cough, sore throat, asthma
Alouatta nigerrima Lönnberg, 1941 -Amazon black howler	Whooping cough, inflammation
Alouatta seniculus *(Linnaeus, 1766)* - Red howler monkey, *"guariba vermelho"*	Whooping cough, inflammation, to accelerate parturition
Ateles chamek (Humboldt, 1812)	Fever, cough, cold shoulder pain, sleeping problems, Leishmaniasis, Spider bite, snake bites.
Aotus azarai (Humboldt, 1811)	To avoid the children to dribble
Cebus apella (Linnaeus, 1758) – Brow capuchin, "capuchin", "macaco", "macaco-prego"	Insect sting, Eye infection
Cervidae	
Blastocerus dichotomus (Illiger, 1815) – Marsh deer, "cervo-do-pantanal"	Diarrhoea, vomit
Mazama americana (Erxleben, 1777) – Red brocket, "veado gaedo"	Stroke, Cold
Mazama simplicicornis (Illinger, 1811)	Diarrhoea, verminosis, evil eye
Mazama cf. *gouazoupira* (G. Fischer, 1814) – Gray brocket, "veado-catingueiro"	Asthma, edema, rheumatism, snake bite, thrombosis, to assit children who take longer than usual to start walking, tootache, wounds, sprains
Ozotocerus bezoarticus (Linnaeus, 1758), veado campineiro	Diarrhoea, verminosis, evil eye
Family / Species / local name	Conditions to which remedies are prescribed
Dasypodidae	
Dasypus novemcinctus (Linnaeus, 1758) – Nine-banded armadillo, "tatu galinha"	Thrombosis, insects bite, scorpions bite, edema, asthma, deafness, earache, evil eye
Euphractus sexcinctus (Linnaeus, 1758) – Six-banded armadillo "tatu peba"	Wounds, earache, evil eye, asthma, sore throat, pneumonia, sinusitis, deafness, coarse throat
Tolypeutes tricinctus (Linnaeus, 1758) – Brazilian three-banded armadillo, "tatu-bola"	Thrombosis, rheumatism
Priodontes maximus (Kerr, 1792)	Embolism, ant bite, visions (hallucinations?), skin diseases
Chaetophractus vellerosus (Gray, 1865)	General diseases
Dasyproctidae	
Dasyprocta prymnolopha Wagler, 1831 – Black-rumped agouti, "Cutia"	Asthma, thrombosis
Dasyprocta variegata - Brown agouti	Childbirth, Afrodisíaco, Picadura de buna, Picadura de víbora
Delphinidae	

Table 1. Continued

Family / Species / local name	Conditions to which remedies are prescribed
Sotalia fluviatilis Gervais & Deville, 1853)[DD/I] – Gray dolphin, gray river dolphin, "boto"	Asthma, headache, rheumatism, hernia, womb disorders, sore throat, injuries caused by the spines of the 'arraia', swelling, haemorrhoids inflammation, wounds, earache, erysipelas, athlete´s foot, tumour, cancer
Sotalia guianensis (P. J. Van Bénéden, 1864) – Guianan river dolphin, "boto"	Asthma, headache, rheumatism, hernia, womb disorders, sore throat, injuries caused by the spines of the 'arraia', swelling, haemorrhoids inflammation, wounds, earache, erysipelas, athlete´s foot, tumour, cancer
Didelphidae	
Didelphis albiventris (Lund, 1840) – Common opossum, "timbú"	Boils, rheumatism
Didelphis marsupialis (Linnaeus, 1758) – Southern opossum, "mucura", "gambá", "saruê"	Acne, wounds, bronchitis, joint pain, stomach ache, rheumatism, diarrhoea, inflammation, erysipelas, pain in gestation, asthma, headache, toothache, earache, sore throat, stomachache, flu, fever, body pain, fatigue
Megalonychidae	
Choloepus hoffmanni Peters, 1858	Visions, hallucination, cramps
Erethizontidae	
Coendou bicolor (Tschudi, 1844)	Hallucination, fever, ant bite, flu, whooping cough, scare, varicose veins
Coendou prehensilis (Linnaeus, 1758) – Brazilian porcupine, "coandú", "porco espinho"	Bronchitis, thrombosis, epilepsy, stroke, abscesses, conjunctivitis, asthma
Equidae	
Equus asinus Linnaeus, 1758 – Asino, ass, "jumento"	Snake bite (antidote), whooping cough, asthma
Equus caballus (Linnaeus, 1758) – Horse, "cavalo"	Cough, deep cuts; dermatosis, wounds
Felidae	
Felis silvestris Schreber, 1775 – Domestic cat, "gato"	Asthma, snake bites
Puma concolor (Linnaeus, 1771) – Mountain lion, "onça"	Wounds , leishmaniosis, arthritis, pain in bones, rheumatism, distend, scare, sthomachache, "evil eye", fever, avoid acne
Panthera onca (Linnaeus, 1758) – Jaguar, 'onça"	Wounds, leishmaniosis, Cough, fatigue, fever, pain in bones
Leopardus jacobitus (Cornalia, 1865)	Self encorage
Leopardus colocolo (Molina, 1782)	Self encorage
Octodontidae	
Ctenomys opimus Wagner, 1848	To make the child's teeth stronger
Chinchillidae	
Lagidium viscacia (Molina, 1782)	Bad memory
Hydrochaeridae	

Table 1. Continued

Family / Species / local name	Conditions to which remedies are prescribed
Hydrochaeris hydrochaeris (Linnaeus, 1766) – Capybara, "capibara", "capivara"	Thrombosis, conjunctivitis, venereal disease, rheumatism, earache, strengthen bones, liver pain, bronchitis, asthma, wounds, erysipelas, cough
Iniidae	
Inia geoffrensis (Blainville, 1817) – Amazon river dolphin, "boto rosa"	Asthma, headache, rheumatism, hernia, womb disorders, sore throat, injuries caused by the spines of the 'arraia', swelling, haemorrhoids inflammation, wounds, earache, erysipelas, athlete's foot, tumour, cancer
Leporidae	
Sylvilagus brasiliensis (Linnaeus, 1758) – Forest rabbit, tapeti, "coelho", "coelho-do-mato"	Thrombosis, conjunctivitis, boils, burns, Ophthalmological problems, embolism, scare, fever, hallucinations
Mephitidae	
Conepatus semistriatus (Boddaert, 1785) – Striped hog-nosed skunk, "cangambá", "gambambá", tacaca	Rheumatism
Conepatus chinga (Molina, 1782) – Gambá, Molina's Hog-nosed Skunk	Thrombosis, Rheumatism, general diseases
Mustelidae	
Lontra longicaudis (Olfers, 1818) – "Lontra"	Thrombosis, Ampollas
Camelidae	
Lama glama (Linnaeus, 1758)	Children "aicados" (a spiritual disease)
Lama guanicoe (Müller, 1776)	Asthma, scare
Vicugna vicugna (Molina, 1782)	Not mentioned
Myrmecophagidae	
Myrmecophaga tridactyla Linnaeus, 1758 – Giant anteater, "tamanduá-bandeira"	Thrombosis, stroke, General body pain, Snake bite, urinary problem, Heart pain, ant bite
Myrmecophaga tetradactyla (Linnaeus, 1758) – Collared anteater, "tamanduá"	Edema, thrombosis, itching, ant bite
Procyonidae	
Nasua nasua (Linnaeus, 1766) – South American coati, "coati", "quati"	Sexual impotence, wounds, skin burns, snake bites, backache, Cold, cough, leg pain, Wounded foot, Earache , neck strain, to help become pregnant, wooping cough
Procyon cancrivorus (G. [Baron] Cuvier, 1798) – Crab-eating raccoon, "guaxinim"	Rheumatism, epilepsy, thrombosis, snake bite
Potos flavus (Schreber, 1774) - Kinkajou	Earache, snake bite, ant bite
Physeteridae	
Family / Species / local name	Conditions to which remedies are prescribed
Physeter catodon Linnaeus, 1758 – Sperm whale, cachelot, "cachalote"	Asthma, backache, rheumatism, sore throat, wounds
Suidae	

Table 1. Continued

Family / Species / local name	Conditions to which remedies are prescribed
Sus scrofa (Linnaeus, 1758) – Wild boar, "porco"	Acne, boils, tumours, asthma, Athlete's foot, warble, wounds,
Tapiridae	
Tapirus terrestris (Linnaeus, 1758) – Brazilian tapir, "anta"	Rheumatism, arthrosis, osteoporosis, bursitis, muscular pain, asthma, tonsillitis, cough, General body pain
Tayassuidae	
Pecari tajacu Linnaeus 1758 – Collared peccary, "porco-do-mato", "caititu"	Thrombosis, bronchitis, stroke
Tayassu pecari (Link, 1795) – White-lipped peccary "porco-do-mato", "queixada"	Thrombosis, stroke, Cold
Trichechidae	
Trichechus inunguis (Natterer, 1883) – Amazonian manatee, "peixe-boi"	Sprains, vaginal discharge, injuries caused by bang, burns, asthma, menstrual cramps, rheumatism, sore throat, wounds, muscle strain, suck a splinter out of skin or fresh, tumour, backache, hernia, arthrosis, luxation, menstrual cramps, insects bite
Trichechus manatus (Linnaeus, 1758) – Manatee, "peixe-boi"	Arthrosis, luxation, menstrual cramps, insects bites, sprains, vaginal discharge, injuries caused by bang burns, asthma, rheumatism, sore throat, wounds, muscle strain

References

[1]   Iwu MM, Gbodossou E. The role of traditional medicine. *Lancet*, 2004 1, 356

[2]   Alves, RRN; Rosa, IL. Why study the use of animal products in traditional medicines?. *Journal of Ethnobiology and Ethnomedicine*, 2005 1, 1-5.

[3]   Alves RRN, Rosa IL. Biodiversity, traditional medicine and public health: where do they meet? *Journal of Ethnobiology and Ethnomedicine*. 2007a 3, 1-9.

[4]   Alakbarli, F. Medical manuscripts of Azerbaijan. 1st ed. Baku, Azerbaijan Heydar Aliyev Foundation, 2006.

[5]   Alves, RRN; Rosa, IL; Santana, G. The Role of Animal-derived Remedies as Complementary Medicine in Brazil. *BioScience*, 2007a 57(11), 1-7.

[6]   David, JP; Anderson, LA. Ethnopharmacology and western medicine. *Journal of Ethnopharmacology*. 1969 25, 61–72.

[7]   Good, C. Ethno-medical Systems in Africa and the LDCs: Key Issues in Medical Geography In: Meade MS editor. *Conceptual and Methodological Issues in Medical Geography*. Chapel Hill, NC, USA: University of North Carolina; 1980.

[8]   Gesler, WM. Therapeutic landscapes: medical Issues in Light of the new cultural geography. *Social Science & Medicine*. 1992 34(7), 735-746.

[9]   WHO – World Health Organization. Millennium Ecosystem Assessment. Ecosystems and Human Well-being: Synthesis. 1st ed. Geneva, Switzerland: WHO, 2005.

[10]   Kang, S; Phipps, M. A question of attitude: South Korea's Traditional Medicine Practitioners and Wildlife Conservation. 1st ed. Hong Kong: TRAFFIC East Asia, 2003.

[11]   Lev, E. Traditional healing with animals (zootherapy): medieval to present-day Levantine practice. *J. Ethnopharmacol*, 2003 86, 107-118.

[12]   Adeola, MO. Importance of wild Animals and their parts in the culture, religious festivals, and traditional medicine, of Nigeria. *Environmental Conservation.* 1992 19(2), 125-134. .

[13]   Alves, RRN; Vieira, WLS; Santana, GG. Reptiles used in traditional folk medicine: conservation implications. *Biodiversity and Conservation* 2008a 17(1), 2037-2049.

[14]   Unnikrishnan, PM. Animals in Ayurveda. *Amruth.* 1998 (Suppl 1), 1-15.

[15]   Vázquez, PE; Méndez, RM; Guiascón, OGR; Piñera, EJN. Uso medicinal de la fauna silvestre en los Altos de Chiapas, México. *Interciencia*, 2006 31(7), 491-499.

[16]   Mahawar, MM; Jaroli, DP. Traditional zootherapeutic studies in India: A review. *Journal of Ethnobiology and Ethnomedicine.* 2008 4, 17 p.

[17]   Van, NDN; Tap, N (editors). An overview of the use of plants and animals in traditional medicine systems in Vietnam. 1st ed. Ha Noi, Vietnam: TRAFFIC Southeast Asia, Greater Mekong Programme, 2008.

[18]   Ashwell, D; Walston, N. An overview of the use and trade ofplants and animals in traditional medicine systems in Cambodia. T 1st ed. Ha Noi, Vietnam: TRAFFIC Southeast Asia, Greater Mekong Programme, 2008.

[19]   Costa-Neto, EM. Animal-based medicines: biological prospection and the sustainable use of zootherapeutic resources. *Anais da Academia Brasileira de Ciências.* 2005 77(1), 33-43.

[20]   Marques, JGW. A fauna medicinal dos índios Kuna de San Blas (Panamá) e a hipótese da universalidade zooterápica. *Anais da 46a Reunião Anual da SBPC.* 1994, 324.

[21]   Robineau, L; Soejarto, DD. TRAMIL: a research project on the medicinal plant resources of the Caribbean In Balick MJ, Elisabetsky E, Laird SA editors. *Medicinal Resources of the Tropical Forest: Biodiversity and its Importance to Human Health.* New York: Columbia University Press; 1996.

[22]   Agra, MF; Baracho, GS; Nurit, K; Basílio, IJLD; Coelho, VPM. Medicinal and poisonous diversity of the flora of "Cariri Paraibano", Brazil. *Journal of Ethnopharmacology.* 2007 111(2), 383-395.

[23]   Uniyal, SK; Singh, KN; Jamwal, P; Lal, B. Traditional use of medicinal plants among the tribal communities of Chhota Bhangal, Western Himalaya. *Journal of Ethnobiology and Ethnomedicine.* 2006 2, 1-8.

[24]   Alves, RRN; Rosa, IL. From cnidarians to mammals: The use of animals as remedies in fishing communities in NE Brazil. *Journal of Ethnopharmacology* 2006 107, 259-276.

[25]   Alves, RRN; Rosa, IL. Zootherapeutic practices among fishing communities in North and Northeast Brazil: A comparison. *Journal of Ethnopharmacology.* 2007b 111, 82-103.

[26]   ITIS-Integrated Taxonomic Information System. Catalogue of Life: 2007 Annual Checklist. 2007 [cited 2007 December]. Available from: http://www.catalogue oflife.org/ search.php.

[27] Almeida, AV. Prescrições zooterápicas indígenas brasileiras nas obras de Guilherme Piso (1611–1679) In Alves AGC, Lucena RFP, Albuquerque UP editors. *Atualidades em Etnobiologia e Etnoecologia.* Recife, Brazil: Nuppea; 2005.

[28] Almeida, CFCBR; Albuquerque, UP. Uso e conservação de plantas e animais medicinais no Estado de Pernambuco (Nordeste do Brasil): Um estudo de caso. *Interciencia.* 2002 27, 276-285.

[29] Alves, RRN. Use of marine turtles in zootherapy in Northeast Brazil. *Marine Turtle Newsletter.* 2006 112, 16-17.

[30] Alves, RRN; Pereira-Filho, GA. Commercialization and use of snakes in North and Northeastern Brazil: implications for conservation and management. *Biodiversity and Conservation.* 2007 16, 969-985.

[31] Alves, RRN; Rosa, IL. Zootherapy goes to town: The use of animal-based remedies in urban areas of NE and N Brazil. *Journal of Ethnopharmacology.* 2007c 113, 541-555.

[32] Alves, RRN; Rosa, IML. Use of tucuxi dolphin *Sotalia fluviatilis* for medicinal and magic religious purposes in North of Brazil. *Human Ecology.* 2008 37, 443-447.

[33] Alves, RRN; Pereira Filho, GA; Lima, YCC. Snakes used in ethnomedicine in Northeast Brazil. *Environment, Development and Sustainability.* 2007b 9, 455-464.

[34] Andrade, JN; Costa-Neto, EM. Primeiro registro da utilização medicinal de recursos pesqueiros na cidade de São Félix, Estado da Bahia, Brasil. *Acta Scientiarum Biological Sciences.* 2005 27(2), 177-183.

[35] Apaza, L; Godoy, R; Wilkie, D; Byron, E; Huanca, O; Leonard, WL; Peréz, E; Reyes-García, V; Vadez, V. Markets and the use of wild animals for traditional medicine: a case study among the Tsimane' Amerindians of the Bolivian rain forest. *Journal of Ethnobiology,* 2003 23, 47–64.

[36] Barbarán, FR. Economía campesina y percepción de la fauna en la Puna: Sus vinculaciones con el comercio legal e ilegal de fibra de vicuña (*Vicugna vicugna*) en el Noroeste Argentino y Sur de Bolivia. *MEMORIAS: Manejo de Fauna Silvestre en Amazonia y Latinoamérica.* 2004, 647-659.

[37] Begossi, A. Food taboos at Búzios Island (Brazil): their significance and relation to folk medicine. *Journal of Ethnobiology.* 1992 12 (1), 117-139.

[38] Begossi, A; Braga, FMS. Food taboos and folk medicine among fishermen from the Tocantins River. *Amazoniana.* 1992 12, 101–118.

[39] Begossi, A; Silvano, RAM; Amaral, BD; Oyakawa, OT. Uses of Fish and Game by Inhabitants of an Extractive Reserve (Upper Juruá, Acre, Brazil). *Environment, Development and Sustainability,* 1999, 1, 73-93.

[40] Branch, L; Silva, MF. Folk medicine in Alter do Chão, Pará, Brasil. *Acta Amazônica.* 1983 13, 737–797.

[41] Campos, E. Folclore do nordeste. 1st ed. Rio de Janeiro: Edições O Cruzeiro; 1960.

[42] Costa-Neto, EM. Faunistic resources used as medicines by an afro-brazilian community from Chapada Diamantina National Park, state of Bahia-Brazil. *Sitientibus.* 1996 15, 211-219.

[43] Costa-Neto, EM. Healing with animals in Feira de Santana city, Bahia, Brazil. *Journal of Ethnopharmacology.* 1999a 65, 225-230.

[44] Costa-Neto, EM. Barata é um santo remédio: introdução a zooterapia popular no Estado da Bahia. 1st ed. Feira de Santana, Brazil: Editora Universitária da UEFS; 1999b

[45]   Costa-Neto, EM. Recursos animais utilizados na medicina tradicional dos índios Pankararés, que habitam no Nordeste do Estado da Bahia, Brasil. *Actualidades Biologicas.* 1999c 21, 69-79.

[46]   Costa-Neto, EM. Traditional use and sale of animals as medicines in Feira de Santana city, Bahia, Brazil. *Indigenous Knowledge and Development Monitor.* 1999d 7, 6-9.

[47]   Costa-Neto, EM. Conhecimento e usos tradicionais de recursos faunísticos por uma comunidade Afro-Brasileira. Resultados Preliminares. *Interciencia.* 2000a 25(9), 423-431.

[48]   Costa-Neto EM. Zootherapy based medicinal traditions in Brazil. *Honeybee.* 2000b 11(2), 2-4.

[49]   Costa-Neto, EM. Introdução a etnoentomologia: considerações metodológicas e estudo de casos. 1st ed. Feira de Santana, Brazil: Editora Universitária da UEFS; 2000c.

[50]   Costa-Neto, EM. A cultura pesqueira do litoral Norte da Bahia. 1st ed. Salvador, Brazil: EDUFBA; EDUFAL; 2001.

[51]   Costa-Neto, EM. The use of insects in folk medicine in the State of Bahia, northeastern Brazil, with notes on insects reported elsewhere in Brazilian folk medicine. *Human Ecology.* 2002 30(2), 245-263.

[52]   Costa-Neto, EM; Oliveira, MV. Cockroach is good for Asthma: Zootherapeutic Practices in Northeastern Brazil. *Human Ecology Review.* 2000 7(2), 41-51.

[53]   Costa-Neto, EM; Pacheco, JM. Utilização medicinal de insetos no povoado de Pedra Branca, Santa Terezinha, Bahia, Brasil. *Biotemas.* 2005 18(1), 113-133.

[54]   Costa-Neto, EM; Dias, CV; Melo, MN. O conhecimento ictiológico tradicional dos pescadores da cidade de Barra, região do médio rio São Francisco, estado da Bahia, Brasil. *Acta Scientiarum.* 2002 24(2), 561-572.

[55]   Figueiredo, N. Os 'bichos' que curam: os animais e a medicina 'folk' em Belém do Pará. *Boletim do Museu Paraense Emílio Göeldi.* 1994 10 (1), 75-91.

[56]   Freire, FCJ. Répteis utilizados na medicina popular no Estado de Alagoas. *Thesis of specialization course.* Universidade Federal de Alagoas, Departamento de Biologia; 1996.

[57]   Lenko, K; Papavero, N. Insetos no Folclore. 1st ed. São Paulo: Plêiade/ FAPESP; 1996.

[58]   Mallmann, MLW. A farmacopéia do mar: invertebrados marinhos de interesse médico e a etnomedicina alagoana. *Thesis of specialization course.* Universidade Federal de Alagoas, Departamento de Biologia; 1996.

[59]   Marques, JGW. Pescando Pescadores: Etnoecologia abrangente no baixo São Francisco Alagoano. 1st ed. São Paulo: NUPAUB/USP; 1995

[60]   Moura, FBP; Marques, JGW. Zooterapia popular na Chapada Diamantina: uma Medicina incidental? [online]. 2007 [cited 2008 August]. URL: http://www.abrasco.org.br/cienciaesaudecoletiva/artigos/artigo_int.php?id_artigo=1395

[61]   Pinto, AAC; Maduro, CB. Produtos e subprodutos da medicina popular comercializados na cidade de Boa Vista, Roraima. *Acta Amazônica.* 2003 33(2), 281-290.

[62]   Seixas, CS; Begossi, A. Ethnozoology of fishing communities from Ilha Grande (Atlantic forest coast, Brazil). *Journal of Ethnobiology.* 2001 21, 107-135.

[63]   Silva, MLV; Alves, ÂGC; Almeida, AV. A zooterapia no Recife (Pernambuco): uma articulação entre as práticas e a história. *Biotemas.* 2004 17, 95-116

[64] Souto, FJB; Andrade, CTS; Souza, AF. Uma abordagem etnoecológica sobre a zooterapia na medicina popular em Andaraí, Chapada Diamantina, Bahia. Proceedings of the first Encontro Baiano de Etnobiologia e Etnoecologia. Feira de Santana, Brazil: EDUFS, 1999.

[65] Vargas, LMA. Estudio comparativo de la caza y uso de mamíferos en dos Comunidades Tsimane. 1st ed. La Paz, Bolívia: Universidad Mayor de San Andrés; 2002.

[66] Gilmore, R. "Fauna e etnozoologia da América do Sul tropical". In: Ribeiro B editor. *Suma Etnológica Brasileira*. Rio de Janeiro: FINEP/Vozes; 1986

[67] Sodeinde, OA; Soewu, DA. Pilot study of the traditional medicine trade in Nigeria. *Traffic Bulletin*. 1999 18(1), 35-40.

[68] El-Kamali, HH. Folk medicinal use of some animal products in Central Sudan. *Journal of Ethnopharmacology*. 2000 72, 279-282.

[69] Kakati, LN; Ao, B; Doulo, V. Indigenous Knowledge of Zootherapeutic Use of Vertebrate Origin by the Ao Tribe of Nagaland. *Human Ecology*. 2006 19, 163-167.

[70] Fitzgerald, LA; Porini, G; Lichtschein, V. El manejo de Tupinambis en Argentina: historia, estado actual, y perspectivas futuras. *Interciencia*. 1994 19(4), 166-170.

[71] De Smet, PAGM. Is there any danger in using traditional remedies? *Journal of Ethnopharmacology*, 1991 32, 43-50.

[72] Schnurrenbergerv, PR; Hubbert, WT. An outline of the zoonoses. 1st ed. Ames, IA, USA: Iowa State University Press; 1981.

[73] Gang, L; Jianqin, X. Application of traditional Chinese patent drugs in pet dog and cat. 1st ed. Beijing, PR China: College of Veterinary Medicine, China Agricultural University; 1996.

[74] Pieroni, A; Giusti, ME; Grazzini, A. Animal remedies in the folk medicinal practices of the Lucca and Pistoia Provinces, Central Italy. In: Fleurentin J, Pelt JM, Mazars G editors. *Des sources du savoir aux médicaments du futur/from the sources of knowledge to the medicines of the future*. Paris, France: IRD Editions; 2002, 371-375.

[75] Albuquerque, UP; Monteiro, JM; Ramos, MA; Amorim, ELC. Medicinal and magic plants from a public market in northeastern Brazil. *Journal of Ethnopharmacology*. 2007 110, 76-91.

[76] Alves, RRN; Santana, GG. Use and commercialization of *Podocnemis expansa* (Schweiger 1812) (Testudines: Podocnemididae) for medicinal purposes in two communities in North of Brazil. *Journal of Ethnobiology and Ethnomedicine*. 2008 4(3), 1-6.

[77] Alves, RRN; Lima, HN; Tavares, MC; Souto, WMS; Barboza, RRD; Vasconcellos, A. Animal-based remedies as complementary medicines in Santa Cruz do Capibaribe, Brazil. *BMC Complementary and Alternative Medicine*. 2008b 8(44), 1-9.

[78] Alves, RRN; Silva, AAG; Souto, WMS; Barboza, RRD. Utilização e Comércio de Plantas Medicinais em Campina Grande, PB, Brasil. *Revista Eletrônica de Farmácia*. 2007c 4, 175-198.

[79] Heiden, G; Macias, L; Bobrowski, VL; Iganci, JRV. Comercialização de carqueja por ervateiros da zona central de Pelotas, Rio. *Revista de Biologia e Ciências da Terra*. 2006 6, 50-57

[80]   Athais, R. Indigenous Traditional Medicine among the Hupd'ah- Maku of Tiquie River (Brazil). London: Indigenous Peoples' Rights to Health Conference and Public Meeting; 2004.

[81]   Sanchez, G. I render services for science don't I?...and I am an indigenous descendant. London: Indigenous Peoples' Rights to Health Conference and Public Meeting; 2004.

[82]   Mata, LJ et al. Latin America. In: McCarthy JJ, Canziani O, Leary N, Dokken D and White K editors. *Climate Change 2001, Impacts,Adaptation, and Vulnerability. A contribution of Working Group II to the Third Assessment Report of the IPCC.* Cambridge, UK and New York: Intergovermental Panel on Climate Change/ Cambridge University Press, 2001.

[83]   IBGE – Brazilian Institute of Geography and Statistic [online]. 2007 [cited 2008 September]. URL: http://www.ibge.gov.br

[84]   Haynes, A. Health care in Brazil. *British Medical Journal.* 1993 306(6876), 503-506.

[85]   Barros, E; Porto, S. Health Care in Brazil: Equity as Challenge [online]. 2002 [cited 2008 September]. URL: www.gdnet.org/pdf2/gdn_library/ global_research_projects/ MERCK_health/Brazil_study.pdf

[86]   Conejo, M. Población indígena y reforma del sector salud. El caso de Ecuador. Iniciativa de Salud de los Pueblos Indígenas. 1st ed. Washington DC: Pan American Health Organisation; 1998.

[87]   PAHO. Health of Indigenous Peoples. 1st ed. Washington DC: Pan American Health Organisation; 1997.

[88]   Raunig, L; Houston, J. Midwives for midwives. Protecting the sacredcircle. Midwifery Today Int Midwife 2002, 51–53.

[89]   Schuler, SR; Choque, ME; Rance, S. Misinformation, mistrust, and mistreatment: family planning among Bolivian market women. *Stud. Fam. Plann.* 1994 25, 211–21.

[90]   Boltanski, L. As classes sociais e o corpo. 1st ed. Rio de Janeiro: Graal; 1977

[91]   Ngokwey, N. Home remedies and doctors' remedies in Feira (Brazil). *Social Science and Medicine.* 1995 40, 1141–1153.

[92]   Sofowora, A. Medicinal Plants and Traditional Medicine in Africa, 2sd ed. Ibadan: Spectrum Books Ltd, 1993.

[93]   Luoga, EJ; Witkowski, ETF; Balkwill, K. Differential utilization and ethnobotany of trees in Kitulanghalo forest reserve and surrounding communal lands, eastern Tanzania. *Economic Botany.* 2000 54, 328–343.

[94]   World Health Organization – WHO. Traditional Medicine Strategy 2002-2005. Geneva: World Health Organization; 2002.

[95]   Tabuti, JRS; Dhillion, SS; Lye, KA. Traditional medicine in Bulamogi county, Uganda: its practitioners, users and viability. *Journal of Ethnopharmacology.* 2003 85, 119–129.

[96]   Nazarea, V; Rodhes, R; Bontoyan, E; Gabriela, F. Defining indicators which make sense to local: Intra-cultural variation in perceptions of natural resources. *Human Organization.* 1998 57. 159-170.

[97]   Convention on Biological Diversity – CBD. Convention on Biological Diversity, article 8(j) [online]. 2007 [cited 2008 August]. URL: http://www.biodiv.org/

[98]   Moran, K; King, SR; Carlson, TJ. Biodiversity prospecting: lessons and prospects. *Annual Review of Anthropology.* 2001 30, 505–526.

[99]   Zhang, X. Traditional medicine and its knowledge. Expert Meeting on Systems and National Experiences for Protecting Traditional Knowledge, Innovations and Practices. Geneva: UNCTAD; 2000.

[100] Svarstad, H. Local interests and foreign interventions: Shaman Pharmaceuticals in Tanzania. In: Svarstad H, Dhillion SS editors. *Responding to Bioprospecting: From Biodiversity in the South to Medicines in the North.* Oslo, Norway: Spartacus Forlag As, 2000.

[101] Smith, D; Binet, L; Bonnevie, L; Hakokongas, L; Meybaum, J. Desequilíbrio fatal: a crise de pesquisa e desenvolvimento de drogas para doenças negligenciadas. 1st ed. Genebra: Médicos Sem Fronteiras, 2001.

[102] Tudela, F. Desarrollo y Medio Ambiente en América Latina y El Caribe Una visión evolutiva. Madrid: Ministerio de Obras Públicas y Urbanismo; 1990.

[103] Mahar, D. Government policies and deforestation in Brazil's Amazon region. Washington DC: World Bank; 1989.

[104] Anyinam, C. Ecology and Ethnomedicine: Exploring Links Between Current Environmental Crisis and Indigenous Medical Practices. *Soc. Sci. Med.* 1995 40(3), 321-329.

In: Low Incomes: Social, Health and Educational Impacts ISBN: 978-1-60741-175-8
Editor: Jacob K. Levine, pp. 207-215

Chapter 9

USE OF MID-UPPER ARM CIRCUMFERENCE AS A MEASURE OF NUTRITIONAL STATUS AND ITS RELATIONSHIP WITH SELF REPORTED MORBIDITY AMONG ADULT BENGALEE MALE SLUM DWELLERS OF KOLKATA, INDIA

Raja Chakraborty[1,2], Kaushik Bose[1,2] and Samiran Bisai[2]
[1]Dinabandhu Mahavidyalaya, Bongaon, West Bengal, India.
[2]Department of Anthropology, Vidyasagar University,
Midnapore, West Bengal, India

Abstract

A cross-sectional study of 474 adult (> 18 years) Bengalee male slum dwellers of Kolkata, (India), was undertaken investigate the use of mid-upper arm circumference (MUAC) as a measure of nutritional status and its relationship with current reported morbidity. Height, weight and MUAC were measured using standard techniques. The body mass index (BMI) was computed following the standard formula. Classification of chronic energy deficiency (CED) was done following the WHO guideline of BMI < 18.5 kg/m^2. Results revealed that MUAC of 24 cm was the best cut-off point to distinguish between CED and non-CED individuals with sensitivity (SN), specificity (SP), positive (PPV) and negative (NPV) predictive values of 86.3, 85.1, 73.3 and 92.9, respectively. Moreover, there was a significant (chi-square = 11.834, p < 0.005) difference in the presence of self reported morbidity between the two MUAC groups (MUACGI: MUAC < 24 cm and MUACGII: MUAC ≥ 24 cm) with subjects in MUACGI 2.09 times more likely to be currently morbid compared with those in MUACGII. Furthermore, morbid subjects had significantly lower mean values of weight (p < 0.005), BMI (p < 0.005) and MUAC (p < 0.001) compared to non-morbid individuals. It can

---

[1] E-mail address: banda@vsnl.net. Address for correspondence: Dr. Kaushik Bose, Reader,Department of Anthropology, Vidyasagar University, Midnapore – 721 102,West Bengal, India..

be concluded that a MUAC value of 24 cm can be used as a simple and efficient cut-off point for the determination of CED and morbidity status in this population.

Keywords: MUAC, Nutritional Status, Health, Morbidity, Blengalee, Males, Slum.

Introduction

The use of anthropometry as an indicator of nutritional and health status of adults has now been well established (WHO 1995). The body mass index (BMI) is an indicator of overall adiposity and low BMI and high levels of undernutrition (based on BMI) is a major public health problem especially among rural underprivileged adults of developing countries (WHO 1995). Although adult nutritional status can be evaluated in many ways, the BMI is most widely used because its use is inexpensive, non-invasive and suitable for large-scale surveys (Lohman et al. 1988, Ferro-Luzzi et al. 1992, James et al. 1994). Thus, BMI is the most established anthropometric indicator used for assessment of adult nutrition status (Lee and Nieman 2003). BMI is generally considered a good indicator of not only the nutritional status but also the socio-economic condition of a population, especially adult populations of developing countries (Ferro-Luzzi et al. 1992, Shetty and James 1994, Nube et al. 1998, Khongsdier 2002). A BMI < 18.5 kg/m^2 is widely used as a practical measure of chronic energy deficiency (CED), i.e., a 'steady' underweight in which an individual is in energy balance irrespective of a loss in body weight or body energy stores (Khongsdier 2005). Such a 'steady' underweight is likely to be associated with morbidity or other physiological and functional impairments (James et al 1988, Shetty and James 1994, WHO 1995,).

Another anthropometric measure that can be used to evaluate adult nutritional status is mid upper arm circumference (MUAC). It has been shown that MUAC is particularly effective in the determination of malnutrition among adults in developing countries (James et al. 1994). It has been noted that MUAC is a simpler measure than BMI requiring a minimum of equipment and in practice has now been found to predict morbidity and mortality as accurately as deficits in weight (Brined et al. 1981). After an extensive study (James et al. 1994) of 8 countries (Mali, India, Senegal, Zimbabwe, Somalia, Ethiopia, Papua New Guinea and China) it was suggested that MUAC could be used for simple screening of nutritional state. It has also been stated that since MUAC is a simpler measure than BMI, it could be used not only in emergencies but also when semi-skilled monitors are available. It can be used as a substitute for BMI when rapid screening of an adult population is required as a prelude to targeting help for the undernourished (James et al. 1994).

Several recent investigations have studied the inter-relationships of socioeconomic status, BMI, CED and morbidity among different populations (Campbell and Ulijaszek 1994, Delpeuch et al 1994, Naidu and Rao 1994, Ahmed et al. 1998, Reddy 1998, Griffiths and Bently 2001, Khongsdier 2002, Pryer et al 2003, Monteiro et al. 2004, Clausen et al. 2006, Mahmud et al. 2006). However, we could not locate any study from India which has tried to establish an efficient cut-off point of MUAC for the evaluation of adult nutritional status among slum dwellers.

In view of this, the present investigation was undertaken to establish an efficient cut-off point of MUAC to evaluate nutritional status and also to investigate the relationship between

MUAC and self-reported morbidity among adult Bengalee male urban slum dwellers of Kolkata, India.

Materials and Methods

Area of Study

The present study was carried out as research project undertaken by the first two authors. The study area comprised of a slum (refugee colony), named *"Bidhan Colony,"* situated on the right hand side of the railway tracks between Dum Dum Junction and The Dum Dum Cantonment Railway Stations, approximately 15 km from Kolkata town center. The subjects had migrated from Bangladesh during the 1970–1971 civil wars in erstwhile East Pakistan. Kolkata (formerly known as Calcutta) is the capital city of West Bengal province. The city lies between 22°32'40" north 70 latitude and 88°24'30" east longitude. Kolkata is 120 km from the sea (Bay of Bengal). It is situated on the eastern bank of the river Ganges (also known as Hooghly River).

Subjects and Information

A total of 474 adult (>18 years of age) male Bengalee Hindu individuals were studied. The vast majority of the subjects belonged to low socioeconomic status. The subjects lived with their families. Ethical approval and prior permission was obtained from Vidyasagar University local community leaders, respectively, before commencement of the study. Informed consent was also obtained from each participant. Information on ethnicity and age were obtained from specific questions in the questionnaire. In addition, information on self-reported morbidity status (illness present or absent during the last month) were recorded for all individuals.

Anthropometry and Evaluation of Nutritional Status

The first author (RC) took anthropometric measurements following the standard techniques (Lohman et al. 1988). Height, weight and mid-upper arm circumference were recorded to the nearest 0.1 cm, 0.5 kg and 0.1 cm, respectively. Technical errors of measurements (TEM) were computed and they were found to be within acceptable limits (Ulijaszek and Kerr 1999). BMI was computed using the following standard equation:

$$BMI = Weight\ (kg)\ /\ height\ (m^2)$$

Nutritional status was evaluated using internationally accepted World Health Organization BMI guidelines(WHO 1995). The following cut-off points were used:

CED: BMI < 18.5
non-CED: BMI ≥ 18.5

Statistical Analyses

The distributions of the anthropometric variables were not significantly skewed. Receiver operating characteristics (ROC) curve analysis was done to determine the best MUAC cut-off point against two categories of BMI, i.e., CED and non-CED. Sensitivity (SN), specificity (SP), positive (PPV) and negative predictive values (NPV) were computed. Two MUAC groups were obtained based on ROC: MUACGI (MUAC < 24 cm) and MUACII (MUAC ≥ 24 cm). Contingency chi-square tests were performed to study the relationship between these two MUAC groups and self-reported morbidity status (illness present or illness absent during the last one month). Lastly, t-tests were performed to test for difference in anthropometric characteristics between these two morbidity status groups (illness present and illness absent). All statistical analyses were undertaken using the Epi-Info6 and SPSS 7.5 Statistical Packages. Statistical significance was set at $p < 0.05$.

Results

The mean and standard deviations of the sample are presented in *Table 1*. *Table 2* presents the SN, SP, PPV and NPV of MUAC with BMI status (CED vs. non-CED). It was observed that MUAC of 24 cm was the best cut-off point to distinguish between CED and non-CED individuals with SN, SP, PPV and NPV values of 86.3, 85.1, 73.3 and 92.9, respectively. The ROC curve is presented in *Figure 1*.

Table 1. Characteristics of the study sample (n = 474).

Variables	Mean	SD
Age (years)	37.5	14.2
Height (cm)	161.5	6.2
Weight (kg)	53.0	9.5
BMI (kg/m^2)	20.3	3.3
MUAC (cm)	25.0	2.9

Table 2. Sensitivity, specificity, PPV and NPV of MUAC with BMI status (CED vs. non-CED).

MUAC (cm)	Sensitivity	Specificity	PPV	NPV
23.0	62.8	94.4	84.2	84.2
23.5	76.5	88.8	76.5	88.8
24.0*	86.3	85.1	73.3	92.9
24.5	92.2	77.9	66.5	95.4
25.0	95.4	69.5	59.8	97.0

PPV = Positive predictive value,
NPV = Negative predictive value.

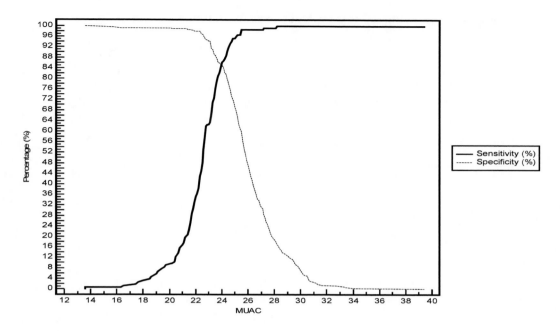

Figure 1. Receiver operating characteristic of MUAC and BMI status (CED vs. non-CED).

Table 3. Relation of MUAC groups with morbidity status.

MUAC Group	Illness Present %	Illness Absent %
MUAC < 24.0 cm	34.5	65.3
MUAC ≥ 24.0 cm	19.8	80.2

* chi-square = 12.564, p < 0.001
OR = 2.13 (95 % CI = 1.37 – 3.33).

Table 3 presents the relationship of the two MUAC groups (MUAC < 24 cm and MUAC ≥ 24 cm) with morbidity status (illness present vs. illness absent during the last one month). There was a significant (chi-square = 11.834, p < 0.005) difference in the presence of morbidity between the two MUAC groups. It was observed that 34.7% individuals with MUAC < 24.0 were currently morbid. Moreover, subjects with MUAC < 24 cm were 2.09 times more likely to be currently morbid compared with those with MUAC ≥ 24 cm.

Comparison of anthropometric characteristics *(Table 4)* between those with illness and those without illness reveled significant differences in mean weight (p < 0.005), BMI (p < 0.005) and MUAC (p < 0.001). Morbid subjects had significantly lower mean values of these variables compared with non-morbid individuals. However, both groups had similar mean age (illness present: mean = 38.9 years, sd = 15.4 years; illness absent: 37.2, sd = 13.9).

Table 4. Comparison of anthropometric characteristics by morbidity status.

Variable	Illness Present (n = 119)	Illness Absent (n = 347)	t
Height (cm)	161.7 (5.9)	161.4 (6.3)	0.35
Weight (kg)	50.7 (8.9)	53.7 (9.6)	3.04*
BMI (kg/m^2)	19.4 (3.3)	20.6 (3.2)	3.45*
MUAC (cm)	24.0 (2.8)	25.3 (2.9)	4.38**

*p < 0.005, ** p < 0.001.

Discussion

The MUAC has recently emerged in the literature as a potential screening tool for poor nutritional status in adults (Khadivzadeh 2002). It has been analysed in adults and cut-off points for CED have been established using a range of datasets from developing countries (UN Sub-Committee on Nutrition 2000). The MUAC measurement reflects adult nutritional status as defined by BMI (Collins 1996). It correlates closely with BMI, is easier to measure and predicts poor outcome better (Powell-Tuck and Hennessy 2003). In undernourished populations, MUAC may be better suited than BMI for screening purposes (Collins 1996). The measurement of MUAC has been used as a useful screening method for the assessment of nutritional status in different ethnic groups (Olukoya 1990, Ferro-Luzzi and James 1996).

Since it is the most reproducible and simplest measurement to perform, its use has been recommended in nutritional studies (Harries et al. 1984).

It is well established that there exists distinct ethnic differences in fat deposition (Bose 1996). The relationship between overall adiposity (measured as BMI) and regional adiposity measured as body circumferences like MUAC and skin folds vary across ethnic groups (Bose 2001). Studies have shown that at the same level of BMI, there exits significant ethnic differences in regional adiposity and body composition measures like percent body fat (Deurenberg et al. 1998, 2002). It is universally accepted that a BMI value < 18.5 kg/m^2 is indicative of CED across ethnic groups (WHO 1995). The MUAC is recognized as an effective means of screening for poor nutritional status in adults (Dorlencourt 2000, Khadivzadeh 2002, Bose et al. 2006). However, although an MUAC value < 23 cm has been recommended for use to define under nutrition (James et al. 1994), this value may not be the most appropriate cut-off point in all ethnic groups. A recent study from Nigeria (Olukoya 1990) reported that a MUAC cut-off point of 23 cm was optimal for the north of the country, while a 24 cm cut-off point was more appropriate for the South. Thus, there is a need to establish ethnic-specific cut-off points of MUAC. The present study attempted to determine the most appropriate cut-off point of MUAC which best relates to CED (measured as BMI < 18.5) among adult slum dwellers of Bengalee ethnicity. It also investigated the relation of undernutrition, as identified using this new cut-off point, with self-reported morbidity status.

Lastly, it also compared the anthropometric characteristics between morbid and non-morbid subjects.

Our study demonstrated that MUAC of 24 cm was the best cut-off point to distinguish between CED and non-CED individuals with SN, SP, PPV and NPV values of 86.3, 85.1, 73.3 and 92.9, respectively. A similar cut-of point of 24 cm was also obtained in a recent study from South India (Rodrigues et al. 1994). Using this cut-off point, it was observed that there was a significant (chi-square = 11.834, p < 0.005) relationship between CED and morbidity status. Individuals with MUAC < 24 cm were 2.09 times more likely to be currently morbid compared with those with MUAC > 24 cm. One of the probable reasons for this cut-off point being higher than that suggested by James *et al* (1994) could be due to the fact that persons of South Asian origin (including Bengalees) have higher levels of regional adiposity (irrespective of BMI) compared to other ethnic groups (Bose 1996, 2001, Deurenberg 1998, 2002).

It can be concluded that a MUAC value of 24 cm can be used as a simple and efficient cut-off point for the determination of CED and morbidity status in this population. Since MUAC is a much simpler measure compared with BMI, the use of this cut-off point will have immense public health implications especially with respect to primary health care related to CED and morbidity. Measuring MUAC has several advantages. The measurement can be taken quickly and at little cost. It requires neither sophisticated equipment nor anything but the most basic literacy level to carry out (Rodrigues 1994). However, one of the limitations of the present study was the small sample size. Therefore, before this cut-off point can be recommended for use among Bengalee males, further validation studies are needed with larger sample sizes. Moreover, similar studies are needed among Bengalee women to determine whether the cut-off point of MUAC < 22 cm recommended by James *et al.* (1994) can be used among them or whether there is a need for a more appropriate and efficient cut-off point. Lastly, it must be mentioned here that studies to assess the capacity of MUAC cut-offs to predict mortality in severe adult malnutrition are needed.

Acknowledgements

All subjects who participated in the study are gratefully acknowledged. This work was partly funded by the University Grants Commission (India) Minor Research Project Grant Number PSW054/03-04 ERO awarded to RC. The authors acknowledge the kind co-operation of Atul Dhali, Gopal Das and Swapan Mallik of Bidhanpally.

References

Ahmed, S.M., Adams. A., Chowdhury, A.M., and Bhuiya, A. (1998): Chronic energy deficiency in women from rural Bangladesh: Some socioeconomic determinants. –*J. Biosoc. Sci.* **30**, 349-358.

Bose, K. (1996): Generalised obesity and regional adiposity in adult white and migrant Muslim males from Pakistan in Peterborough. –*J. R. Soc. Health* **116**(3),161-7.

Bose, K. (2001): The interaction of waist-hip ratio and conicity index with subcutaneous adiposity in two ethnic groups: native British and migrant Pakistani men. - *Anthropol. Anz.* **59**(3),275-82.

Bose, K., Chakraborty, F., Mitra, K., and Bisai, S. (2006): Nutritional status of adult Santal men in Keonjhar District, Orissa, India. - *Food Nutr. Bull.* **27**(4),353-6.

Briend, A., Garenne, M., Maire, B., Fontaine, O., and Dieng, K. (1989): Nutritional status, age and survival: the muscle mass hypothesis. – *Eur. J. Clin. Nutr.* **43**(10), 715–26.

Campbell, P and Ulijaszek, S. J. (1994): Relationships between anthropometry and retrospective morbidity in poor men in Calcutta, India. – *Eur. J. Clin. Nutr.* **48**(7),507-12.

Clausen, T., Charlton, K. E., and Holmboe-Ottesen, G. (2006): Nutritional status, tobacco use and alcohol consumption of older persons in Botswana. – *J. Nutr. Health Aging.***10**, 104-110.

Collins, S. (1996): Using middle upper arm circumference to assess severe adult malnutrition during famine. – *J. Am. Med. Assoc.* **276**(5), 391-395.

Delpeuch, F., Cornu, A., Massamba, J. P., Traissac, P., and Maire, B. (1994): Is body mass index sensitivity related to socio-economic status and to economic adjustment? A case study from the Congo. – *Eur. J. Clin. Nutr.* **S3**, S141-S147.

Deurenberg, P., Deurenberg-Yap, M., and Guricci, S. (2002): Asians are different from Caucasians and from each other in their body mass index / body fat per cent relationship. - *Obes. Rev.* **3**(3),141-6.

Deurenberg, P., Yap, M., van Staveren, W. A. (1998): Body mass index and percent body fat: a meta analysis among different ethnic groups. - *Int. J. Obes. Relat. Metab. Disord.* **22**(12),1164-71.

Dorlencourt, F., Priem, V., and Legros, D. (2000): Anthropometric indices used for the diagnosis of malnutrition in adolescents and adults: review of the literature. - *Bull. Soc. Pathol. Exot.* **93**(5), 321-4.

Ferro- Luzzi, A. and James, W. P. (1996): Adult malnutrition: simple assessment techniques for use in emergencies.- *Brit. J. Nutr.* **75**(1),3-10.

Ferro-Luzzi, A., Sette, S., Franklin, M., and James, W. P. T. (1992): A simplified approach of assessing adult chronic deficiency. – *Eur. J. Clin. Nutr.* **46**, 173-186.

Griffiths, P. L., and Bentley, M. E. (2001): The Nutrition Transition Is Underway in India. – *J. Nutr.* **131**, 2692-2700.

Harries, A. D., Laura, A. J., Heatley, R. V., Newcombe, R. G., and Rhodes, J. (1984): Precision of anthropometric measurements: the value of mid-arm circumference. – *Clin. Nutr.* **2**(3-4), 193-196.

James, W. P. T., Ferro-Luzzi, A., and Waterlow, J. C. (1988): Definition of Chronic energy deficiency in adults. Report of a Working Party of the International Dietary Energy Consultative Group. – *Eur. J. Clin. Nutr.* **42**, 969-981.

James, W. P., Mascie-Taylor, G. C., Norgan, N. G., Bistrian, B. R., Shetty, P. S., and Ferro-Luzzi, A. (1994): The value of arm circumference measurements in assessing chronic energy deficiency in Third World adults. – *Eur. J. Clin. Nutr.* **48**(12), 883-94.

Khadivzadeh, T. (2002): Mid upper arm and calf circumferences as indicators of nutritional status in women of reproductive age. - *East Mediterr. Health J.* **8**(4-5), 612-8.

Khongsdier, R. (2002): Body mass index and morbidity in adult males of the War Khasi in Northeast India. – *Eur. J. Clin. Nutr.* **56**, 484–489.

Khongsdier, R. (2005): BMI and morbidity in relation to body composition: a cross-sectional study of a rural community in North-East India. – *Br. J. Nutr.* **93**, 101–107.

Lee, R. D., and Nieman, D. C. (2003): Nutritional Assessment. - New York: McGraw Hill.

Lohman, T. G., Roche, A. F., and Martorell, R. (1998): Anthropometric Standardization Reference Manual. - Chicago: Human Kinetics Books.

Mahmud Khan, M., Hotchkiss, D. R., Berruti, A. A., and Hutchinson, P. L. (2006): Geographic aspects of poverty and health in Tanzania: does living in a poor are matter? - *Health Pol. Plan.* **21**, 110-122.

Monteiro, C. A., Conde, W. L., and Popkin, B. M. (2004): The burden of undernutrition and overnutrition in countries undergoing rapid nutrition transition: a view from Brazil. - *Am. J. Pub. Health* **94**, 433-434.

Naidu, A. N., and Rao, N. P. (1994): Body mass index: a measure of nutritional status in Indian populations. – *Eur. J. Clin. Nutr.* **48**, S131-140.

Nube, M., Asenso-Okyere, W. K., and van den Bloom, G. J. M. (1998): Body mass index as an indicator of standard of living in developing countries. - *Eur. J. Clin. Nutr.* **77**, 1186-1191.

Olukoya, A. A. (1990): Identification of underweight women by measurement of the arm circumference. – *Int. J. Gynecol. Obstetr.* **31**(3), 231-235.

Powell-Tuck, J. and Hennessy, E. M. (2003): A comparison of mid upper arm circumference, body mass index and weight loss as indices of under nutrition in acutely hospitalized patients. - *Clin. Nutr.* **22**, 307-312.

Pryer, J. A., Rogers, A., and Rahman, A. (2003): Factors affecting nutritional status in female adults in Dhaka slums, Bangladesh. - *Soc. Biol.* 2003; 50, 259-269.

Reddy, B. N. (1998): Body mass index and its association with socioeconomic and behavioral variables among socio-economically heterogeneous populations of Andhra Pradesh, India. – *Hum. Biol.* **70**, 901-917.

Rodrigues, V. C., Rao, R. S., and Lena, A. (1994): Utility of arm circumference as a screening instruments to identify women at nutritional risk. - *Tropical Doctor* **24**, 164-6.

Shetty, P. S. and James, W. P. T. (1994): Body Mass Index: A measure of Chronic Energy Deficiency in Adults. - *Food and Nutrition Paper* No. **56**. Rome: Food and Agricultural Organization.

Ulijaszek, S. J., and Kerr, D. A. (1999): Anthropometric measurement error and the assessment of nutritional status. - *Br. J. Nutr.* **82**, 165-177.

United Nations Sub Committee on Nutrition (ACC/SCN). (2000): *4th report on the world nutrition situation: Nutrition through out the life cycle.* New York, United Nations, 1-21.

World Health Organization (1995): Physical Status: the Use and Interpretation of Anthropometry. - *Technical Report Series* no. **854**. Geneva: World Health Organization.

In: Low Incomes: Social, Health and Educational Impacts   ISBN: 978-1-60741-175-8
Editor: Jacob K. Levine, pp. 217-225   © 2009 Nova Science Publishers, Inc.

Chapter 10

COST-EFFECTIVENESS OF SURGERY IN LOW-INCOME COUNTRIES: EXAMPLES IN SIERRA LEONE AND CAMBODIA

Richard A. Gosselin[*1] *and Amardeep Thind*[2]

[1] UC Berkeley School of Public Health; 506 Warren Hall;
Berkeley, CA, USA

[2] Department of Family Medicine, Department of Epidemiology
and Biostatistics, University of Western Ontario, Canada

Abstract

Surgery has long been considered too costly to be part of basic health care packages in low-income countries. Very little data are in fact available from resource-poor settings. Cost-effectiveness analysis is a widely used tool to inform decision makers in the resource allocation process. It is particularly valuable where resources are very scarce. This paper reports on two cost-effectiveness analyses conducted at two surgical centers of the Italian non-governmental organization Emergency, in Sierra Leone and in Cambodia. Data on both the costing and effectiveness sides were collected and analyzed using the same methodology. The results are presented in dollars per DALY averted. Although both hospitals have a slightly different vocation, they were found to be very cost-effective at $32.78 per DALY averted in Sierra Leone and $77.40 per DALY averted in Cambodia. This compares favorably to other public health interventions in similar contexts, such as vaccination or nutritional supplementation. The reasons for the difference between the two sites, and the significance of the findings are discussed.

Abbreviations

BKA	below-knee amputation
DALY	disability-adjusted life-year
ENT	ear, nose and throat

---

[*] E-mail address: froggydoc@comcast.net

GBD	global burden of disease
GIEESC	global initiative for emergent and essential surgical care
ICU	intensive care unit
NGO	non-governmental organization
OPD	outpatient department
WHO	world health organization
YLD	years lived with disability
YLL	years of life lost

Introduction

Only fairly recently has surgery been recognized as a potentially effective and cost-effective intervention in developing countries. For the first time a chapter was devoted to surgery in the latest edition of the "Disease Control Priorities for Developing Countries" textbook [1]. There is still a dearth of data on the burden of surgical diseases in developing countries, but recent evidence suggests it is steadily increasing, in large part because of the worldwide increase in perinatal conditions and injuries [2,6,7]. The recent study by Weiser et al showed that the unmet surgical burden in developing countries is huge [12]. The World Health Organization (WHO) recognizes this, and has instituted the Global Initiative for Emergent and Essential Surgical Care (GIEESC) which aims at improving human and technical capacity to decrease mortality and morbidity from certain surgical conditions in low-income countries [13]. Train-the trainer workshops have been held in over 20 countries so far, with encouraging initial results.

There is even less data on the cost-effectiveness of surgical interventions in developing countries. Until recently, sparse data were available only for cataract surgery, and to a lesser extent, hernia repair. In 2003, McCord and Chowdhury published a landmark study on the cost-effectiveness of a mid-sized obstetrical hospital in Bangladesh [8]. The methodology was original and the results, at $11 per Disability Adjusted Life-Year (DALY) averted, showed that surgical obstetrical care could be highly cost-effective in such environments, comparing favorably with other highly cost-effective non-surgical interventions such as vaccination or tuberculosis treatment. This went against conventional public health wisdom that deemed surgery too expensive to be incorporated in standard basic health packages for developing nations, and sparked an interest in furthering research in this field [5]. There is now a working group affiliated with the Institute of Health Metrics whose goal is to quantify more precisely the burden of surgical diseases (www.gsd2008.org/).

This paper will review the methodology and results from 2 studies done at Emergency Surgical Centers in Sierra Leone [3] and in Cambodia [4].

Context

Emergency is an Italian non-governmental organization (NGO) based in Milan, whose mission is to provide free surgical care for civilian victims of wars and conflicts. It has been active for nearly two decades and is presently mainly involved in Afghanistan, Sudan, Cambodia and Sierra Leone. The same guiding principles are applied at all sites:

strengthening of local human resources with a minimum of expatriate physicians, nurses, administrators and logisticians, building standard infrastructures that will eventually be handed over to the local authorities, and insuring a steady and reliable supply chain with regular shipments from Italy of containers full of equipment, drugs and disposables, supplemented as needed with local or regional purchases. Treatment is provided at no cost to patient or family. The organization is financed solely through private donations.

In Sierra Leone, The Emergency Surgical Center is located in Goderich, a suburb of the capital, Freetown. It has been operational since 2001 and has progressively increased its capacity to over 95 beds at present: 70 surgical beds, including 9 Intensive Care Unit (ICU) beds, and around 25 beds in the medical pediatric ward. There are two operating rooms, well equipped for basic anesthesia and surgical care. The country was ravaged by a brutal civil war from 1992 to 1999, which resulted in a massive brain drain and almost complete destruction of the health sector infrastructures. The country is just beginning to rebound from this national catastrophe, but, except for a few private clinics, the health sector remains almost non-functional, and the only health care available for the vast majority of the population, other than traditional healers, is through NGOs. Sierra Leone consistently ranks at or near the bottom for many health indicators such as maternal mortality, less than 5 mortality, life expectancy and human development index. Over time, the Emergency Surgical Center has evolved from providing surgical care strictly to war victims to a more general surgical hospital which today offers emergent and elective general and orthopedic surgery, but no obstetrics. To better meet the population needs, an outpatient pediatric clinic was started a few years ago, soon followed by an in-patient medical pediatric ward. The hospital runs at 100% capacity or more throughout the year. So far, over 100,000 patients have been seen in the outpatient department, over 17,000 have been admitted and over 16,000 surgical procedures have been performed

In Cambodia, the hospital is located in Battambang, the nation's second largest city approximately 300 kilometers northwest of the capital Phnom Penh. It is in the heart of an area where many landmines were laid, particularly during the bloody Khmer Rouge revolution of 1975-1979, which killed roughly a quarter of the population. Fresh landmine injuries are now relatively rare, the hospital admitting on average two per month. Since its inauguration in 1998, the Emergency Surgical Center has also evolved and is now purely dedicated to the surgical management of injuries, fresh and old. The only exception occurs when a subspecialist group of plastic or ENT surgeons comes for a few weeks per year to do select elective procedures. There are no pediatrics, or elective general surgery. The Cambodian health care system, although still under-developed by western standards, is much more developed than in Sierra Leone, and there are other centers, governmental and non-governmental, to provide care for the pediatric and general surgical populations. So the in-patient population is much more homogenous than in Sierra Leone. On a yearly basis, 96% of all surgeries are performed for trauma. There are three well-equipped operating theaters, one of which is used exclusively for clean cases. There are 106 beds, including 9 ICU beds, and the occupancy rate is always 100% or higher.

Methodological Considerations

The WHO guidelines for cost-effectiveness analysis were followed whenever possible [11]. At both sites, data were collected for age, sex, diagnosis, treatment, complications and status at discharge, for a 3-month period, and results extrapolated over 12 months, as there was no evidence of a seasonality effect on either costs or outputs. Records and logbooks from the outpatient department (OPD), ICU, the operating theater and all wards were reviewed and cross-referenced to identify all patients. All available charts (>96% in Cambodia, >90% in Sierra Leone) were reviewed. In Cambodia, the OPD records were not suitable for analysis, and thus no DALYs were attributed.

A simplification of the methods described by McCord was used to calculate the DALYs averted [8]. The severity of any given condition/disease was given a weight between 0 and 1: 1 if the condition/disease is assumed to be fatal >95% of the time without treatment, 0.7 for conditions assumed to be fatal between 50% and 95% of the time, 0.3 for those assumed to be fatal between 5% and 50% of the time, and 0.0 for those assumed to be fatal less than 5% of the time. The presumed effectiveness of treatment was similarly weighted between 0 and 1. A weight of 1 was given if the probability of permanent cure of a given ailment by treatment is 95% or greater, 0.7 when it is between 50% and 95%, 0.3 when it is between 5% and 50%, and 0.0 when the chance of permanent cure is less than 5%. This is summarized in table 1. DALYs were calculated according to the Global Burden of Disease study (GBD), using the discounted figures for the Years of Life Lost (YLL), and the disability weights for the Years Lived with Disability (YLD), when available [10]. The sum of all DALYs therefore represented the overall burden of disease seen at that hospital for that period. Factoring in the weights for severity of disease and effectiveness of treatment allowed calculating the effectiveness of any intervention for each patient, in terms of DALYs averted. For example, a 20-year-old male has successful surgery for peritonitis:

35.02 (YLL value for male 20yo) x 1.0 (>95% mortality if untreated) x 1.0 (>95% chance of permanent cure) = 35.02 DALYs averted.

A 20-year-old male has a unilateral below-knee amputation (BKA) after a road traffic injury:

35.02 x 0.7 (mortality between 50% and 95% if untreated) x 1.0 (>95% chance of permanent cure) x 0.281 (BKA disability weight in GBD) = 6.9 DALYs averted.

It is important to note that for both studies we have made great efforts to consistently err on the conservative side. Table 2 summarizes the comparative monthly distribution of all cases and DALYs averted for both sites. Of interest is the fact that although 644 patients on average are treated each month in the Cambodian OPD, no DALYs averted were attributed because the records were not reliable enough in terms of diagnosis and/or treatment. These represented 9% of the total burden averted in Sierra Leone, where the total monthly caseload is about three times that of Cambodia, as are the DALYs averted. Table 3 is specific for surgical cases. The burden avoided per general surgery case is much higher in Cambodia where all cases were life threatening, whereas in Sierra Leone most procedures were done on an elective basis for non-life-threatening conditions. The burden averted per orthopedic procedure in Cambodia (2.66 DALYs per case) is lower than in Sierra Leone (3.95 DALYs per case). This is mainly attributable to the fact that there were more patients in Cambodia who underwent more than one surgical procedure (re-debridement, skin grafting, etc) than in Sierra Leone, without any further contribution to DALYs averted.

Table 1. Scoring System

SEVERITY OF DISEASE		WEIGHT
	> 95% FATAL WITHOUT TX	1.0
	<95% and >50%	0.7
	<50% and >5%	0.3
	<5%	0
EFFECTIVENESS OF TREATMENT		
	>95% CHANCE OF CURE	1.0
	<95% and >50%	0.7
	<50% and >5%	0.3
	<5%	0

Legend: This table explains the different weights given for severity of disease and effectiveness of treatment.

Table 2. Monthly distribution of all cases, and DALYs averted

	SIERRA LEONE		CAMBODIA	
	# CASES	Dalys Averted	# CASES	Dalys Averted
OUTPATIENT DEPT	1,751	333	644	0*
PEDIATRIC IN + OUT PATIENTS	933	2,333	0	0
GENERAL SURGERY IN-PATIENTS	49	567	19	509
ORTHO SURGERY IN-PATIENTS	134	529	283	754
TOTAL	2,867	3,762	946	1,263

* DALYs Averted were impossible to calculate.

Legend: This table compares the monthly distribution of patients for different services in each hospital, and the corresponding DALYs averted.

Table 3. Monthly distribution of surgical cases, and DALYs averted

	SIERRA LEONE		CAMBODIA	
	# CASES	DALYs Averted	# CASES	DALYs Averted
General Surgery	49	567	19	509
Orthopedic Surgery	134	529	283	754
TOTAL	183	1096	302	1263

Legend: This table compares the number of general and orthopedic surgical cases in each hospital, and the corresponding DALYs averted.

Costs in $US were divided into fixed and operating costs. Land purchase and building construction costs were straight line depreciated to zero over 30 years. The initial equipment costs (medical equipment, generators, vehicles, etc) were straight line depreciated over 10 years for the Sierra Leone study, and, after reviewers said they thought that 10 years was too much, over 7 years for the subsequent Cambodia study. Local operating costs included all salaries and benefits, all local purchases (equipment, consumables, drugs, supplies, etc), maintenance costs of buildings, equipment and vehicles, fuel, transportation, utilities and miscellaneous costs such as office supplies or banking fees. The only non-local cost is that of the shipping containers of equipment and supplies sent 2 or 3 times a year from Italy. These costs were prorated on a monthly basis and included in the operating costs. The total costs for the 3 month period were divided by the estimated DALYs averted for the same period to give the cost per DALY averted.

Table 4 shows comparative costs between the two sites. The difference in the depreciated monthly fixed costs for equipment reflects the difference between the depreciation schedules, but much more importantly the fact that more equipment was available locally or regionally in Cambodia, whereas almost none was available in Sierra Leone, and almost everything had to be shipped from Italy, at obviously much higher costs. The significant difference in local operating costs for equipment/drugs/consumables reflects the higher utilization of more expensive operating room equipment and supplies. On a monthly basis, there are on average 302 surgical procedures performed in Cambodia and only 183 in Sierra Leone, as shown in Table 3. The last significant difference is in fuel and transportation costs, and is explained by the fact that the vehicle flotilla in Sierra Leone is much bigger, as they provide transportation to and from work to the entire staff, and also includes an often-utilized ambulance. In Cambodia, the much smaller number of vehicles is used only for administrative purposes and transportation of expatriates. All national staff came to work by their own means. The remaining cost inputs are fairly similar between the two sites.

Table 4. Comparative costs

		SIERRA LEONE ($US)	CAMBODIA ($US)
FIXED COSTS			
	Land & Infrastructures	1,597	2,083
	Equipment	6,731	2,976
OPERATING COSTS Local			
	Expat staff salaries/benefits	38,641	30,459
	Local staff salaries/benefits	28,741	23,585
	Equipment, Drugs, Consumables	3,899	21,358
MAINTENANCE			
	Infrastructures and Equipment	4,921	1,514
	Fuel and Transport	12,670	1,948
	Utilities	2,078	5,280
OPERATING COSTS Non-Local		13,329	11,530
MISCELLANEOUS		10,651	4,123
TOTAL		123,258	104,856

Legend: This table compares fixed, operating, maintenance and miscellaneous costs for each hospital.

Results

The two series were heterogeneous in terms of patient population. In Sierra Leone, the medical treatment of pediatric conditions accounted for one-third of the caseload but almost two-thirds (62%) of the DALYs averted. In-patient general and orthopedic surgery accounted for 7% of the caseload but 29% of the DALYs averted. 61% of the entire caseload came from the OPD, but represented only 9% of the DALYs averted. The overall cost per DALY averted was estimated at $32.78. In Cambodia, the situation was quite different. Except for the few subspecialty elective cases as already mentioned, every admission was trauma-related. Of those, 90% were fresh injuries and 10% were chronic problems, such as painful stumps, retained foreign bodies, chronic post-traumatic osteomyelitis, etc. Only 4% of all surgeries were for non-trauma related conditions. During the study period, there were 957 admissions, and 895 surgical procedures. Most of the non-surgical admissions were patients treated conservatively in the ICU for head/face injuries, or more rarely for burns. By non-surgical, we mean that these traumatic conditions were treated conservatively, without surgery. One could easily argue that non-surgical management of some injuries (head trauma, splenic rupture in a child) still requires surgical expertise and availability, and as such, should be seen as part of the "surgical process". The conservative estimate of DALYs averted was 1,355 per month, and the monthly total costs were $104,856, for a cost per DALY averted of $77.40.

The differences between the two series can be attributed almost entirely to the different patient populations and volumes of services. The higher volume in Sierra Leone probably creates some economies of scale, but the overall significance and magnitude are unknown. The methodological differences are few: the OPD accounted for 9% of all DALYs in Sierra Leone, but as already mentioned, none were attributed to the Cambodia OPD, thus underestimating the total burden averted. Also, using a 7-year depreciation schedule instead of a 10-year one, and adding a 10% treatment failure "premium" both contribute to increasing the costs per DALY averted. Nevertheless those are probably a relatively minor contribution compared to the difference in type and volume of patients. In Sierra Leone, 62% of all DALYs averted were from the in and out-patient non-surgical pediatric population. It is extremely unlikely that this group contributes to 62% of the costs, since they exclude "costly" surgical interventions. If they were excluded from the calculations, the cost per DALY averted would be significantly higher. It should come at no surprise that it is more costly to run a purely surgical hospital than a more general hospital with a large non-surgical component. Still, both series are significantly higher than the $11 per DALY averted reported by McCord[8]. Although part of it might be attributed to methodological differences, again the explanation mostly lies in the difference in patient population. McCord's series is almost exclusively obstetrical patients, where the surgical "bang for the buck" is at its highest: one surgery saves the lives of an infant and a young mother, thus averting many DALYs. His overall costs were also lower than ours, which is likely contextual.

There are many potential flaws to this methodology. Firstly, the weights assigned for the severity of a condition/disease, or for the effectiveness of treatment, are subjective: based on experience, consensus, and best educated guess but not on hard data. While most of the time weights are self-evident, this is not always the case and the only way to avoid overestimating the number of DALYs averted is by consistently erring on the conservative side, which we have systematically done both for the assumptions and the estimates. Secondly, the disability weights from the GBD are themselves controversial, often having the same value whether a condition is treated or not, and not factoring in some important regional disparities. Until a better tool is introduced, the systematic use of these weights at least provides consistency in allowing relative comparisons, if not necessarily accuracy. Thirdly, for some diseases/conditions, there are no formal disability weights (e.g. osteomyelitis, club feet) and assigning weights is very subjective. In many instances these patients were not able to be included in the calculations, causing a possibly significant underestimation of DALYs averted. Nevertheless, the methodology is coherent and reproducible, and its consistency allows comparisons between settings, conditions, and over time.

We believe that this type of hospital-based cost-effectiveness analysis may be more useful to policymakers and managers than procedure-based ones (e.g. cataract surgery, hernia repair) when there are only scarce resources to be allocated [9]. Most health economists were not expecting such low costs per DALY averted for surgical interventions. Obstetrical and perinatal conditions, and injuries combine for an ever-increasing share of the global burden of diseases. Surgical management of these problems can be done in a cost-effective manner, and should be given serious consideration by those who allocate resources and determine the content of basic health packages for low-income countries.

References

[1] Debas HT, Gosselin RA, McCord C, Thind A, "Surgery" in Jamison D, Breman J, Measham A, Alleyne G, et al. [Eds]. *Disease Control Priorities in Developing Countries* (2nd Edition), ed. 2006, 1245-1260.

[2] Fingerhut LA, Harrison J, Holder Y, Frimodt MB, et al: Addressing the Growing Burden of Trauma and Injury in Low and Middle Income Countries. *Am. J. Public Health.* 2005, 95(1): 13-17.

[3] Gosselin RA, Thind A, Bellardinelli A : Cost/DALY Averted in a Small Hospital in Sierra Leone: What Is the Relative Contribution of Different Services? *World J. Surg.* Vol. 2006, 30(4): 505-511.

[4] Gosselin RA, Heitto M: *Cost-Effectiveness of a District Trauma Hospital in Battambang,* Cambodia. World J Surg, on-line first, available 8/26/08 at http://www.springerlink.com/content

[5] Jamison D, Breman J, Measham A, Alleyne G, et al, editors (2006): Disease Control Priorities in Developing Countries, Oxford University Press, Washington

[6] Lopez AD, Mathers CD, Ezzati M, et al, editors (2006): *Global Burden of Disease and Risk Factors.* Oxford University Press, Washington: 119-125.

[7] Mathers CD, Loncar D. Projections of global mortality and burden of disease from 2002 to 2030. *PLoS Med.* 2006;3:e442.

[8] McCord C, Chowdhury Q: A Cost Effective Small Hospital in Bangladesh: What it can Mean for Emergency Obstetric Care. *Int. J. Gynaec. Obstet.* 2003, 81: 83-92.

[9] Mills AJ, Kapalamula J, Chisimbi S: The cost of the district hospital: a case study in Malawi. *Bull. WHO.* 1993, 71(3-4):329-339.

[10] Murray CJL, Lopez AD, eds. *The global burden of disease: A comprehensive assessment of mortality and disability from diseases, injuries, and risk factors in 1990 and projected to 2020.* Boston, MA, Harvard School of Public Health, 1996.

[11] Tan Torres-Edejer T, Baltussen R, Adam T, Hutubessy R, et al, (2003): *WHO Guidelines to Cost-Effectiveness Analysis*. Geneva: World Health Organization

[12] Weiser TG, Regenbogen SE, Thompson KD, Haynes AB, et al: An estimation of the global volume of surgery: a modeling strategy based on available data. *Lancet*. 2008, 372: 139-144.

[13] WHO- Global Initiative for Emergent and Essential Surgical Care, at www.who.int/surgery/en

In: Low Incomes: Social, Health and Educational Impacts   ISBN: 978-1-60741-175-8
Editor: Jacob K. Levine, pp. 227-243   © 2009 Nova Science Publishers, Inc.

Chapter 11

EFFICACY OF A STAGE-MATCHED PHYSICAL ACTIVITY MESSAGE FOR LOW-INCOME WOMEN

Roberta Hoebeke[*]

University of Southern Indiana, College of Nursing and Health Professions,
Evansville, IN, USA

Abstract

Physical inactivity is most prevalent among low-income women, yet a paucity of physical activity research exists with this population. Primary care practitioners can play a critical role in promoting physical activity to decrease adverse health outcomes among low-income women. The purpose of this study was to test a stage-matched message developed from the Transtheoretical Model to increase physical activity. From a primary care clinic women (N=32) at or below 185% of poverty level in Contemplation or Preparation stages of change completed measures of physical activity, stage of change, perceived physical activity benefits and barriers, and demographic data. Participants were randomized to receive a stage-matched physical activity message or a standard message with two follow-up phone contacts over 10 weeks. Pre and post difference scores, Mann-Whitney U and independent t-tests were used to analyze data. The groups did not differ pre-intervention on demographic variables, mean number of steps measured by pedometer, benefits or barriers scores. Participants were 78% White, with a mean age of 37.5 years, 11.8 years of education, and BMI of 34. The experimental group progressed significantly more in stage of change (m = 21.24) than the control group (m = 11.13; U = 47.00, p < .000). The experimental group had significantly ($t(30)$ = 2.60, p = .015) higher step counts (m = 7826.24, sd = 4559.45) than the control group (m = 4137.27, sd = 3280.03) and significantly lower ($t(30)$ = -2.52, p = .017) barriers scores (m = 12.88, sd = 5.13) than the control group (m = 17.47, sd = 5.15) post-intervention. Further research is needed that targets this at-risk population, but it appears that practitioners in primary care settings could implement this counseling approach to increase physical activity in low-income women.

---

[*] E-mail address: rhoebeke@usi.edu. Phone: 812-465-1171; Fax: 812-465-7092.

Introduction

According to the American Heart Association, cardiovascular disease is the leading cause of death among women in the United States. More women than men die each year of cardiovascular disease. Of the nearly one million deaths due to cardiovascular disease in 2004, 459,096 (52.8%) were women while 410,628 (47.2%) were men. The number of women's deaths that year due to cardiovascular disease exceeded the number of women's lives claimed by all cancers, accidents, diabetes, chronic lower respiratory disease, and Alzheimer's combined. Since 1984, the trend has been that more women than men have died each year of cardiovascular disease (Rosamond et al., 2008).

Physical inactivity is a major risk factor for cardiovascular disease, and carries nearly the same increased risk (from 1.5 to 2.4) as hypertension, hyperlipidemia, or smoking. Women who accumulate less than one hour per week of physical activity increase their risk of developing cardiovascular disease by 1.58 times compared to women who engage in physical activity more than three hours per week (World Heart Federation, 2008). Our national physical activity health objectives propose that 30% of adults engage in physical activity for at least 30 minutes 5 or more days per week for health benefits, and that the proportion of adults who engage in no physical activity be reduced to 20% by the year 2010 (U.S. Department of Health and Human Services [USDHHS], 2000). In spite of the evidence that physically active women can significantly reduce their risk for cardiovascular disease, 43% of U.S. women engaged in no leisure-time physical activity, and only 13% engaged in the recommended 30 minutes of physical activity 5 or more days per week (USDHHS, 2000).

Disparities in levels of physical activity exist among population groups. Women with lower incomes are the least likely to be physically active (Crespo, Ainsworth, Keteyian, Heath, & Smit, 1999; National Center for Chronic Disease Prevention and Health Promotion [NCCDPHP], 2008; USDHHS, 2000) and they have a higher prevalence for two or more risk factors for cardiovascular disease when compared to women with higher incomes (Mosca et al., 2007; National Center for Chronic Disease Prevention and Health Promotion [NCCDPHP], 2008). According to the U.S. Surgeon General's Report *Physical Activity and Health* (1996), the rate of physical inactivity for Americans with annual household incomes of $15,000 was 41% compared to 17.3% for those with annual household incomes of $50,000 and above.

This study was guided by constructs from the Transtheoretical Model of behavioral change (TTM), which integrates five stages of motivational readiness to change, ten processes of change, self-efficacy, and decisional balance (the "pros" and "cons" of changing), from across theories to explain behavioral change (Prochaska, DiClemente & Norcross, 1992). The TTM has shown promise in providing a framework for understanding physical activity behavior in adults. The TTM has been used to describe the temporal stages of change individuals move through to adopt new behaviors. The stages of adopting physical activity and their definitions are described in Table 1. The stages focus on both the behavioral intention and actual behavior (Prochaska, DiClemente, & Norcross, 1992).

Table 1. Stages of Change for Physical Activity (PA) and Definitions

Stage	Definition
Precontemplation	Do no PA and do not intend to start in the next 6 months
Contemplation	Do not do PA but intend to start in the next 6 months
Preparation	Intend to change PA behavior in the next month; Have made some attempts to do PA but not regularly
Action	Have been doing PA regularly for less than 6 months*
Maintenance	Have been doing PA regularly for 6 months or longer

*Accumulating moderate-intensity PA for at least 30 minutes $\geq$ 5 days/week.
Definitions adapted from Marcus & Simkin (1993).

Integrally linked to the stages are ten *processes of change*, which individuals use to progress through the stages. These processes are categorized as either cognitive or behavioral strategies. The number and types of processes used depends upon the individual's stage of change. The processes are: 1) *Consciousness Raising*: increasing one's awareness about a problem through seeking information; 2) *Dramatic Relief*: increasing emotional experiences related to the behavior; 3) *Self-Re-evaluation*: one's self-image and emotional and cognitive appraisal of values related to the problem; 4) *Environmental Re-evaluation*: how the habit affects one's social and physical environment; 5) *Self-Liberation*: belief that one can change and commitment to act on that belief; 6) *Social Liberation*: increase in social opportunities through empowerment; 7) *Counter-conditioning*: learning healthier behaviors to substitute for problem behaviors; 8) *Stimulus Control*: remove cues for unhealthy habits and add prompts for healthy habits; 9) *Contingency Management*: rewards, positive self-statements for taking steps in the right direction; and 10) *Helping Relationships*: utilizing support from others for the healthy behavior change (Prochaska, DiClemente, & Norcross, 1992). Those in the earlier stages of change such as Contemplation and Preparation use a mix of behavioral and cognitive processes to modify their behavior. Specifically, behavioral processes such as *self-liberation* (to believe in the ability to change and commit to setting goals), *counter-conditioning* (where one learns to replace sedentary behaviors with physical activity), *helping relationships* (enlist the support of others), and cognitive processes such as *environmental re-evaluation* (caring about the consequences of one's physical inactivity behavior on others) are used primarily by those in Contemplation and Preparation to move to the Action stage of change for physical activity (Prochaska, DiClemente, & Norcross, 1992).

Perceived *self-efficacy* is belief in one's capability to perform a specific action in order to attain a desired outcome. Self-efficacy beliefs affect the intention to change, the amount of effort it will take to attain the goal, and the persistence to continue on even though barriers could undermine motivation. In the TTM, self-efficacy is the situation-specific confidence individuals have to perform healthy behaviors (such as physical activity) and resist relapse. Within the TTM, *decisional balance* reflects an individual's weighing of the perceived benefits ("pros") and the perceived barriers ("cons") to changing behavior. The decision to move from one stage to the next is based upon the relative weight of the perceived benefits and barriers. People in the earlier stages of change perceive more barriers to being physically active than benefits, while those in the later stages of change perceive more benefits than barriers to being physically active (Prochaska, DiClemente, & Norcross, 1992).

Sedentary behavior in adults has been consistently associated with perceived barriers to engaging in physical activity in reviews of the physical activity determinants literature (Sherwood & Jeffery, 2000). Current research attributes barriers to physical activity for low-income women to being too tired, lack of time due to family and work roles, and lack of encouragement (Eyler, Matson-Koffman, Vest, Evenson, Sanderson, Thompson, et al., 2002; Hoebeke, 2008; King, Castro, Eyler, Wilcox, Sallis, & Brownson, 2000). The transtheoretical model (TTM) of behavior change has been used to explain the relationship between perceived barriers and physical activity behavior, primarily in middle to higher income adults. Physical activity interventions guided by TTM constructs have been shown to be more effective in moving individuals to higher stages of physical activity than standard approaches of advising people to increase their physical activity without assessing their stage of readiness for behavior change in community, workplace, and primary care settings (Marcus, Banspach, Lefebvre, Rossi, Carleton, & Abrams, 1992; Marcus & Owen, 1992; Marcus, Rakowski, & Rossi, 1992; Marcus, Pinto, Simkin, Audrain, & Taylor, 1994; Cardinal & Sachs, 1995; Calfas, Sallis, Oldenburg, & Ffrench, 1997; Marcus, Emmons, Simkin-Silverman, Linnan, Taylor, Bock, et al., 1998; Bock, Marcus, Pinto, & Forsyth, 2001). A recent physical activity intervention study specific to low-income women showed that application of the TTM constructs did result in stage progression and improvements in physical activity behavior in a small sample of women (Fahrenwald, Atwood, Walker, Johnson, & Berg, 2004). However, a paucity of physical activity research exists with this population and little is known about promoting physical activity among low-income women. Therefore, the purpose of this study was to test a stage-matched message developed from the TTM to increase physical activity among sedentary low-income women.

Design

This study used a randomized, two-group experimental design. The specific aims were to compare the efficacy of an intervention to positively affect changes in the outcome variables stage of change for physical activity, physical activity behavior, and perceived barriers to physical activity. The research question was, "Will a stage-matched physical activity message for low-income women result in increased physical activity participation and decreased perceived barriers to physical activity compared to a standard message approach to promoting physical activity"? Three research hypotheses were tested. The author hypothesized that as a result of the intervention, the experimental group would:

1. Increase their physical activity behavior, as measured by pedometer step counts, compared to the standard message (control) group;
2. Progress in stage of change for physical activity more than the control group; and,
3. Have decreased perceived barriers to physical activity compared to the control group.

Participants were randomized to either the experimental stage-matched message intervention group or to the standard message control group after enrollment using the Statistical Package for the Social Sciences (SPSS) version 13.0.

Methods

Population, Sample, and Setting

The population chosen for this study was comprised of low-income sedentary women. Low-income was defined as an annual household income at or below 185% of the federal poverty level for the year 2005. According to these income criteria, the upper income limit for a single individual was $17,705; annual income for a family of four was $35,798 (USDHHS, 2005). Women in the Contemplation and Preparation stage of change for physical activity according to the Transtheoretical Model were defined as sedentary. Potential participants were recruited from a family practice primary care clinic for uninsured and underinsured families in the Midwestern United States. Families eligible to receive health care services at the clinic had annual household incomes at or below 185% of federal poverty level. Eligibility criteria included women who were: (a) age 18 years or older, (b) able to speak, understand, and read English, (c) able to have access to a telephone, and (d) in either the Contemplation or Preparation stage of change for physical activity. Exclusion criteria were women who were: (a) under age 18 years, (b) not able to speak, understand, or read English, (c) unable to have access to a telephone, (d) pregnant or postpartum for 6 weeks or less, and (e) advised by a health care provider to not engage in physical activity (e.g., walking) as measured by a *yes* answer to any question on the Physical Activity Readiness Questionnaire (PAR-Q). The Physical Activity Readiness Questionnaire (PAR-Q) was used to screen out any women who might have a medical condition that precludes them from performing moderate physical activity. The PAR-Q has a specificity of 80% and a sensitivity of 100% for identification of persons who have contraindications to exercise (Thomas, Reading, & Shepard, 1992).

Procedures

This study was approved by the institutional review boards of the principal investigator's University and the hospital that was affiliated with the clinic where the participants were recruited. Recruitment and data collection procedures were conducted over a three-week period during May, 2005. The principal investigator approached women as they signed in at the reception desk of the clinic for appointments, provided information that explained about the study, answered any questions, and invited the women to participate. Ninety-nine women were approached and invited to participate in the study. Of the 99 women invited, 18 did not meet eligibility inclusion requirements and 9 declined to participate. Reasons for potential participants to not take part in the study due to ineligibility included lack of access to a telephone (n=6), not in the Contemplation or Preparation stage of change for physical activity (n=10), and a *yes* answer on the PAR-Q (n=2). Reasons given by those who declined to take part in the study included issues related to the time required to complete the study instruments that day, moving to a new address out of town, and the randomization process. Seventy-two participants who met eligibility criteria and agreed to participate were enrolled in the study. Participants were provided written informed consent by the principal investigator. Participants were randomly assigned to either the experimental or the control group following eligibility and informed consent using an SPSS version 13.0 computer-generated program for randomization.

Data were collected during the initial face-to-face clinic visit on the day of enrollment, at two weeks, and on two subsequent follow-up telephone contact calls (at 4 weeks post two-week visit and at 8 weeks post two-week visit) over a 10-week period. At the initial clinic visit, participants completed a self-report questionnaire consisting of demographic data including: age, race/ethnicity, educational level, marital status, children living at home, employment status, household size and annual household income. Actual weight and height were measured and recorded at the initial clinic visit. Weight and height were measured using a digital medical office scale and stadiometer. Participants completed additional instruments that measured perceived benefits and barriers to physical activity and stage of change for physical activity at the initial clinic visit. At two weeks following the initial clinic visit data were collected again on stage of change for physical activity, and perceived benefits and barriers for test-retest reliability, and these results were used for baseline data. At two weeks following the initial clinic visit women also reported their baseline pedometer step counts. These instruments were also completed during two telephone follow-up calls at four weeks and eight weeks after baseline during the course of the 10-week study. Each participant was given a *Sportline* pedometer that was set to the individual's personal step length and weight by the principal investigator, and then the participant was instructed in how to use the pedometer. A packet of information was given to each participant consisting of: (a) a log for recording physical activity, (b) a sheet to record physical activity goals and barriers, (c) the physical activity pyramid, and (d) the *10,000 Steps a Day* instruction sheet on wearing a pedometer. Before participants left the clinic a copy of the consent form was placed in the packet and dates were set for the follow-up contacts over the 10-week period. Each participant was given a $5.00 gift card to be used at a Target store as a thank-you for participation. Those women who were not eligible but who took the time to talk to the principal investigator were given a water bottle or a Frisbee to thank them for their time.

Measures and Instruments

A *Sportline* pedometer was used to count steps as an objective measure of physical activity. A standard digital medical office scale and stadiometer were used to measure each participant's weight and height without shoes to calculate body mass index (BMI). Self-report questionnaires were used to measure the Transtheoretical Model constructs of stages of change for physical activity and perceived benefits and barriers.

A pedometer was selected to measure physical activity behavior since walking has been reported as the most popular form of physical activity among low-income women (Hoebeke, 2002). A *Sportline* pedometer was worn on the clothing waistband at the hip to count steps. Participants in the experimental and control groups kept a log of their steps each day throughout the study. The average of the step counts for 3 consecutive days at the start of the study from the participant's log was used as the baseline (time 1) activity level. The average of the step counts for 3 consecutive days from the participant's log at the week of the final follow-up phone contact was used to represent the ending (time 2) activity level.

Stage of change for physical activity was measured using the Transtheoretical Model self-report Physical Activity Stages of Change questionnaire (Marcus, Rossi, Selby, Niaura,

& Abrams, 1992). Physical activity was defined and examples of moderate-intensity physical activities were given (such as walking briskly, riding a bike, or fast dancing). *Regular* engagement in physical activity was described in terms of the frequency (at least 5 days per week) and the amount (at least 30 minutes a day). Participants circled *yes* or *no* to four questions that categorized their intended and actual physical activity behavior into one of five stages when scored. For example, if a participant answered *no* to "I am currently physically active" and *yes* to "I intend to become more physically active in the next 6 months", they were in the Contemplation stage of physical activity (i.e., inactive but thinking about becoming more active). If a participant answered *yes* to "I am currently physically active" and *no* to "I currently engage in *regular* physical activity", they were in the Preparation stage (i.e., infrequently doing physical activity). Concurrent validity for this questionnaire has been established by means of this measure's significant association with other self-reported physical activity questionnaire data (Marcus & Simkin, 1993). The Kappa index of reliability for the stage of change question has been demonstrated to be .78 over a two-week period (Marcus, Selby, Niaura, & Rossi, 1992). For this study (N=32), two-week test-retest reliability ($r = .76$) was congruent with that of published studies.

Perceived benefits and barriers to physical activity were measured using the self-report 10-item Exercise Benefits Scale and the 6-item Exercise Barriers Scale questionnaire (Marcus, Rakowski, & Rossi, 1992). These items represented the pros and cons to physical activity. Participants were asked to rate how important each statement was in deciding whether to be physically active *right now*, rather than how they would like to feel or how they may have felt in the past. Items were rated on a five-point Likert scale, with 1 = not at all important, to 5 = extremely important. The 10 benefits items were summed to create a benefits score that could range from 10 to 50. A lower score indicated fewer perceived benefits to physical activity, while a higher score indicated more perceived benefits. The six barriers items were summed to create physical activity barriers scores with a potential range from 6 to 30. A lower score on this scale represented fewer perceived barriers to physical activity, while a higher score indicated more perceived barriers. For this study (N=32), internal consistency was high for the 10-item Benefits scale (Cronbach's alpha = .94), which is comparable to .95 found in the literature for this scale (Marcus, Rakowski, & Rossi, 1992). For this study (N = 32), internal consistency was high for the 6-item Barriers scale (Cronbach's alpha = .89), and this is similar to .79 reported for this scale in the literature (Marcus, Rakowski, & Rossi, 1992). Two-week test-retest reliability in this study was high for the Benefits scale ($r = .88$) and the Barriers scale ($r = .82$).

Intervention

The principal investigator made telephone contact with participants in the experimental and control groups at 4 weeks post-baseline and 8 weeks post-baseline at a pre-determined time and date set up during the baseline week 2 visit. A written script of 10 items was followed for the intervention. Those in the experimental group were asked all 10 items, while those in the control group were only asked the final 3 items. None of the participants knew what group they were randomly assigned to. The script consisted of 7 items developed from TTM constructs that were used to counsel those in the experimental group, and 3 items that were asked of participants of both groups. The 7 items incorporated processes that would most likely be used by those in either the Contemplation or Preparation stage of change to motivate behavior. Participants in the experimental group were asked to tell the principal investigator about the activity goal they had written on their sheet they received in their packet. This incorporated the process of *self-liberation,* which entails setting goals and committing to a healthy behavior change. The principal investigator asked how they were doing with meeting the goal, and this gave opportunity to discuss whether the goal needed to be revised and if encouragement was needed. Next, barriers were discussed in terms of "what things get in the way of you being physically active?" The principal investigator asked about barriers they had recorded on their sheet, which one was the biggest barrier, and discussed strategies to overcome barriers. Participants were encouraged to write down their ideas to overcome their biggest barriers to physical activity. The process of *helping relationships* was incorporated into the script items by asking participants in the experimental group whether they could identify someone who could help them be more active or engage in walks or other physical activity with them. Participants in the experimental group were asked how they had been fitting physical activity into their day in place of more sedentary activities. Discussion on how to replace less active pursuits for active ones incorporated the process of *counter-conditioning* into the counseling. Participants were asked to list examples of how they could fit more physical activity into their day and write them down. The process of *environmental re-evaluation* was utilized in the telephone script items by discussing with the participant their thoughts about how their own physical activity behavior as mothers would influence their children to be healthy. Lastly, perceived benefits of physical activity were discussed, and participants in the experimental group were asked to write down benefits that applied to them.

The remaining 3 items of the script were asked of all participants. These were questions related to the amount and type of physical activity of the participants, and a standard physical activity message statement. Participants were asked about whether they had recorded steps on their physical activity log for that week and how many steps they had taken each day of the week. They were asked what types of physical activity they were doing and how much time they were spending on the activity. Lastly, each participant was encouraged to keep getting physical activity for at least 30 minutes a day on most, preferably all days of the week. They were referred to the physical activity pyramid and the *10,000 Steps a Day* instruction sheet in their packet for ideas. They would then be reminded that they would receive another phone call on the specified date in 4 weeks, or if this was the final end-of-study call, they were congratulated for staying with the study for the entire 10 weeks.

Data Analysis

Data analysis included descriptive statistics, Pearson's *r*, Cronbach's alpha, Chi-square, one-way analysis of variance (ANOVA), pre and post difference scores, Mann-Whitney-*U*, and independent *t*-tests. Descriptive statistics were conducted on all variables. Frequencies were conducted for categorical data. Means and standard deviations were conducted on continuous variables, and pair-wise correlations were examined. Cronbach's alpha values were obtained to measure the internal consistency of scale items. Chi-square tests were conducted to assess for differences between groups on nominal-level variables at baseline. One-way ANOVA analyses were conducted to assess for differences between groups on age in years, highest number of years of education attained, and BMI variables at baseline. Mann-

Whitney-U tests were used to test the difference between two independent groups based on ranked scores at baseline and when determining if the experimental group had progressed in stage compared to the control group. Independent t–tests were conducted to analyze differences in step counts, benefits and barriers scores of the experimental and control groups at baseline and post-intervention. Two-tailed p values < 0.05 were considered statistically significant. Sample size was calculated using the sample sizes for two-sample t-test (Cohen, 1969) and a moderate effect size ($d = .54$) for the two main outcomes of change in stage of physical activity and change in physical activity behavior as measured by step counts. This effect size was based on a meta-analysis of applications of the Transtheoretical Model to physical activity (Marshall & Biddle, 2001), where the mean effect size for moving from Contemplation to Preparation across all types of physical activity interventions was .54. A sample size of 26 subjects per group (total sample size 52) was calculated to achieve a power of .80 at the .05 alpha level of significance. Because the author anticipated that the drop-out rate for the study might be high in this population, the desired sample size was oversampled by 38% (N = 72).

Results

Of the 72 participants that were recruited, a total sample of 32 women who were randomly assigned (17 to the experimental group and 15 to the control group) completed the 10-week study. Loss to follow-up occurred during the telephone contact phase of the study due to: land line phones were disconnected or cell phones were no longer in service (n = 18), participants said they stopped keeping track of their steps or said lost their log (n = 13), participants lost the pedometer and did not want to go back to the clinic to pick up another one (n = 4), participants had lost interest (n = 2), were unavailable each time the author called day or night (n = 2), or they had moved away (n =1). Baseline comparison data were analyzed on those participants who completed the study (N = 32). There were no significant differences

Table 2. Baseline Sample and Group Demographic Characteristics

Characteristic	Total Sample (N=32)	Control Group (N=15)	Experimental Group (N=17)	X^2 or F^d	p
Age (years)[a]	37.50 $\pm$ 11.98	38.4 $\pm$ 12.62	36.72 $\pm$ 11.72	.155	.70
Education [b]	11.88 $\pm$ 2.32	12.2 $\pm$ 2.08	11.59 $\pm$ 2.55	.544	.47
BMI [c]	34.06 $\pm$ 11.38	33.5 $\pm$ 13.03	34.55 $\pm$ 10.10	.066	.80
Employed Full-time	10 (31%)	4 (27%)	6 (35%)	.276	.60
Employed Part-time	4 (12.5%)	3 (20%)	1 (6%)	1.452	.23
White	25 (78%)	10 (67%)	15 (88%)	2.169	.14
Married or Partnered	10 (31%)	5 (33%)	5 (29%)	.057	.81
Children $\leq$ 5 years at home	14 (44%)	4 (27%)	10 (59%)	3.348	.07
Children 6-18 years at home	19 (59%)	7 (47%)	12 (71%)	1.890	.17
Children $\leq$ 18 years at home	25 (78%)	10 (67%)	15 (88%)	2.169	.14

[a] Range = 19-65 years. [b] Range = 8-18 years. [c] BMI Range = 19-70. [d] $df = 1$.

between the experimental and control group on any of the demographic variables or body mass index (BMI). Table 2 shows the baseline demographic characteristics of the sample and comparison of the control and experimental groups. Participants in the sample were predominantly White (78%), with a mean age of 37.5 years and a mean BMI of 34. The mean level of education was 11.8 years of school. The majority of women (78%) had children living at home. Of those with children, 44% had children under the age of 5, and 59% had school-age children living at home ranging in age from 6 to 18 years. Nearly one third (31%) of the women worked full-time. The majority of the women were single, (68%), and 31% were married or partnered.

Physical Activity Behavior

The first hypothesis was that women in the experimental group would demonstrate increased physical activity behavior as measured by pedometer step counts compared to the women in the control group. The mean daily step counts pre-intervention for the experimental group (N = 17) were (m = 3863.29 $\pm$ sd 2755.96) and for the control group (N = 15) mean daily step counts were (m = 3519.67 $\pm$ sd 2596.69) at baseline. There were no significant differences between the two groups at baseline for step counts ($t(30)$ = .362, p = .720). To assess the efficacy of the intervention on the outcome variable physical activity behavior, independent samples t-tests were conducted to examine whether there were significant differences in step counts between the two groups as a result of the intervention. Mean daily step counts post-intervention for the experimental group (N = 17) were (m = 7826.24, sd = 4559.45) and for the control group (N = 15) were (m = 4137.27, sd = 3280.03). The differences between the two groups post-intervention on mean daily step counts was statistically significant ($t(30)$ = 2.60, p = .015). Cohen (1988) defined effect sizes as "small, d = .2", "medium, d = .5", and "large, d = .8". The effect size (Cohen's d) for increase in step counts in this study was large (d = .93). Figure 1 depicts the mean daily step counts for the control and experimental groups before and after the intervention.

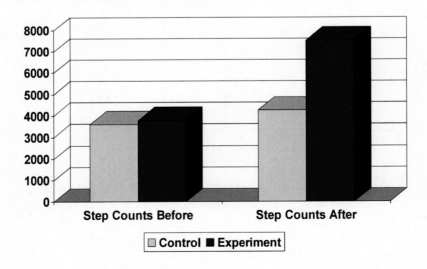

Figure 1. Mean Daily Step Counts Pre and Post Intervention by Group.

Stage of Change for Physical Activity

The second hypothesis was that women in the experimental group would progress in stage of change for physical activity more than the control group. Participants were in either the Contemplation or Preparation stage of physical activity when they enrolled in the study as assessed by the Physical Activity Stages of Change questionnaire (Marcus, Rossi, Selby, Niaura, & Abrams, 1992). Stage of physical activity was again assessed at two weeks, and this stage was used as the baseline. For data analysis, stages were described using 1 = Precontemplation, 2 = Contemplation, 3 = Preparation, 4 = Action, and 5 = Maintenance. Mann-Whitney U tests showed there were no significant differences between the experimental (N = 17) and control (N = 15) group in stage of physical activity at baseline (m = 19.03; U = 84.50, p = .105). At post-intervention, 13 of the control group participants had stayed in the same stage and two had progressed in stage. At post-intervention, the experimental group had four participants who stayed in the same stage, and 13 had progressed in stage. None of the participants regressed in stage. The experimental group progressed significantly more in stage of change (m = 21.24) than the control group (m = 11.13; U = 47.00, p < .000). Figure 2 presents the stage progression for the control and experimental groups as a result of the intervention. The effect size (Cohen's d) for stage progression in this study was large (d = 1.75).

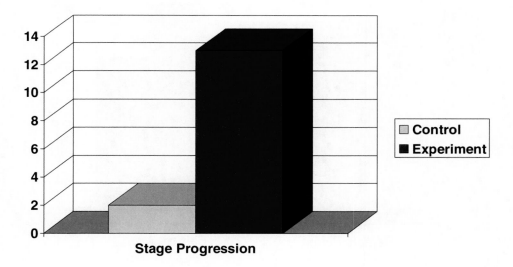

Figure 2. Numbers of Stage-Progressed Participants by Group Post-Intervention.

Perceived Barriers and Benefits to Physical Activity

The third hypothesis was that women in the experimental group would have decreased perceived barriers to physical activity compared to the control group as a result of the intervention. Independent t-tests were done to analyze differences between the two groups in perceived barriers scores before and after the intervention. The pre-intervention mean sum of barriers scores for the experimental and control groups were examined at baseline using the 6-

item Exercise Barriers Scale questionnaire (Marcus, Rakowski, & Rossi, 1992). The possible range for barriers scores was 6 to 30. The mean barriers score for the control group (N = 15) at baseline was (m = 16.07, sd = 4.48) and for the experimental group (N = 17) was (m = 14.41, sd = 5.00). The two groups were not significantly different on mean barriers scores at baseline pre-intervention ($t(30)$ = .980, p = .335). The greatest individual barrier for both groups at baseline was "At the end of the day, I am too exhausted to be physically active" (m = 2.88 for this barrier for the experimental group; m = 3.33 for the control group) with no significant difference between the groups on this barrier (p = .363). Post-intervention (see Figure 3), the barriers scores for the experimental group decreased (N = 17, m = 12.88, sd = 5.13), which indicated they perceived fewer barriers to physical activity as a result of the intervention, while the control group's barriers scores increased post-intervention (N = 15, m = 17.47, sd = 5.15). The difference between the experimental group's perceived barriers scores and those of the control group was significantly different post-intervention ($t(30)$ = -2.52, p = .017). The effect size (Cohen's d) for change in barriers scores post-intervention in this study was large (d = .89). The individual barrier that was ranked the highest for both groups post-intervention remained the same as at baseline (m = 2.59 for the experimental group; m = 3.47 for the control group) with no significant difference between the two groups (p = .254).

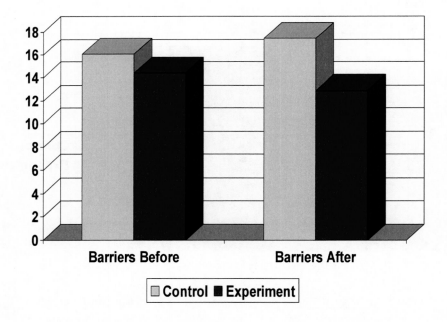

Figure 3. Mean Barriers Scores by Group Pre and Post Intervention.

Independent t-tests were done to analyze differences between the two groups in perceived benefits scores before and after the intervention. The pre-intervention mean sum of benefits scores for the experimental and control groups were examined at baseline using the 10-item Exercise Benefits Scale questionnaire (Marcus, Rakowski, & Rossi, 1992). The possible range for benefits scores was 10 to 50. The mean benefits score for the control group (N = 15) at baseline was (m = 38.33, sd = 8.91) and for the experimental group (N = 17) was (m =

41.94, sd = 6.78). The two groups were not significantly different on mean benefits scores at baseline pre-intervention ($t(30)$ = 1.315, p = .262). Post-intervention, the benefits scores for the experimental group remained essentially unchanged (N = 17, m = 41.65, sd = 6.96), while the control group's benefits scores increased post-intervention (N = 15, m = 39.27, sd = 8.19). The difference between the experimental group's perceived benefits scores and those of the control group was not significantly different post-intervention ($t(30)$ = .880, p = .387).

Discussion

This study provided preliminary information on the efficacy of a stage-matched physical activity message intervention to increase physical activity behavior and decrease perceived barriers to physical activity in low-income sedentary women. The study was guided by the transtheoretical model (TTM) of behavioral change. Constructs of the TTM were incorporated into the intervention's stage-matched message when counseling the women on physical activity and how to overcome perceived barriers. This study used a randomized experimental design which controlled for extraneous variables. Participants were blinded as to group status. The instruments that were used to measure the outcome variables of interest were tested with this target population prior to the intervention, which methodologically served to strengthen the findings. Two different measures of physical activity behavior, stage of change and pedometer step counts, were used to assess physical activity in this study. The intervention was delivered entirely by the principal investigator, who is a registered nurse and a family nurse practitioner, using a script to ensure consistency. The intervention employed principles of experiential learning, active engagement, reflection, and evaluation. The principal investigator kept track of the length of time for each phone contact, and endeavored to keep each conversation from 15 to 20 minutes for both the experimental and the control groups. The experimental group, as hypothesized, progressed statistically significantly more in stage of change for physical activity and in reported mean daily pedometer step counts than the control group that received the standard physical activity message. Also as hypothesized, the experimental group demonstrated decreased perceived barriers to physical activity as a result of the intervention compared to the control group. Each of these hypothesized desired outcomes had large effect sizes.

The findings in this study with respect to significant stage progression in physical activity behavior as a result of a tailored, stage-matched intervention are consistent with other published studies that used approaches guided by constructs from the TTM to achieve this outcome in community, workplace, and primary care settings (Marcus, Banspach, Lefebvre, Rossi, Carleton, & Abrams, 1992; Marcus & Owen, 1992; Marcus, Rakowski, & Rossi, 1992; Marcus, Pinto, Simkin, Audrain, & Taylor, 1994; Cardinal & Sachs, 1995; Calfas, Sallis, Oldenburg, & Ffrench, 1997; Marcus, Emmons, Simkin-Silverman, Linnan, Taylor, Bock, et al., 1998; Bock, Marcus, Pinto, & Forsyth, 2001) and with low-income women enrolled in the Women, Infants, and Children (WIC) program (Fahrenwald, Atwood, Walker, Johnson, & Berg, 2004). The majority of the participants in this study were single mothers of pre-school and school-aged children, and nearly one third of the women worked full-time outside the home. The greatest perceived barrier to physical activity that was reported by the participants was being too exhausted at the end of the day. This is consistent with published studies that have shown that women with parenting, family and work demands perceive more barriers, particularly fatigue, to engaging in physical activity (Eyler, Matson-Koffman, Vest, Evenson, Sanderson, Thompson, et al., 2002; Hoebeke, 2008; King, Castro, Eyler, Wilcox, Sallis, & Brownson, 2000). The participants in the experimental group of this study demonstrated a significant decrease in their perceived barriers to physical activity, compared to the control group, as a result of the tailored, stage-matched intervention.

Low-income populations are often harder to reach than middle to higher income primary care setting participants. In this tailored stage-matched telephone counseling intervention study there was a large loss to follow-up with this low-income population of women. Fortunately, the large effect sizes that were demonstrated for the outcomes of interest made it possible to see significant differences even though the sample sizes for the control and experimental groups were below the desired numbers calculated in the power analysis. These results are very encouraging.

Limitations

Limitations of this study include small sample size and predominantly White participants which limits generalizability of these findings. It is possible that the intervention group participants received more attention than those in the standard message group, even though attempts were made to keep the phone conversations to approximately the same length of time (15 to 20 minutes). This study was only 10 weeks long, therefore the short follow-up time period limits interpretation regarding whether adoption of physical activity would be maintained. This study was conducted during the summertime in the Midwestern United States, when the weather is conducive to being outdoors. Since walking is the most frequent physical activity in low-income women, the results may have been different if the study had been conducted during the winter months. The stage of change and perceived benefits and barriers for physical activity instruments used in this study had good psychometric properties, but self-report measures of physical activity have limits, and participants may have given answers that were socially desirable. The pedometer step counters were an objective measure of physical activity, but the author has no way to verify actual physical activity that the steps represent. Few women kept records of how many minutes they spent engaged in physical activity, so this could not be used to determine if the women met the *Healthy People 2010* national physical activity health objectives.

Conclusion

This study demonstrates that a tailored, stage-matched telephone counseling intervention derived from the TTM was effective in decreasing perceived barriers and increasing physical activity behavior outcomes in low-income women from a primary care setting. The clinical applications of this study require further testing to determine the feasibility of delivering TTM-guided physical activity counseling by primary care providers with this population. It may be that other methods of delivering the tailored stage-matched physical activity message, such as CDs or scheduled group counseling sessions, once tested, might be as effective as and less time-intensive than a telephone-delivered message. Further research is needed that targets this at-risk population, but it appears that practitioners in primary care settings could implement this counseling approach to increase physical activity in low-income women.

Acknowledgements

This research study was supported by a competitive Excellence through Engagement Summer Research Fellowship funded by the Lilly Endowment, Inc. The author thanks the Deaconess Family Practice Clinic staff and patients for their assistance and participation in this research. A portion of this research was presented at the Midwest Nursing Research Society (MNRS) 30th Annual Research Conference, Milwaukee, Wisconsin (paper presentation), and as a poster presentation at the National Organization of Nurse Practitioner Faculties (NONPF) 32nd Annual Meeting, Orlando, Florida, in 2006.

References

Bock, B.C., Marcus, B.H., Pinto, B.M., & Forsyth, L.H. (2001). Maintenance of physical activity following an individualized motivationally tailored intervention. *Annals of Behavioral Medicine,***23**, 79-87.

Calfas, K.J., Sallis, J.F., Oldenburg, B., & Ffrench, M. (1997). Mediators of change in physical activity following an intervention in primary care: PACE. *Preventive Medicine,* **26**, 297-304.

Cardinal, B.J., & Sachs, M.L. (1995). Prospective analysis of stage-of-exercise movement following mail-delivered, self-instructional exercise packets. *American Journal of Health Promotion,* **9**(6), 430-432.

Cohen, J. (1969). *Statistical Power Analysis for the Behavioral Sciences,* New York: Academic Press.

Cohen, J. (1988). *Statistical Power Analysis for the Behavioral Sciences* (2nd ed.). Hillsdale, NJ: Lawrence Earlbaum Associates.

Crespo, C.J., Ainsworth, B.E., Keteyian, S.J., Heath, G.W., & Smit, W. (1999). Prevalence of physical inactivity and its relation to social class in U.S. adults: Results from the Third National Health and Nutrition Examination Survey, 1988-1994. *Medicine and Science in Sports and Exercise,* **31**, 1821-1827.

Eyler, A.A., Matson-Koffman, D., Vest, J.R., Evenson, K.R., Sanderson, B., Thompson, J.L., Wilbur, J., Wilcox, S., & Young, D.R. (2002). Environmental, policy, and cultural factors related to physical activity in a diverse sample of women: The Women's Cardiovascular Health Network Project – summary and discussion. *Women & Health,* **36** (2), 123-134.

Fahrenwald, N.L., Atwood, J.R., Walker, S.N., Johnson, D.R., & Berg, K. (2004). A randomized pilot test of "Moms on the Move": A physical activity intervention for WIC mothers. *Annals of Behavioral Medicine,* **27** (2), 82-90.

Hoebeke, R. (2002). *Low-income women's barriers to engaging in physical activity for health benefits.* Unpublished doctoral dissertation, University of Wisconsin, Madison.

Hoebeke, R. (2008). Cardiovascular disease prevention in women: The role of the NP in primary care. *Critical Care Nursing Clinics of North America,* **20** (3), 297-304.

King, A.C., Castro, C., Eyler, A.A., Wilcox, S., Sallis, J.F., & Brownson, R. C. (2000). Personal and environmental factors associated with physical inactivity among different racial/ethnic groups of U.S. middle-aged and older-aged women. *Health Psychology,* **19,** 354-364.

Marcus, B.H., Banspach, S.W., Lefebvre, R.C., Rossi, J.S., Carleton, R.A., & Abrams, D.B. (1992). Using the stages of change model to increase the adoption of physical activity among community participants. *American Journal of Health Promotion,* **6**(6), 424-429.

Marcus, B.H., Emmons, K.M., Simkin-Silverman, L.R., Linnan, L.A., Taylor, E.R., Bock, B.C., Roberts, M.B., Rossi, J.S., & Abrams, D.B. (1998). Evaluation of motivationally tailored versus standard self-help physical activity interventions at the workplace. *American Journal of Health Promotion,* **12**(4), 246-253.

Marcus, B.H., & Owen, N. (1992). Motivational readiness, self-efficacy, and decision making for exercise. *Journal of Applied Social Psychology,* **22,** 3-16.

Marcus, B.H., Pinto, B.M., Simkin, L.R., Audrain, J.E., & Taylor, E.R. (1994). Application of theoretical models to exercise behavior among employed women. *American Journal of Health Promotion,* **9,** 49-55.

Marcus, B.H., Rakowski, W., & Rossi, J.S. (1992). Assessing motivational readiness and decision making for exercise. *Health Psychology,* **11,** 257-261.

Marcus, B.H., Rossi, J.S., Selby, V.C., Niaura, R.S., & Abrams, D.B. (1992). The stages and processes of exercise adoption and maintenance in a worksite sample. *Health Psychology,* **11,** 386-395.

Marcus, B.H., Selby, V.C., Niaura, R.S., & Rossi, J.S. (1992). Self-efficacy and the stages of exercise behavior change. *Research Quarterly for Exercise and Sport,* **63**(1), 60-66.

Marcus, B.H., & Simkin, L.R. (1993). The stages of exercise behavior. *The Journal of Sports Medicine and Physical Fitness,* **33,** 83-88.

Marshall, S.J., & Biddle, S.J.H. (2001). The transtheoretical model of behavior change: A meta-analysis of applications to physical activity and exercise. *Annals of Behavioral Medicine,* **23**(4), 229-246.

Mosca, L., Banka, C.L., Benjamin, E. J., Berra, K., Bushnell, C., Dolor, R. J., et al. (2007). Evidence-based guidelines for cardiovascular disease prevention in women: 2007 update. *Circulation,* **115**(11): 1481-1501.

National Center for Chronic Disease Prevention and Health Promotion. (2008). *Wisewoman: A crosscutting program to improve the health of uninsured women.* Retrieved October 30, 2008 from http://www.cdc.gov/nccdphp/aag/aag_wisewoman.htm

Prochaska, J.O., DiClemente, C.C., & Norcross, J.C. (1992). In search of how people change: Applications to addictive behaviors. *American Psychologist,* **47,** 1102-1114.

Rosamond, W., Flegal, K., Friday, G., Furie, K., Go, A., Greenlund, K., et al. (2008). Heart disease and stroke statistics – 2008 update: A report from the American Heart Association Statistics Committee and Stroke Statistics Subcommittee. *Circulation,* **117**(4): (e25-146).

Sherwood, N.E., & Jeffery, R.W. (2000). The behavioral determinants of exercise: Implications for physical activity interventions. *Annual Review of Nutrition,* **20,** 21-44.

Thomas, S., Reading, J., & Shepard, R.J. (1992). Revision of the Physical Activity Readiness Questionnaire (PAR-Q). *Canadian Journal of Sport Science,* **17,** 338-345.

U.S. Department of Health and Human Services. (1996). *Physical activity and health: A report of the surgeon general.* Atlanta, GA: Centers for Disease Control and Prevention, National Center for Chronic Disease Prevention and Health Promotion.

U.S. Department of Health and Human Services. (2000). *Healthy People 2010* (Conference Edition, in Two Volumes). Washington, DC: Author.

U.S. Department of Health and Human Services. (2005). The 2005 HHS poverty guidelines. Retrieved May 1, 2005 from http://aspe.hhs.gov/poverty/index.shtml

World Heart Federation. *Cardiovascular disease risk factors.* Retrieved October 30, 2008, from http://www.world-heart-federation.org/cardiovascular-health/cardiovascular-disease -risk-factors/

In: Low Incomes: Social, Health and Educational Impacts   ISBN 978-1-60741-175-8
Editor: Jacob K. Levine, pp. 245-281   © 2009 Nova Science Publishers, Inc.

Chapter 12

AN EMPIRICAL LOOK AT LOW INCOME CONSUMERS AND THE RENT-TO-OWN INDUSTRY

Michael H. Anderson[a] and Sanjiv Jaggia[b]
[a] Charlton College of Business
University of Massachusetts, North Dartmouth, MA, USA
[b] Orfalea College of Business
California Polytechnic State University, San Luis Obispo, CA, USA

Abstract

The rent-to-own (RTO) industry is popular among low income consumers in part because it offers immediate access to merchandise along with the ability to cancel a transaction at any point without adverse consequence. This paper studies consumer use of RTO using a unique data base of more than 11,000 completed transactions originating between 2001 and 2004 inclusive and drawn from four RTO stores in the southeast United States. Descriptive statistics are produced on customer characteristics, e.g., income level and martial status; and on contract structure, e.g., maximum duration and the periodicity of the payment schedule. While it is understood that the main categories of RTO products are appliances, computers, furniture, electronics and jewelry to produce a fuller picture of a typical transaction, the data is used to tabulate the actual merchandise being acquired. Further, contracts must conclude in one of four manners: return, contract payout, early purchase or default (i.e., a "skip"—the customer does not fully discharge their obligation but the store is unable to recover the merchandise). This paper explores the likelihood of these various outcomes using a multinomial logit methodology. This has two advantages. One, we are able to see the significance of various customer characteristics and contractual features in impacting these probabilities as well as comparing the direction of any affect against a priori hypotheses. Two, we are able to compare and contrast the simulated probabilities of different types of customers, e.g. a single, young, man receiving government aid versus a married, older, female getting no aid. In sum, this paper seeks to add to our understanding of an important but little studied acquisition mechanism. Among other benefits, this piece could play a role in the policy debate about the nature of rent-to-own and its contribution to consumer welfare. Additionally, the paper adds novel insights into the picture of how financially-disadvantaged consumers conduct their affairs while also providing some insights applicable to all consumers whether financially constrained or not.

1. Introduction

The rent-to-own (RTO) industry from its beginnings in the 1960s has grown into an important sector of the retailing industry. The heart of the RTO arrangement is that consumers gain immediate access to new or used merchandise—most commonly appliances, electronics or furniture—with neither a credit check nor down payment in exchange for a fixed rental payment due either weekly, biweekly, semi-monthly or monthly. The agreement has a predetermined time period, usually between 12 and 24 months; however, the consumer may terminate the contract at any point by returning the merchandise or by exercising an early purchase option. Should all payments be made, or the lump sum payment option used, the customer takes ownership of the merchandise. However, no adverse credit action occurs if the consumer decides to terminate after only one payment or after just a few. By offering immediate access to household goods for a small periodic fee, this type of arrangement has strong appeal to low income and financially distressed consumers.

As an industry serving to a large extent lower income consumers, RTO transactions are often grouped with other alternative financial services such as check-checking stores, payday lenders and pawn shops—see, e.g., Swagler, Burton and Lewis (1995) and Stegman and Faris (2003). Many studies have been conducted studying the economics of rent-to-own. For instance, Anderson and Jackson (2004), Lacko, McKernan and Hastak (2002), McKernan, Lacko and Hastak (2003) and Swagler and Wheeler (1989) examine various aspects of the consumer experience. The industry has been subject to criticism by consumer advocates who argue that RTO exploits low income individuals who have no other option to acquire necessary household goods—see, e.g., Renuart and Keest (1999) and Swagler and Wheeler (1989).[1] This high cost has been argued in, e.g., Freedman (1993) and Hill, Ramp and Silver (1998). For a good overview of typical contractual terms and customer demographics see Anderson and Jaggia (2008) or FTC (2000), see also Cheskin+Martin (1993) for a somewhat earlier longitudinal study.

Consumer advocates tend to advise that financially constrained consumers simply save or use layaway instead of RTO. One can argue that rent-to-own could well be rational if the item is viewed as having high enough intertemporal utility. While layaway as a forced saving plan aimed at a specific goal can be very helpful as a discipline and accumulation mechanism, possession of the merchandise is obtained only after the entire amount has been paid. So while undeniably more expensive, RTO provides immediate access to desired items which is something the consumer may feel is worth the cost.

One attempt to characterize the underlying consumer demand for RTO is Anderson and Jackson (2001). They propose a trichotomy of types: renters who have a short term need for the product; tentative buyers who have significant purchase probabilities yet for whom return is the most likely outcome; and, finally, denied buyers who are attracted to buying but either do not have access to conventional financing or place a high value on the termination option due to uncertainty over finances or the length of their need. Implicit in this categorization is the notion that consumers are rational decision makers and that rent-to-own

---

[1]Andreasen (1993) presents an introduction to the issues of consumer advocacy for the disadvantaged. Additionally, Martin and Huckins (1997) reviews legal and legislative moves to curtail rent-to-own. While most states have defined RTO as akin to a lease, Keest, Langer and Day (1995) relates how Minnesota and Wisconsin ruled it a credit sale and so subject to state usury ceilings.

is filling a genuine consumer need. Viewing the question more broadly, Zikmund-Fisher and Parker (1999) conjecture four economic and psychological explanations for demand for RTO. Namely, (1) liquidity constraints caused by insufficient credit access, (2) high intertemporal discount rates, (3) a self-management method to deal with myopic preferences for immediate reward, and, (4) valuing highly the escapability of these contracts as a method of dealing with variable and unpredictable cash flows. Their findings generally support the latter two explanations.

The nature of the rent-to-own transaction—whether it is a rental or purchase agreement—is a key policy question. The industry is pursuing national legislation classifying it as a lease while some states have classified it as an installment credit agreement. Clearly, if it is most appropriately described as a purchase then this transaction is usurious and should be the subject of further legislation. This is partly an empirical question judged by how the contract is actually being used by consumers, e.g., the probability of purchase and the expected duration of the agreement. Indeed, one goal of the current paper is to contribute to our understanding of how these agreements are used in practice, which in turn will shed light on the rationality of the consumers, albeit indirect. Further, the RTO market affords insights into the impact of factors, especially those related to contract structure and repeat customers, in other consumer loan markets.

The contribution of the current piece is the analysis of detailed store-level transactional data. We use this in an attempt to provide new insights into both the rent-to-own market as well into the economic behavior of low income consumers. While the extant literature has relied on relatively small scale customer interviews or surveys,[2] the richness of our data allows quantification of variables otherwise unavailable. Two general themes emerge from our analysis. First is a demographic picture of rent-to-own customers. As one might expect, the typical RTO customer can be described as a member of the "working poor," and we show how variations in demographic characteristics impact the amount of rent that a customer pays. These results are consistent with and complementary to the existing literature. The second theme relates to the actual transactional details of the contracts; for instance, payment frequency and contractual length. Exploration of such features is only possible due to the nature of our data. Much of our analysis revolves around descriptive statistics derived from our data base, but we also present some regression results which show the direction of relationship and statistical significance for various parameters.

In the next section, the origin and creation of the data set is described and various summary statistics are derived. A multinomial logit model is specified and run in section 3.. Further, that section discusses various implications of the results and then constructs some scenarios along with associated simulated probabilities to better illustrate the impact of various customer and contract characteristics. Conclusions appear in section 4..

2. Data Analysis and Descriptive Statistics

The data for this study was drawn from proprietary information from four stores of a small rent-to-own (RTO) chain in the Southeast United States. The stores were located in three states: Alabama, Louisiana and two in Mississippi. It represents all available

---

[2]FTC (2000) is an exception as it surveys 524 customer identified from a sample of 12,000 consumers.

transactional records as of the date(s) gathered and was filtered only to remove personal information to ensure consumer confidentially. At the store level, the detailed history of an individual transaction—from which we draw our data—is automatically purged 14 months after concluding to free up system storage (transactions involving stolen merchandise are kept longer). To extend the available data window, the data were regathered in several later periods and merged—in all, the data represent five gatherings spaced 14 months apart (the last being September 2007).

There are both truncation and censoring issues present in the raw data, these issues needed to be corrected in order to construct the data set. To address the truncation issue, we eliminated all records whose origination was more than 14 months prior to the data gathering, thereby ensuring that no transaction contemporaneous to one in the data set could be omitted. This resulted in removing many old transactions with relatively long lives as an unknown amount of transactions originating around the same time but having shorter durations would be missing; so as not to have removed those old records would have introduced several biases into the data set. The censoring issue has an opposite cause; for transactions originating closer and closer to the final data collection date, only short running transactions would have concluded, the remainder will still be active and so their outcome is unknown, i.e., knowledge of their resolution is censored. To address this problem, we placed restrictions on the range of permissible origination dates so that all agreements considered would be sufficiently old, relative to the last collection date, to have naturally concluded. Correcting for the truncation and censoring issues resulted in considering transactions originating between August 2001 and August 2004 inclusive. The data spans just over five years as the most recent termination date in the set is December 2006. After filtering out spoiled records—those voided at origination but retained for auditing purposes—as well as any transaction with missing information, our final data set contained 11,113 observations.

2.1. General Data Analysis

Detail on each individual payment made on every transaction is tracked in the data base. In sum, there are 136,275 payments or an average of 12.26 payments per agreement. It is noteworthy that 89% of these payments represent the customer physically going into the store to pay (120,693) and, of those, 93% of the payments are in cash (112,405). By contrast, among all payments only 233 were charged using a credit or debit card.[3] This is consistent with, but starker than the finding in FTC (2000) which reported that among those households using rent-to-own, their ownership of both credit cards and checking accounts was significantly lower than the ownership rates among households in general. However, their study did reject the hypothesis that most RTO customer were "unbanked."[4] At the same time though, such direct involvement in making each individual payment, instead of mailing a check, pre-authorizing a debit or using some other such mechanism, is an interesting commentary on the economic circumstances of consumers who utilize rent-to-

---

[3]Regarding location, an additional 6.1% of payments are picked up at the customer's home, the rest are dropped off or mailed. Of payment method, 88.9% are cash, 6.7% are check or money order, 0.2% are charge, the remainder are unspecified.

[4]This issued is discussed in, for example, Hogarth and O'Donnell (1999). For further discussion of the use of traditional credit and bank accounts by rent-to-own customers (and more generally, by "alternative financial sector customers") see Swagler et al. (1995), Caskey (1994) and Caskey (1997).

own. This point is further buttressed by considering the rent-to-own customers' ability to make their payments on time.

One needs to be careful in analyzing late payment behavior. Generally, a customer makes a payment at the time of contract initiation (time zero), so by definition that payment would be on-time. However, if the contract terminated before another payment was made—because, say, there was an adverse change in the customer's economic circumstances—then that customer would misleadingly have a perfect on-time record. By contrast, one could imagine a customer who acquires the merchandise after, e.g., 25 on-time payments; this would be a very different case which would need to be distinguished from the prior example. Another interesting case arises if the store has chosen to run a promotion allowing "free days"—an initial period before any payments are due—in this case, it would actually be possible for a customer to skip with the merchandise having paid nothing and yet, having made zero payments he/she made zero late payments. To control for such issues, we considered only contracts for which at least ten payments were made; this represented some 35% of the agreements (3,889 out of 11,113). In this subsample, the mean (median) percentage of payments made late was 43.76% (42.86%)—more than two out of every five payments.[5] Additionally, some 45% (1,745) of the agreements had at least 50% of their payments made late and 17% (645) had 75% late. Finally, considering the number of days the payments were late, the mean (median) was 2.95 (2.11) days past the due date.[6]

It is also interesting to consider the actual amount of the payment due each period. Contracts with weekly, bi-weekly and monthly schedules have median payments of $16.88, $33.99 and $62.38, respectively. Likewise, in terms of means (standard deviations) they are $19.63 ($11.53), $39.02 ($21.76) and $72.49 ($43.98), respectively. These statistics are constructed conditional on the chosen payment structure, however each agreements details its whole price menu. Thus, we can also construct overall (unconditional) statistics, finding that the mean (median) is $19.37 ($15.99), $38.73 ($31.99), and $77.03 ($63.99) for weekly, bi-weekly and monthly, respectively. In the overall median numbers, one can see the marketing aspect of pricing as they all end in 99. Also, comparison of the conditional and unconditional statistics shows a tendency among the clientele to structure more expensive contracts weekly or bi-weekly and less expensive contracts monthly—e.g., for weekly agreements, the conditional median of $16.88 is greater than the unconditional value of $15.99 which necessarily implies that expensive contracts are over-represented in the sample. Finally, note we excluded contracts structured semi-monthly here because they are not very popular (less than 2% of the total) and their statistics are very similar to those associated with bi-weekly agreements.

In examining the concluded transactions, a number of contract outcomes are considered. First is RETURN whereby the contract concludes with the return of the merchandise to the store and the cessation of payments. This could occur because, among other reasons, there was only a short term need for the product (e.g., renting an air conditioner for the summer), because the customer's needs or desires changed (e.g., wanting a different colored sofa or a different sized television), or the customer found meeting the payment schedule too onerous for whatever reason.

---

[5] These proportions were quite consistent in the sample. The mean percent late for those making at least 6, 18 and 24 payments was 43.09%, 43.53% and 42.76% with sample size 5,361, 2,394 and 1,752, respectively.

[6] For more analysis of late payment behavior among RTO customers see Anderson and Jaggia (2008).

The second outcome is PAYOUT, this is the acquisition of the item under agreement by making all scheduled payments. As a practical matter, this term is employed by a store if the agreement goes nearly to the end with the customer having paid almost all the total rent—i.e., periodic payment times the number of scheduled payments—the overall median amount paid is 97.67%. Third is EARLY PURCHASE here, again, ownership transfers to the customer, the difference from the previous classification is that the agreement terminates prior to its specified end with the customer paying a portion of the remaining payments—in effect by making a balloon payment. The percentage of remaining rent to be paid is pre-specified and set by the contract, it is typically set at about one half (FTC (2000)). Notice that the earlier this option is exercised the less is the total cost of purchase or, alternatively, the less is the financing cost, and so the relative rent paid speaks to the degree of financial constrains of the consumer, this information is examined below.

The final classification is DEFAULT, this is the customer keeping the merchandise but failing to make the payments required to own the underlying item. In other words, the customer is illegally "skipping" with a good which does not belong to him/her and the store was unable to recover the merchandise. Notice that the four outcome classifications that we consider are mutually exclusive and collectively exhaustive. Additionally, they answer if ownership is transferred (as with PAYOUT and EARLY PURCHASE) and if the merchandise is returned to store inventory (as with RETURN).

The paper provides a number of descriptive tables, all of which share the same format. The results are always presented as the outcome of the agreements as a function of various customer- and contract-specific characteristics, e.g., type of merchandise, maximum con-tract length or customer income. The table is in two parts where the first part gives raw counts and percentages for each subgroup. The percentages are relative to the breakdown within each category (column); further, the last row is an "overall" group which presents the size of each column's category relative to the total. The second part of the table pro-vides information on the percentage rent paid on a given agreement using the exact same breakdown of transactions.

The variable "percentage rent paid" is defined as the rent actually paid by the customer relative to total rent where total rent is the required periodic payment times the maximum possible number of periods as set by the agreement. The second part of the table summa-rizes percentage rent paid in terms of mean and median for the same subgroups as in the first part of the table. Also, an "overall" row is provided—here it represents the mean and median for all the agreements fitting that particular column's category.

The study of the percentage rent paid variable is attractive for several reasons. For in-stance, one common concern of consumer groups is the very high cost of RTO as an acqui-sition mechanism. In the extant literature, such cost calculations have been made assuming payment to term. If, in contrast to this, the average "purchaser" acquires the merchandise relatively early in the contract paying only a fraction of the total then the effective interest rate would be much less. Further, a complaint lodged against RTO is that they let the cus-tomer get close to ownership and then somehow manipulate the contract so that the item gets returned. These are both concerns that need to be addressed to make informed public policy. At the same time, they are empirical questions addressed by examining this variable.

It should be noted that, like many other consumer transactions, sales tax may need to be collected and a variety of fees may be assessed—among other things for late payments, bounced checks, having to hand collect the payment from the customer or if the agreement lapsed and needed to be reinstated. We exclude all such taxes and fees from our analysis, considering only "pure" rent payments. Such a pure rent analysis should not impose any methodological bias as the sample appears fairly homogeneous with respect to contract terms.

Table 1 disaggregates the data set with respect to the eventual outcome of the transactions as a function of merchandise under agreement. There are five categories considered: appliances, computers, electronics, furniture and jewelry. Looking at the breakdown of merchandise, furniture is most important with more than a third of the transactions, following that are appliances and electronics with these three categories collectively representing over 85% of transactions. Expressed another way, a majority, some 61%, of transactions are for basic household necessities—major appliances and furniture. One implication is that consumers appear to be using rent-to-own for essential household formation needs as opposed to acquiring more marginal luxury goods. To better illustrate this point, the merchandise categories are further decomposed into item groupings.

The appliance category contains, in order of importance, washing machines (880 transactions, 29.5% of the appliance total), air conditioners (559, 18.7%), clothes dryers (533, 17.8%), refrigerators (499, 16.7%), freezers (290, 9.7%), stoves/ranges (172, 5.8%), microwaves and vacuums (55, 1.8%). Computers are primarily desktop machines (517 agreements, 86.5% of the total) along with computer desks and printers (81, 13.5%). Electronics includes televisions (1,656 transactions, 57.8% of the total in electronics), stereos (491, 17.1%), video games (310, 10.8%) along with VCRs, DVD players and camcorders (408, 14.2%). Furniture breaks down into pieces for the living room (1,304 agreements, 33.9% of the furniture total), bedroom (1,245, 32.3%), general—lamps, rugs, wall units, et cetera (927, 24.1%) and dining room (376, 9.7%). Jewelry is rings (248 transactions, 34.4% of total jewelry), necklaces (219, 30.4%), wedding rings (146, 20.3%), and bracelets and miscellaneous (107, 14.9%). One observation is that living room and bedroom items (a total of 2,549 agreements) dominate the outstanding contracts. Further, at 1,656 transactions, televisions represents the largest single item while washing machines and dryers—a total of 1,413 agreements–are also very important. Finally, it is quite striking that 20% of jewelry transactions are for wedding rings. Looking at the outcome of those wedding ring transactions we see 85 (58.2%) ended in return, 29 (19.9%) in payout, 13 (8.9%) in early purchase and 19 (13.0%) were recorded as skip/stolen.

Regarding contract outcomes, notice almost two thirds of agreements end up as a return. With that rate being highest (lowest) for computers (jewelry) at 79.43% (54.58%). Also 30.86% are early payout or purchase; with this purchase rate much higher for furniture and jewelry at over 35% while it is slightly less for electronics (about 27%) and much less for computers (about 18%).

One interesting aspect of this RTO data is the strikingly high default (skip) rate of 3.57%. This is below average for appliances, computers and furniture while above average for electronics and is almost three times higher for jewelry (10.28%). Overall, these skip rates point out the high business risk present in this industry.[7] This is further dramatized in the second part of Table 1 which suggests that default, in addition to being all too common,

---

[7]For an analysis of additional aspects of business risk, see Anderson and Jackson (2006).

Table 1. Outcome as a Function of Merchandise.

(a) Raw Counts (Percentages) and Cross Tabs.

	All	Appliances	Computers	Electronics	Furniture	Jewelry
Return	7,287 (65.57)	2,009 (67.24)	475 (79.43)	1,984 (69.25)	2,372 (61.58)	393 (54.58)
Payout	1,768 (15.91)	454 (15.19)	73 (12.21)	404 (14.10)	668 (17.34)	152 (21.11)
Early Purchase	1,661 (14.95)	464 (15.53)	34 (5.69)	363 (12.67)	690 (17.91)	101 (14.03)
Default	397 (3.57)	61 (2.04)	16 (2.68)	114 (3.98)	122 (3.17)	74 (10.28)
Overall	11,113 (100.00)	2,988 (26.89)	598 (5.38)	2,865 (25.78)	3,852 (34.66)	720 (6.48)

(b) Mean (Median) Percentage Rent Paid.

	All	Appliances	Computers	Electronics	Furniture	Jewelry
Return	14.43 (7.70)	15.09 (8.15)	12.80 (7.03)	12.73 (6.14)	15.82 (9.31)	12.56 (6.41)
Payout	95.60 (97.67)	95.51 (97.53)	96.37 (98.17)	94.54 (97.25)	95.81 (97.47)	97.16 (99.26)
Early Purchase	39.51 (33.81)	40.40 (33.66)	38.54 (34.62)	39.90 (32.31)	37.13 (32.54)	52.79 (57.70)
Default	29.68 (20.00)	33.67 (22.36)	16.80 (16.61)	26.78 (14.91)	32.53 (25.25)	28.06 (18.59)
Overall	31.64 (15.38)	31.62 (15.39)	24.57 (10.57)	28.27 (11.54)	34.04 (18.39)	37.66 (19.23)

is likely to be costly to the store given the amount of rent paid at the point when the customer skips. While the percentage rent paid in a default is, overall, more than twice as much as in the average return, half the agreements in default have paid less than 20% of the total rent. Thinking about portability and resale potential, it is not surprising that the relatively worst hits happen within the electronics, computers and jewelry categories, in that order.

Looking at the overall row, average percentage rent paid is about 32%—lower for computers and electronics, slightly higher for furniture and jewelry, ranging across categories from 25% to 38%. At the same time, the distribution of percent rent paid is very right skewed—note the median runs from 11% to 19%. Figure 1 presents the distribution graphically. Casually, the figure suggests the presence of two clienteles, at least, one paying little rent—renters with short term needs and those unable to proceed very far into the contract due to personal circumstances—and a smaller but still significant number who make basically all of the payments (payout), and so pull up the average paid.

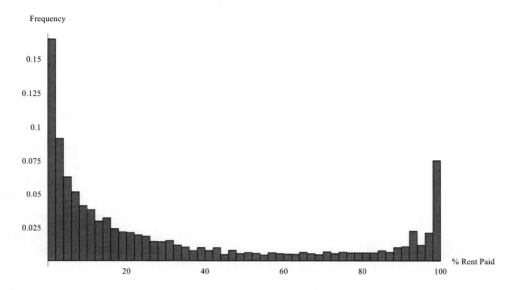

The figure is a relative frequency histogram of actual percentage rent paid for all 11,113 agreements.

Figure 1. Distribution of Percentage Rent Paid.

It is important to note that our finding of some 65% of transactions ending in return is a reversal of the common perception that 60-70% of goods are acquired under RTO contracts.[8] One issue, which partly reconciles this difference but does not eliminate it, is that our data set is based on transactions while the extant literature focuses on consumer surveys. Survey data suffers from misreporting, either simple memory errors or something more.[9] Further, survey data may pick up customer intent which, of course, can diverge from the actual outcome. One can also argue there is bias toward over-reporting purchases if that is perceived as a positive outcome while returns, particularly if involuntary, may be perceived negatively and under-reported. A related issue is consumer fraud; our sample shows a significant amount of items being charged off by stores as unrecoverable (stolen or damaged) and it is unlikely that such behavior would be reported in a telephone interview. Finally, there is the issue of merchandise exchanges. Another empirical regularity of our data set is a surprisingly high proportion of goods being returned in order to exchange them

---

[8]For example, FTC (2000) reports that 66.8% of customers intended to purchase the item being rented (their Table 5.1) and that, of the transactions completed at the time of survey, 64.3% resulted in acquistion (their Table 5.2).

[9]FTC (2000), for instance, asked about transactions originated up to five years prior.

for a similar item.[10] This represents an important consumer option to resolve uncertainty over a good's utility without having to suffer "buyer's remorse." It seems likely that on a survey this would be reported as a single transaction while, in our data set, it would constitute several.

For another take on this question, we consider the number of underlying customers represented in the set of transactions. There are a total of 4,354 unique customers in the data base and so, on average, each customer generated 2.55 transactions. Further, considering those agreements which ended with acquisition (either by payoff or early purchase), they were associated with some 1,614 customers. That is, in our sample, 37.07% of the consumers acquired merchandise using rent-to-own—moving our estimate somewhat closer to that found in the survey-based literature. Looking further at those customers who did acquire merchandise in our sample, 943 (58.4%) got one item while the average acquisition was for 2.12 items with a standard deviation of 4.42; further, the 99th-percentile was 9 items.

To provide a better sense of contract creation, Figure 2 graphs the total number of agreements, organized by the month that they were originated. The first and last months, August 2001 and August 2004, were excluded as they are only partial months. As the figure shows, September 2001 was an outlier as its contract volume of 192 was only 77% of the next lowest month. Showing the impact of 9/11 on this market, we note that while the acquisition volume was comparable to other months, the return rate is less than two thirds of the next lowest month. So that, while life went on, short term plans were apparently suspended by the RTO clientele. Excluding September 2001, contract volume ranged from 249 to 418 with a median of 315.5 and a standard deviation of 38.77. A linear trend line was fitted and while it has a positive slope, it is virtually flat—showing that variation over the period is what is important as opposed to growth per se. Figure 3 organizes the raw contracts, by month of origination, into the four tracked outcomes to give a more dynamic sense of contract resolution over time. This covers the period from October 2001 through July 2004 as we excluded the September 2001 outlier, for a total of 34 months of data. Due to scale differences, the RETURN outcome was graphed separately.

Presenting a casual look at seasonality, Figure 4 shows the relative percentage breakdown of the various outcomes. For clarity, contracts were aggregated into their associated calender quarter—from fourth quarter 2001 through second quarter 2004. Consequently, for each outcome there are eleven points each corresponding to the percentage of agreements ending in that particular outcome relative to the total number originated in that quarter. Again, due to differences in scale, the return outcome is graphed separately. We note that returns seem to be higher in the first two quarters of a calender year, that payout tends to dominate early purchase as an acquisition mechanism and that the default rate seems relatively constant. In terms of distributions, the median return rate is 66%, ranging from 61% to 71%. The total purchase rate has a median of 31% and a range from 25% to 38%, with the median payout proportion being 16% with range 14% to 19% and the median early purchase rate is 15%, ranging from 11% to 19%. The default rate has median 3.6% and ranges from 2.7% to 4.7%.

---

[10]To illustrate, imagine a customer renting a suite of living room furniture only to return that and, nearly simultaneously, rent another grouping of living room furniture, possibly repeating such an exchange several times.

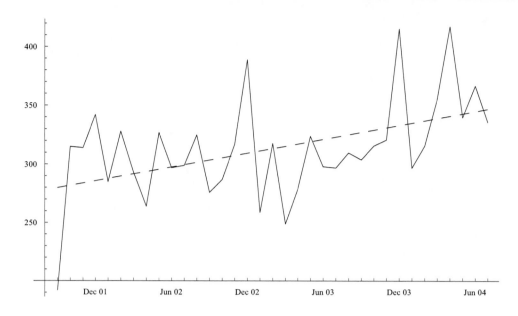

The graph shows the raw total of contracts generated each month from September 2001 through July 2004. The dotted line is a least squares trend line with equation: $277.86 + 1.978mn$, where mn is the integer position of the month in the data series, e.g., September 2001 = 1, October 2001 = 2, and so forth.

Figure 2. Total Monthly Contract Production.

2.2.   Descriptive Statistics

Tables 2 through 10 present detail on contract outcome and percentage rent paid as a function of various attributes. Some attributes are customer-specific, e.g., age, income and employment status, while others are contract-specific, e.g., maximum contract duration and how the payment schedule is structured. In all cases, the information is presented in the same manner as it was in Table 1.

Table 2 looks at the impact of marital status, gender and home ownership. Less than 30% are married and fewer than 20% report owning their own home. Most striking is the gender statistics, in particular that three quarters of the customers in the sample are female. Women are somewhat more likely to use rent-to-own to acquire the underlying item (either by payout or early purchase) and less likely to default. Homeowners had purchase rates almost 20% higher than do renters; further, not only is their default rate less than renters, it is only two thirds of the overall average default rate. With respect to percentage rent paid, married customers, when they exercise their early purchase option or default on the agreement, pay more rent than do those who are unmarried. This is suggestive of a greater desire to use RTO as an acquisition mechanism as well as a more constrained budget. Likewise, while homeowners have a higher overall purchase rate, they exercise their early purchase option later paying 41% of total rent relative to renters who pay 32%.

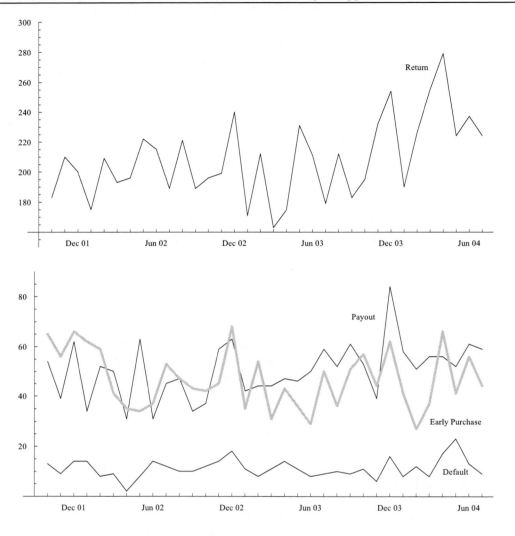

The graph shows the raw number of contract for each of the outcomes—return, payoff, early purchase and default—for every month from October 2001 through July 2004.

Figure 3. Raw Contract Outcomes as a Function of the Month of Origination.

This suggests that these may be "house poor" consumers, i.e., those for whom maintaining their dwelling and servicing its mortgage is a major burden on their finances. Finally, it is interesting to note, across all three categories, the sharp swing in median percentage rent paid for those using the early purchase option with more rent paid by those who are married, by men and by homeowners.

Table 3 considers employment status where only 41% report being employed at least six months. Consistent with expectations, those unemployed are less likely to purchase and more likely to return. Somewhat surprising is that the default rate is 25% lower for those unemployed. The second part of the table sheds more light on this showing that those

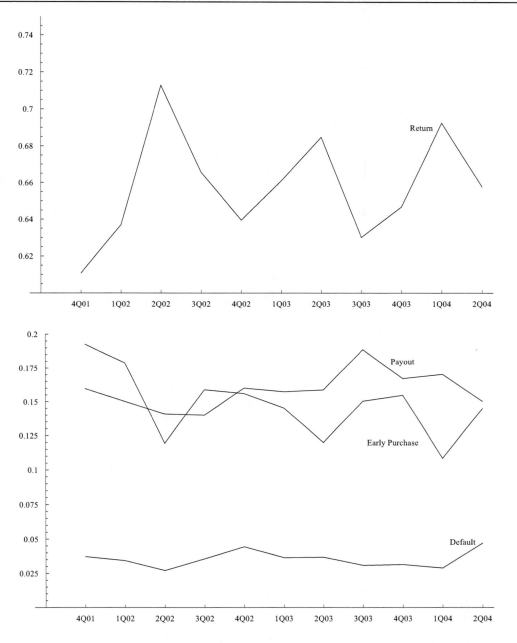

The graph shows the relative percentage breakdown by outcome for those contracts which originated in one of the eleven complete calender quarters—i.e., from 4th quarter 2001 through 2nd quarter 2004.

Figure 4. Contract Outcomes as a Function of the Originating Calender Quarter.

unemployed pay less rent both when they exercise their early purchase option and when they default. This is somewhat suggestive that there are two populations in the unemployed

Table 2. Outcome as a Function of Customer Characteristics—Part One.

(a) Raw Counts (Percentages) and Cross Tabs.

	Marital Status		Gender		Homeownership	
	Single[a]	Married	Female	Male	Renter	Owner
Return	5,229 (65.96)	2,058 (64.62)	5,421 (64.88)	1,866 (67.66)	5,993 (66.55)	1294 (61.39)
Payout	1,241 (15.65)	527 (16.55)	1,370 (16.40)	398 (14.43)	1,365 (15.16)	403 (19.12)
Early Purchase	1,170 (14.76)	491 (15.42)	1,294 (15.49)	367 (13.31)	1,300 (14.44)	361 (17.13)
Default	288 (3.63)	109 (3.42)	270 (3.23)	127 (4.60)	347 (3.85)	50 (2.37)
Overall	7,928 (71.34)	3,185 (28.66)	8,355 (75.18)	2,758 (24.82)	9,005 (81.03)	2,108 (18.97)

(b) Mean (Median) Percentage Rent Paid.

	Marital Status		Gender		Homeownership	
	Single	Married	Female	Male	Renter	Owner
Return	14.04 (7.69)	15.4 (8.83)	14.42 (7.88)	14.44 (7.69)	14.49 (7.79)	14.14 (7.69)
Payout	95.33 (97.28)	96.24 (98.70)	95.44 (97.44)	96.16 (98.90)	95.61 (97.71)	95.58 (97.62)
Early Purchase	37.26 (31.73)	44.87 (39.04)	38.01 (32.31)	44.79 (37.81)	37.96 (32.06)	45.1 (41.41)
Default	28.36 (18.71)	33.19 (24.56)	29.67 (19.98)	29.72 (20.36)	29.55 (19.80)	30.61 (21.44)
Overall	30.71 (14.41)	33.93 (17.69)	31.85 (15.39)	30.97 (14.10)	30.75 (14.77)	35.4 (18.68)

[a] Single, divorced or widowed.

category: those who lost their job and hope for an improvement in their prospects–which may or may not happen—and those voluntarily unemployed, e.g., a student, but who are in decent financial shape. The receipt of government aid—received by some 40%—is also considered. Two observations stand out here. First, the default rate for those with aid is

Table 3. Outcome as a Function of Customer Characteristics—Part Two.

(a) Raw Counts (Percentages) and Cross Tabs.

	Employment Status		Government Aid		Repeat Customer	
	Unemployed	Employed[a]	No Aid	Aid	New	Repeat
Return	4,404	2,883	4,265	3,022	3,319	3,968
	(67.70)	(62.57)	(64.14)	(67.71)	(64.79)	(66.24)
Payout	957	811	1106	662	852	916
	(14.71)	(17.60)	(16.63)	(14.83)	(16.63)	(15.29)
Early Purchase	938	723	994	667	768	893
	(14.42)	(15.69)	(14.95)	(14.95)	(14.99)	(14.91)
Default	206	191	285	112	184	213
	(3.17)	(4.14)	(4.29)	(2.51)	(3.59)	(3.56)
Overall	6,505	4,608	6,650	4,463	5,123	5,990
	(58.54)	(41.46)	(59.84)	(40.16)	(46.10)	(53.90)

(b) Mean (Median) Percentage Rent Paid.

	Employment Status		Government Aid		Repeat Customer	
	Unemployed	Employed	No Aid	Aid	New	Repeat
Return	14.07	14.98	14.98	13.64	14.76	14.15
	(7.69)	(8.79)	(8.42)	(7.17)	(7.76)	(7.69)
Payout	94.83	96.51	96.5	94.11	95.48	95.71
	(96.63)	(98.72)	(98.71)	(95.16)	(97.62)	(97.81)
Early Purchase	35.74	44.4	44.23	32.48	39.97	39.11
	(29.84)	(38.46)	(38.46)	(25.22)	(34.16)	(33.52)
Default	28.02	31.48	30.44	27.77	30.41	29.06
	(15.39)	(24.00)	(21.12)	(14.42)	(21.30)	(19.23)
Overall	29.52	34.63	33.57	28.75	32.53	30.87
	(12.82)	(18.75)	(17.74)	(11.70)	(15.66)	(14.99)

[a]Report employment at current job for at least six months.

40% lower than for those without aid. Second, while the early purchase rate is identical, those on aid are able to purchase much sooner, having paid on average 65% of the total rent relative to those not on aid.

Table 4. Outcome as a Function of Employment Length.

(a) Raw Counts (Percentages) and Cross Tabs.

	Unemployed	0-3 Months	3-6 Months	6-12 Months	1-2 Years	2 Years+
Return	732	2,786	886	830	822	1,231
	(62.94)	(69.08)	(67.69)	(65.72)	(65.45)	(58.93)
Payout	185	560	212	210	204	397
	(15.91)	(13.89)	(16.20)	(16.63)	(16.24)	(19.00)
Early Purchase	208	571	159	183	181	359
	(17.88)	(14.16)	(12.15)	(14.49)	(14.41)	(17.19)
Default	38	116	52	40	49	102
	(3.27)	(2.88)	(3.97)	(3.17)	(3.90)	(4.88)
Overall	1,163	4,033	1,309	1,263	1,256	2,089
	(10.47)	(36.29)	(11.78)	(11.36)	(11.30)	(18.80)

Table 4. Continued

(b) Mean (Median) Percentage Rent Paid.

	Unemployed	0-3 Months	3-6 Months	6-12 Months	1-2 Years	2 Years+
Return	13.92	13.4	16.28	14.15	14.29	15.99
	(7.70)	(6.98)	(8.61)	(7.45)	(8.79)	(10.10)
Payout	94.22	94.4	96.48	96.05	96.38	96.83
	(93.51)	(96.23)	(98.69)	(97.99)	(99.08)	(98.90)
Early Purchase	45.76	29.61	44.64	44.81	43.71	44.55
	(42.31)	(20.52)	(44.17)	(38.76)	(36.27)	(39.01)
Default	36.59	23.98	30.79	30.95	23.96	35.29
	(26.91)	(10.75)	(15.58)	(26.25)	(15.93)	(25.34)
Overall	33.13	27.25	33.29	32.74	32.24	37.2
	(17.31)	(10.39)	(16.80)	(17.07)	(16.34)	(21.72)

This is suggestive that the government aid is helping the consumer through some type of transitional period in his/her life. Finally, whether the transaction is being initiated by a repeat customer is considered, with us finding that for a slight majority (54%) of the transactions, the underlying customer has initiated at least one other transaction in this data set. The comparison here shows little difference between repeat and first-time customers, except a slightly higher return probability for repeat customers. Note, however, that one motivation for making a return is in order to do a exchange which would make one a repeat customer—although the consumer could view it as being the same transaction.

Table 4 disaggregates the employment variable and sheds additional light on consumer behavior. Notice that the purchase rates (both payout and early purchase) generally increase with employment length—going from a total acquisition rate of 28% at 0-3 months up to 36% for two years plus. At the same time, so does the default rate, starting at 2.88%, well below the overall average (of 3.57%), but rising to more than a third above the average, at 4.88%. This is consistent with the natural diminution of prospects, i.e., the longer one works at a job with low wages the less likely it becomes that there would be an improvement. Further support for this hypothesis comes from the second part of Table 4 where we note that the percentage rent paid in both early purchase and default also generally increases with employment length; arguing that customers in such circumstances would both be more dependent on the rent-to-own mechanism and find making the payments harder. On this point, note that for those who have worked at their current job for at least three months, payout dominates early purchase as the most common method of acquisition by some 15%. Contrasting the outcome of those employed to those unemployed, we see that the acquisition rate at 33% is the second highest in the table, while the default is below average at 3.27%. This argues that "unemployment" in the data is capturing a transitional or even voluntary event, or that they are receiving government aid or some other form of assistance, e.g., from a family member.

Table 5 considers outcome as a function of customer age and tells a very interesting life cycle story. Overall purchase rates (both payout and early purchase) increase with age before dipping slightly at 56+ group. Further, the rent paid in early purchase generally increases with age as well—from a low of 24% for 18-25 year olds to a high of 46% for 56+; this same pattern repeats for rent paid in default going from 14% to 41%. This suggests a curtailment of options similar to that observed with length of employment. That is, the older one gets, still employed at low wages, the lower becomes the likelihood that there will be some future improvement and hence the greater would be the reliance on rent-to-own as a means of merchandise acquisition. Additionally, possibly consistent with expectations, the proportionate default rate also generally declines with age, and for those consumers over 40 years of age is below the overall average.

Table 6 looks at customer income. In the sample, 92% report income below $20,000 while fully 39% report income below $5,000. We note that, generally, return rates are increasing in income level while the purchase rates decline. Further, percentage rent paid is generally declining with the income level as well. These observations are consistent with the notion that higher income consumers have more financial options and/or a greater chance of future economic improvement and so would be less reliant on rent-to-own as an acquisition mechanism.

Table 7 looks at the impact of payment structure. One very interesting aspect of rent-

Table 5. Outcome as a Function of Customer Age.

(a) Raw Counts (Percentages) and Cross Tabs.

	18-25	26-30	31-40	41-55	56+
Return	3,352 (69.36)	1,414 (66.11)	1,390 (60.96)	744 (59.95)	387 (62.42)
Payout	658 (13.61)	335 (15.66)	437 (19.17)	227 (18.29)	111 (17.90)
Early Purchase	668 (13.82)	305 (14.26)	349 (15.31)	233 (18.78)	106 (17.10)
Default	155 (3.21)	85 (3.97)	104 (4.56)	37 (2.98)	16 (2.58)
Overall	4,833 (43.49)	2,139 (19.25)	2,280 (20.52)	1,241 (11.17)	620 (5.58)

(b) Mean (Median) Percentage Rent Paid.

	18-25	26-30	31-40	41-55	56+
Return	13.79 (7.15)	14.84 (8.09)	14.69 (8.56)	15.44 (9.37)	15.54 (8.79)
Payout	95.23 (97.25)	96.17 (98.36)	96.5 (98.66)	95.66 (97.54)	92.42 (93.02)
Early Purchase	31.55 (24.13)	43.45 (37.24)	46.09 (43.12)	44.2 (39.02)	46.4 (46.56)
Default	24.57 (14.10)	27.21 (15.57)	34.69 (27.27)	35.7 (24.18)	45.91 (41.33)
Overall	27.68 (11.54)	32.15 (15.75)	36.09 (19.23)	36.12 (21.31)	35.36 (19.64)

to-own is that the customer has a choice over the frequency of payments. One motivation for this choice would be to match up the payments to the cash flow stream. That is, a customer with little in the way of back up liquidity would be dependent on his/her paycheck to make the required payments and so would pick a payment structure consistent with the timing of that paycheck. A second, not necessarily mutually exclusive, motivation is pre-selection by customers based on their expectation over the outcome, either rental or purchase. That is, those expecting to rent would prefer a weekly arrangement for the

Table 6. Outcome as a Function of Customer Income.

(a) Raw Counts (Percentages) and Cross Tabs.

	$0-5K	$5-10K	$10-15K	$15-20K	$20-25K	$25K+
Return	2,832	1,321	1,721	830	388	195
	(65.68)	(62.31)	(66.65)	(67.15)	(66.55)	(69.64)
Payout	684	402	410	156	77	39
	(15.86)	(18.96)	(15.88)	(12.62)	(13.21)	(13.93)
Early Purchase	663	306	375	194	89	34
	(15.38)	(14.43)	(14.52)	(15.70)	(15.27)	(12.14)
Default	133	91	76	56	29	12
	(3.08)	(4.29)	(2.94)	(4.53)	(4.97)	(4.29)
Overall	4,312	2,120	2,582	1,236	583	280
	(38.80)	(19.08)	(23.23)	(11.12)	(5.25)	(2.52)

(b) Mean (Median) Percentage Rent Paid.

	$0-5K	$5-10K	$10-15K	$15-20K	$20-25K	$25K+
Return	13.83	14.86	14.83	15.02	13.21	16.52
	(7.35)	(8.03)	(8.17)	(8.79)	(8.24)	(9.50)
Payout	94.87	96.54	95.86	95.38	95.95	96.24
	(96.63)	(99.02)	(97.67)	(98.01)	(97.71)	(98.90)
Early Purchase	32.58	44.71	45.26	42.34	40.71	45.24
	(25.14)	(42.31)	(42.31)	(34.91)	(30.78)	(41.18)
Default	26.37	33.57	32.26	30.37	30.78	14.87
	(15.46)	(22.97)	(26.70)	(19.11)	(24.57)	(13.10)
Overall	29.95	35.46	32.63	30.15	29.21	31.04
	(12.66)	(19.23)	(17.06)	(15.39)	(14.10)	(15.67)

greater flexibility offered while those expecting to purchase would prefer monthly for the greater convenience.[11] Contrasting weekly to monthly schedules bears out the second explanation as the return rate drops from 72% to 52% while the acquisition rate (payout plus early purchase) rises from 24% to 45%, respectively. Countering that is the early purchase rates whereby those on weekly schedules only pay one third the rent then do those making monthly payments. Interestingly, looking at the percent rent paid on a payout shows a hid-

---

[11]For a discussion of underlying customer motivations along these lines, see Anderson and Jackson (2001).

den cost of weekly schedules. Weekly and bi-weekly pay about 97% of the maximum rent due while monthly and semi-monthly only pay about 91%. This occurs because the former are paying a quarter of the monthly payment every week or half of it every two weeks, i.e., over the course of the year they effectively pay 8.33% more than would a customer whose schedule is based on monthly amortization.[12] So, in effect, an implicit fee is charged for high frequency payment schedules.

Table 8 considers how outcome varies as a function of the maximum payable amount—i.e., the total undiscounted amount due on a payout. The data tell a fairly clear and interesting story. Notice that as the merchandise becomes more expensive, the return rate strictly rises while both the payout and early purchase rates strictly fall. Also, the default rate roughly increases with merchandise cost. Additionally, as the maximum payable amount increases, the percentage rent paid on a return falls while it generally rises for an early purchase. It may be that more expensive goods are being viewed as luxury items for which acquisition is not intended—consistent with the rising return and falling purchase rates. Alternatively, it may be that the customer, given his/her financial circumstances, finds successfully achieving the required payment schedule very difficult—consistent with the increasing rent paid on an early purchase. The general financial constraints of these consumers is also suggested by the fact that as the payable amount increases, payout comes to dominate early purchase as an acquisition mechanism.

Table 9 considers the contractual length. An interesting tension exists here: all else equal, the longer the contractual length the lower, and so the more affordable, are the periodic payments. At the same time, however, a customer is "building equity" slower. It not clear, ceteris paribus, which effect would dominate. Suppose one views that longer terms correspond to more expensive items. Then there are two possible hypotheses. First, as the underlying merchandise represents harder to afford items, the RTO mechanism would be more valuable for these consumers in financial distress and so, purchase rates would be higher, the greater the term. Second, if more expensive translates into the view that the underlying merchandise is a luxury item then return rates might be higher, reflecting the necessary emphasis on supplying household necessities first and foremost. Consistent with longer term contracts representing less affordable items, we see that as length increases, the percentage rent paid increases fairly dramatically when the item is acquired by exercising the early purchase option; likewise, percentage rent paid is also positively related to length in the default outcome. Also consistent with the affordability hypothesis, as contract length increases we see a notable rise in return and default rates along with a drop in the acquisition rate—but this set of observations is not inconsistent with the luxury-good hypothesis as well.

Table 10 looks at the outcome of several individual items. The 11,113 transactions in the data base involve some 1,787 unique items—thus, on average, each item has been rented out 6.22 times. The total number of items being rented is somewhat overstated as the count is by part number and so some items effectively appear several times, e.g., furniture pieces available in multiple colors. For additional context, we note that 1,313 items (73.48%) appear in no more than five transactions, while a total of 1,547 of the items (86.57%) are in less than ten transactions apiece. At the other extreme, the top 25 items each went out

---

[12]For instance, with a weekly schedule, 52 weekly payments will be made—each a quarter of what would have been charged on a monthly schedule—adding up to 13 full payments instead of 12.

Table 7. Outcome as a Function of Payment Structure.

(a) Raw Counts (Percentages) and Cross Tabs.

	Weekly	Bi-Weekly	Semi-Monthly	Monthly
Return	4,339 (72.41)	1,758 (61.30)	122 (65.24)	1,068 (51.69)
Payout	746 (12.45)	555 (19.35)	35 (18.72)	432 (20.91)
Early Purchase	714 (11.92)	427 (14.89)	26 (13.90)	494 (23.91)
Default	193 (3.22)	128 (4.46)	4 (2.14)	72 (3.48)
Overall	5,992 (53.92)	2,868 (25.81)	187 (1.68)	2,066 (18.59)

(b) Mean (Median) Percentage Rent Paid.

	Weekly	Bi-Weekly	Semi-Monthly	Monthly
Return	10.59 (4.84)	21.59 (15.87)	19.07 (12.64)	17.68 (12.31)
Payout	97.29 (99.45)	97.28 (98.90)	91.03 (91.77)	90.9 (92.35)
Early Purchase	27.77 (16.92)	48.73 (44.51)	51.13 (53.10)	47.91 (49.48)
Default	21.85 (8.88)	37.35 (27.72)	35.65 (35.75)	36.72 (28.10)
Overall	23.8 (6.86)	40.98 (27.84)	37.35 (25.28)	40.88 (28.38)

on at least 50 agreements and represent some 20% (2,181) of the transactions. Table 10 considers five of the top ten most frequently rented items which involve a total of some 774 agreements (6.96% of the total). In particular, there are two appliances (a Maytag Washer and a Frigidaire Dryer), two pieces of consumer electronics (a Sony PlayStation 2 and a 25" Sanyo television) and one furniture item (a Fraenkel queen-sized bedroom set). It is interesting to note the similarity of outcome and rent paid across this variety of merchandise. The return rate is in the upper sixties except for the PlayStation 2 at 62%.

Table 8. Outcome as a Function of Maximum Payable Amount.

(a) Raw Counts (Percentages) and Cross Tabs.

	$0-500	$500-1,000	$1,000-2,000	$2,000-4,000	$4,000+
Return	798 (39.68)	2,327 (64.75)	2,398 (70.99)	1,462 (82.18)	302 (86.04)
Payout	538 (26.75)	550 (15.30)	492 (14.56)	172 (9.67)	16 (4.56)
Early Purchase	612 (30.43)	581 (16.17)	363 (10.75)	89 (5.00)	16 (4.56)
Default	63 (3.13)	136 (3.78)	125 (3.70)	56 (3.15)	17 (4.84)
Overall	2,011 (18.10)	3,594 (32.34)	3,378 (30.40)	1,779 (16.01)	351 (3.16)

(b) Mean (Median) Percentage Rent Paid.

	$0-500	$500-1,000	$1,000-2,000	$2,000-4,000	$4,000+
Return	16.99 (9.76)	15.22 (8.24)	13.74 (7.69)	13.3 (7.05)	12.51 (4.95)
Payout	93.72 (96.20)	96.1 (97.67)	96.72 (98.36)	96.56 (98.45)	96.9 (99.45)
Early Purchase	27.55 (24.56)	40.92 (32.61)	52.06 (64.31)	59.35 (72.93)	50.72 (59.46)
Default	33.66 (28.05)	26.31 (19.32)	30.56 (20.37)	31.75 (19.21)	28.7 (21.98)
Overall	41.25 (27.92)	32.17 (16.48)	30.56 (13.74)	24.23 (9.89)	18.88 (6.87)

The combined purchase rates are around 30%, with the clear majority of purchases being made by making all the payments (payout) for the dryer and bedroom set, while it is exactly opposite (most acquistions made by early purchase) for the other three items. Further, there is quite a spread of percentage rent paid, given early purchase, with the median ranging from 26% for the PlayStation 2 to 63% for the Maytag Washer.

Table 9. Outcome as a Function of Contractual Length.

(a) Raw Counts (Percentages) and Cross Tabs.

	0-6 months	6-12 months	12-18 months	18-24 months	2 years+
Return	90	1,078	3,099	2,566	454
	(16.89)	(55.40)	(70.03)	(70.42)	(80.35)
Payout	241	386	582	512	47
	(45.22)	(19.84)	(13.15)	(14.05)	(8.32)
Early Purchase	189	427	617	388	40
	(35.46)	(21.94)	(13.94)	(10.65)	(7.08)
Default	13	55	127	178	24
	(2.44)	(2.83)	(2.87)	(4.88)	(4.25)
Overall	533	1,946	4,425	3,644	565
	(4.80)	(17.51)	(39.82)	(32.79)	(5.08)

(b) Mean (Median) Percentage Rent Paid.

	0-6 months	6-12 months	12-18 months	18-24 months	2 years+
Return	20.67	15.85	13.98	14.38	13.09
	(12.31)	(8.42)	(7.69)	(8.06)	(6.18)
Payout	93.07	93.79	96.56	96.97	96.68
	(96.24)	(94.85)	(98.35)	(98.73)	(99.23)
Early Purchase	7.92	33.49	43.18	54.15	54.53
	(1.43)	(31.73)	(37.04)	(65.12)	(67.69)
Default	48.81	26.57	28.22	29.21	37.71
	(48.42)	(10.88)	(20.36)	(19.14)	(37.67)
Overall	49.57	35.49	29.33	30.94	24.02
	(46.15)	(23.08)	(14.04)	(14.10)	(8.93)

3. Regression Analysis

Multinomial logit models are often employed to model a nominal dependent variable with multiple discrete outcomes (a good basic reference is Greene (2003)). For instance, we may want to model consumer choice of occupation with the consumer having various possible choices among menial, blue collar, craft, white collar and professional jobs. The objective would then be to study the influence of explanatory variables such as education, experience, race, and gender on the ultimate choice of occupation. Other examples include the choice of health plans, college, product brand, transportation mode and so forth.

Table 10. Outcome as a Function of Specific Merchandise.

(a) Raw Counts (Percentages) and Cross Tabs.

	GLER331A[a]	PS2[b]	MAV6200A[c]	DS25390A[d]	RA50[e]
Return	136	121	101	91	65
	(68.00)	(62.37)	(67.79)	(68.42)	(66.33)
Payout	24	40	28	23	11
	(12.00)	(20.62)	(18.79)	(17.29)	(11.22)
Early Purchase	37	25	17	16	18
	(18.50)	(12.89)	(11.41)	(12.03)	(18.37)
Default	3	8	3	3	4
	(1.50)	(4.12)	(2.01)	(2.26)	(4.08)
Overall	200	194	149	133	98
	(1.80)	(1.75)	(1.34)	(1.20)	(0.88)

(b) Mean (Median) Percentage Rent Paid.

	GLER331A	PS2	MAV6200A	DS25390A	RA50
Return	15.52	15.88	12	12.16	15.8
	(9.28)	(8.71)	(6.41)	(6.37)	(8.53)
Payout	96.18	94.94	95.51	94.6	95.86
	(97.11)	(95.49)	(98.05)	(96.24)	(96.21)
Early Purchase	44.82	33.99	51.52	46.9	39.41
	(43.04)	(25.64)	(63.03)	(57.55)	(34.62)
Default	32.2	23.99	41.67	27.05	42.94
	(8.88)	(10.25)	(26.93)	(19.97)	(37.09)
Overall	30.87	34.85	32.8	30.93	30.23
	(15.10)	(21.15)	(11.54)	(13.19)	(17.31)

[a] GLER331A is a Frigidaire basic clothes dryer (Appliance)
[b] PS2 is a Sony PlayStation 2 (Electronics)
[c] MAV6200A is a Maytag deluxe washing machine (Appliance)
[d] DS25390A is a Sanyo 25" Television (Electronics)
[e] RA50 is a Fraenkel queen-sized bedroom set (Furniture)

The rent-to-own industry and, in particular, our finely grained transactional data provide a very good avenue for this technology. That is, a multinomial logit model can be employed to analyze the termination probabilities of the various outcomes of RTO agreements—

return, payout, early purchase, and default—on the basis of a number of explanatory variables, broadly representing both customer characteristics and contract structure.

3.1. Methodology

Consider a nominal dependent variable with J discrete outcomes. The probabilities based on a logistic distribution are given by

$$Pr(y_i = j \mid \mathbf{x_i}) = \frac{exp(\mathbf{x'_i}\beta_j)}{\sum_{h=1}^{J} exp(\mathbf{x'_i}\beta_h)} \tag{1}$$

where $j = 1, 2, \ldots, J$; $\mathbf{x_i}$ represent the specific attributes of agreement i and $\beta_1, \ldots, \beta_J$ are J vectors of unknown regression parameters. Note that, by construction, these probabilities are contained in the $[0, 1]$ interval. Further, since the probabilities sum to one, the J sets of parameters are not unique and so for identification purposes we need to normalize one of the regression coefficients, β_k, to zero.

In this application, we let $j = r, p, \epsilon, d$ correspond to return, payout, early purchase, and default, respectively. After setting β_r equal to the null vector, we can derive the following probabilities using equation (1):

$$Pr(y_i = r \mid \mathbf{x_i}) = \frac{1}{1 + exp(\mathbf{x'_i}\beta_p) + exp(\mathbf{x'_i}\beta_\epsilon) + exp(\mathbf{x'_i}\beta_d)}$$

$$Pr(y_i = p \mid \mathbf{x_i}) = \frac{exp(\mathbf{x'_i}\beta_p)}{1 + exp(\mathbf{x'_i}\beta_p) + exp(\mathbf{x'_i}\beta_\epsilon) + exp(\mathbf{x'_i}\beta_d)}$$

$$Pr(y_i = \epsilon \mid \mathbf{x_i}) = \frac{exp(\mathbf{x'_i}\beta_\epsilon)}{1 + exp(\mathbf{x'_i}\beta_p) + exp(\mathbf{x'_i}\beta_\epsilon) + exp(\mathbf{x'_i}\beta_d)}$$

and

$$Pr(y_i = d \mid \mathbf{x_i}) = \frac{exp(\mathbf{x'_i}\beta_d)}{1 + exp(\mathbf{x'_i}\beta_p) + exp(\mathbf{x'_i}\beta_\epsilon) + exp(\mathbf{x'_i}\beta_d)}$$

These probabilities are, in turn, used in the maximum likelihood estimation of the model.

Table 12 presents the parameter estimates of the multinomial logit model. Although multinomial logit models are easy to estimate, care must be exercised in interpreting their regression coefficients. The partial effect of a variable on the probability of a particular outcome is based on the estimated regression coefficients of all outcomes which makes the interpretation difficult. To help make sense of the results, we use simulations to better elucidate the influence of variables representing customer characteristics and contract structure on the termination probabilities of return, payout, early purchase, and default. Also, for reference, Table 11 presents the sample means and standard deviations for every independent variable that is used in the regression. To enable ready comparison, this information is presented both on an overall basis as well as relative to the subsamples corresponding to the various contract outcomes.

Table 11. Sample Mean (Standard Deviation) of the Independent Variables.

Variable	Overall	Return	Payout	Early Purchase	Default
Age	2.161	2.094	2.320	2.280	2.179
	(1.250)	(1.236)	(1.263)	(1.292)	(1.166)
Gender (1 if male)	0.248	0.256	0.225	0.221	0.320
	(0.432)	(0.436)	(0.418)	(0.415)	(0.467)
Marital Status (1 if married)	0.287	0.282	0.298	0.296	0.275
	(0.452)	(0.450)	(0.458)	(0.456)	(0.447)
Government Aid (1 if aid)	0.402	0.415	0.374	0.402	0.282
	(0.490)	(0.493)	(0.484)	(0.490)	(0.451)
Employment (1 if > 6 mn)	0.415	0.396	0.459	0.435	0.481
	(0.493)	(0.489)	(0.498)	(0.496)	(0.500)
Income	2.325	2.342	2.240	2.303	2.479
	(1.355)	(1.368)	(1.288)	(1.346)	(1.417)
Own Home	0.190	0.178	0.228	0.217	0.126
	(0.392)	(0.382)	(0.420)	(0.413)	(0.332)
Referral	0.175	0.165	0.214	0.168	0.229
	(0.380)	(0.371)	(0.410)	(0.374)	(0.421)
Repeat Customer (1 if repeat)	0.539	0.545	0.518	0.538	0.537
	(0.498)	(0.498)	(0.500)	(0.499)	(0.499)
Transactions To Date	3.644	3.909	2.872	3.515	2.738
	(10.098)	(11.176)	(6.736)	(9.019)	(3.891)
December Dummy	0.103	0.095	0.118	0.118	0.121
	(0.304)	(0.294)	(0.323)	(0.323)	(0.326)
Maximum Payable Amount	1.332	1.517	1.005	0.854	1.377
	(1.102)	(1.164)	(0.843)	(0.770)	(1.202)
Contractual Length	1.252	1.334	1.080	1.057	1.327
	(0.454)	(0.409)	(0.509)	(0.472)	(0.437)
Weekly Payment	0.539	0.595	0.422	0.430	0.486
	(0.498)	(0.491)	(0.494)	(0.495)	(0.500)
Monthly Payment	0.186	0.147	0.244	0.297	0.181
	(0.389)	(0.354)	(0.430)	(0.457)	(0.386)
Computers	0.054	0.065	0.041	0.020	0.040
	(0.226)	(0.247)	(0.199)	(0.142)	(0.197)
Electronics	0.258	0.272	0.229	0.219	0.287
	(0.437)	(0.445)	(0.420)	(0.413)	(0.453)
Furniture	0.347	0.326	0.378	0.415	0.307
	(0.476)	(0.469)	(0.485)	(0.493)	(0.462)
Jewelry	0.065	0.054	0.086	0.061	0.186
	(0.246)	(0.226)	(0.280)	(0.239)	(0.390)

Table 12. Estimates of a Multinomial Logit Model.

Variable	Payout	Early Purchase	Default
Constant	0.834***	0.500***	-2.766***
	(5.740)	(3.338)	(-9.172)
Age	0.144***	0.084***	0.020
	(5.420)	(3.064)	(0.401)
Gender (1 if male)	-0.139*	-0.096	0.144
	(-1.954)	(-1.300)	(1.178)
Marital Status (1 if married)	0.117*	0.142**	-0.270**
	(1.711)	(1.997)	(-2.115)
Government Aid (1 if aid)	-0.261***	-0.208**	-0.627***
	(-3.260)	(-2.527)	(-4.016)
Employment (1 if > 6 mn)	0.447***	0.310***	0.115
	(5.684)	(3.803)	(0.849)
Income	-0.273***	-0.154***	-0.015
	(-9.091)	(-5.052)	(-0.289)
Own Home	0.249***	0.177**	-0.563***
	(3.330)	(2.272)	(-3.439)
Referral	0.223***	-0.044	0.236*
	(3.127)	(-0.566)	(1.847)
Repeat Customer (1 if repeat)	-0.025	0.008	0.081
	(-0.430)	(0.132)	(0.717)
Transactions To Date	-0.014***	-0.004	-0.020**
	(-3.440)	(-1.400)	(-2.010)
December Dummy	0.193**	0.265***	0.081
	(2.167)	(2.892)	(0.498)
Maximum Payable Amount	-0.130***	-0.594***	-0.06
	(-2.846)	(-10.367)	(-0.883)
Contractual Length	-1.357***	-0.936***	-0.034
	(-14.998)	(-10.067)	(-0.193)
Weekly Payment	-0.765***	-0.535***	-0.499***
	(-11.771)	(-7.696)	(-4.216)
Monthly Payment	0.299***	0.680***	0.145
	(3.739)	(8.323)	(0.928)
Computers	-0.322**	-0.724***	0.045
	(-2.173)	(-3.700)	(-0.153)
Electronics	-0.103	-0.230***	0.551***
	(-1.302)	(-2.839)	(3.513)
Furniture	0.135*	0.206***	0.428***
	(1.887)	(2.896)	(2.750)
Jewelry	0.523***	0.018	1.668***
	(4.521)	(0.137)	(9.243)

The vector of Return outcome coefficients (β_r) is normalized to the null vector.
**, **, * denotes significance at the 1, 5, 10% level, respectively.

3.2. Regression Results

Inspection of Table 12 reveals that all the independent variables are significant at the 99% level for at least one outcome, except for gender, marital status and repeat customer. Further, only the repeat customer variable fails to be significant at the 90% level or better for some outcome.

Regarding customer age, the regression results were very consistent with those in the descriptive section. Age is highly significant in increasing the purchase probabilities—both payout and early purchase—but not significant at raising default risk. Also, looking at the subsample statistics, we see that the average age varied from oldest to youngest going from payout to early purchase to default and, lastly, to return. Adding all these factors up, a very clear picture emerges that among such consumers, increasing age is associated with ever diminishing economic opportunities and financial options and so, an ever greater reliance on rent-to-own as an acquisition mechanism.

In the regression, gender was barely significant. It shows that, with 90% significance, men are less likely to acquire merchandise using the payout method. Also, although not statistically significant, we note, looking at sample means, that men are over-represented in the default category. However, again, the most noteworthy aspect of the gender classification is the dramatic predominance of women (at 75.2%) as rent-to-own customers.

The marital status variable contrasts those who self-report being in a marriage from those who are not, i.e., those who are single (4,266 out of the total of 11,113), divorced (3,518) or widowed (144). The variable is significant for all three destinations at the 90% or 95% level. As one might expect, those married are more likely to acquire the merchandise and are less likely to default. This argues that married RTO customers are more established and stable consumers but, at the same time, the implication is that, with their stability, they become less likely to be able to substantially improve their economic status.

Receiving government aid is very significant statistically in the regression. In the sample, 40% reported receiving government aid in the form of TANF (temporary assistance for needy families, 75% of aid recipients), Social Security (23%) or welfare (2%)—for totals of 3,329, 1,027 and 107, respectively. The regression results suggest that the variable is capturing aid primarily for transitional events as receiving aid reduces the chance of purchase by either method, while it also reduces the default rate. This also squares with the fact that the bulk of aid is coming in the form of TANF which is only meant to be available short term. Looking at Table 11 clearly illustrates this transitional aspect of government aid in that, while the sample mean for receiving aid is 40.2%, the sample mean among defaulters is only 28.2%.

Making an interesting comment on the type of consumer that uses rent-to-own, we see that being employed actually increases the probability of purchase; likewise, the higher the reported income, the lower the purchase probabilities. This is true for both payout and early purchase and is highly statistically significant for both outcomes with both variables. However, for neither variable is default significant. Additionally, noting that the dummy variable for employment is defined as one only if the customer has been at his/her job six months or longer, we see that these two variables together are measuring long term employment at relatively low wages. Hence, the longer the employment period and the lower the wage level, the tighter would be one's budget and the less likely it would be that one could expect future improvement, thus leading to greater reliance on rent-to-own. This is bolstered looking at sample means which show that, within the payout outcome, employment has its highest subsample mean while income has its lowest.

The home ownership dummy is also very interesting. It is significant for all outcomes and raises both the payout and the purchase rate while decreasing the default rate. Strikingly, the sample mean for default is only two thirds of that overall. The latter affect makes intuitive sense, as a homeowner is effectively much less of a "flight risk" than is a renter; while the former effect speaks to probable constraints in the budget of such consumers—including possibly being "house poor."

The referral variable comes about from the stores in the sample trying to track advertising effectiveness. In addition to the 1,949 rent-to-own customers who were referred by someone (17.5% of the total), 3,289 (32.0%) came because of a door-hanger or mailer that they received, 628 (5.7%) because of an ad on TV, radio or in a newspaper while the remaining 4,983 (44.8%) were simply "walk-ins." The referred customers are noteworthy as they have a higher likelihood of acquiring the underlying items by paying to term (payout) but they also have a higher chance of defaulting on the agreement. These consumers thus seem to be in the target market for the rent-to-own industry, those for whom financial circumstances preclude other options, while budgetary constrains dictate paying to term but also for whom default remains a distinct possibility. Further, it is interesting to see such a tangible example of consumer self-selection as well as the degree that RTO is promoted by word-of-mouth.

The raw numbers suggest some seasonal variation may be present in this business—see, for example, Figure 3. As one aspect of this, we were interested to see if there was a "santa effect." In particular, we considered a dummy variable for whether the agreement originated in December. The idea is simply that such agreements are more likely to represent gifts and so one would hope that the purchase rates would be higher, which is indeed the finding whereby the probability of both payout and early purchase are both higher and statistically significant.

The remaining independent variables considered in the regression are all features inherent to the contract itself. We find that longer, more expensive contracts are less likely to end up purchased. That is, the greater the maximum payable amount or the longer the contractual length, the less the probability that the agreement will end in either a payout or early purchase. This is statistically significant at the 99% level for both outcomes under either variable (default, however, is not significant for either). This is consistent with the hypothesis that the underlying merchandise on such a contract is being viewed as a luxury good which was only intended to meet a short term need. Alternatively, it could be that while rent-to-own serves as an important conduit to enable a consumer to try and acquire such merchandise, the inherent financial strain makes successful acquisition hard to achieve. While it is not clear what is the correct underlying explanation, looking at the sample means in Table 11 shows a higher average contract length for both the return and the default outcomes than for the other categories; further, the exact same statement is true for maximum payable amount as well.

A dummy variable was included in the regression testing whether the agreement has a payment schedule which requires weekly payments (as do some 53.9% of the agreements), and a second dummy was used testing for a monthly payment schedule (another 18.6% of agreements)—the remaining agreements were scheduled biweekly (25.8%) or semimonthly (1.7%). The finding is that agreements with the payments structured weekly are much less likely to end with purchase, either by exercising the early purchase option or via a pay-out; by contrast, monthly-structured contracts are much more likely to end in an acquisition outcome. One possible explanation is that the payment schedule is selected based on the consumer's expected income stream and other available resources. This would imply that a consumer needing a weekly schedule has a more marginal financial existence than does someone opting for monthly and consequently is more likely to end up terminating—or be-ing terminated in—the relationship. Another explanation is that this captures pre-selection by the customer based on his/her expectation for the outcome, either rental or purchase. That is, those expecting to rent would prefer a weekly arrangement for the greater flexibil-ity offered while those expecting to purchase prefer monthly for greater convenience. One can also hypothesis a behavioral component whereby the more frequent attention required to maintain a weekly agreement leads the consumer into taking positive action to terminate the contract. This fits the general notion that consumers mentally track the cost and benefits of a transaction with a symbolic linkage between consumption and the way the purchase is financed (see, e.g., Prelec and Loewenstein (1998) and Thaler (1985)).

At the same time, it is also very interesting that contracts on a weekly schedule are less likely to default; this is an appealing result, as the greater frequency of payments not only may make the consumer more likely to return the item, it also affords better monitoring of the customer from the standpoint of the store. Finally, all these effects are statistically significant at the 99% level.

The impact of different types of merchandise was examined by adding dummy vari-ables. The five product categories that we consider are uniquely identified through the use of four dummies. Computers and electronics are alike in that each is less likely to be early purchased, this is true for both at the 99% significance level. Additionally, computers are also less likely to be acquired by an agreement payout, while electronics have a greater default rate. This suggests that computers and electronics are more likely to be viewed as rental items. Customers executing agreements within the furniture category are more likely to acquire the items—either by payout (90% statistical significance) or early purchase (99% significance). This is an appealing result, for instance if one is using rent-to-own to get bunk beds for his/her children, the expectation would be that this customer probably is trying to acquire the item or, at least, desires ownership. At the same time, the default rate is also higher (significant at the 99% level) which, in part, probably speaks for somewhat greater mobility among the clientele. For the jewelry variable, alone among these dummies, the likelihood of acquisition via payout and the likelihood of default are both higher with these effects being significant at the 99% level. Hence, these rent-to-own jewelry customers are more likely to be either making payment after payment until the end of the agreement or simply skipping with the (highly portable) goods.

In reviewing these regression results, an important observation can be made. Com-paring the customer- and transaction-specific variables, it seems that as interesting as *who* these customers are, more important is *how* the contacts are being used. Qualitatively, the transaction-specific variables have somewhat greater explanatory power over a given contractual outcome. A reasonable conclusion is that rent-to-own customers, despite the demographic variation, are actually fairly homogeneous. That is, the defining factor is their membership in this group, which is determined primarily by economic factors. Given this, the variation observed can be traced to the duration of stay in such an economic situation which is better explained by contract usage. To provide more intuition into our results, the next subsection presents some scenario-based simulations.

3.3. Simulation Results

The estimated regression coefficients are not directly comparable as they interact in a fairly sophisticated manner as can be seen in equation (1). However, we provide some simulations to better illustrate the impact of various parameters. In particular, four simulations are provided in Tables 13 through 16, the first two involve customer-specific factors and the latter two contract-specific factors. These are produced by setting the indicated factors to the values specified below while evaluating all other parameters at their mean levels.

The first simulation, Table 13, contrasts a relatively old, married female who is not receiving government aid—call her Ms. X—from a relatively young, single male who is getting aid—Mr. Y. Interestingly, X is almost twice as likely to acquire her merchandise than is Y; in particular, X has a better than a one in three chance of her agreement ending in acquisition while it is only one in five for Y. Further, while Y is about equally likely to use the two acquisition methods, X shows a definite preference for the payout method. Given the difference in purchase rates, it is not too surprising that X has a return rate which is much higher at 77% relative to Y's 61%. However, it is somewhat surprising that they have near identical default rates of 3%—which is also below the overall average.

Table 13. Simulated Probabilities—Scenario One.

	Return	Payout	Early Purchase	Default
41-55 year old Married Female with no Gov't Aid	0.607	0.207	0.155	0.030
18-25 year old Single Male on Gov't Aid	0.770	0.102	0.098	0.029

The second simulation, detailed in Table 14, contrasts two consumer types. The first type is a homeowner who has been employed at his/her current job at least six months receiving total income under $5,000—which represents, for instance, roughly half-time employment at minimum wage[13]—denote him/her as A. The second person rents and although unemployed reports income above $25,000—possibly he/her is disabled and receiving social security—denote him/her as B. Notice that A is 3.5 times more likely to purchase the

---

[13]Note that if this characterization of employment is correct, such a job would probably not come with any benefits—further stressing the consumer's budget.

underlying merchandise than is *B*, and is more than five times as likely to use the payout method. Strikingly, *B* has a return probability of 83.7%, 1.5 times that of *A*. However, at the same time, the default probability of *B* at 4.0% is 2.2 times that of *A* and is 10% higher than the overall average rate. So while *B* may not be that attractive, it seems that *A* is an ideal customer for rent-to-own mechanism in that the very constrained budget that *A* faces would likely mean that he/she would have few alternatives and so would benefit from having access to RTO and, at the same time, being relatively tied to their home would make for low business risk from the standpoint of the store.

Table 14. Simulated Probabilities—Scenario Two.

	Return	Payout	Early Purchase	Default
Employed Homeowner, Income < $5,000	0.551	0.264	0.167	0.018
Unemployed Renter, Income > $25,000	0.837	0.051	0.072	0.040

The third simulation—Table 15—looks at the impact of contract length and merchandise expense. A relatively short term contract on an inexpensive item is contrasted to one that is long running and written on an expensive item. The latter contract has a return probability more than twice as high as the former contract; further, at 88.1% it is, by far, the most likely outcome for such an agreement. Perhaps this is capturing the impact of the greater financial burden placed on the customer by longer and more expensive agreements. Alternatively, such items may be viewed by consumers as luxury goods intended only for short-term rental. By contrast, for the relatively inexpensive contract the most likely outcome is acquisition occurring with a 55.8% chance and which is equally likely to be via payout or by exercising the early purchase option. The probability of default is very interesting here, it is 2.2% for the short running contract and 3.7% for the longer running contract. Thus, benchmarked against the overall average default rate of 3.6%, the former contract has a rate that is only three fifths of the average while for the latter contract it is slightly higher than average. This suggests that the default behavior observed in our data set does not represent opportunistic behavior on the part of consumers but rather is due to constraints related to their current economic situation.

The final simulation given in Table 16 considers the affect of the timing of payments. That is, what is the impact of having chosen to make weekly payments as opposed to monthly payments or to the intermediate option of a bi-weekly or semi-monthly schedule. The table clearly shows that as the frequency of payments increase, the probability of return sharply increases while the chance of acquisition decreases. For example, the probability that the contract ends with a return is 1.45 times higher with a weekly schedule relative to a monthly schedule. Alternatively, the probability of an acquisition occurring is 2.15 times higher with monthly payments than with weekly. These results are consistent

Table 15. Simulated Probabilities—Scenario Three.

	Return	Payout	Early Purchase	Default
$300 Maximum Payable, 6 Month Contract	0.420	0.279	0.279	0.022
$3,000 Maximum Payable, 2 Year Contract	0.881	0.054	0.029	0.037

with the three hypothesis introduced earlier. Namely, that those choosing weekly schedules are in more tenuous economic circumstances and so are more likely to have to return the merchandise; that the schedule chosen represents pre-selection based on expected outcome, so renters would choose weekly payments; or, that there are behavioral aspects whereby the more frequent payments result in greater introspection and a greater likelihood of terminating the agreement. Notice that, conditional on acquisition, payout is somewhat more likely than is early purchase for all payment structures except monthly payments for which this preference is reversed. By arguing for the financial constraints faced by these consumers, this preference for the payout method tends to support the first hypothesis. Further, examination of the default rates across payment schedules is very interesting. Consistent with an improved monitoring hypothesis, the weekly default rate is only 60% of the monthly rate. However, countering this monitoring hypothesis is the fact that the highest rate present is associated with bi-weekly/semi-monthly schedules.

Table 16. Simulated Probabilities—Scenario Four.

	Return	Payout	Early Purchase	Default
Weekly Payment	0.770	0.107	0.094	0.028
Bi-Weekly or Semi-Monthly Payment	0.637	0.191	0.133	0.038
Monthly Payment	0.530	0.214	0.219	0.037

4. Conclusions

This work examined rent-to-own contracts using a data set of some 11,000 actual transactions. This contrasts with most existing literature which has relied on interview or survey data. Our data set allowed us to look at the outcome of the agreement—return, payout, early purchase or default—as a function of customer- and contract-specific characteristics. A considerable amount of descriptive statistics were developed to provide a snapshot look at the variation in the underlying features in these contracts and in the various attributes of the consumers as well as their associated impact on contract outcome. In addition, the relationship of different factors on the outcome was more formally examined by developing a multinomial logit model which estimated the probabilities that a specific agreement would ultimately conclude in each of the outcomes considered, given the underlying set of characteristics for that agreement. Additionally, to better illustrate our regression results, we simulated some representative contractual outcome probabilities, associated with some customer- and contract-based scenarios that we developed. We next briefly summarize some of our findings.

We found that merchandise return was the most likely outcome overall; that acquisition occurred in more than a third of the contracts; and, at 3.6%, there is a high chance of default—skipping—by customers. Looking at payment details, we found the majority of agreements were structured with weekly payments each averaging about $20 per week and that about 40% of these payments were made late. Also interesting was that some 89% of payments were made by the customer physically returning to the store to pay.

We can make a number of observations regarding our multinomial logit regression analysis. Considering only the most statistically significant regressor variables, we found that acquisition, via payout or early purchase, was more likely for older, employed, homeowners; while government aid and higher income levels reduced the chance of acquisition. Further, customers who were referred to a rent-to-own store were more likely to acquire via payout and that there was evidence of a "santa effect" in that agreements originated in December were more likely to end in ownership. Regarding contract-specific variables, merchandise acquisition has a lower probability the greater the maximum payable amount and the longer the duration of the agreement. Also, agreements with weekly payment schedules are less likely to end in acquisition; by contrast, those with monthly schedules are much more likely to be acquired. There is interesting variation among types of merchandise. For instance, early purchase is less likely with computers and electronics while it is more likely with furniture. Jewelry is more likely to be purchased by making payments to term (payout) as well as being much more likely to have a default. In reviewing the statistical significance of the various regressors, one can note that the transactional-specific variables had somewhat greater explanatory power on the outcome than do customer-specifc ones. That is, rent-to-own customers seemed to be more defined by their economic circumstances than by their demographics.

Taken together, a very clear picture emerges from this analysis. Rent-to-own customers are the "working poor" who, while frequently viewed as financially unsophisticated, clearly have few financial options. Rent-to-own is quite possibly a valuable option given a choice not between cash or charge but rather between layaway or deferring consumption. The present detailed portrait of the customer base and the underlying contractual relationship is meant to contribute to the policy debate regarding rent-to-own and, more generally, financially disadvantaged consumers.

References

Anderson, M. H. and Jackson, R. 2001, A reconsideration of rent-to-own business, *Journal of Consumer Affairs* **35**(2), 295–307.

Anderson, M. H. and Jackson, R. 2004, Rent-to-own agreements: purchases or rentals?, *The Journal of Applied Business Research* **20**(1), 13–22.

Anderson, M. H. and Jackson, R. 2006, Managing high risk in a retail operation: the rent-to-own business, *Southern Business and Economic Journal* **29**(1 & 2), 68–86.

Anderson, M. H. and Jaggia, S. 2008, Rent-to-own agreements: customer characteristics and contract outcomes, *Journal of Economics and Business* .

Andreasen, A. R. 1993, Revisiting the disadvantaged: old lessons and new problems, *Journal of Public Policy and Marketing* **12**(2), 270–275.

Caskey, J. P. 1994, Fringe banking: check-cashing outlets, pawnshops, and the poor. The Russell Foundation, New York, NY.

Caskey, J. P. 1997, Lower income americans, higher cost financial services. Filene Research Institute Report, Madison, WI.

Cheskin+Martin 1993, Rent-a-center longitudinal research in rent-to-own: providing opportunities or gouging consumers? Submitted to the Committee on Banking, Finance and Urban Affairs, House of Representatives, 103rd Congress, 1st Session. Serial No. 103-24, Washington, D.C.

Freedman, A. M. 1993, Peddling dreams: a marketing giant uses its sales prowess to profit on poverty. Wall Street Journal, pp. A1, A10.

FTC 2000, Survey of rent-to-own customers. Federal Trade Commission, Bureau of Economics Staff Report, Washington, D.C.

Greene, W. H. 2003, *Econometrics Analysis*, Prentice Hall.

Hill, R. P., Ramp, D. L. and Silver, L. 1998, The rent-to-own industry and pricing disclosure tactics, *Journal of Public Policy and Marketing* **17**, 3–10.

Hogarth, J. M. and O'Donnell, K. H. 1999, Banking relationships of lower-income families and the governmental trend toward electronic payment, *Federal Reserve Bulletin* **85**, 459–473.

Keest, K. E., Langer, J. I. and Day, M. F. 1995, Interest rate regulation developments: high-cost mortgages, rent-to-own transactions, and unconscionability, *The Business Lawyer* **50**(3), 1081–1091.

Lacko, J. M., McKernan, S. M. and Hastak, M. 2002, Consumer experience with rent-to-own transactions, *Journal of Public Policy and Marketing* **21**, 126–138.

Martin, S. L. and Huckins, N. W. 1997, The cost of credit: regulation and legal challenges.

McKernan, S. M., Lacko, J. M. and Hastak, M. 2003, Empirical evidence on the determinants of rent-to-own use and purchase behavior, *Economic Development Quarterly* **17**(1), 33–52.

Prelec, D. and Loewenstein, G. 1998, The red and the black: mental accounting of savings and debt, *Marketing Science* **17**, 4–24.

Renuart, E. and Keest, K. E. 1999, The cost of credit: regulation and legal challenges. National Consumer Law Center, Boston, MA.

Stegman, M. A. and Faris, R. 2003, Payday lending: a business model that encourages chronic borrowing, *Economic Development Quarterly* **17**(1), 8–32.

Swagler, R. M., Burton, J. and Lewis, J. K. 1995, The alternative financial sector: an overview, *Advancing the Consumer Interest* **7**(2), 7–12.

Swagler, R. M. and Wheeler, P. 1989, Rental-purchase agreements: a preliminary investigation of consumer attitudes and behaviors, *Journal of Consumer Affairs* **23**, 145–160.

Thaler, R. 1985, Mental accounting and consumer choice, *Marketing Science* **4**, 199–214.

Zikmund-Fisher, B. J. and Parker, A. M. 1999, Demand for rent-to-own contracts: a behavioral economic explanation, *Journal of Economic Behavior and Organization* **38**, 199–216.

INDEX

F

G

T